IN
MADELEINE'S
KITCHEN

Books by Madeleine Kamman

MADELEINE KAMMAN'S SAVOIE *1989*

MADELEINE COOKS *1986*

IN MADELEINE'S KITCHEN *1984*

WHEN FRENCH WOMEN COOK *1976*

DINNER AGAINST THE CLOCK *1973*

THE MAKING OF A COOK *1971*

IN MADELEINE'S KITCHEN

Madeleine Kamman

INTRODUCTION BY JAMES BEARD

MACMILLAN • USA

Macmillan General Reference
A Simon & Schuster Macmillan Company
1633 Broadway
New York, NY 10019

10   9   8   7   6   5   4   3

PRINTED IN THE UNITED STATES OF AMERICA

Library of Congress Cataloging-in-Publication Data
Kamman, Madeleine.
  In Madeleine's kitchen: a personal interpretation of the modern
French cuisine / Madeleine Kamman; introduction by James Beard.

    p.   cm.
  Originally published: New York: Atheneum, 1984.
  Includes index.
  ISBN 0-02-009745-X
  1. Cookery, French.   I. Title.
TX719.K255   1992   92-16739   CIP
641.5944—dc20

FOR

Ann Baum

Richard Black

Jacqueline Cattani

Thomas Connors

Deirdre Davis

Myra Dorros

Judith Flewelling

Brett Frechette

Ethel Goralnick

Maria Hausmann

Richard Kzirian

June Levine-Connors

Linda Marino

Lynnwood McManus

Roy Palmeri

Lea Sharp

James Schmidt

Bruce Tillinghast

who helped me build and sustain the reputation of Chez la Mère Madeleine and Modern Gourmet Inc. in Massachusetts and continue the tradition in Annecy. Their devoted cooperation made the 1973–83 decade the happiest, most rewarding, and most productive time of my professional life.

My book is also dedicated to all those, not mentioned here, who were members of the last restaurant crew in 1979. Their work and help all through that summer will remain a very special and warm memory.

INTRODUCTION

Several years ago I did a series of cooking demonstrations with Julie Dannenbaum in Philadelphia, to benefit an art gallery. The demonstrations took place in a large auditorium, and a startlingly large audience turned out for the occasion. On the second or third day, Julie and I were somewhat taken aback to find ourselves the combined object of a positive bombardment of questions from a lady in the audience. They were not gentle, hesitant questions, either. The lady wanted to know all we knew, and she wanted to know now. Professionalism and a sense of humor carried us through, but it was difficult to keep track of what we were supposed to be doing! Well, that lady turned out to be Madeleine Kamman, and we have since become the best of friends.

Madeleine has never been shy in speaking out. She is a very outspoken person on the subject of food. And well she might be. French by birth, she grew up in the best of all possible food worlds, and absorbed the art of cooking from a variety of relations. She studied languages at the Sorbonne. She has taught cooking in this country since 1962, writes for a number of periodicals both here and in France, and she has done something else that I consider to be quite extraordinary: she ran a chef's training school and restaurant in a village outside Boston. Her whole staff consisted of graduate students, who would take turns working at the stoves, as restaurant manager, as waiters. These young people were exceedingly enthusiastic about what they were doing, and the food at that restaurant was quite extraordinary. No less a personage than Paul Bocuse had nothing but praise for it, as did a great many residents of Boston and its environs, not to mention a constant stream of passing visitors.

Madeleine has a gift for instilling in others her love of good food, her feeling for ingredients, her sense of the rightness of one flavor or texture with another, and she is a most exciting person to know. Often peppery, she knows damn well what she is talking about! Her knowledge is profound, and she can transmit it so well. She is now teaching cooking classes in New York, San Diego, San Francisco, Portland, Seattle . . . her energy is boundless. But she has not lost sight of her original goal. She has opened a school and is planning a small restaurant in New Hampshire. I can only predict that, given her love and attention and expertise, it will become one of the great training spots for aspiring chefs and food writers in this country. Madeleine's beliefs and tastes and experience in matters of food and wine deserve to be perpetuated, to become part of the fabric of gastronomy in this great country of ours. To read her books is an adventure, as I am sure you will discover in the following pages.

JAMES BEARD

PREFACE

This book is for all cooks: home cooks, fancy cooks, good cooks, professional cooks, bad cooks aspiring to become better cooks. Everyone will be able to find, in the pages that follow, some new ideas, some old ideas rejuvenated, some grand ideas, and also a share of crazy ideas.

Those cooks who are interested in learning how concepts and ideas about cooking developed from the historical point of view may find the first twenty pages or so quite interesting. Those whose profession it is to present to the public new food ideas—the restaurateurs as well as the cooking teachers—will either love those twenty pages or hate them; they represent my point of view on many current burningly interesting cooking topics, and my views have always been either hated or dearly beloved. Controversy, after all, keeps the mind nimble.

I know that there are cooks who would rather cook without wondering where ideas come from, just for the pleasure of putting food together for good fare and good fun; they should start reading the book on page 18 and forget my literature; I wholly understand their point of view.

There is definitely a measure of risk in reading my impassioned statements on the state of the Culinary Arts. I have been known to bring into the ranks of professional cooks a solid number of engineers, teachers, nurses, physicians, and lawyers who have switched occupations and are now happily practicing cooking as a vocation.

There is something known as "getting the call of the kitchen," and it is my wish that all my readers, the old fans as well as the newcomers to my kitchen, either "get the call" or see their energies renewed by the reading and use of this book.

MADELEINE KAMMAN

Annecy, France, and Glen, New Hampshire
September 1982 to April 15, 1983

Contents

IN
MADELEINE'S
KITCHEN

NOUVELLE CUISINE OR CUISINE PERSONNELLE?

Being French born, I have that Gallic fascination with food, especially since I belong to a generation of French people who, during the war, never quite saw its hunger satisfied. I was working in a restaurant at an early age. When transplanted to America in my late twenties, I went into "transcultural" shock and saved my soul by teaching French cuisine. In my kitchen, borders disappeared and oceans became nonexistent. Teaching gradually became more demanding as I aimed not only at training home cooks but at developing a more meaningful education for younger people wanting to make a profession out of cooking.

The challenge led me to operate a restaurant for the second time in my life. I became very controversial, which probably meant that I was in a place I was not supposed to be. I had transcended the limits imposed on women by generations of professional chefs and found myself succeeding in a so-called male profession.

Even more confusing was the fact that all the while I was working, I persisted in producing cuisine of professional quality without always having professional equipment and in surroundings I insisted on keeping feminine rather than businesslike and impersonal. Nothing is easier to understand, however; a human soul always functions better and expresses more of its own inherent talents when surrounded by warm colors rather than by stainless steel.

Stainless steel is a symbol of the dehumanization of the profession of cook and chef. It promotes stereotyped behavior and lack of personality. I kept my work surroundings human for both my cooperators and myself, because to be a good cook, one always needs to tap the inner, emotional layers of one's personality. Statistics, percentages, charts, written or imposed recipes are, as one of my witty students put it one day, "antiestetico." I truly do not care how many tons of foie gras and truffles are produced annually in France. The statistics will not cook the "foie"; my understanding of the qualities present in the specimen I am preparing will. So I kept the restaurant kitchen as any other kitchen, at home or in the school: an inner sanctum with another little room, the worst in the place, for all the statistics—since statistics and calculations there must be— keeping them hidden and limiting the damage they could do to the quality of the work surroundings.

It took me ten years, working my way through a maze of material, to evolve the long professional course I now teach. I used the works of the classic cuisine as well as older books of previous centuries; I restudied the history of France, dug into many parts of the Durants' *History of Civilization*, plundered knowledge from the *Britannica*, the *Americana*, the *Hachette*, and the *Larousse* encyclopedias. I studied thousands of books on French provincial food in order to understand the relationship between the soil, the food, and the people of all the provinces; I investigated Italy and did the same with her regions, and I am still deeply involved in learning about the rest of Europe and that hopelessly complex study of mycology (the study of fungi).

Most difficult of all proved to be the science of food chemistry, for as research goes on in laboratories, the picture is changing every day. Facts are always reviewed, and explanations of culinary reactions have changed some- what over the last ten years. I am often asked the question: "Why do you place such emphasis on a scientific background?" Because Escoffier himself in *Le Guide Culinaire* went beyond the empirical knowledge transmitted both by chefs and women, and he caught my fancy. His approach felt rational and sane.

Saying that one cannot cook without knowledge of chemistry or physical reactions is, of course, nonsense, but the quality and creativity of one's cooking is greatly enhanced if one understands the behavior of proteins or starches when submitted to heat, or the importance of protein foams. Mistakes can be pre- vented and money saved if one is aware of the most important reactions liable to take place when one cooks. Ninety-nine percent of curdled sauces could be avoided if the cook were aware of the effects of heat on proteins.

Food chemistry has developed so considerably in the last thirty years that its font of knowledge can be tapped intelligently by any cook. All that is needed is comprehension and conceptualization of reactions; the memorization of chemical formulae is not for the cook and better left to the chemist. My students insist that they enjoy their kitchen chemistry because it gives them a freedom to play with textures and compositions that they never had while they cooked only by recipes.

It is important to focus on the state of French cuisine, upon whose evolution during the last fifty years depends the type of curriculum that should be offered to the younger generations.

First, there is "classic cuisine." Contrary to certain claims, classic cuisine is not dead. When I arrived in Annecy in July 1980, I asked people at random: "What do you think of nouvelle cuisine?" Out of twenty-five persons asked, only two knew what it was: the owners of two Annecy restaurants. The others— professional persons, teachers, housewives, women cooks in smaller restaurants —all said to me wide-eyed: "What is that?" I had to laugh, because I had known that this would be the type of answer I would receive.

Annecy is a very typical bourgeois city where lots of capital is spent and invested every day while at the same time a steady stream of tourists from all over the world pours in and out. If there is a town where one can see what the French population likes to eat, this is it: good "bourgeois" fare prepared without much imagination or extremes of style. The most popular places offer steak with the old classic sauces, trout—since the area is full of it—gratins in great quantities and not always of the best quality, with here and there an adventure into a new style of cuisine that meets with more or less success.

What remains of the classic cuisine in France is its bourgeois aspect, and the population is most attached to it. I understand the classic cuisine to consist of the *haute cuisine classique* as it was served by many renowned chefs between the death of Carême in 1825 and the First World War. Auguste Escoffier and Prosper Montagné both rank among the masters, since they codified the classic cuisine in large volumes still accessible to us.

The *cuisine bourgeoise* evolved out of the haute cuisine by process of simplification. As the bourgeoisie came into social preeminence all through the nineteenth and twentieth centuries, the upper-class haute cuisine was adapted to its needs. A comparison between *Le Guide Culinaire* and *Ma Cuisine* by Escoffier shows the attempts at simplification by the author from the former style to the latter. Often local provincial dishes were executed by chefs according to the techniques of classic cuisine and incorporated into the *cuisine bourgeoise.* The best twentieth-century text on cuisine bourgeoise is *La Bonne Cuisine de Madame Saint-Ange.* Although the methods used in the book appear somewhat outdated, the fare is delicious and the book is still widely used by well-known food authorities. I learned a great deal from it since it was my mother's kitchen bible.

There is no doubt that the bulk of the knowledge a professional cook should have is included in the classic cuisine and pastry work. I, therefore, dedicate one-third of my course to its dissection. Stocks, sauces, pastries and breads, as well as egg preparations, are examined with "a fine-tooth comb." This is as taxing a part of the course for the teacher as it is for the students, but it must be done exhaustively. An occasional student, never the best, may become impatient with it.

Classic cuisine is to nouvelle cuisine what classical ballet is to neoclassical ballet. In cooking as in the dance, one cannot do the second one well without being thoroughly familiar with the first. But before I ever come to what is called nouvelle cuisine, it is absolutely necessary for me as a teacher to familiarize my students with the bulk of the food of the people, which is done during the second third of the course.

Known in America as "ethnic" foods, the foods of the humble people represent the enormously rich font of cuisine provided by all the women in the world. One look at the cuisine of all nations will reveal that it exists everywhere: in the Orient, in the Islamic countries, through Africa, all over the Americas, and all over Europe. Humble earthy foods and food combinations were produced by generations and generations of women in an attempt to feed families economically with what was at hand. The French provincial and regional cuisines, sometimes called *cuisine de terroir, cuisine de femmes, cuisine de misère,* or in more gallant, more modern terms, *cuisine du coeur,* and the *cucine casalinghe* of all the regions and provinces of Italy belong to this category.

Some of the women's dishes can be traced back almost to protohistory. They are all issued of the local soil and its productions or have been brought to an area by large population movements, invasions, wars, crusades, or nomadism. The *confit* of the French Occitania, for which I have tried to give the possible origins on page 312, belongs to this category.

This pool of women's foods is our ancestral patrimony. It is the material we are all made of whether we were born wealthy or poor, for one must remember that in Europe, particularly in France, almost all the way to the dawn of the twentieth century, infants and young children from the upper classes were raised until age seven by country women, with whom they ate their meals and by whom their meals were cooked.

The food lore put forth by women across the world is so rich a treasury that it can be tapped almost endlessly by the serious student of cookery in order to link the past to the present and forever create new compositions.

The difficulty of trying to re-create provincial and regional foods is that we have no record previous to 1925 of the original ingredients with which they were produced, so we can no longer be sure what their true taste and textures were. For example, flours as they existed in France in 1882 have very little in common with the commercial flours produced in France in 1982 and even less with the flours of modern America.

Most of the recipes existing in the depths of the French countryside were passed orally until at least 1890, for it took all that time to make the French peasant literate (loi Jules Ferry 1880–81 made school mandatory for all French children). By the time Austin de Crozes and Curnonsky attacked with gusto the project of recording in book form most of the material they could gather by oral interrogation, it was almost too late. The great industrial push had already emptied many villages and small towns, and it would take until at least 1950 to see the interest in country cuisine revive and the publication of books on the subject by Huguette Couffignal, Suzanne Robaglia, Simone Morand, Jeanne Levatois, and Marie Thérèse Hermann. These women have recorded most of what is remembered nowadays of our provincial gastronomic past and have used all possible sources from farm women of advanced age to ancient books available in local libraries. Once in a while a handwritten personal book will still surface from the cleaning of an attic, such as my grandmother's book that I used in one of the chapters of *When French Women Cook*.

The recipes as they are printed and presented are mostly unworkable, and that is where the pleasure for the modern cook comes in. Reinterpretation can be used; ingredients added here or removed there. The extra-light flour of the twentieth century works wonders, but one cannot help feeling sorry that the dusky, smoky ham remembered from childhood is not quite adequately replaced by modern factory-processed ham. All in all, reinterpretation really works, however, and all of a sudden one finds that one has created a new dish, very nice, lighter than the ancient dish, almost a dish of the nouvelle cuisine.

Nouvelle cuisine—what is it really? I often fear that it will become old before it has been adequately defined. Isn't it already on its way to becoming *cuisine nouvelle internationale?* Here is how I understand it; the reader can agree or disagree. Although little attention was paid to it, I wrote about some of it in *The Making of a Cook* in 1970–71 and about plenty of it in *When French Women Cook* in 1974–75. When, in 1975, Roy Andries de Groot wrote the *Esquire* article that brought the attention of America to nouvelle cuisine, I had been cooking more and more of it no farther away than Boston for at least five years, only I called it *cuisine personnelle*. I had already abandoned all or most of the flour-bound sauces (see *The Making of a Cook*, pp. 139–49) and used quite a bit of the French provincial food, rejuvenating and making usable in modern kitchens quite old ideas from my great-grandmothers, great-aunts, grandmothers, and mother (see *When French Women Cook*, all chapters).

Also, during the ten years I lived in America, I realized that the Chinese and Japanese cook their vegetables, fish, and shellfish much better than the French do. Consequently, I abandoned the French methods in favor of some of the Oriental methods. In essence, I had mastered *cuisine personnelle/nouvelle* and had already communicated some of its principles to my students.

Some want to see the advent of nouvelle cuisine in Escoffier. Maybe; he indeed recognized the necessity of simplifying and started to advocate an emphatic "Faites Simple," especially after 1918. He went so far as to recommend a pure starch in the preparation of the roux for the espagnole sauce, but he remained an opulent chef for an opulent, overfed, *grande bourgeoise* society, and his food, as magnificent as it may be, is now dating seriously. Two facts point to its aging: the length of his menus and the disaster that usually occurs when one tackles Escoffier in the modern kitchen. Most of the hotel kitchens in the world must make the poor man roll over in his grave. Escoffier is wonderful if one takes time to cook his food the way it should be, with care and technique. But few cooks care anymore, and their techniques are rough or nonexistent. The results are conclusive: let's leave Escoffier on the bookshelf and tackle simpler ideas that the unskilled modern cook can understand better. Basing a whole culinary education on Escoffier nowadays is a severe mistake. His fare is too expensive to produce as he himself produced it, and replacement products disgrace his style fundamentally. Also his food offerings are ill-adapted to "Homo sapiens sapiens"* under massive stress at the end of the twentieth century.

It was probably Fernand Point who first seriously pointed the way back

* The term is used by anthropologist Louis Leakey.

to simpler foods and cuisine in France. The book that has been put together from his papers and memories clearly points out that for him the best cooking was his mother's cooking. Two Point disciples, Messrs. Bocuse and Chapel, are now in the forefront of the nouvelle cuisine movement, and each of them makes great use of the ancestral cooking ideas of their respective provinces. The influence of the *mères cuisinières* cannot be doubted there.

After World War II, travel became everyone's habit and pleasure. The famous hotel school in Tokyo attracted the greatest chefs in France. Once there, they in turn were impressed by the Oriental food offerings: colors, textures, tastes. Everything was intriguing to them, and pretty soon they started introducing these ideas in their restaurant dishes. The most extreme Orientalization of French cuisine could be found at Le Camélia in Bougival in 1978. The influence of the Far East was and still is strong in modern French cuisine, especially in the new cooking methods.

Having accepted the Oriental influence, one was only one step away from incorporating other ethnic influences. Dominique Nahmias, of Italian origin, incorporated some Italian ideas in her food; I did the same out of love for the basic Italian foods such as *Parmigiano* and *pancetta*. Greek or Spanish concepts were adopted by others.

There is also a return to the ideas and concepts of the Middle Ages. The medieval influence came with the reimpressions in rare editions of many ancient texts. As a matter of fact, older ideas often pass for original when they are to be found well described in ancient texts not available to the general public. The trick of using the "leaf" to wrap various foods goes all the way back to the ancient Greeks, with a brief reappearance in the seventeenth century; now one wraps in lettuce, cabbage, other greens and even plastic wrap.

Would it perhaps be possible at this point to state that the airplane also had something to do with the development of nouvelle cuisine? Most probably yes, because from 1945 on, the world started to shrink. Foods began to travel as air freight; Maine and South African lobsters reached Europe; French cheese and wines came to America; seasons began to disappear as fruit was shipped to the northern hemisphere from the southern and vice versa. Many types of new fruit and vegetables found their way to kitchens that had before been content with European and/or American crops. At this point, is there a cook in the world who does not pray for the invention of a new fruit to displace the kiwi?

The development of new social laws and unions, which have made labor and workmanship more and more difficult to afford in Europe and America, created the necessity for simplifying a lot of time-consuming techniques. The simplification knelled the death toll of the already menaced *haute cuisine classique.*

To the development of social laws and unions one must add the influence of the no less important modern dietetics. Dietetic considerations are primarily responsible for the development of that cousin to nouvelle cuisine known as cuisine minceur. For a while, 95 percent of the United States even confused nouvelle with minceur, probably because it was never brought to the attention of the public that cuisine minceur was Michel Guérard's personal interpretation of diverse dietetic types of cuisines that had already existed in France for twenty-five years. When his book was published in 1976, a lot of work had already been done in this area by male and female dietitians. I was teaching my version of it in Philadelphia as far back as 1968, having gathered my basic knowledge from several French books on the subject.*

To sum up the definition, nouvelle cuisine, if there really is such a cuisine, is cuisine as it has always been—updated for the twentieth century, simplified quite a bit, rejuvenated by foreign and ethnic ingredients, lightened in texture by both the adoption of Oriental techniques of cooking and modern man's worry about his arteries and the expanse of his waistline, and truly personalized by each cook or chef who cares to bring to the stove her/his font of technical and historical knowledge while at the same time exercising her/his own creativity at combining ingredients. So is it *cuisine nouvelle* or *cuisine personnelle?* I prefer the second nomenclature. It corresponds more with the individualist mentality of the twentieth century.

Having defined *cuisine personnelle* for myself, I was faced with the problem of teaching it in a way that would relate to my whole philosophy of teaching. I have always applied the principle that teaching cooking by recipes is fine for the man or woman who will never go farther than cooking a fancy dinner, but totally useless for the future professional, who needs a much deeper training.

After a future professional chef has been indoctrinated in depth in the basic techniques and basic proportions of the classic cuisine and after she/he has been given an idea of the tremendous variety of culinary concepts offered by all the foods of the world, the creative education must begin. In 1977–78, I started

---

* Simone Martin-Villevielle, *Cuisine sur Ordonnance* (Paris: Pierre Houe, 1967) and Germaine Deloge, *Cuisine Rapide et Techniques Nouvelles* (Paris: Dupuis, 1969).

teaching with the help of lists of ingredients, and gradually I found myself putting more and more emphasis on this pedagogical tool. Now I provide my students simply a tableful of ingredients so that they can appreciate their quality, freshness and appearance. I begin with relatively simple combinations and build to more varied and complex assortments as time goes on. The students are asked to formulate a personal menu from the available ingredients, so that at the end of the hour there is, among the six students and myself practicing with them, a list of approximately thirty-five recipes, brand-new and very personal to each of us. At the beginning of this part of their training, especially in the short seminars, the students are often intimidated and awkward. But in the longer courses, everyone quickly gets used to the procedure and starts enjoying it thoroughly. From the third list on, it is not unusual to see several possible menus thought out by one single student. There is a great diversity of proposed dishes, and the food is always very personal, imaginative and delicious.

It would be boasting to pretend that all of my students are geniuses of imagination. What I can truly say, however, is that some of them are truly endowed with a wonderful creativity, often more developed than mine. Most do very well and are proud of their own work and style; some will never be anything more than "Madeleine clones," mimicking me and my methods; a few plainly waste their potential; and mercifully, those who are nothing but unprincipled merchants are very few and far between.

As we go together through all the ideas presented, I steer students toward the correct flavor and taste combinations and compositions and toward color schemes that will enhance the appearance of the plate. It should be remembered, however, that this type of training is valid only if a student already knows the basics in depth. Otherwise it is useless. Anyone not able to recognize at first sight the cut of meat presented on the table cannot, obviously, choose the correct method of cooking it.

This is as far as the students who attend my eight-week seminars go, but the training goes on for those who study with me longer. For the last two months of the course, they learn how to demonstrate their creations so that they, too, can start teaching by demonstration if they wish to. Also, they proceed to handle the kitchen as if they owned it and were the *patron* or *patronne*. We have a "chef-of-the-day" who improvises his/her own menu and practices at having his colleagues execute and serve it to the class as is done to the public in a restaurant. It is a most rewarding and warm experience to see a young person who five months earlier was close to a baby in the kitchen develop into a proficient cook with professional chef capacities. These methods of teaching develop self-confidence, pride in one's work and eagerness to present one's own material to the public. Those who have undergone this type of experience will never again serve other people's recipes, and if this method becomes popular enough to be used by other teachers, America will soon be able to develop its own three-star restaurants without having to draw from those of the French chefs.

The state of the food world in France and in the United States at the present time is fascinating. If there is a so-called haute cuisine left in France today, it revolves entirely around expensive ingredients. Cooking in the haute cuisine style now truly consists in using every possible luxury ingredient under the sun out-of-season: truffles in August; foie gras year round, even if it loses texture with the heat of summer; lobster; expensive wild mushrooms that are not wild anymore; luxurious cuts of meat only, and barely mature salmon that could advantageously have spent another year in Middle Atlantic feeding waters. In a word, one startles the public with expensive ingredients not always treated with supreme technique or efficiency.

There is, according to some somber prophets, a distinct possibility that French cuisine is on an irreversible downhill course. It may be. In the last ten years, I have had only two perfect meals at the whole array of starred restaurants I have visited—and one was not even in France.

I know only too well from personal experience that it is barely possible to produce that elusive perfect meal when one works at 200 miles per hour moving like a machine to just "get" that food out. All one can do is produce the best possible meal, given the ingredients and the time one has to produce it. I have steadily sent my plates to the dining room with an inner regret for the time I did not have at my disposal to really finish my sauce, so I am pretty sure that I am not unique and that this same feeling has echoed in the minds of many of my colleagues.

The truth of the matter is that great restaurant cuisine is in decline not only in France, but also in Italy, in the United States and everywhere. Less and less craftsmanship is taught, and a forever spreading union mentality nips all creativity in the bud. Everything considered, I cannot see why a French restaurateur should have an easier time producing great food than an American or Italian one just because he or she is French. The pressures are the same everywhere: taxes, regulations that are nonsensical, lack of qualified personnel, irregularity in the quality of ingredients.

In big cities there is hardly a hope that the situation will ever improve. Right now attention is too focused on New York, Paris, Chicago, London, and San Francisco. The general public does not quite realize that some of the most serious restaurants in the world are outside of big cities, sometimes in villages close to main centers of communcation, but at the same time embedded in the rich and lush countryside that produces plentifully for them.

People do travel considerably to find good food. They even came from France and the rest of Europe to my hole in a semibasement in Newton Centre, Massachusetts. Then why are so many restaurants both in France and the United States suffering because customers do not take the time to drive to their small towns and villages?

There may be too many restaurants. There is no doubt that a smaller number of better restaurants would make a lot of sense. In France and in America, in big cities, in small cities, everywhere, every person with a bit of capital to invest seems to open a restaurant. The result is a great many establishments owned by people who have no feeling for the profession whatsoever.

Then there is the case of the owner who inherits a restaurant from parents. Although the heir is not too keen on the profession and would rather be painting, he carries on against his better judgment, and in order to try to redeem the whole affair, sends his own son or daughter to school to become a chef. If by bad luck the latter would rather be a drummer, he or she will end up drumming out the same boring fare for the duration of a sad life, and for years the public will only trickle in. In the tiny town where I apprenticed, the toll on three such ancestral institutions was heavy: one restaurant became a gas station, another one a retreat for Catholic sisters, and the third a pinball machine game room. I could also cite at least ten such examples around Annecy.

Being a restaurateur in our difficult days necessitates a true personal gift for cooking combined with a fine business acumen. Everywhere in the French countryside "great chefs" do their tricks with foie gras and lobsters; great creations here, great creations there, and a steadily growing temper because not enough people visit the restaurant to allow the modern *maîtres-queues* (master cooks) to eke out a decent living.

Meanwhile there is an Emilie down the street who owns a hole in the wall with stone walls and terribly old chairs and tables. She fills this shapeless joint to the brim every day for lunch and chock-full every Friday and Saturday night for dinner. Why?

She really could not explain. Most of the time she brings you her modest and delicious fare herself, sets a huge dish of something or other in the middle of your table, and lets you cope. She has to let you cope or else give up the seventy-five cents or so she makes on the dinner, for which she is charging only between eight and ten dollars. Ten minutes later she is back: is everything okay and as you want it? Smiles here, smiles there. A conversation is struck, good pleasant feelings pass between guests and *patronne*. Everyone loved it.

Et voilà! Never a chance not to be successful. She will probably never attract the attentions of Gault and Millau, but she may be doing more for the survival of French cuisine than the chef down the street who tortures a magnificent pike into a doughy and bready loaf of unidentifiable something.

The two styles of cooking are, at first sight, almost irreconcilable, but elements have come in during the last thirty years that may bring them closer together. The economic situation is giving the men tremendous problems. Running a serious, formal restaurant is a steady migraine, and the men find themselves slowly pushed from the glorious ingredients toward the more humble and modest ones traditionally reserved to the women.

The women, on the other hand, have come out of their homes, some writing more intelligent and better researched books than the men, precisely on the food of the women, some going to cooking schools and opening more intimate and comfortable restaurants than women had previously owned. The food cooked by women has been moving toward a higher level of execution, so that right now, men and women are going toward a meeting on equal ground. It seems safe to say that the new generation of great chefs will be American rather than French and that it will consist of a fifty-fifty ratio of women and men.

The stereotyped image of a formal restaurant is changing. The Senderens, Girardet, and Surmain dining rooms are already less formal and more relaxing and closer in feeling to some women's dining rooms.

Nothing will change in the area of quality: those who are good will remain good; those who are average will remain average whether they are female or male. One thing appears fairly certain: the creativity, opinions, and new points of view being brought into the cooking profession by a growing number of women probably account for the uneasiness and the more than vague discomfort of some male chefs. All women in professional kitchens, especially those pioneers who have been able to reach the rarefied heights of so-called haute cuisine, will be a challenge to the men and will remain a puzzle to them until the men settle down to realize that quality work will always be recognized whether it is produced by men or women; it is the public who decides very firmly, and the public is difficult and choosy.

This book is an expression of my deep, sincere, and personal commitment to the survival of all the styles and multiple facets of my national cuisine, as well as a celebration of the definite emergence of women and their *cuisine personnelle* into the cooking professions. I want it to express my gratitude that food is *there*: there to use as the medium of my art and to enjoy at my dinner table, mercifully not as a necessity for which I am starving or as a symbol that is "in" or "out" in good society. To paraphrase Voltaire, that essence of French controversy, *"Cuisinons notre Cuisine"* (Let's cook and cook well).

BEFORE YOU START
COOKING...

THE RECIPES GIVEN in the chapters that follow are but a few of the thousands I created in Newton Centre, Massachusetts, and Annecy, France, between 1972 and 1983. Any resemblance to compositions read or found elsewhere is strictly fortuitous.

To develop these recipes, I studied many historical culinary texts in several languages, I read French magazines or I simply looked at food stands in markets all over the world. I did borrow a few ideas and have given their authors credit for their original work. I never copied an idea straight from a book or a magazine; rather I thought about the concept for a few days, then reworked the idea into a context that was mine. As an example I can cite the combining of smoked salmon and asparagus. I read a recipe in *Gault & Millau* for a salad containing those two eminently compatible ingredients. A few days later, I had rendered this food combination concept into the Cream of Asparagus Soup with Smoked Salmon Quenelles to be found in this book on page 90.

All through the years that I was actively building and constantly changing restaurant menus, I carried a small book in my pocketbook in which I noted all ideas, good or bad, that came to my mind. It was essential to carry this little book, for intuitive work is fickle and fleeting; insights appeared as fast as they disappeared and had to be noted or they would have been forgotten. If you are creative in any art or craft, you will know about those sharp insights that will wake you up at 3:00 A.M. and make you jump out of bed to immediately make a note. Rolling over and being too lazy to get up means losing forever the idea that promptly returns to the recesses of the subconscious never to resurface in the middle of the day.

In spite of their apparent complexity, the recipes presented here are quite simple, the fruit of common sense and good techniques. To understand the techniques in depth, the reader may want to consult my book *The Making of a Cook*. Though written in 1970–71, it is still very much in use by cooking teachers, restaurateurs, and serious cooks across the nation. Also published by Atheneum, it presents a lay person's approach to the physical and chemical reactions that occur on the stove or the pastry table. Trained chemists may raise their eyebrows at this volume, but many a cook has found it interesting and useful because of its everyday language and the total absence of intimidating chemical formulae.

A recipe cannot ever be a magic formula that will work uniformly from San Francisco to the Baffin territories or from Thule to Madagascar. When an author writes a recipe, she or he uses the ingredients available in her/his area and in his or her climate. There will always be variations in all ingredients: no two flours have exactly the same starch content; some people consider thick and heavy a stock that I would call shockingly thin or vice versa. The degree of humidity is different in each and every area, so that sauces will reduce at very different speeds. The problem of your skills is also important; if when I instruct you to fold, you fold all topsy-turvy and deflate the whole batter, you may think my recipe is crazy, though it will be your technique that is at fault, not my formula. How well the recipes work out will depend on the quality of your ingredients and the quality of your skills.

So, before you start cooking, read the recipe, understand it, and arrange a tray with your ingredients all prepared and measured out. Make sure that you understand the techniques involved; it is wiser to postpone cooking a recipe until you become secure about its preparation. Basically, it is essential not to worry excessively when you cook and to let yourself relax into the pleasure of cooking. Use your own good sense, thin what is too thick and thicken what is too thin, and always remember that the first try at something is always the hardest. Repetition of hand movements and techniques builds security and expertise, so repeat until you get there. All great chefs have done just that before you. Bon appetit and have fun.

The Bases of Modern French Cuisine

THE STOCK PROBLEM

THE CLASSIC CUISINE was very rich and generous in stocks. To obtain the diverse sauces recommended by the old masters, one had to have a constant supply of brown stock, white stock, fish fumet, and essences—all of which took a long time to cook and used an enormous amount of energy during the time they were simmering.

Modern cooks started taking very noticeable steps to remedy this expensive situation immediately after World War II. A look at almost any modern French cookbook will immediately reveal that of the numerous stocks only one or two remain. There are two essential survivors: the golden veal stock and the white stock. Beef stock is much more rarely made as a routine item and is mostly produced at the same time one prepares pot-au-feu at home for the family or for the staff dinner in a restaurant.

Almost immediately after *The Making of a Cook* was published, I switched my style of cooking from the classic manner to faster cooking techniques, and devised for myself a method of stock and sauce making that proved practical for our very difficult economy. I decided that at all times there would be only one stockpot on the stove, not three as there had been before.

To obtain a solid stock that reduces quickly, I chose to work exclusively with golden veal stock—the one that contains the largest amount of available gelatin—and from that base I built all my meat sauces and made all my braisés for the more expensive meat items such as quails, pigeons, and filets of beef. For items requiring a less powerful stock, such as soups, grain pilafs, braisés made with pungent or very strong-tasting meats such as beef, lamb, etc., I used a white stock that I shall call here a secondary stock. This I made with those bones that are still gelatinous after the cooking of the golden veal stock, giblets, and other trimmings of diverse meats. I use this method to this day, and it works very well. It limits the utilization of energy, takes advantage of any scraps coming from the boning of chickens, uses roast bird carcasses and the trimmings from pieces of veal and other meats. The only meats one should not use in any basic stock destined for general use are lamb and other animals with very strong characteristic flavors such as game birds, venison, and browned beef. But this is nothing new; the rule already existed in the classic cuisine, and the reasons for it are as obvious now as they were then.

Restaurateurs, chefs, and cooks use great quantities of stock all the time; they have no storage problem as the stocks are kept very cold either in a high-speed refrigerator or in a walk-in. Here are a few instructions for the home cook who will be, after cooking a generous batch of stock, the proud owner of 3–4 quarts of expensive "elixir of pure gold" with very little space to keep it.

a. If you own a freezer, store the stock in 1-quart or 2-cup mason jars leaving some space for expansion during freezing, label and date the jars and store in the freezer. Remember as you freeze that you will need 1 quart of stock to prepare a modern brown sauce and approximately 2 cups to prepare a modern white sauce for 6 people; hence, the sizes of jars indicated. Prior to being filled, the jars must be boiled or sterilized in the dishwasher. Freezer shelf life: 3 months.

b. If you live in a small apartment and are very limited in freezer space, cook the stock down—the correct culinary expression is "reduce the stock"—by three-quarters and store the obtained reduction, which is now "meat glaze," in 1-cup mason jars in the coldest part of your refrigerator. Check the reduction every week for mold. Any trace of the tiniest spot of mold must be removed with a clean spoon and the reduction reboiled for 5 full minutes.

Sterilize all jars before storing the reduction and after reboiling it. If no dishwasher is available, boil the jars 5 minutes in clear water and let them air dry. Refrigerator shelf life: 2 months. To reconstitute meat glaze to a stock texture, add 3 parts water to 1 part meat glaze.

c. Everyone may want to consider freezing approximately 1 quart of stock in ice cube trays, then transferring the cubes to plastic storage bags. The cubes are easy to use for the quick deglazing of a frying pan. Freezer shelf life: 1 month.

GOLDEN VEAL STOCK

Elements of Golden Veal Stock

Preparing veal stock is, at current inflated prices, not a very cheap endeavor, but in the long run the sauces produced with it reduce so fast and so well that there is a resulting measure of economy. If there is one situation where the old rule, "If you go, go first class or do not go at all" applies, this is it. Veal stock is the guarantee of excellent sauces. Too many sauces nowadays do not taste or look as they should because their base, the stock, is too weak or not made with the correct ingredients. So let us look at those ingredients in a critical manner.

Most modern French recipes in the books used by the French state cooking schools indicate as their main ingredient "veal bones" without further comment. Not only are bones needed, but also good meat able to render taste into the water, so the cut of meat is important. Over the years, I have come to the conclusion that the best veal for a good veal stock is the breast. The meat is not that good for eating and the ribs are separated from one another by most useful gelatinous discs containing collagen, which will melt into the stock during the long cooking process and make it syrupy with good gelatin. Try to make the stock with two-thirds very meaty veal and only one-third veal bones as given by butchers. The latter, being very bare of meat, give to the stock nothing more than gelatin and not very much taste. The choice bone is, of course, the knuckle, which releases a very large quantity of gelatin while cooking. If you can afford the shoulder shank, it may also be used, but not, in any case, the leg shank or *osso bucco*, which is terribly expensive and makes too good eating to be thrown into a stockpot.

Of course, in restaurant trade all the trimmings that come from large pieces such as racks, loins, shoulders, and shanks of veal must be used. For the home cook, trimmings from chops, shoulders, and shanks bought in supermarkets can be saved and frozen if necessary while waiting to be used in stock making. Cooks with little storage space will find on page 24 a quick recipe that can be done within 2 hours, just in case they have no freezer to keep all these precious meat "scraps."

The choice of the vegetables is as important as that of the meat:

- Onions must be of the ordinary yellow type that makes everyone cry. Sweet Bermuda, white, or red onions are too sweet and will deliver an oversweet stock.
- Carrots must be used with great discretion. Their sugar should be a hint, not a statement.
- Wrap thyme and bay leaf into the parsley stems to obtain what is customarily known as a bouquet garni, which is added to the pot as is, never wrapped in cheesecloth, so it can render all of its flavor by floating freely around in the liquid.
- The leek is the soul of the stock, but do not be extravagant. Use the light green part and approximately 2 inches of the dark green part of each leek. The very dark green top is useless and can be discarded; the white wonderful part is eminently edible and will make a royal garnish for a meat or even a wonderful vegetable dish.

Why add white wine? First because its flavor is a great enhancer and also because its acid will work on the bones to release a maximum of gelatin.

Quantities to Prepare Good Veal Stock

Professional and home cooks both should use the following proportions, which will allow everyone to adapt the recipe to the size of the stockpot used, be it an ugly functional 45-quart aluminum or a pretty 5-quart home-size copper stockpot.

One quart of water yields approximately 3 cups of good stock.

You will need per quart of water used:

1 pound veal (⅔ pound meat,
  ⅓ pound bones)
⅓ cup dry white wine
1 medium onion, stuck with 1 clove
A 2½-inch-long piece of carrot
  (1 inch in diameter)

3 thick parsley stems
¼ teaspoon dried thyme leaves
⅓ of a Turkish bay leaf
1 leek

Cooks who do not feel that they should be bothered weighing all the meat have a point, for, if one simply puts the browned meat at the bottom of the stockpot and adds water to reach 1 inch above the meat, one automatically obtains the correct proportions. This is probably how they were empirically calculated over the centuries.

METHOD OF PREPARATION FOR
GOLDEN VEAL STOCK

1. Remove all visible traces of fat from the meat. Cut it into large chunks or ask the butcher to do it for you.

2. Place the meat in a large, flat roasting pan. Roast the meat in a preheated 400°F. oven until the chunks are golden and a lovely thin layer of meat juices has coagulated to a warm russet color on the surface of the roasting pan. You may, if you wish, brown onions and carrots at the same time as the veal. The browning time varies between 35 and 45 minutes.

3. Transfer the meat and, if applicable, the onions and carrots to the stockpot and pour the white wine into the hot roasting pan. Scrape well to dislodge and melt every bit of the beautiful meat glaze from the bottom of the pan; add it to the stockpot.

4. Cover the meat with the appropriate amount of lukewarm water and bring it to a boil. Add all the vegetables and aromatics. Turn down to a simmer and cook "until tasty." The lid should be placed on the pot slightly askew so as to leave ½ inch of space for evaporation, and warm water should be added to the pot at regular intervals to keep the water level approximately even. A home-size batch will be cooked in 3–4 hours; a large restaurant batch will require close to 12 hours. Very little skimming is needed since all available surface blood and other impurities have been deeply cooked during the oven roasting.

5. Strain the stock carefully. Cool it very quickly by filling the sink with cold water and immersing the pot containing the stock into the water bath until it is cold. Refrigerate immediately.

6. If you are going to use some of the stock immediately, set it aside and refrigerate it. Immediately process the remainder for storage in the freezer or as a reduction (see p. 19). It is a good idea to sterilize all storage jars while the stock cools in its cold water bath.

Salting or not salting a stock is vital for the production of the sauces that will result from it. Some say do not, others say do.

I have developed a very personal method, which I have found very satisfactory. I use a small—⅓–½-inch—chicken bouillon cube for each 5 quarts water. This does not salt the stock, but it releases into it a very very tiny amount of monosodium glutamate, which rounds the stock's flavor for the best. As much as I object to monosodium glutamate used in quantities as large as ½ teaspoon or even less, the tiny amount used in the bouillon cube is enough to give the stock the small hint of salt it should have.

Using no salt at all in the stock results in sauces that are much too sweet in background, while any amount of pure salt can lead to sauces that are so salty they become objectionable and damage both the meat they cover and the palate of the diner.

SECONDARY STOCK

Meats that have been used in the preparation of stock have lost all flavor and are nothing more than a mass of exhausted fibers. They can safely be discarded unless one is willing to grind them and add to them an awful lot of good eggs, bread crumbs, and all kinds of seasonings to revive them, then enclose the forcemeat between 2 layers of mashed potatoes to prepare a shepherd's pie. But if the stock has been well prepared and the meats truly drained of their nutritive elements, this will be a very "basic" shepherd's pie.

As you discard the meats, look for the larger bones; on many of them there will remain quite a lot of yet unmelted gelatin, recognizable immediately as white opaque sheets and blobs pulling off the bone. Reserve those bones;

they may still be used to make secondary stock for the less important preparations.

Since you are in possession of an excellent golden veal stock already, cook the secondary stock without browning the meats so that you will have both brown and white stocks at our disposal. If you feel, however, that you would prefer your secondary stock to have more taste and color, do not hesitate to oven brown whatever other meats you are using. Those meats may be anything you have: trimmings of veal, giblets of chicken, chicken breast, or other chicken bones; even a little trimming or two of beef and/or pork will not be an offender really. Just stay away from lamb and gamey meats.

To prepare the stock, proceed exactly as described for the Golden Veal Stock, but since the bones will be less tasty, you may want to add a couple more onions "for the pot" and 2 good cloves of garlic, and make sure that your bouquet garni is nice and fat. Do not weigh anything. Fill the pot with the meats. Add enough water to reach 1 inch above the meats. Bring to a boil and skim; add the vegetables. Bring to a second boil and skim again. Then let simmer until tasty and handle with every bit as much care as the Golden Veal Stock while cooking, storing, and cooling.

STOCK IN A HURRY

This special method of making a quick stock is for anyone who, because of radical lack of time or radical lack of storage, has absolutely no way to produce and store any amount of the two stocks mentioned above. Here is a super-quick stock that will be excellent for producing a quick sauce for 6 to 8 persons:

2 tablespoons butter or oil
1 large onion, sliced thick
1/2 a small carrot, sliced thick
1 leek (white part only), sliced thick
1 pound veal meat, from shoulder
    shank or breast, cut into 1/2-inch
    cubes, or an equal quantity of
    chicken wings chopped in small
    pieces

2 cups dry white wine
5 cups water
Bouquet garni made from 1/4
    teaspoon dried thyme leaves,
    1/3 of a Turkish bay leaf, and
    12 thick parsley stems

1. Heat half the butter in a sauté pan. Add the onion, carrot, and leek and toss into the butter until they have all browned. Remove to a plate.

2. In the same pan, add and heat well the remainder of the butter and brown the pieces of veal or chicken until they appear golden, caramelized, and the browning fat is visible on the bottom of the pan. Discard the fat. Remove veal or chicken to a plate.

3. Add 1 cup of the white wine. Scrape the bottom of the pan well to loosen up all the glaze. Return the meats to the pan and reduce to a mere 3 tablespoons of syrupy liquid.

4. Repeat the same operation twice more, the first time with the second cup of wine, the second time with 1 cup of the water.

5. Finally, add the remaining quart of water, return the browned vegetables to the pot, add the bouquet garni and simmer for 2 hours, adding warm water as needed to maintain the level of liquid.

6. Strain and use as needed. Will keep several days refrigerated and can be frozen as are other stocks.

A WORD ABOUT SANITATION AND STOCKS

Please be careful; nothing is more dangerous than rich stocks. If you are tempted to be careless and let a stock stand around, do remember that heavy, gelatinous stocks are used in laboratories to prepare bacterial cultures.

As much as this seems an unattractive topic to discuss in a cookery book, I find it necessary to bring up the subject of bacterial development for everyone's protection. Stock should never stand around just "waiting"; either it should be involved in some preparation to be served immediately or it should be refrigerated or frozen.

To be on the safe side, if you think that a stock has been standing at room temperature for just a bit too long, reboil it a full 5 minutes.

In home preparations, frozen stocks should be defrosted by immersing the jar in a large pot of cold water and heating slowly to prevent the jar from cracking. As soon as the stock is loose enough from the sides of the jar to pour out (even if a block of frozen stock still exists), empty the stock into a pot and bring it to a boil promptly. Reboil it a full 5 minutes.

FISH FUMET

As much of a cook as I feel I am by birth and vocation, I have to admit that making fish stock—to be precise, fish fumet—is not an attractive occupation. But if a cook wants to serve a fish sauced lightly with something a little less boring than lemon butter or the sempiternal *beurre blanc*, there is no escape: fish fumet must be prepared, and it is not always an easy task, depending on where one lives. I give here as much information as I have been able to gather through my peregrinations demonstrating across the United States.

CHOICE OF FISH FOR FISH FUMET

Generally, only the heads and bones of white-meat fish should be used. All types of blue fish are unacceptable because their taste is too oily. No skins in any category must ever be used.

East Coast
Sea fish: all the flounders, gray sole, whiting, haddock, conger eels, ocean perch, salmon
Freshwater fish: trout of all breeds (small and large), landlocked salmon, pike

Southern Coast and Gulf
Sea fish: red snapper, ocean perch, pompano
Freshwater fish: pike, muskelunge, bayou crayfish thorax and shells

West Coast
Sea fish: sole petrale, sand dabs, red rock cod, halibut, salmon, all rock fish
Freshwater fish: trout of all breeds, pike

Central and Landlocked States
(*See Special Instructions for Emergency Fish Fumet on p. 30*)
Some fish bring mostly taste to a fumet, as in the case of all the flounders, sole, and whitings; some bring only texture in the form of an abundant supply of gelatin, as in the case of haddock and halibut, which give a very sticky broth.

Whereas one can use the taste-giving fish in as large a quantity as one likes, the proportion of gelatin-giving fish should be limited to one-quarter of the total volume of bones used or the fumet will be too heavy and, when used in sauces, will reduce to a flocculent mass that will string from the spoon and appear and taste too thick.

CHOICE OF WINE FOR FISH FUMET

The choice of white wine is of the utmost importance, not only for the appearance but also for the final taste of the sauce. Wines made from *vitis labrusca* are not usable, nor are any sweetish or sweet wines made from *vinifera*. The following, all made from *vitis vinifera*, are acceptable:

- From France—Entre-deux-Mers, Mâcon, Alsatian Edelzwicker or Riesling.
- From California—Sauvignon Blanc, as low in alcohol as possible.
- Pinot Chardonnay from either country may of course be used. The choice must be in accordance with the cook's purse and to her/his capacities in the kitchen. In restaurant operation the "bottom line" remains the dictator of which wine to use.

    Positively no Sauternes or other sweet wines should be used. Although some French chefs use them for shellfish sauces, they are much too sweet, and the sweetness of the reduced wine clashes miserably with the sweetness of the shellfish.

PREPARATION OF THE FISH TO MAKE FUMET

Since this is an unappetizing task, to say the least, there is a tendency to "sweep the cleaning of the fish under the rug"—washing the fish heads and bones perfunctorily and throwing the mass into the pot without further ado.

    It is important to remember the horrible fight the poor fish goes through when being landed. Anything can happen, especially internal injuries that often make the liver and gall bladder explode, polluting the fillets and the bones alike.

    Fish merchants usually give away fish heads or "frames" (they call a head with the whole backbone attached as it comes off the filleting bench a "frame").

This is how you must clean all these: Work in the sink. Wash each frame or head individually. Put all frames on a board; with a heavy knife, chop away the "triangle," or the part containing all remnants of viscera, and discard this without touching it by pushing it into the trash can with the back of your knife blade. Rinse the frame again to discard all traces of blood, fold it in two or three (the backbone will break very easily), and put it in the stockpot.

For fish heads, cut the pointed underside of the head and around the gills, pull the whole bottom part of the head off and throw it away. Scrape out any trace of internal organs left in the top part of the head, rinse again and put into the pot.

TIME INVOLVED IN THE PREPARATION OF FUMET

Take time to make absolutely certain that no traces of organs or egg sacs are left. These often contain oils and bitter-tasting materials that will do very little for the final taste of a sauce.

The cook should not be discouraged by the mention of time involved. In home quantity work, where no more than 3 frames or heads are handled at once, it takes no more than a few minutes to clean them. The person to feel sorry for is the restaurant cook who handles 100 pounds of frames at a time and is employed by a taskmaster of my type!

BASIC PROPORTIONS AND PREPARATION
OF FISH FUMET

Beware of two important points before you start:

1. Your pot should not be made of aluminum or any other oxidizing material. Stainless steel and enameled cast iron both do well, as no discoloration of the stock is noticeable.
2. Use a pinch of salt with freshwater fish and no salt at all with ocean fish. Adapt the amount of salt in case of a mixture of salt and freshwater fish. Respect this rule. Since all sauces will be made by reduction, the level of salt will intensify while the sauce cooks.

For each quart of finished fish fumet you wish to obtain, use the following:

1 large onion, sliced thin
1 tablespoon chopped parsley stems
2 pounds fish frames and heads,
  cleaned
¼ of a bay leaf
¼ teaspoon thyme

Any available mushroom peelings
  (optional)
1 quart water (approximate)
½ cup dry white wine
Salt if needed (see above)

Place the aromatics at the bottom of the pot. Add the fish frames, bay leaf, thyme, and mushroom peelings, if available. Fill the pot with water to come ⅓ inch below the level reached by the fish. Add the wine. Bring quickly to a boil, turn down to a simmer, and simmer no longer than 35 minutes.

Important: As soon as the stock has come to a simmer, push on the pieces of fish to destroy them systematically and force all the enclosed natural juices out of the bones. Repeat this destruction of the bones several times during the cooking, until the bones appear totally broken down.

Strain the finished stock into a clean bowl, using a fine *chinois* or "China cap" type strainer. Push well on all the bones to release all the stock locked into them and all the flavor. Spoon off any fat visible on the surface of the fumet.

If you taste the stock and find that it is too thin, reduce it *after straining, never before.* Boiling down in the presence of the bones results in a "bony"-tasting stock and ultimately a "fishy" sauce.

Store in the refrigerator and use within 48 hours.

Fish fumet can easily be frozen in sterilized mason jars, but its freezer shelf life is only one month. The ice cube tray method is not recommended. Fish fumet is so quickly done in small quantities at home that one can, without worry, make it fresh the few times it is needed.

The managing of fish fumet in restaurant operation is an art that depends upon strict control of refrigeration temperatures and of the shelf life of the fumet; this will vary with the scope of the restaurant menu. Every cook must be trained carefully in this matter. Safety requires a shelf life of no more than 4 days for fumet kept in a high-speed refrigerator or walk-in.

RED WINE FISH FUMET

There is no more necessity in modern cuisine to prepare such a fish fumet. Modern sauces are made by blending ordinary fumet with reduced red wine.

EMERGENCY FISH FUMET FOR LANDLOCKED AREAS

The supply of fish frames and heads is so limited in landlocked areas that making a fish sauce sometimes becomes difficult. Two cases must be considered:

a. Landlocked areas with a limited supply of available freshwater fish (the Great Lakes, for example). Prepare the basic recipe for fumet, using whatever freshwater fish frames are available and use as liquids:

> *2 cups water*
> *1 cup bottled clam juice (never use canned clam juice)*
> *1 cup dry white wine*

b. Landlocked areas with no supply of available freshwater fish (the desert areas, for example). If you really want a base for sauces, you must locate shrimp in shells. Good fish stores everywhere receive them frozen from the Gulf at the same time they receive all ocean fish filleted and boned. Purchase 1 pound of shrimp. Sauté the shrimp in a pat of butter; shell the shrimp; set aside for a salad. Proceed as follows to prepare a fish fumet with the following ingredients:

The shrimp shells	*3 large onions, sliced*
3 cups water	*2 shallots, sliced*
1 cup bottled clam juice (never use canned clam juice)	*1 clove garlic, sliced*
1 cup dry white wine	*Large bouquet garni*

Liquefy the shrimp shells in the blender with the water, clam juice, and wine. Empty into a saucepan. Add the onions, shallots, garlic, and bouquet garni and bring to a boil. Cook until 3½ cups tasty liquid is left.

This truly cannot replace a good fish fumet in a fine sauce, but it provides an excellent soup base that can be garnished with diverse shellfish to make a creditable first course.

Those in landlocked areas can also use the broiling and panfrying methods of cooking fish rather than the poaching ones, thus skipping the necessity of a sauce. Or you can make the basic plain wine and butter sauces, or those based on reduced court bouillon, in conjunction with compound butters for very acceptable results. See the chapter on fish, pages 178–260.

ALL-PURPOSE WHITE WINE AND VINEGAR COURT BOUILLON

All cooks must be aware of the difference between fish stock or fumet and court bouillon. Whereas fumet is made with fish bones as described above, court bouillon is strictly a flavored bath of various liquids in which one poaches a piece of fish or a whole fish.

In the decadent classic cuisine, there developed the bad practice of using a court bouillon to prepare a flour-bound sauce of the velouté style. Since court bouillon has no body, the sauce was thin and unattractive. Sauces of the emulsified Hollandaise style were also often made by using some of the court bouillon as a lightly acid base in which the egg yolks were whisked and fluffed up.

Nowadays, it is common to use a reduced quantity of court bouillon to prepare a plain fish butter sauce. The court bouillon is reduced, the butter is fluffed into it, and a seasoner or garnish is added to give the sauce its final character. The underlying fish taste that relates the fish to the sauce is provided by the fish juices that always escape into the court bouillon in small but definitely traceable quantities as the fish poaches. For a specific example, see page 229.

PREPARATION OF COURT BOUILLON

Court bouillon is to be prepared directly in the fish poacher. The following is an all-purpose court bouillon for all fish, either white or blue meat. If you wish to prepare a red wine court bouillon, you may want to remember that the color will always turn bluish purple unless you use a good wine of breed and quality. This is an expense not really justifiable at current prices for good red wines. I, therefore, use a white wine and vinegar composition for all fish. I am giving here the proportions for home use and for small restaurant or catering service uses.

Home Use Proportions	*Restaurant Use Proportions*
2 quarts water	*1½ gallons water*
1 bottle Entre-deux-Mers or other	*2 bottles Entre-deux-Mers or other*
acceptable wine (see p. 27)	*acceptable wine (see p. 27)*
1 cup cider vinegar	*2 cups cider vinegar*
2 large carrots	*½ pound carrots*
1 pound onions	*2½ pounds onions*
Large bouquet garni made from	*Large bouquet garni made from*
⅓ cup chopped parsley stems,	*1½ cups chopped parsley,*
2 bay leaves, and 1 teaspoon	*4 bay leaves, 1½ teaspoons*
thyme leaves	*thyme leaves*
½ teaspoon peppercorns	*1½ teaspoons peppercorns*
2 tablespoons salt	*3 tablespoons salt*

Put all the elements of the court bouillon into the fish poacher. Bring to a boil, turn down to a simmer and cook 35 minutes for the small bath and 50 minutes for the large bath.

The vegetable garnishes can be left in the fish poacher and will find themselves squeezed between the rack and the bottom of the pot while the fish is poaching.

In restaurant use where the court bouillon is kept on the stove a whole evening, take care at regular intervals to cut it with some boiling water or else the concentration will become unbearable and the taste of the fish will be damaged, especially in fillets and steaks. If the court bouillon is predominantly salty, also add vinegar; if it is predominantly acid, add salt.

A court bouillon that has been used can be "renewed"; that is, those with available refrigerator or freezer space can strain the leftover court bouillon into a large container and freeze it. To reuse it, all one need do is defrost it and extend it with more wine, more water, more vinegar, and more fresh vegetables.

Note: Once fish has been cooked in it, court bouillon contains many fish proteins and must be treated as carefully as fish fumet and refrigerated or frozen diligently. A court bouillon can stand around only when it is in the process of cooling off for easier handling. As soon as it is no longer in use, it must be refrigerated or frozen.

FISH MOST OFTEN POACHED IN COURT BOUILLON

Salmon, trout of all breeds, salmon trout, landlocked salmon, pike, bass, mullets, skate, haddock, cod in slices, conger eel and monkfish can all be poached successfully in the above court bouillon.

Carp, mackerel and bluefish are rarely poached nowadays. Should they be, the white wine in the court bouillon should be changed to red wine and the amount of vinegar increased slightly.

Poaching in milk is almost never done anymore. It is good to remember, however, that this is the best method for poaching pieces of turbot or finnan haddie. For milk court bouillon, see *The Making of a Cook*, page 255.

About Basic Ingredients and Kitchen Implements

SPICES

Aromatic Pepper for All Uses

OVER THE LAST FEW YEARS I have taken the habit of using the following aromatic pepper that I blend myself. I found the idea at Hédiard, Place de la Madeleine in Paris. This mixture is not Hédiard's mixture and represents strictly my own proportions of each spice. If you like more allspice, by all means change the formula to increase the quantity. I use by volume 15 percent allspice berries and 42.5 percent each of white and black peppercorns. Calculated for 1 cup of mixture, this would be approximately:

2 tablespoons allspice berries
7 tablespoons white peppercorns
7 tablespoons black peppercorns

Restaurant cooks can prepare a large jar that will last longer by using:

½ cup allspice berries
3 ¼ cups white peppercorns
3 ¼ cups black peppercorns

Chinese Pepper

I like to use Szechuan pepper, plain and coarsely ground, for its flavor and flower; since I am not looking for its "fire," I do not toast it.

"So-called" Pink Peppercorns

These are not peppercorns but freeze-dried berries from the Bourbon Islands. Their use has been outlawed in the United States by the Department of Health, Education and Welfare because they are considered dangerous for consumption in large quantities.

Quatre-Epices

This is the mixture I already recommended in *The Making of a Cook* (p. 27), less the tarragon and marjoram. For home use:

1 teaspoon ground cinnamon	*½ teaspoon ground cardamom*
2 teaspoons ground allspice	*1 teaspoon grated nutmeg*
⅛ teaspoon ground cloves	*2 teaspoons ground coriander*

This is a quantity that will not last too long and will not get too stale. Restaurant cooks who prepare a lot of terrines can use the following proportions, which will last approximately 3 months:

½ cup ground cinnamon	*¼ cup ground cardamom*
1 cup ground allspice	*½ cup grated nutmeg*
1 tablespoon ground cloves	*1 cup ground coriander*

This mixture represents strictly my personal taste, and both the spices and their quantity may be changed any way one desires.

Worcestershire Sauce

I use good old Lea & Perrins when I use some, which is not too often. Any kind you enjoy will be fine, especially if you make your own.

Anchovy Paste

I use anchovy paste both as a Mediterranean seasoning and, in some cases, as a salt corrector in a fish sauce. Any brand you like is fine *provided* it does not contain any sugar. If you have the time, mash your own anchovies after rinsing the fillets.

Meat Extract

Diluted meat extract is never used as a replacement for broth in good cuisine, but only as a taste modifier and corrector to intensify the flavor of sauces. It adds body and salt (see the chapter "Generalities on Sauces in Modern French Cuisine," pp. 169–177). Use semisolid extract, in which salt crystals are palpable, or semiliquid, the thick, most syrupy meat extract. It is important that the list of ingredients on the label mentions meat proteins rather than yeasts.

Bitters

I use simple Angostura bitters when I want to accentuate the bitter character of a sauce. There is no need to use orange bitters, as it is better to use some orange or other citrus rind in the sauce.

FRENCH-STYLE MUSTARDS

Since many cooks have been looking back to the Middle Ages and using a lot of the homemade concoctions of the French provincial cuisines, more and more vinegars, mustards, and fancy oils are being used and sold in fancy grocery stores for prices that can be shocking.

The cost of these items is all the more insulting in that most of them can be prepared at home for about one-quarter the price. So, if you can find the time, prepare them yourself. If not, go to the store and purchase them. The occasional expense will still prove worthwhile.

Dijon Mustard

Dijon mustard is Dijon mustard is Dijon mustard. That means: read the labels carefully and purchase mustard made in Dijon, capital of Burgundy, and use it as a base for all other preparations.

Mustard came to Gaul and especially to Dijon with the Roman legions, and the first recipe for it seems to have been written by Columella in the first century A.D. in his book *De Re Rustica*. By 1200 A.D., mustard was in general use in Dijon and Burgundy. The formulae have varied over the centuries and still vary from house to house, but in any case, Dijon mustard comes in two strengths: *forte*, or strong, and *extra-forte*, or extra strong. Using the strong type is amply sufficient to obtain an all-around typical French taste.

Fancy Mustards Based on Dijon Mustard

Using the basic strong Dijon mustard, you can prepare the following condiments yourself. They are excellent in some sauces and always provide a very pleasant change in salad dressings. Their refrigerator shelf life is 2 to 3 months.

MOUTARDE A L'ESTRAGON {Tarragon Mustard}

> *One 6½-ounce jar Dijon mustard*
> *⅓ cup packed fresh tarragon leaves*
> *A few drops lemon juice*
> *Salt and pepper*

Empty the mustard into the blender or food processor container. Blanch the tarragon leaves as follows: place them into a *chinois* or "China cap" conical strainer. Plunge the *chinois* into a pot of boiling water for 2–3 minutes until the leaves wilt. Drain well and add the blanched leaves to the blender or food processor container at the same time as the lemon juice, salt and pepper. Process to your taste—either smooth or slightly grainy.

MOUTARDE AUX HERBES VERTES {Green Herb Mustard}

One 6½-ounce jar Dijon mustard	*¼ cup basil leaves*
1¼ cups fresh mixed herbs	*¼ cup chopped chives or green*
consisting of:	*scallions*
¼ cup tarragon leaves	*⅓ teaspoon honey*
¼ cup chervil leaves	*1 tablespoon lemon juice*
¼ cup parsley leaves	*Salt and pepper*

Proceed as described in the preceding recipe, but process until the mixture turns bright green. Rebalance the taste with salt and pepper after adding the lemon juice.

MOUTARDE AU POIVRON ROUGE
{Red Bell Pepper Mustard}

2 medium very ripe red peppers	*1 tablespoon red wine vinegar*
1 tablespoon olive oil	*One 6½-ounce jar Dijon mustard*
Salt and pepper	*A pinch of cayenne pepper*
1 teaspoon tomato paste	*2–3 drops lemon juice*

Cut the peppers into ⅓-inch strips. Heat the olive oil in a 1½-quart saucepan; add the pepper strips and sauté them in the oil. Add the salt, pepper, tomato paste, and vinegar. Cover the pan and let the peppers cook for approximately 20 minutes, until they have rendered all their juices. Remove the cover and let the liquid in the pan evaporate completely. Let the peppers fall into mush. Strain the mixture into a clean bowl. Process the mustard as follows: blend together in the blender or food processor the Dijon mustard, pepper purée, cayenne, and lemon juice. Correct the seasoning with salt and pepper.

MOUTARDE DE FRAMBOISES *{Raspberry Mustard}*

½ cup fresh raspberries or ⅓ cup frozen raspberries in sugar syrup	*1 teaspoon tomato paste*
	½ teaspoon dry mustard
1 teaspoon honey	*One 6½-ounce jar Dijon mustard*
1 tablespoon red wine vinegar	*Salt and pepper*

Toss the fresh raspberries with the honey and vinegar and let stand for 4 hours, or until the berries look sadly depleted and flat. If using frozen raspberries, omit the honey. Separate the frozen berries well from the sugar syrup after defrosting and add the vinegar. The frozen berries will need 6 hours of marinating. Process the mixture in the blender and strain through a fine conical strainer to remove the seeds. Return the purée to the blender with the tomato paste, dry mustard, and Dijon mustard. Blend well. Empty the mixture into a saucepan or the top of a double boiler and stir over simmering water until the mustard thickens slightly. Correct the seasoning with salt and pepper. Turn into a jar and cool completely. Keep refrigerated.

MOUTARDE AU POIVRE VERT
{Green Peppercorn Mustard}

> *4 teaspoons green peppercorns (saltwater packed)*
> *2–3 drops lemon juice*
> *One 6½-ounce jar Dijon mustard*
> *1 tablespoon olive oil*

Mash the peppercorns with the lemon juice and 2 to 3 tablespoons of the mustard. Gradually mix in the remainder of the mustard and the olive oil. Turn into a jar and keep refrigerated.

CONDIMENTS MOUTARDES A L'ITALIENNE
(Italian-style Fruit Purée Mustards)

I love Italian cuisine so much that I have really made a serious study of it in the last ten years and have found the fruit mustards of Tuscany, Mantua, and the Piemonte attractive additions to my poultry dishes. The few mustards described here are very interesting concoctions for birds baked in salt or for the usually too bland white meat of chicken. See recipes on pages 336 and 345.

Where the Italians have the habit of using this type of fruit mustard with meat or pasta dishes, corresponding versions found in the French provinces probably issue from distant Gallo-Roman origins and are strictly sweet items. However, in fourteenth-century French cookbooks there is a mention of home-made mustard mixed with jams or sauces.

The recipes given below are made in the French style with modern ingredients and require very little preparation. They cook by themselves. All that is needed is to stir once in a while to prevent the mixture from sticking to the bottom of the pan.

CONDIMENT MOUTARDE AUX POMMES ET AUX POIRES *{Apple-and-Pear Mustard Condiment}*

6 Granny Smith apples	*3 cloves*
6 ripe Bartlett or Bosc pears	*1 teaspoon cardamom*
½ cup cider vinegar	*Grated rind of 1 lemon*
12 ounces white grapes, as green as possible	*½ teaspoon cinnamon*
	A pinch of salt
⅓–½ cup sugar	*Dijon mustard to taste*

Peel the apples and pears. Slice both fruits paper thin and put into a saucepan. Add the vinegar and cook over medium heat. Blend the grapes in the blender and strain the juice into the pot. Add the sugar, cloves, cardamom, lemon rind, cinnamon, and salt. Bring to a boil and then simmer until all the fruit has fallen apart and becomes a purée. Return to the blender and blend until smooth. Continue cooking until the sauce tastes good to you (everyone has a personal taste). Add mustard to taste and more sugar if desired.

The mixture can be used as is on all roasted poultry, especially turkey, white meat of chicken, or even on veal and duck. It is also very good on noodle dishes.

CONDIMENT MOUTARDE AUX FRAMBOISES *{Raspberry-and-Rhubarb Mustard Condiment}*

1 pound rhubarb	*Salt*
½ quart fresh raspberries	*Pepper from the mill in large flakes*
Sugar to taste (approximately ⅓ cup)	*Dijon mustard to taste*

Peel the rhubarb well. Cut it into 1-inch-long pieces. Place them in a saucepan with the raspberries, sugar, and salt. Cook until a saucelike mixture results. Strain it well to remove all seeds and fibers. Flavor with Dijon mustard to your taste.

This is excellent with plain roasted duck, pigeon, or quail. It also goes well on lukewarm asparagus.

CONDIMENT MOUTARDE AUX QUETSCHES
{Italian Prune-Plum Condiment}

1 pound Italian prune-plums
1 cup red wine (Côte-du-Rhône)
1/3 cup sugar, or more to taste
1/2 teaspoon Quatre-Epices
   (p. 35)

1/3 cup red wine vinegar
Dijon mustard to taste

Pit the prune-plums. Cut them into quarters and put them in a saucepan with the red wine, sugar, *quatre-épices*, and red wine vinegar. Cook to a sauce-like consistency. Strain to remove the skins of the prune-plums and add mustard to taste. Correct the seasoning.

This condiment is excellent on pasta and on all grain dishes such as polenta or spaetzle. It is also quite delicious on white meat of chicken, Cornish hens, turkey, etc.

VINEGARS

Vinegars come in diverse strengths of acetic acid. They are more or less sour, come in all colors, and are made from diverse substances such as red or white wine, pure white dilute of alcohol in water, pure apple juice fermented and turned sour, apple cider turned sour, and rice wine turned sour.

All this happens quite slowly and by itself. All you have to do to start a bottle of whatever vinegar you like is to remove one-third of the wine or cider from its bottle and replace it with the same amount of wine vinegar or cider vinegar. This method will give you the type of vinegar you prefer within 6 months. Letting wine simply turn to vinegar all by itself is a longer process that takes months and goes at its own pace without anyone being able to accelerate matters. Cider turns faster than wine.

The older a vinegar, the better I like it, so the cupboard in my house is always full of all kinds of vinegars. If you do not have the time or space to make your own, purchase good average-acidity vinegar made from red or white wine. The bottle will always indicate the degree of acetic acid, usually from

4 percent to 7.5 percent. The stronger the vinegar, the less of it you should use in dressings, reductions of sauces, or marinades.

Sherry vinegar, with its 7.5 percent acetic acid, can be the best or the worst depending entirely on you and how much you use. One will never make a mistake using cider vinegar, the strength of which is never above 4.5 percent or 5 percent. Wine vinegar usually reaches 6 percent acid, and alcohol vinegar for pickling can reach as high as 10 percent.

Good quality vinegars produced in France and Italy (*aceto balsamico*, for example) contain a residue of alcohol that mellows their acidity. You can tame a strong vinegar yourself by cutting it with a small amount of wine.

Whether you make your own basic vinegar or not is immaterial, for there are some very good products on the market. You should never buy a flavored vinegar, however, for you can make it yourself and skip the expense involved. Time and patience are again required. There are two ways to proceed.

The quick way consists in bringing the vinegar to a boil and pouring it over the flavoring agent. The smaller the cut of the flavoring, the faster the vinegar gets flavored. Crushed garlic cloves and coarsely chopped shallots render more taste faster than whole cloves of garlic and whole shallots. Herbs that have been bruised with the back of a knife act faster also. Shallot and garlic vinegars and those made with dried herbs are best prepared by this method. For other vinegars made with fresh herbs, I prefer the slow method of steeping the herb in the raw vinegar, which then remains unpasteurized and natural. Simply pour approximately ⅔ cup vinegar from the bottle and slide the herbs, singly or in combination, into the bottle until it is fairly well filled. From then on it will take at least 2 months for the characteristic flavor to be clearly discernible. All these "witch's brews" are extremely pleasant to have on hand.

Fruit vinegars that fetch such a price on the market can easily be made at home with berries (raspberries, strawberries) or other fruit (peaches, pears). Use *very* ripe berries or fruit and 6 percent red or white wine vinegar. For each bottle to be flavored, use ⅔ cup berries or sliced fruit (skins on). Put the berries or fruit into a bowl. Sprinkle with a tablespoon of the vinegar. Cover the bowl with cheesecloth and let stand at room temperature for 2 days. Remove ⅔ cup vinegar from the bottle and slide the berries or fruit slices into the bottle opening. The ripening of the vinegar takes a good 6 months.

In homes without much available space, working with bottles is simpler than dealing with a barrel in which the "mother" develops ever so slowly. It is surely romantic to have a vinegar barrel, but not always practical in the "sardine cans" people live in these days. If you have space, no problem; have fun with the barrel and make sure you keep it where it will not get too cold. I always place my bottles in a cupboard adjacent to the dishwasher where the temperature keeps things going!

Prepare a collection of vinegars every year. You will love them. Throw the old bottle away when it is finished. A good vinegar cupboard can offer the following varieties:

- garlic and rosemary, started from boiled vinegar (red or white wine)
- shallot, started from boiled vinegar (red or white wine)
- basil, started from raw vinegar (white wine)
- tarragon, started from raw vinegar (white wine)
- chervil, started from raw vinegar (white wine)
- raspberry, strawberry, started from raw vinegar (red wine)
- peach, pear, started from raw vinegar (white wine)
- rose petal, started from raw vinegar (red wine)—the old *vinaigre rosat* of the sixteenth century

Once a week, gently turn the bottles upside down. Do not shake madly. The most important ingredient is patience, since you cannot rush nature. It does what it feels like doing at the speed it feels like doing it!

From Verjus to Aceto Balsamico

Verjus is a condiment made of fresh green grapes, sugar, pure alcohol, and vinegar for which I gave my own old family recipe in *When French Women Cook*. Since 1976, however, I have made a number of such mixtures, and I would like to give here my favorite of all the formulae I have used. This is a wonderful mixture to use on salads, either plain for a low-calorie dressing or in combination with walnut or hazelnut oil. It also replaces wine in the sautéing of chicken, rabbit, squabs, quail, and pork.

You can make this *verjus* with sugar or with honey, with plain alcohol or with pisco, grappa, aquavit, or vodka (even Armagnac or Cognac if you feel rich), so that you will obtain very diverse mixtures. I found that by using a combination of sherry vinegar, honey, and plain grappa, one obtains a mixture that is a very useful imitation of *aceto balsamico*. Like Dijon mustard, *aceto balsamico* is *aceto balsamico*. Since chasing after a bottle of *aceto balsamico* is often almost like an epic adventure, I replace it sometimes with a mixture of nice, old *verjus* with sherry vinegar added, although the replacement would be totally inadequate by Italian standards.

Both *verjus* and *aceto balsamico* came to us from the Middle Ages. In grape-producing areas especially, but also all over France, women produced both their own *verjus* and their own vinegar. There was a use for each of them in the household. *Verjus* is mentioned in the 1392 *Le Ménagier de Paris* and is probably traditional to many grape-producing countries. Some areas poor in oil used *verjus* exclusively as a condiment for their salad greens, with nothing more than a dash of salt added, since pepper was too expensive for the common folk.

Aceto balsamico, according to Felice Cunsolo in *La Guida Gastronomica d'Italia*, is made in Modena from white wine that has, as the author says, been *"opportunamente trattato"* (properly treated). It is kept a long time in small barrels known as *vascelli*, which are made of woods as diverse as juniper, chestnut, oak, or mulberry. Each barrel—and the colony of acetobacter it contains—is transmitted from generation to generation. The finished vinegar is passed from barrel to barrel. The diverse woods give the unique flavor, aroma, and bouquet to the vinegar.

Nowadays, there are two types of *aceto balsamico*: the mass-produced type and the old traditional type. Tasted side by side, one recognizes immediately those coming from smaller production houses. They have, to say the least, more personality. The artisanal products do not, by any means, all taste the same, since no producer has the same combination of barrels. If the reader is interested, the purchase of diverse labels is recommended. All the vinegars will be good; some will be truly excellent. *Aceto balsamico* never has less than 6 percent acetic acid and a residue of pure alcohol of approximately 1.5 percent.

VERJUS

30 large green grapes, unwashed
1 quart grape juice made from
   crushed grapes, as sour as possible
2/3 cup honey (thyme, evergreen,
   blossoms)

2 quarts 90 percent alcohol or other
   distilled spirit such as grappa,
   vodka, aquavit, or brandy
2 cups sherry vinegar

Prick the whole grapes with a needle. Place them at the bottom of a half-gallon jar.

Filter the grape juice through a paper coffee filter placed on the opening of the jar, dripping the juice onto the grapes. Add the honey and stir until dissolved. Add the alcohol and the vinegar. Seal the jar with several layers of cheesecloth. Do not disturb for at least 2 months. The *verjus* is ready to use when the berries have fallen to the bottom and the liquid mixture has completely clarified. A fine layer of sediment will appear at the bottom of the jar. It keeps several years and ages very gracefully.

EMERGENCY ACETO BALSAMICO

Make this mixture only if you cannot find the original product.

> ½ cup sherry vinegar
> 1 teaspoon honey
> ¾ cup verjus, *well finished and aged*

OILS

This is another product of tremendous expense that one simply cannot escape. One can, however, be parsimonious.

Corn Oil
The old passe-partout oil, corn oil, is, of course, available everywhere, although those sold in natural food stores are better than those sold in supermarkets.

Olive Oil
Olive oil comes in many qualities and flavors. My very favorite is the Italian, extra-virgin, pale green olive oil from the area of Lucca in Tuscany. Make sure that the label on the bottle or container reads "extra-virgin." It has become less difficult to find but is still worth "schlepping" across the Atlantic when returning from a trip to Italy.

French virgin olive oil varies enormously in quality, color, and flavor. It depends who processes it. My compatriots do not all have the same standards of production, I must admit to my greatest regret. Brand naming would not help, as the quality varies from vintage to vintage.

California olive oil is no worse than the lesser grades of Provençal olive oils. One should be critically aware of the fact that "Made in France" or "Made in Italy" are not magic words. Made in the U.S.A. can be extremely good. Sure, they can be difficult to find, but there are people in California who have pride in their production, and consequently there are some excellent olive oils. The challenge is to hunt for them. Change brands until you find the one with uniformly favorable characteristics.

Walnut Oil

Beware of walnut oils sold in the United States. Many are old and downright rancid. If, when you open the bottle, the oil smells strong and has that awful acrid and aggressive taste, it is too old. Take it back where you bought it and ask that your money be returned. Good walnut oil is sweet and gives the impression when one tastes it of eating a liquid walnut meat without the tannic skin. Use walnut oil sparingly—only for dressings. Frying in it is done only very, very rarely.

Hazelnut Oil

Hazelnut oil is a delicious luxury. It is so good that it is well worth the monetary investment. It lasts a long time when kept cool in an opaque container, and a little bit goes a long way, so do not overuse. Again, one does not usually fry in hazelnut oil; it is used mostly for dressings on vegetables or high-protein salads. One of its best uses is in making chocolate *couverture* (see Chocolate Tuiles, p. 506).

Avocado Oil

This is one of the wonderful treats California has to offer. Purchase in very small bottles for two reasons: price and quick spoilage. Wrap the little bottle in foil and use sparingly on melon or other fruit salads.

CREAMS

The two basic creams for cooking, heavy cream and sour cream, will remain the staples used from one end of this book to the other. They replace the French *crème fraîche* in my American kitchen. In France, of course, I use *crème fraîche* and nothing else.

I am totally aware that "making" *crème fraîche* is a favorite sport of the American cook; all I can say is if cooks enjoy themselves making *crème fraîche*, they might as well go ahead and do it. The taste of any of those products, however, has nothing at all to do with true *crème fraîche*; sometimes the texture is right, but the taste is never in the least reminiscent of the French or European unpasteurized products. Even in Europe, the taste of *crème fraîche* varies enormously from the masterpieces of "nature made" *crème fraîche* found in Normandy and the Alps to the "dairy made" products found in big cities.

As you read the recipes in this book, remember that true, unpasteurized *crème fraîche* "pits" the texture of the sauce if boiled hard. You will see tiny bits of protein floating in the sauce; straining will eliminate this problem. The dairy made *crème fraîche* will not pit, nor will reduced heavy cream. Please read carefully the instructions on using cream in the sauces for meats and fish.

Ultrapasteurized Heavy Cream
Use it only if you have nothing else. It does not "pit" sauces while reducing and can be used in all fish mousselines (see pp. 184–208).

Reduced Heavy Cream
Since heavy cream is often used reduced rather than plain, it is wise both at home and in the restaurant to always keep a jar of it on the refrigerator shelf. It is prepared by cooking down by one-half on medium-low heat and whisking at regular intervals to prevent the formation of a skin. Any amount can be prepared at once. The reduced cream is perfectly sterile and must be stored in a sterile jar. It keeps at least 3 weeks in the refrigerator.

BUTTERS

Use exclusively Grade AA 93 Score unsalted butter for all your preparations. Only unsalted butter will make a good sauce, because it must be emulsified into an already well seasoned essence or reduction.

Clarified butter is obtained by melting the butter on medium-high heat, then skimming off both the casein scum that forms at the top and the liquid whey that settles at the bottom of the pan.

Noisette butter is made by cooking the butter until the casein precipitates to the bottom of the pan and cooks there to a dark russet brown deposit. The butter grease also turns a deep russet brown and smells like toasting hazelnuts, hence its French name—noisette (or hazelnut) butter. Once the butter has reached the correct color and taste, it must be decanted of all solids. This is best done by using a large sauce spoon to transfer the clear butter grease into a clean jar. The brown deposits can be discarded. Note that if the deposits turn black, the butter grease smells and tastes burned, so avoid overcooking.

FLOURS

I will keep the same philosophy in this book as in all my other books and use all-purpose, unbleached flour.

It is good, nevertheless, to learn to evaluate the percentage of proteins in a flour so as to know how "strong" it is, that is to say, whether it is usable for pastry or bread or both. This can be done by reading the nutritional information on the side of each bag of flour. It will give you the amount of protein grams per cup of flour, which weighs 4 ounces, or 114 grams. For example, should the label indicate 12 protein grams, the percentage of protein is:

$$\frac{12 \times 100}{114} = 10.5 \text{ percent}$$

Should the label say 14 protein grams, the percentage would be:

$$\frac{14 \times 100}{114} = 12.28 \text{ percent}$$

A flour containing 10.5 percent protein can be used to make pastries but will be a bit soft to make bread. On the contrary, a flour with 12.28 percent protein will be fine for bread but require a little more shortening when used for pastry making.

Most of the time, the label will list 12 to 14 protein grams. The percentage will then be an average of $\dfrac{12 + 14}{2} = 13$, and the flour will have a protein of

$$\frac{13 \times 100}{114} = 11.3 \text{ percent}$$

which places the flour right in the all-purpose range.

Such a flour will make a good homemade loaf and can be transformed into pastry flour by removing 2 tablespoons of flour per pound (4 cups sifted) and replacing them with 2 tablespoons of cornstarch.

To obtain cake flour, ¼ cup of flour must be removed per pound and replaced with ¼ cup of cornstarch.

FOIE GRAS

From the revered and rarely used item it was until the 1950s, foie gras has become a very much used and favorite item in French cuisine today.

I feel compelled to say a few words about it. Yes, it is extremely interesting to see the ducks and geese force-fed and to examine the resulting fat livers at a "Marché au Gras" (Foie Gras Market) in the diverse areas of their production. I have seen several in the Chalosse and in Périgord, and found that the market at Samatan in the Gers department in the heart of Gascony was simply the most interesting of all for me.

The American mind and heart usually revolt at the thought of force-feeding the birds, a process that is so old it goes as far back as the Egyptians and is done with love and dedication by women called *"Gaveuses."* But considering Spinoza's opinion that man is a wolf to man, how can man not be a wolf to animals, including ducks and geese? I fail to understand Americans who thoroughly enjoy their sirloin steaks and yet feel upset because a duck or goose is force-fed on solid natural corn kernels. Is shooting a steer full of hormones and antibiotics any more ethical? Let us be a bit reasonable and face the fact that either one is a meat eater and admits it, or one simply sticks to a vegetable diet.

Anyhow, at this writing, good quality American-made foie gras is first becoming available to restaurant owners in the United States, and will probably become available to the general public within a very short time. I have tasted the American-made livers both in the summer and in the winter. The winter livers, like the French products, are firmer and superior to the warm weather livers. American livers are huge—a large duck liver in France weighs up to 1½ pounds; in the United States it is a good 2 pounds, and the quality is in no way inferior to the French hand-fed and force-fed livers. For the reader who will consider affording the fresh fattened liver, the way to cook it is indicated on pages 364–65. Those who find the price prohibitive can substitute a simple liver mousse prepared with Armagnac and served on plain French bread, as on page 79.

A bit of raw foie gras can be used to bind a sauce, just as a bit of a regular fowl or unfattened liver can be used. See page 276. A liver mousse cannot be used to bind a sauce, because the liver, being already cooked to prepare the mousse, would be overcooked if added to a hot sauce and would cause the sauce to turn greenish and slightly grainy.

TRUFFLES

I have omitted all but one recipe in which truffles are essential, as their price is extremely prohibitive. You can import fresh black truffles into the United States, since they are not on the forbidden list of the Department of Commerce. I used to import them weekly between December 1 and March 1. The best truffles in France now come from Tricastin (département de la Drôme). You can order them by airmail from:

SICA FRANCE TRUFFES
La Baume de Transit
St. Paul-Trois-Châteaux, Drôme

If you find yourself in France and want to see truffles dug out by a dog, contact these people. They organize trips every Saturday morning from December 1 to February 15. The dogs are legitimate and the truffle hunting and finding absolutely authentic. Be prepared for a very rustic meal for lunch, but on the whole it is a most interesting experience, and the Provençaux are congenial and will easily sing in a group while you eat your lunch.

USING MODERN IMPLEMENTS

May I restate here my oft expressed opinion that one cooks with the implements one has and can afford. Good food comes from good understanding of what one is executing, not from expensive pots, pans, and other paraphernalia.

There is no doubt, however, that owning an electric mixer, a blender, and a food processor is most useful at home and absolutely indispensable in the restaurant trade, however small the restaurant. It is silly to stand there puréeing fish meat for a mousseline in a foodmill when a blender or a food processor can do the work in one-tenth the time.

The attitude that should be avoided is that having a food processor is a replacement for one's brain or hands. The food processor can do almost anything. There are, however, a few things it does not do quite as well as a pair of hands holding a good sharp knife.

You will find me tolerant in the pages that follow, and I will always indicate "by hand" or "in a food processor." Take your pick! . . . I know what I like as look and texture, and I know what the knife or the food processor can produce. I never hesitate to use the food processor when it gives me the texture and quality I like. When it does not, I switch to other implements.

An Honest Loaf of Bread

MUCH HAS BEEN WRITTEN about bread during the last twenty years, and some of the best French bread produced in the whole world is made in American homes. There is, as a result, very little wisdom I can add to the volumes written, so I shall limit myself to a few very easy recipes preceded by a few words on the value of a leaven.

When I was growing up, I always loved the slightly sour taste of the massive round "*meules*" (round loaves 20 inches wide and 7–8 inches high) of country bread neatly floured. Questioning my wonderful baker in Annecy in an informal conversation, I found out that that taste is obtained by letting a very small amount of yeast, a pinch each of cumin powder, flour, and water stand and ferment for 48–72 hours before being kneaded into a bread dough. The leavening method was not new to me, but the use of cumin to sour it slightly was. So I tried it, and it worked.

First I want to talk about how to prepare the leaven. Then I will give you several recipes that can be built on that leaven and indicate what each bread is best used for.

LEAVEN

For each batch of bread, you will need 2 cups of flour for the leaven. The making of the leaven takes 3 days, so *plan* your bread 3 days before you serve it, 4 days if you like your bread day-old.

The amount of work involved is minimal; the yeast does the work, not you.

Day One

½ envelope dry yeast
1 cup all-purpose flour (12 percent protein)
¼ teaspoon cumin powder
⅔ cup lukewarm water

Mix the yeast, flour, cumin powder, and water into a semiliquid batter. Let stand at room temperature in a bowl covered with cheesecloth for 24 hours.

Day Two

Add I cup flour and enough lukewarm water to make your batter semiliquid again. Cover and let stand at room temperature for another 24 hours.

Day Three

Finish the bread. Add to the leaven as much flour as is called for in each of the following recipes in this chapter and knead well.

WHY ONE SPRAYS A LOAF OF BREAD WITH WATER WHILE BAKING

After you have kneaded a bread dough and let it rise to double its original bulk, you must punch it down, then form it into the desired shape. You must then "dock" it (slash its surface deeply in several places with a razor blade) and let it rise again until it is four-fifths larger than it was at the onset of that last rising. Notice that a dehydrated crust has already formed on the surface of the bread and that this crust is thinner within the slashes cut with your razor blade.

The heat of the oven will cause the crust to continue hardening through dehydration, and as the internal dough, which is still very wet, expands, you will see the dockings expand, thus keeping the superficial crust from breaking open under the internal pressure of steam and dilating carbon dioxide. It may happen that even if you have docked the loaf, internal pressure will make it break on one of its sides, and you will see a longitudinal crack run on one whole side of the loaf.

To prevent this, spray the loaf with water 2 or 3 times during the first 10 minutes of the baking time. The fine spray of water droplets will rehydrate the surface of the loaf and allow better expansion of the bread.

The first spraying is the most important; the following two are proportionally less important since the loaf, by the third spraying, will have developed to its maximum size.

To prevent a crust as hard as a rock, brush the finished loaf, while hot right out of the oven, with a bit of olive or walnut oil.

THE BEST FLOUR FOR BREAD

Use all-purpose flour for which the protein content is marked on the bag as 12–14 grams (see explanation of how to calculate the percentage of protein in flour on p. 48) or use a flour sold under the label "bread" flour.

COMPOSITION OF BASIC FRENCH BREAD DOUGH

Notice the total absence of any ingredients other than flour, water, salt, and yeast in basic bread doughs. French breads never contain any sugar; sugar is reserved for breakfast breads.

PAIN PROVENÇAL AU FENOUIL
{Olive Oil and Fennel Bread}

For all Mediterranean meals and all fish soups and stews.

L E A V E N :

> *⅓ teaspoon cumin powder*
> *2 cups all-purpose white flour (12 percent protein)*
> *½ envelope dry yeast*
> *Lukewarm water*

B R E A D :

> *4 cups flour*
> *1 tablespoon salt*
> *1½ tablespoons fennel seeds*
> *Lukewarm water*
> *½ cup olive oil*

1. Have your leaven ready and fermenting for 2 days. Place the 4 additional cups of flour on the table or counter top. Make a large well in it, and add the leaven, salt, and fennel seeds.
2. Gather leaven and flour into a bread dough, adding as much lukewarm water as needed to make a smooth dough that shows a wee bit of tackiness. Knead the dough for 10 minutes, no more.
3. When the dough is ready, put it into a large bowl that has been lightly rubbed with some of the olive oil. Let rise until double in bulk.
4. Preheat the oven to 425°F. Punch the dough down, gradually adding the olive oil by working it into the dough. Shape into a large, round loaf 12–13 inches in diameter and, with a razor blade, slash a cross ⅓ inch down into the top of the loaf. Let it rise again until it is 1⅔ times its original size.
5. Bake until crisp and golden, about 20–30 minutes, spraying it with water 3 times during the first 10 minutes of baking. No brushing of the crust with olive oil is necessary afterward.

PAIN DE CAMPAGNE {*French Country Bread*}

This is an all-purpose bread for all meals.

The French whole-wheat flour, also called *farine integrale*, meaning that it contains all the essential parts of the wheat kernel—bran membrane, endosperm, and germ—is extremely finely milled and has a uniform beige color due to the presence of the bran. *Pain de campagne* is made with 50 percent white bread flour and 50 percent *farine intégrale*. To reproduce the fine texture of the *farine intégrale*, blend your whole-wheat flour in the blender until no trace of the bran flakes appears in it.

LEAVEN:

> *¼ teaspoon cumin powder*
> *2 cups all-purpose white flour*
> *½ envelope dry yeast*
> *Lukewarm water*

BREAD:

> *1 cup all-purpose white flour*
> *3 cups whole-wheat flour blended to a uniform powdery texture*
> *1 tablespoon salt*
> *Lukewarm water*
> *2 tablespoons walnut oil*

1. Prepare the leaven. When it is ready, place the white flour mixed with the whole-wheat flour on the table or counter top. Make a well.
2. Add the leaven, the salt, and enough lukewarm water to gather it into a ball. Knead 10 minutes or until completely smooth but still ever so slightly tacky.
3. Put the finished dough in a bowl rubbed with 1 tablespoon of the walnut oil. Let rise until doubled in bulk.
4. Preheat the oven to 425°F. Punch the dough down and cut it into 2 equal parts. Shape each part into a loaf 3 inches wide and 10 inches long. Cut a deep slash, approximately ⅓ inch deep, down the center of each loaf from one end to the other. Let rise until it is 1⅔ times its original size. Bake for 25–30 minutes, spraying with water 3 times during the first 10 minutes of baking. When the loaves are baked, brush each one with the remaining tablespoon of walnut oil.

PAINS AUX NOIX DIVERSES
{Breads with Diverse Nuts}

Walnuts, hazelnuts, pignoli, or any other nut of your choice can be added to a bread dough to give it taste and to vary the texture.

Walnut Bread
Excellent with all soft paste French cheese such as Camembert, Brie, and Triple Crème; also with cabbage-based soups.

Hazelnut Bread
Excellent with all fresh goat cheeses, with salads containing asparagus and sweetbreads, with terrines of light meats such as rabbit and sweetbread.

Pignoli Bread
Extremely expensive; reserve it for Mediterranean-style fish soups.

In all cases, prepare a bread dough with the flour(s) of your choice, using either 100 percent white flour or 50 percent white flour and 50 percent whole-wheat flour blended to a uniform texture. See bread recipes 54–56.

The quantity of nuts used for each bread made with a total of 6 cups flour is:

> *1 cup walnut meats, chopped coarse*
> or
> *½ cup hazelnut, chopped coarse, or pignoli meats, whole*

PAIN AU BLE GERME *{Sprouted Wheat Bread}*

You can either use the olive oil bread on page 54 and replace the fennel seed with 1 cup sprouted wheat kernels or introduce the same amount of wheat kernels into the *Pain de Campagne* recipe on page 55.

To sprout the wheat, place the kernels in a bowl and barely cover them with water. Stretch cheesecloth over the surface of the bowl and let the wheat stand until well puffed up. Within 24 hours you will see the sprouting start, and within 48 hours hours the kernels will start showing green sprouts that, after 3 days, will weave into one another. You can add the sprouts to the bread dough of your choice.

Plan your sprouting and dough preparation so both are finished at the same time, remembering that you need 3 days for each to be ready for blending.

Shape the dough into 2 loaves well rubbed with olive or other oil and brush the top of each loaf with oil also before baking.

PAIN DE SEIGLE POUR LES HUITRES
{Rye Bread for Oysters}

In France this bread is customarily served with oysters on the half shell. The following recipe will yield 3 loaves baked in small loaf pans.

LEAVEN:

> 2 cups all-purpose white flour
> ½ envelope dry yeast
> ¼ teaspoon cumin powder
> Lukewarm water

BREAD:

> 1 cup all-purpose white flour
> 2 cups rye flour, milled fine
> 1 tablespoon salt
> 4 tablespoons butter

1. Prepare the leaven.
2. When the leaven is ready, mix the white flour with the rye flour and make a well. Add the leaven, salt, and enough lukewarm water to gather it into a ball. Knead into a soft, elastic, and slightly tacky dough. Do not knead more than 10 minutes.
3. Melt 2 tablespoons of the butter. Rub a clean bowl with 1 tablespoon of the melted butter. Put the dough in the bowl and let rise. When double in bulk,

punch it down, shape into 3 small loaves and fit into 3 small loaf pans, greased with the 2 tablespoons unmelted butter.

4. Preheat the oven to 375°F. Let the loaves rise until the dough is within ¼ inch of the rim of the pan. Brush the top of each loaf with the remaining tablespoon of melted butter and bake for 35 minutes.

Amuse-Gueule

A<small>N AMUSE-GUEULE IS AN INSIGNIFICANT</small>, delicious little piece of food that a good restaurateur puts on the table to keep his guests busy while the serious food is cooking. Americans would call any of these tidbits an appetizer or an hors d'oeuvre, but I like that truculent expression reeking of Bocuse because it is a familiar and funny word. I am not even sure that it yet appears in the French dictionary as a legitimized word or that the Académie Française has yet established whether the plural form of the word should or should not take an "s." I guess it depends whether one means to amuse one *gueule* or several *gueules*.

Amuse-gueule are not so insignificant that prepared in larger quantity they cannot become serious dishes. You will find the recipes written so they can be multiplied to obtain main courses or first courses. The omelets will be easier to prepare in large quantity if you follow the directions at the beginning of the recipe.

AMUSE-GUEULE AUX OEUFS
(Egg Appetizers)

The effect on guests of a tiny, well-prepared, and nicely shaped omelet is won-derful. There is something in that fat, rounded, golden cigar that is comforting and so appetizing it makes the gastric juices flow immediately. And yet . . . look at the lowly ingredients: eggs, shallots, bread crumbs; so as not to frighten the reader into cholesterol fits, I use butter to cook the omelets, but in the original provinces, these omelets are cooked in *confit* (rendered duck) fat (see p. 311).

OMELETTE DE LA MERE BOURGAIN DE BEYNAC {Marie-Antoinette Bourgain's Omelet}

Marie-Antoinette Bourgain was exiled from her native Périgourdian village of Beynac in the late 1890s at the same time my great-grandmother was exiled from her native Poitou. They had lost their vines in the phylloxeria epidemic and ended up neighbors in a fourteenth arrondissement Paris tenement and became as close as sisters. Marie-Antoinette passed on to Marie-Charlotte several of the omelets she had brought with her from her native province. This first one is made with buttered coarse bread crumbs, garlic, shallots, and parsley all rolled into 1 egg and cooked in 20 seconds. To make larger omelets, multi-ply by the number of eggs you wish. Two eggs make a nice luncheon or brunch dish, three a handsome dinner if complemented by a salad.

SERVES 1

1 egg
1 tablespoon chopped parsley
½ a small clove garlic, chopped fine
½ a shallot, chopped fine
1½ tablespoons coarse bread crumbs from French or light rye bread

Coarsely cracked pepper from the mill
½ tablespoon butter or rendered duck [confit] fat
Salt

1. Mix the egg, parsley, garlic, and shallot very well together.
2. Place the bread crumbs and pepper together with the butter or fat in a small

omelet pan. Heat the mixture gradually until the bread crumbs turn golden and the pepper starts smelling of flowers.

3. Pour the egg mixture over the bread crumbs. Add a pinch of salt. Stir once or twice with a fork; when the omelet is cooked, roll it and invert it onto a small plate. Serve very quickly.

OMELETTE AUX PEAUX DE CANARD
{Omelet with Duck Skins}

On page 315, amidst the explanations of the duck and goose *confit*, you will find the recipe for preparing the skins of both animals so that they turn into very crisp and very tasty little strips. These duck and goose skins are prepared all over the areas whose main occupation is *"Le Gras"* or "artisanal" fattening of geese and ducks. Everything is used from the poor animals to prepare a multitude of excellent little dishes and tidbits. Here is what can be done with some of the crisp skins.

SERVES I

1 tablespoon chopped parsley
½ small clove garlic
Salt
Pepper from the mill
1 egg

½ tablespoon butter or rendered duck
  [confit] fat
1½ tablespoons confit *duck skins as*
  prepared on page 315

1. Put the parsley, garlic, salt, pepper, and egg into a small bowl and beat well.
2. Heat the butter or fat in a frying pan; add the skin strips and heat well until the latter start frying.
3. Add the egg and aromatics mixture and stir several times. Roll the omelet and invert on a plate to serve.

OMELETTES AUX AULX CONFITS

There are several interesting little morsels resulting from the cooking of a *confit* (see pp. 315–17) and taught to my family by Madame Bourgain. One of these uses the wing tips and the garlic cloves that were put to candy with the larger pieces of duck or goose. The omelet made with these is indescribably delicious, especially the mixture of cooked and raw garlic. One goose wing produces enough meat for 2 omelets; 1 duck wing enough for 1.

SERVES 1–2

1 tablespoon meat removed from 1
  duck or goose confit-*ed wing tip*
  (see p. 315)
1 tablespoon confit-*ed garlic cloves*
  (see p. 317)
½ tablespoon butter or rendered
  duck (confit) *fat*

½ a tiny raw clove garlic, mashed
1 tablespoon chopped parsley
A pinch of salt
Pepper from the mill
1 egg

1. Dice the duck or goose meat. Put in the omelet pan to heat slowly. Add the *confit*-ed garlic cloves and the butter or fat.
2. Mix the raw garlic, parsley, salt, pepper, and egg in a small bowl and beat until homogenized.
3. Pour over the meat and garlic cloves. Stir 2 or 3 times with a fork and roll into an omelet. Invert onto a small plate.

AMUSE-GUEULE AUX FROMAGES DIVERS
(Cheese Appetizers)

CLAQUERET

Lyon, the silk capital of France, was kept affluent by the toil of its silk workers, the *Canuts*. The ancestral beaten white cheese of the Lyonnais was called the *Claqueret* because it was "*claqué*" (beaten), says the chronicle, "as if it were a woman." The white cheese was rebaptized *Cervelle de Canuts* (*Canuts'* brains) —perhaps by the *Canuts* in self-mockery, or maybe by the bourgeoisie of Lyon in mockery of the *Canuts'* heads and brains, made mellow by too much work and not enough education.

Here is a version eminently feasible in the United States, to be eaten on whatever you like, from vegetable sticks to toasted French bread. If you have access to unpasteurized milk, of course use your own well-dripped white cheese.

1 pound small-curd creamed cottage
    cheese
1/4 cup sour cream
1 1/2 tablespoons vinegar of your
    choice, preferably white wine
    vinegar
3 tablespoons dry white wine of the
    Mâcon Villages type

2 large shallots, chopped very fine
1 clove garlic, chopped very fine
1 1/2 tablespoons each chopped parsley,
    chervil, tarragon, and chives
Salt to taste
Coarsely cracked pepper from the mill
    to taste
1/3 cup heavy cream

1. Process in the blender until smooth the cottage cheese and sour cream. Empty into a strainer or colander fitted with cheesecloth and let drip for 36–48 hours.
2. Place the dripped cheese into the large bowl of an electric mixer. While beating, add gradually the vinegar, wine, shallots, garlic, and herbs. Remove to a bowl. Add the salt and pepper.
3. Whip the cream to the light Chantilly stage and fold into the cheese. Correct the final seasoning. Let stand in the refrigerator 2 hours before serving.

Note: It is essential that the sour cream used in this recipe be plain and unadulterated and contain no moisture-retaining stabilizer or the cheese will not drip properly.

FROMAGE FORT

Strong cheese! Wow, is it ever strong! The name connotes mashed cheese that, in diverse areas of France, is fermented in pottery jars with marc or other potent spirits. It is chiefly prepared in the Beaujolais, in Lyon, in Lorraine where it is called *fromage en pot*, and in the Dauphiné where it has the refined name of *Pétafine*. The Vivarais has its version called *Foudjou*. The north of France does not leave the custom only to the ancient Roman world; it uses its old *Maroille* the same way.

    This version is more a marinated cheese than a *fromage fort*, but it still gets potent. Serve a dish of salted red onion slices with it and nice buttered slices of crusty French bread. This will show off a Châteauneuf-du-Pape or a Californian Petite Sirah with great gusto. Prepare 3 months before eating. Just put it in the refrigerator or the cellar and forget about it.

3 small half-dry goat cheeses
1 leek, sliced thin
1 cup dry white wine
1 ounce marc, Cognac, Armagnac,
    or brandy
Approximately 1½ cups olive oil

1 bay leaf
1½ teaspoons each dried thyme and
    rosemary
10 each of black peppercorns, white
    peppercorns, and allspice berries
3 cloves garlic, peeled and bruised

1. Place the goat cheese into a pint-size canning jar.
2. Place the sliced leek in a saucepan and top it with the wine. Boil together until only ¼ cup of liquid is left. Cool.
3. Pour this liquid in the blender container. Add the spirits and the olive oil and blend until homogenized.
4. To the canning jar add the bay leaf, well crushed, and the thyme and rosemary. Add the peppercorns, allspice, and bruised garlic cloves. Pour the marinade over. Close the jar and shake well.
5. Store in the refrigerator for 3 months before serving. Shake the jar at regular intervals.

PETITS FROMAGES ROTIS AUX AMANDES
{Almond Coated and Roasted Goat Cheeses}

A Provençal idea, using the ewe's milk *Banon* in the spring, the goat *Banon* from the end of spring to the beginning of fall, and cow's *Banon* year round.

The cheese comes wrapped in chestnut leaves tied into a neat package with natural raffia fibers. Remove the chestnut leaves and the crust should appear fresh, but a bit viscous. Do not use the *"Pebre d'aï"* or *Banon* flavored with wild savory; the plain one is better.

SERVES 8 AS AN APPETIZER

3 tablespoons very fine-chopped blanched almonds
1½ tablespoons coarse bread crumbs from stale French Country Bread (p. 55)
1 Banon *cheese without chestnut leaves*
2 tablespoons butter, melted

1. Mix the ground almonds with the bread crumbs.
2. If the cheese is creamy and sticky enough on the outside, coat it well with

the mixture. If it is not, brush it with butter, then coat it with crumbs and nuts.

3. Preheat the oven to 425°F. Put the cheese on a cookie sheet and dribble melted butter all over its surfaces. Bake until the crust is golden and slightly crisp. It should become warm at the center, not brightly hot.

4. Serve with toasted French Country Bread (p. 55).

PETITS CHAUSSONS AU REBLOCHON
{Reblochon Turnovers}

This is a favorite pastry savory of my beautiful city of Annecy. I have modified the recipe with an addition of thick white sauce to prevent the cheese from running through the edges of the pastry and all over the oven. Filling and pastry both can be prepared up to 2 days ahead of time.

Although I am not fond of the vegetable shortening that enters their composition, cooks who lack either the time or the knowledge to make puff pastry may want to use frozen puff pastry bought from a catering service or can roll out paper thin a supermarket-bought puff pastry shell and cut their turnovers out of that. For those cooks who will consider making puff pastry, the method described on page 461 is quick and beats all others.

SERVES 6–8

FILLING:

1 pound Reblochon, Beaufort, or
    Swiss Gruyère cheese
1½ tablespoons butter
1½ tablespoons flour

½ cup milk, scalding
Salt
Pepper from the mill
Nutmeg to taste

PASTRY:

2 cups sifted all-purpose white flour
1 cup unsalted butter, cut into large
    chunks
¾ teaspoon salt

½ teaspoon fine-grated nutmeg
⅓–½ cup water
1 egg yolk
3 tablespoons milk

1. *To prepare the filling*: Remove all crust from the cheese and cut it into ⅓-inch cubes. With butter and flour prepare a roux, bind it with the scald-

ing milk, and thicken over medium heat. Season with only a little salt, plenty of coarsely cracked pepper, and nutmeg. Cool to barely lukewarm. Add the cheese, mix well, and let cool completely. Taste the seasoning before using.

2. *To prepare the pastry*: Mix the flour, butter, salt, nutmeg, and water into a rough, unhomogeneous paste. Let it rest for 30 minutes. Give it 6 turns (see puff pastry directions on p. 461).

3. *To prepare the turnovers*: Roll the pastry ¹⁄₁₆ inch thick. Cut the pastry into as many 6-inch circles as you can make (from 8 to 10). Put 1 teaspoon of the cheese mixture at the center of each round. Brush the edge of the pastry with a wash made from mixing the egg yolk and the milk and seal into a turnover by rolling the crinkled edge of the cutter on the cut edge of the turnover. Brush with egg wash.

4. Refrigerate—as long as you wish—to prevent shrinkage. Preheat the oven to 425°F. Bake turnovers for 15 minutes. For best flavor serve lukewarm.

TARTES AU M'GIN DE LORRAINE
{Lorraine White Cheese Tart}

Mougin, or *M'gin* in old Lorraine, was the name given to very fresh white cheese still containing a good proportion of whey. Here is a savory version of it; the basic idea is that of my Great-Aunt Orelly, who was a farm woman from between Mirecourt and Portieux. She used plain onions; I find the shallots better.

MAKES EIGHTEEN 2-INCH
TARTLETS OR A 9-INCH PIE
TO SERVE 10–12
SMALL COCKTAIL PORTIONS

PASTRY:

1½ cups sifted all-purpose white flour
½ teaspoon allspice
½ cup butter, cut into large chunks
1 egg
½ teaspoon salt

FILLING:

7 tablespoons butter

½ pound shallots, sliced into ¼-inch
    rings

Salt

Pepper from the mill

1 tablespoon poppy seeds, crushed

¼ cup good stock of your choice

4 ounces cream cheese

2 tablespoons flour

4 ounces small-curd cottage cheese

⅓ cup sour cream

2 large eggs

A large pinch each of fine-ground
    nutmeg and allspice

1. *To prepare the pastry*: Make a well in the flour, add the allspice and the butter. Work together with your fingertips until a meal results. Add the egg beaten with the salt and work into a pastry. Refrigerate at least 1 hour before using.

2. *To prepare the filling*: In 1 tablespoon of the butter, sauté, then cover the shallots and stew them until they are well done and quite soft; season with salt and pepper, add the poppy seeds and the stock to coat the shallots, then let it reduce completely. Set this mixture aside. Cream the remaining butter, gradually add the cream cheese and the flour. Set aside. Put the cottage cheese, sour cream, eggs, nutmeg, and allspice in the blender container and process until very smooth. Gradually blend into the butter–cottage cheese mixture and season to your taste.

3. *To prepare the pies:* Roll the pastry out ⅛ inch thick and cut into 2¼-inch circles. Fit into buttered cocktail tartlet shells. Spread a teaspoon or so of shallot mixture on the bottom of each shell and top with 2 tablespoons or so of the liquid batter, or prepare one large tart that you can cut in wedges. Preheat the oven to 350°F. Bake 15 minutes for the tartlets and 35–40 minutes for a larger, 9-inch tart. Bake half the baking time on the bottom rack of the oven and half on the top rack of the oven. The pies are done when puffed and golden brown. Serve warm, not hot.

CROUTES DE COURMAYEUR
{Spinach and Cheese Tart}

One large, beautiful food store on the main street of Courmayeur sells a wonderful *Torta Valdostana*, a huge pie of puff pastry enclosing layers and layers of spinach and fontina. Here is a simplified version, faster, fresher in taste; cut 12 slivers 1½ inches wide from a layer pie or prepare in twelve 3½-inch tart shells.

SERVES 12

1 loaf unseeded rye bread, sliced	½ pound boiled ham, cut in slices
6 tablespoons butter, melted	3 inches by 1½ inches by ¼ inch
1 pound spinach, preferably young	1 pound fontina (preferably Italian),
tender leaves	cut in slices 3 inches by 1½ inches
Salt	by ¼ inch
Pepper from the mill	2 eggs
Freshly grated nutmeg to taste	1½ cups heavy cream

1. Preheat the oven to 375°F. Remove the crust from the slices of bread. Flatten them with a rolling pin and brush them on both sides with melted butter. Fit 1 bread slice into each of twelve 3½-inch tart shells, or arrange the bread slices into a tight-fitting pattern on the bottom of the larger pie plate. Bake 7 to 10 minutes for a large pie, 5 to 6 minutes for a small one, or until set and light golden. Set aside. This operation can be done hours ahead of time; leave the bread slices in their pans.

2. *To prepare the filling*: Wash the spinach well; blot the leaves dry and chop them very coarsely. Sauté them until just wilted in the remainder of the melted butter. Salt and pepper them and season with nutmeg to your taste. Drain into a colander placed over a saucepan until well dripped.

3. *To prepare the tarts*: Spread 1 tablespoon of spinach on the bottom of each crust. Top with a slice of boiled ham, then 1 or 2 slices of fontina. For the larger pie, build the filling in successive layers of spinach, ham, and cheese. Beat the eggs with the heavy cream; season with salt, pepper, and nutmeg. Preheat the oven to 375°F. Pour enough egg mixture over the filling just to bind it. Bake until heated through and set. The fontina usually melts just as the egg and cream mixture sets. Serve warm, not hot, on small plates.

AMUSE-GUEULE AUX LEGUMES
(Vegetable Appetizers)

CROUTES D'ASPERGES AU THYM ET ACETO BALSAMICO
{Asparagus and Aceto Balsamico *Tartlets}*

This is truly a personal recipe, and it was extremely successful as an *amuse-gueule* in the restaurant. It is as tasty in America with the green asparagus as it is in France with the white ones.

A lighter version can easily be made by omitting the pastry and using a larger quantity of asparagus.

If *aceto balsamico* is not available, use the replacement indicated on page 45, or a mixture of 50 percent cider vinegar, 50 percent sherry vinegar, and 1 drop of honey in the sauce reduction.

A note on the pastry: I know that puff pastry and asparagus are very fashionable today, but a plain, very short, and very thin pastry lets the asparagus flavor come through much better.

SERVES 6–8

PASTRY:

1½ cups all-purpose white flour
½ cup butter
2 tablespoons sour cream
2 tablespoons water
1 teaspoon Aceto Balsamico *or other vinegar (p. 45)*
1 teaspoon salt

FILLING:

18 large asparagus
½ cup water
Salt and pepper
2 tablespoons Aceto Balsamico *or other vinegar (p. 45)*
⅓ teaspoon thyme leaves
½ cup butter
1 tablespoon heavy cream, whipped

1. Prepare the pastry as described on page 458. Refrigerate at least 1 hour. Then roll out and cut into 2-inch circles and fit into 1½-inch tartlet shells.

Preheat the oven to 400°F. Fit a piece of foil over the pastry in each shell and fill with beans or aluminum nuggets. Bake for 7 minutes. Keep shells warm.

2. Peel the asparagus from tip to root, then snap off the root end at the spot where the asparagus breaks naturally. Cook the asparagus in boiling, salted water until done to your personal taste. They are best when still al dente if green, and rather well done if white. Cut each asparagus into three or four 1-inch-long pieces.

3. Put the water, salt, pepper, and vinegar in a small, enameled cast-iron saucepan and reduce to a small ¼ cup. Add the thyme. Keep the contents of the saucepan boiling and whisk in 4 tablespoons of the butter in its un-melted, cold state. Remove from the heat. Melt the remainder of the butter and cook it to the "noisette" stage (see p. 48). Let it cool to warm, then strain it whisking it into the vinegar base. Finally, add the heavy cream and correct the seasoning.

4. Arrange 1 asparagus cut into 1-inch-long chunks in each shell, putting the tip to rest over the other pieces. Keep warm in the oven and, just before serving, spoon 1½ teaspoons of the flavored butter over the asparagus. Serve warm.

TOURTE A L'CHITROUILLE {Savory Pumpkin Pie}

This is truly an "heirloom" pie. The recipe originated in the mining town of Somain, in Flanders, and has been passed among all the women of our family with great care. This *"flamiche"*—as this type of pie is called in the Northern counties—can be made with any baked pumpkin or yellow winter squash but tastes smashing with buttercup and just great with butternut squash.

It is best presented in a 9–10-inch round porcelain pie plate, cut into ten or twelve 1-inch wedges for appetizers and six 2½-inch wedges for lunch or dinner.

SERVES 10–12 AS AN APPETIZER;
SERVES 6 FOR LUNCH OR DINNER

PASTRY:

1½ cups sifted all-purpose flour   ½ teaspoon salt
1½ teaspoons dry yeast   ¼ teaspoon Quatre-Epices (p. 35)
½ cup lukewarm water
½ cup plus ½ tablespoon butter, melted

FILLING:

4 tablespoons butter   1 cup heavy cream
2 large onions, minced fine   1½ cups fine-puréed cooked squash
3 large leeks (white part only),   or pumpkin meat
   minced fine   3 eggs
Salt and pepper to taste   Freshly grated nutmeg
6 rashers of thick-sliced bacon

1. *To make the pastry*: Make a well in the flour. Add yeast and mix in luke-warm water. Incorporate approximately 2 tablespoons of the flour into the water. Let stand until the mixture bubbles well. Add ¼ cup of the melted butter. Gradually mix in the flour, salt, and *quatre-épices* until a soft dough is obtained. *Do not knead*. Roll out immediately and fit into a 9-inch porcelain plate brushed with the remaining ½ tablespoon of butter. Let the shell remain at room temperature, uncooked, until ¼ inch thick.

2. *To prepare the filling*: Heat the butter until it turns golden brown. Toss in the minced onions and leeks; add salt and pepper and cover to cook until soft and translucent.

    Cut the bacon crosswise into ¼-inch-wide slivers and, without blanching them, sauté gently in a frying pan; they should turn golden but not crisp. Remove to a double layer of paper towels and set aside. Discard the fat in the frying pan and deglaze the pan with the heavy cream without boiling or reducing it.

    Put the cream, the squash, and the egg into the blender or food processor and homogenize well. Mix the onions, leeks, and bacon in a bowl and combine with the pumpkin mixture. Correct the seasoning with salt, pepper, and nutmeg to your taste.

3. *To bake the pie*: Preheat the oven to 375°F. Pour the filling into the shell. Bake for 20 minutes on the bottom rack of the oven and 20 minutes on the top rack, until puffed up and well set.

    Cool to lukewarm and serve with the *daussade* on page 161.

FLAMIQUES A PORIONS {Leek Tartlets}

Another Flemish family concoction that will be most popular. You can, if you want, prepare it as a pie, using the pastry dough on page 70. It is presented here for more convenience as a small appetizer on round slices of top-quality white bread.

SERVES 6–8

18 slices of white bread of excellent
   quality
9 rashers of bacon
12 leeks of average size (white and
   light green part only)

2 tablespoons butter
Salt and pepper
1½ cups heavy cream
6 tablespoons grated Gruyère cheese

1. Out of the slices of white bread, cut 18 round pieces 2½ inches in diameter, using a cutter or a thin narrow glass. Toast them lightly on 1 side only.
2. Render the bacon in a frying pan until golden but not too crisp. Remove to a layer of paper towel and cut each slice in half crosswise.
3. While the bacon renders, cut the leeks into ⅛-inch slices; wash and parboil them for 3 minutes. Drain well.
4. Discard all the bacon fat; replace it in the skillet with the butter. Heat it well, then add the leeks. Toss them into the hot butter, salt and pepper them, cover the skillet and let them cook slowly until tender, tossing the contents of the pan occasionally.
5. When the leeks are cooked, add the heavy cream and reduce until thick, creamy, and well bound. Almost no cream should remain in the skillet.
6. Top each slice of toast on the untoasted side with half a rasher of bacon. Top with 1 tablespoon of the leek mixture and 1 teaspoon of grated Gruyère. Gratiné 1 or 2 minutes under the broiler.

TIMBALES DE POIVRON ROUGE/SAUCE ASPERGES {Timbales of Red Pepper with Asparagus Sauce}

As an *amuse-gueule*, serve in tiny 1-ounce timbale molds. If you double the amounts per serving, this can be used either as a first course or as a vegetable to garnish any meat broiled or simply panfried.

SERVES 12

6 large, very ripe red peppers
1 tablespoon olive oil
Salt and pepper
1⅔ cups heavy cream
2 tablespoons fino (dry) sherry
4 eggs
1 teaspoon cornstarch
½ teaspoon fine-ground Szechuan
    pepper, untoasted

2–3 tablespoons butter
12 large asparagus stalks
1 cup Golden Veal Stock (p. 20)
    or other stock
1 tablespoon chopped fresh coriander
    beans

1. Cut the pepper up into quarters. Remove seeds and stem.
2. Heat the olive oil in a small sauté pan, add the peppers, toss them in the oil, and season with salt and pepper. Cover the pot and steam the peppers until they are very soft and the skins are separated from the pulp. Strain through a conical strainer.
3. Place the obtained purée, 1 cup of the heavy cream, the sherry, eggs, cornstarch, and Szechuan pepper into the blender container and process to a smooth custard.
4. Preheat the oven to 325°F. Butter the timbale molds and fill with the custard. Cover with a sheet of buttered parchment paper. Bake in a hot water bath until set, approximately 20 minutes.
5. Peel and blanch the asparagus stalks. Remove the tips to use as garnish. Set aside.
6. Mix the remaining ⅔ cup of the heavy cream with the veal or other stock and reduce to 1 cup. Put the blanched asparagus stalks and reduced cream-stock mixture into the blender container and purée very fine. Strain into a clean saucepan. Reheat well, correct seasoning, and add the chopped coriander.

7. To serve, unmold each timbale onto a plate of appropriate size, top with an asparagus tip, and surround the base of the timbale with the tender green asparagus sauce.

TIMBALES DE COURGETTE/SAUCE CREME PARMESAN *{Timbales of Zucchini with Parmesan Cream Sauce}*

As an *amuse-gueule*, serve in tiny 1-ounce timbale cups. If you double the amounts per serving, the preparation can be used as a first course or as a vegetable to garnish any meat broiled or simply panfried.

SERVES 12

2 medium zucchini
½ cup butter
1 onion, chopped fine
3 cloves garlic, chopped fine
2 tablespoons chopped parsley
Salt
Coarsely cracked pepper from the mill

3 tablespoons flour
1 cup milk, scalding
2 eggs, lightly beaten
¼ cup fine-scissored basil leaves
⅔ cup grated true Parmigiano-Reggiano cheese
1½ cups heavy cream

1. Wash and dry the zucchini, cut off both ends, and cut into a ¼-inch julienne by hand or in a food processor.
2. Heat 2 tablespoons of the butter in a large sauté pan. Add the onion, garlic, and parsley. Cook until all three have lightly browned. Add the zucchini, mix well, season with salt and pepper, cover and cook until the zucchini have lost all their water. Uncover and let all moisture evaporate.
3. Meanwhile heat 3 tablespoons of the butter in a saucepan. Add the flour and cook into a golden roux. Off the heat, whisk in the scalding milk and bring to a boil. Cool slightly, blend in the eggs, the basil leaves, and ⅓ cup of the Parmigiano cheese. Blend this mixture with the prepared zucchini julienne.
4. Preheat the oven to 325°F. Butter the timbales with the remaining butter and fill them with the custard mixture. Cover with buttered parchment paper, and bake for 20 minutes. The timbales are done when a skewer inserted at their center comes out clean.

5. While the timbales bake, bring the cream to a boil and reduce to approximately 1¼ cups. Add the remaining Parmigiano and stir until well melted. Let cook to coating texture and season with salt as needed. Pepper well.

6. To serve, unmold the timbales onto small plates. Spoon some of the Parmesan cream onto the timbales and dot generously with coarsely cracked pepper from the mill.

A FEW AMUSE-GUEULE WITH
FISH, SHELLFISH, AND CHICKEN LIVERS

You will find that I have put snails in the shellfish category. This is a point of view taken from the food lore of the mountain back country of the Nice area. Since people had no access to shellfish, due to poor communications with the coast, the gathering and preparing of snails as fare for fasting days was most important. I've also included two fish pâtés, one from the lake and one from the sea.

These *amuse-gueule* are varied in cost and taste as well as time needed for preparation. But all have proved extremely popular in the restaurant dining room.

Note that all tartlet shells involved can be prepared ahead of time and stored in a canister for later reheating (see recipe p. 458). Also, all tartlet shells may be replaced by a slice of buttered white bread rolled thin with a rolling pin, fitted in a tartlet mold, and baked in a preheated 350°F. oven until golden.

TARTELETTES PERSILLEES AUX ESCARGOTS
{Snails in Pastry Shells}

A favorite combination of snails and vegetables. Hide the snails so they are not visible and thus become a tasty surprise.

SERVES 9–10

18 *tartlet shells (prepared with the*   1 *small zucchini, diced into ¼-inch*
    pastry from p. 458 or 67)   *cubes*
18 *snails*   6 *large mushrooms, diced into ¼-inch*
2 *tablespoons chopped parsley*   *cubes*
1 *large clove garlic, mashed*   *Salt and pepper*
1 *shallot, chopped fine*   ¾ *cup heavy cream*
⅓ *cup butter*

1. Prepare and bake cocktail pastry shells 2 inches in diameter (see p. 68). Set aside.
2. Drain the snails well. Mix the parsley, garlic, and shallot well into a persillade. Toss the snails into half of the mixture and let stand in a small bowl, covered, while you finish the dish.
3. Mix very well 4 tablespoons of the butter with the remaining persillade to obtain a very good "snail butter."
4. Heat the remainder of the butter in a skillet. Add the zucchini and sauté until they turn bright green. Add the mushrooms, toss well, season with salt and pepper, cover the skillet and let cook until all the moisture has run out of the mushrooms. Add the cream and let cook until barely any of the cream is left and the mixture is well bound. Keep hot or let cool and reheat when ready to use.
5. Heat the tartlet shells; remove from oven and raise temperature to 400°F. Place a snail at the bottom of each and add a dab of snail butter the size of a hazelnut. Top with as much as possible of the zucchini and mushroom mixture. If any snail butter is left, top each tartlet with a tiny bit and reheat well in oven. Serve very hot.

TWO VARIATIONS OF A CHICKEN LIVER MOUSSE

Here are two presentations for the same "old" chicken liver mousse so popular with everyone. You can easily change the garnish in the mousse by using chopped toasted hazelnuts or pignoli nuts. Beware of walnuts; they can release a lot of their tannin into the mousse even if sautéed in oil beforehand and can communicate a cheesy, fermented taste to the liver.

In *When French Women Cook*, I had suggested caramelized apples and Calvados; here I use currants and vodka in the Russian style and raisins and Armagnac in the Languedocian version. Also try diced prunes and Slivovitz or a small amount of dried apricot in Cognac. Adapt the bread to the garnish as done here. *Keeps only 48 hours well refrigerated.*

SERVES 18

BASIC MOUSSE:

1 pound chicken livers
½ cup plus 2 tablespoons butter
1 large onion, chopped fine
2 shallots, chopped fine
Salt
Pepper from the mill

1½ ounces vodka or Armagnac
½ cup heavy cream
1 tablespoon sour cream
⅛ teaspoon each of Quatre-Epices
  (p. 35) and plain allspice
Macerated dried fruit of your choice

1. Clean the chicken livers very well. Heat 2 tablespoons of the butter in a skillet. In it sauté the onion and shallots over medium heat until translucent. Raise the heat to very high and add the livers. Toss them in the hot butter until they just turn gray, but remain pink at the center; season with salt and pepper. Heat the chosen spirit in a small saucepan and flambé the livers, tossing well. Remove to a large plate to cool, keeping the livers well separated.

2. When the livers are quite cool, put them into the blender container and purée. Strain through a tamis or conical strainer.

3. In an electric mixer, cream the remaining butter with a pinch of salt and pepper. Mix and flavor the two creams with the *quatre-épices* and allspice and a pinch of salt and pepper and beat to a light Chantilly. Set the cream aside.

4. To the creamed butter in the mixer bowl, gradually add the liver purée still on creaming speed. Correct the seasoning of both the buttered liver purée and the cream mixture so they are seasoned evenly. Fold the cream into the buttered purée.

Note: Any garnish of nuts or dried fruit must be placed on top of the cream with whatever is left of its maceration liquid and folded into the mousse at the same time as the cream.

Russian version: Flambé the livers with 1½ ounces vodka and fold into the mousse ¼ cup currants macerated in 2 tablespoons vodka until most of the spirit has been absorbed by the fruit. To serve, present the mousse in a small crock and surround it with thin slices of very dark Russian rye bread.

Languedocian version: Flambé the livers with 1½ ounces excellent Armagnac and fold into the mousse ¼ cup light raisins macerated in 2 tablespoons Armagnac until most of the spirit has been absorbed by the fruit. To serve, present the mousse in a small crock. Cut 18 slices of French bread slightly slantwise and toast them lightly on each side. Butter each with a mixture made of 2 tablespoons butter and 1 tablespoon mashed Roquefort (please use true Roquefort).

PATE DE TRUITES FUMEES AU RAIFORT
{Smoked Trout and Horseradish Pâté}

Smoked trout is available across the United States in the best fish stores. If you cannot get it, do not hesitate to use any other smoked fish such as whitefish or sable, which is always available in delicatessens. If the fish is very oily, cut the amount of butter by 1 or 2 tablespoons.

SERVES 12–15

8 smoked trout	*2 tablespoons chopped fresh dill weed*
4 ounces butter, at room temperature	*¼ cup sour cream*
Coarsely cracked pepper from the	*⅓ cup heavy cream, whipped semistiff*
mill	*1½ tablespoons prepared creamed*
A dash of Quatre-Epices *(p. 35)*	*horseradish*
Salt if and as needed	*12–15 light rye toasts*

1. Remove the fillets from each trout and put in the food processor container.
2. Add the butter, pepper to taste, and *quatre-épices*, and process until smooth. Add more salt and pepper if needed.
3. Strain, if you desire, for a lighter texture, pressing a tablespoon at a time of the mixture through a conical strainer with a large rubber spatula. Straining will remove any trace of small bones that the processor may have missed.

4. Pack the pâté in a 2-cup earthenware container and sprinkle the top heavily with the chopped dill.
5. Place the sour cream in a bowl. Fold both the heavy cream and the creamed horseradish at once into the sour cream. Season with salt and pepper.
6. To serve, spread each rye toast with ¼ inch of the trout pâté and dot with a bit of the horseradish cream.

PATE DE SARDINES AUX CAPRES
{Sardine and Caper Pâté}

For this recipe you will spend a little more money but save time if you use boned and skinned sardines. If you do not, you must remove the center bone before processing and the pâté will be somewhat stronger in taste, but certainly still very pleasant. Use sardines canned in any oil according to your budget, but remember that if you can afford it, olive oil is always the best.

SERVES 12–15

3 cans sardines, preferably canned in olive oil, skinned and boneless
4 ounces unsalted butter, at room temperature
Pepper from the mill

Salt
Lemon juice to taste
Store-bought garlic melba rounds
¼ cup tiny capers packed in brine, well drained

1. Open each sardine can and, leaving the lid on, squeeze the can between thumb and index finger to extract the oil. Empty the oil into a bowl. If the sardines have skins and bones, remove bones in any case, and as much of the skin as possible. Place the sardines in the food processor container.
2. Add the butter and pepper to your taste and process until smooth. Strain through a conical strainer, correct final seasoning with salt and lemon juice, and pack into a 2-cup earthenware container.
3. Serve on very dry garlic rounds and top with a few tiny capers.

Soups

SOUPS HAVE ALL BUT DISAPPEARED from French restaurant menus. An occasional luxury restaurant still serves a delicious potage here and there, but the good old delectable fillers of my young days have gone forever. Between 1950 and 1980 most of society became comfortable enough to afford a piece of meat, and people no longer had to tax their stomachs with a lot of liquid at the onset of a meal.

In restaurants, the "soupe du jour" was traditionally and artistically prepared with the cores of some vegetables and some leftovers of others artfully blended, to make the leftovers magically into a pleasant new dish. Nowadays, since the one and only vegetable served in the majority of restaurants is French fries—mostly frozen at that—there is little or no material left over to prepare the soup, which, since it must then be made of fresh vegetables, has become an expensive item to produce.

Soups were traditionally poor people's food. They stretched a long way and fed a lot of people. During World War II my mother's soups were the epitome of ingenuity, made as they were with all the possible trimmings of anything at hand; when one is truly hungry, everything is edible and tastes good.

Although soup is not exactly inexpensive anymore, it can still provide a wonderful meal when complemented with bread and cheese. I have separated the soups listed in this chapter into *Potages de Campagne* and *Potages de Reception*. The first can be made with a lot of leftovers: a few sliced carrots from last night's dinner, a handful of green beans or broccoli flowerets that cannot go unused while their price keeps going up at the market. Years ago I invented the term Garbage Soup and on television showed the New England public how to prepare it from all kinds of tidbits. My own garbage soups raised two sons.

All the soups "de campagne" were served in my restaurant for the weekday dinners of the *cuisine de misère* style we started after the small recession of 1978. They brought very positive reviews, as did, for other reasons, the soups "de réception." Those are the "studied" or thought-out soups, which always appeared on my weekend *grande cuisine* menus. They were extremely popular. We never prepared a pot of soup that was not empty by the end of the evening.

At the onset of each recipe I have mentioned which of the ingredients can be found in the kitchen, either at home or in a restaurant, at very little expense, but I have also indicated which fresh ingredients can be used to replace the leftovers. In the country soups I use water as a cooking medium with a chicken bouillon cube instead of salt, and I lean heavily on the country food ideas of my native France.

In the upper-class concoctions, do not hesitate to save time by using the food processor both to shred the vegetables and to prepare the compound butters that you will find garnishing each soup.

There is a conspicuous absence of cold soups. Cold soups are not truly a French concept, our colder climates being probably responsible for this fact. I have enjoyed cold soups during my travels to hot climates or during a torrid Philadelphia summer, but they are not my idea of a cooler; for me, soup remains a warmer.

Notice in most soups the presence of a bouquet garni. It will always be made of 10 parsley stems, 1 bay leaf, and ¼ teaspoon dried thyme, wrapped into one another and tied with a string—never wrapped in cheesecloth.

I. POTAGES DE CAMPAGNE
(Country Soups)

PAPIN NORMAND AU VERT
{Bread and Onion Soup Garnished with Watercress}

Which household or restaurant does not have leftover chopped or forgotten onions and bread? Here is a way to use them as well as those leaves of watercress that, without being wilted, have lost their prime fresh look and can no longer be used as garnish. No watercress? Use any green at your disposal: parsley, chives, etc.

SERVES 6

SOUP:

3 tablespoons butter
2 onions, chopped by hand or in a processor
6 shallots, chopped by hand or in a processor
3 leeks (white and light green parts only), chopped by hand or in a processor
3 cloves garlic, mashed

Six ½-inch-thick slices of day-old French bread, crusts removed
⅔ cup scalding whole milk
6 cups water
1 chicken bouillon cube
Bouquet garni (see p. 82)
½ cup each heavy and sour cream
Salt and pepper

GARNISH:

½ cup chopped watercress or parsley leaves
1 tablespoon chopped chives

1. Heat the butter well in the soup pot. Add the onions, shallots, leeks, and garlic and sauté until all the vegetables start browning at their edges.
2. Meanwhile, crumble the bread into the milk; mix well to obtain a purée. Mix into the water. Add the mixture to the soup pot and bring to a boil. Add the bouillon cube and bouquet garni and simmer until reduced to approximately 5 cups. Remove the bouquet garni, pour into the blender to homogenize, and return to the pot.

3. Add the creams and reheat well. Just before serving, add the watercress and the chives. Correct the seasoning with salt and pepper and serve very hot.

CREME DE RUTABAGAS AU BEURRE D'ESCARGOTS {Cream of Yellow Turnips with Snail Butter}

Besides being wonderful for glazing and puréeing, rutabagas make a mean soup. To gain time, julienne the root in the food processor and, in a restaurant operation, use those leftovers of julienne that are no longer quite sparkling enough to be used as a vegetable.

SERVES 6

SOUP:

2 tablespoons butter
2 medium onions, chopped
1 yellow turnip (rutabaga), peeled and julienned
7 cups water

1 chicken or beef bouillon cube
Bouquet garni (see p. 82)
1 cup light or heavy cream
Salt and pepper

GARNISH:

6 tablespoons butter
1 tiny clove garlic
1 small shallot, chopped and squeezed into the corner of a towel

1/3 cup parsley leaves
Salt and pepper
Grated nutmeg

1. Heat the butter in a soup kettle. In it sauté the onions until translucent. Add the julienned turnip and approximately 1/2 cup of the water. Toss well, cover and cook until the turnip starts to fall apart.
2. Add the remaining water, bouillon cube, and bouquet garni. Cook for approximately 30 minutes. Empty into the blender or food processor to purée. Strain back into the soup pot. Add the cream, correct the final seasoning, and keep warm until ready to serve.
3. To prepare the snail butter, put butter, garlic, squeezed shallot, parsley

leaves, salt, pepper, and nutmeg into the food processor and process into a smooth compound butter.

4. Serve the soup in bowls and float a dollop of snail butter on the surface of each serving.

GARBURE AUX PEAUX DE CANARD
{Vegetable Soup with Duck Skin Cracklings}

After you have made the *confit* on pages 315–17 or roasted 1 or 2 ducks, you will have duck carcasses at your disposal to prepare this soup. To save time, process all the vegetables in the food processor, making sure that you do not forget to soak the dried beans overnight. This soup is a whole meal in itself. Serve it with a basket of homemade breads. If you are not too worried about your arteries, toast the slices of bread lightly, rub them with garlic, and spread them with a fine layer of *confit* (rendered duck) fat (see p. 315). No duck skins available? Replace them with garlic croutons fried in *confit* fat or in oil, or with a slice of *pancetta*, diced fine.

SERVES 6

SOUP:

½ pound dried white beans, soaked overnight

1 duck carcass

A large piece of prosciutto rind and/or a pork hock

3 cloves garlic, chopped

Bouquet garni (see p. 82)

2 onions, sliced thin

2½ quarts cold water

1 chicken or beef bouillon cube

2 carrots

2 white turnips

2 leeks

½ a small head of cabbage

A tiny pinch of ground clove

2 potatoes

Salt and pepper

GARNISH:

⅓ cup chopped parsley

2 cloves garlic, chopped fine

⅔ cup duck skin cracklings (see p. 315), or ⅔ cup garlic croutons, or 3 ounces fine-diced pancetta, sautéed

1. Put the soaked white beans in a large soup pot. Add the duck carcass and the chosen meat, the garlic, bouquet garni, and onions. Cover with the water and bring to a boil. Add the bouillon cube, turn down to a simmer, and cook for approximately 1 hour.
2. Meanwhile, process the carrots, turnips, leeks, and cabbage into a julienne ¼ inch wide and add to the soup after it has cooked 1 hour. Cook for another 30 minutes. Add the clove and potatoes, season with salt and pepper; finish cooking another 15 minutes.
3. Remove all the pieces of duck carcass or the prosciutto rind. If you have used a hock, dice the meat into the soup and discard the bones.
4. Just before serving, add the chopped parsley and garlic to the soup along with the duck skins or the *pancetta*. If you use croutons, pass them in a small bowl for guests to help themselves.

BOUILLON AUX SEPT POULES
{*Périgord-style Bouillon with "Seven Hens"*}

This soup is the result of an improvised dinner prepared on my cousin's farm in Sainte Nathalène, Périgord. It is a whole meal, to be served with extra-strong Dijon mustard. Complete the dinner with walnut bread (p. 57) and a cheese course. Any good fruity white or red wine will do. The first hen is the bird, the other "hens" are the stuffed cabbage leaves, called "poules vertes" in Périgord.

SERVES 6–8

SOUP:

1 stewing hen
Salt and pepper
3 quarts cold water
4 leeks, tied into a bundle
4 carrots, cut into quarters
4 white turnips, cut into quarters
2 large onions, each stuck with

1 clove
1 large head of white cabbage
One 5-ounce piece of pancetta, *left whole*
Bouquet garni (see p. 82)
2 large ribs of Swiss chard, diced
1 chicken bouillon cube

GARNISH:

6 large outside cabbage leaves

2 eggs

½ cup milk

Reserved liver of the hen, chopped
   fine

1 cup bread cubes from French bread,
   oven dried

2 links Italian sweet sausage

3 cloves garlic, chopped fine

¼ cup chopped parsley

2 shallots, chopped fine and squeezed
   dry in a towel

Salt

Pepper from the mill

Extra-strong Dijon mustard

1. Reserve the hen's liver, salt and pepper the cavity and truss it. Put the hen in a soup kettle, cover it with the water, bring to a boil, skim. Add the leeks, carrots, turnips, onions stuck with cloves, and the heart of the cabbage cut into quarters. Reserve 6 large outside cabbage leaves to prepare the "poules vertes." Add the piece of *pancetta*, the bouquet garni, the diced Swiss chard ribs, and the bouillon cube; bring to a second boil, skim again and simmer until tasty, approximately 2 hours.

2. When the soup is ready, ladle the broth into another pot and keep the solid ingredients ready and hot.

3. Blanch the outside leaves of cabbage. Remove their rib.

4. Beat the eggs with the milk and the liver. Pour this over the bread cubes and let them completely absorb the mixture. Mix in the Italian sausage, the garlic, parsley, shallots, and salt and pepper as needed. Work until blended and homogenized.

5. Wrap an equal amount of stuffing into each of the cabbage leaves. Tie them into neat little packages. Bring the strained broth to a boil and add the stuffed cabbage leaves. Cook for at least 30 minutes.

6. To serve, carve the hen into serving pieces and surround them with the stuffed cabbage leaves and vegetables. Turn the broth into a tureen and pass both the tureen and the platter of solid ingredients with the jar of mustard, and the walnut bread. The mustard should either be added to each plate of broth or be spread on the walnut bread.

TOURIN A LA DOUCETTE
{White Onion Soup Garnished with Lamb's Lettuce}

Originating in the Pyrenees, this soup is still very popular locally. The Prince of Talleyrand reports in one of his letters to a friend that while traveling in the Pyrenees he stopped at a farm to purchase food. The farm woman, too poor to own a knife, was preparing a *tourin* and cutting the onions in small pieces . . . with her front teeth. The addition of lamb's lettuce and goat- or ewe's-milk cheese are my idea. Thyme, also called *herbotte* in Basque and Béarnaise countries, is a favorite of those two areas.

SERVES 6

SOUP:

3 tablespoons butter or, better, confit
   (rendered duck) fat (see p. 315)
8 large onions, sliced paper thin
4 shallots, sliced paper thin
2 tablespoons flour
3 cups water

3 cups hot milk
1 chicken or beef bouillon cube
Pepper from the mill
1 teaspoon fresh thyme leaves or ½
   teaspoon dried

GARNISH:

1 cup lamb's lettuce leaves, cut into ⅛-inch chiffonade
4 tablespoons butter
2 tablespoons goat- or ewe's-milk cheese
1 small clove garlic, mashed

1. In the soup pot, heat the butter or *confit* fat and in it sauté the onions and shallots until translucent.
2. Add the flour and cook for 3–4 minutes. Mix water and milk, bring to a boil and, off the heat, gradually add it to the onions and shallots, using a wooden spoon. Return to the heat and bring to a second boil, stirring constantly with the wooden spoon. Add the bouillon cube, pepper from the mill, and the thyme. Simmer until tasty.
3. When the soup tastes good, and just before serving, correct its seasoning and add the chiffonade of lamb's lettuce.
4. Cream the butter for the garnish, mashing the cheese and garlic into it.

Ladle the soup into bowls and float a dollop of cheese-and-butter mixture on the surface of each portion. Let your guests stir the butter into their soup.

LA VALAISANNE {Alpine Tomato and Cheese Soup}

This is a wonderful soup for the months of September through November when tomatoes are superabundant. I enjoyed a first cousin of it in a mountain refuge, just below the Trient Glacier, years and years ago. A good opportunity to use tomatoes that are too ripe for a salad or broiling.

SERVES 6

SOUP:

3 tablespoons butter
2 onions, chopped
1 clove garlic, chopped
2 leeks (white and light green parts only), chopped
2 tablespoons flour
Salt

2 pounds fresh tomatoes, peeled, seeded, and chopped or one 29-ounce can Italian plum tomatoes, chopped
Bouquet garni (see p. 82)
½ cup dry white wine
7 cups water
1 chicken or beef bouillon cube
Pepper from the mill

GARNISH:

½ cup shredded Gruyère cheese
⅔ cup heavy cream, lightly whipped
Coarsely cracked pepper

1. Heat the butter in a soup pot. Add the onions, garlic, and leeks and sauté over medium-low heat until translucent. Add the flour and cook for 5 minutes. Salt very lightly. Add the tomatoes, toss well, and cook for another 5 minutes.
2. Add the bouquet garni, the white wine, and the water. Bring to a boil. Add the bouillon cube and a dash of pepper from the mill and bring to a second boil. Turn down to a simmer and cook until tasty, approximately 45 minutes.

3. Fold the grated Gruyère into the cream and add coarsely cracked pepper to your taste. Ladle the soup into bowls and add to each bowl an equal amount of Gruyère and cream. Serve piping hot.

II. POTAGES DE RECEPTION
(Soups for Entertaining)

PUREE D'ASPERGES A LA QUENELLE DE SAUMON FUME
{Cream of Asparagus Soup with Smoked Salmon Quenelles}

The asparagus used need not be of the best caliber; all it needs is freshness. Note that the price of the soup can be slashed in half by using other greens such as Swiss chard leaves or early soft spinach mixed with one-third sorrel. The method and quantities are the same. The soup tastes better made with fish fumet than with clam juice.

SERVES 6

SOUP:

2 pounds fresh asparagus
2 tablespoons butter
2 onions, sliced
1 shallot, sliced
2 cups asparagus cooking water

2 cups Fish Fumet (p. 28) or clam juice
1 cup heavy cream
1 1/2 teaspoons ground coriander
Salt and pepper

QUENELLES:

3 ounces fine salmon meat, no skin, connective tissues, or bones, ice cold
1 ounce smoked salmon, ice cold
1 egg

1/2 teaspoon salt
Pepper from the mill
2 tablespoons very soft butter
1/2 cup heavy cream
2 tablespoons chopped fresh dill

1. Peel and blanch the asparagus for 3 minutes. Reserve the blanching water and 12 to 16 green tips for soup and garnish. Melt the butter in a sauté pan

and sauté the onion and shallot until translucent. Add the blanched asparagus and let cook uncovered until tender but still bright green.

Pour 2 cups of the reserved asparagus cooking water and half the
fumet or clam juice in the blender and add the asparagus, shallot, and
onion. Process to obtain a bright green purée. Strain into a saucepan and
add the remaining fumet, the cream, and the coriander. Add salt and pepper
to your taste. Keep warm.

2. Place the salmon meats, egg, salt, and pepper into the container of the food
processor. Process until smooth. Open the top of the processor, add the soft
butter and process until super smooth. Then add the cream in a steady
stream. The quenelle paste is ready in 3 minutes. Empty into a bowl and
chill well.

3. To serve the soup, shape 12 small quenelles using 2 teaspoons. Poach them
in the remaining asparagus blanching water. Put 2 ladlefuls of soup into a
white soup plate or bouillon cup and add 2 quenelles. Sprinkle the dark
green dill all around the quenelles on the surface of the pale green soup
and garnish with the reserved asparagus tips. (In restaurant operation, use
only 1 quenelle and serve in a bouillon cup for better budgeting.)

CONSOMME EN CHINOISERIE
{Chinese-style Consommé}

You can refine the soup by clarifying it or decide to serve without clarification.
Also, since all the spices are frankly traceable, you can use any type of stock at
your disposal. The decision is yours. The tea idea results from the combined
efforts of my student Peter Hoffman and myself; I put the tea on a list of ingredients used in creative cookery; he used it to flavor a vegetable broth.

SERVES 6

CONSOMME:
2 quarts excellent broth of your
   choice
1 teaspoon Lapsang Souchong tea
1 teaspoon coriander seeds

½ teaspoon ground ginger
2–3 egg whites
3 tablespoons dry sherry

GARNISH:

½ a red pepper, preferably peeled

½ a green pepper, preferably peeled

½ a yellow pepper, if available, preferably peeled

½ a gingerroot

½ a small zucchini

½ a small carrot

½ a small white turnip

¼ cup tiny green peas, ¼ inch in diameter

Green and white scallion rings

1. Prepare the stock for clarification. If you do not clarify completely, defatten at least. To clarify, heat 1½ quarts of the stock with the tea, coriander seeds, and powdered ginger. Beat the egg whites well and gradually add to them the remaining cold stock. Then beat this mixture into the hot stock.

   Beat over medium heat until the boiling point is reached. Simmer for 20–30 minutes. Let stand, off the heat, for 10 more minutes. Strain through a fine *chinois* or "China cap" strainer or another strainer lined with several layers of cheesecloth. Add the dry sherry.

2. Whether or not you peel the peppers is your choice; I like to. In any case, cut them into ⅛-inch julienne; repeat with the gingerroot, zucchini, carrot, and turnip. Blanch all the vegetables except the peas in salted water, keeping them al dente. Blanch the peas last, keeping them bright green. Add all the vegetables to the broth and reheat well. Season carefully and serve in white soup plates or bouillon cups.

CREME DE VOLAILLE AU SAFRAN
{Cream of Chicken with Saffron Threads}

This soup was inspired by the rich broth traditionally made for funerals in the Rouergue. A good sprinkling of saffron at the last minute turns it bright yellow. The broth here is turned into a velouté and creamed before adding the saffron.

SERVES 6

SOUP:

1 large veal bone

1 ½ pounds fowl, chicken, or turkey
   wings, cut up

1 pound chicken gizzards

2 quarts water

2 onions, each stuck with 1 clove

1 clove garlic, mashed

2 small carrots, cut up

2 small white turnips, cut up

Large bouquet garni (see p. 82)

3 leeks (white and light green parts
   only)

Salt and pepper

6 tablespoons butter

6 tablespoons flour

⅔ cup heavy cream

⅓ cup sour cream

GARNISH:

   1 small vial saffron threads (approximately 16)

   ½ cup true fresh baby peas, sorted to measure no more than ¼ inch in
      diameter, blanched

1. Place the veal bone, wings, and gizzards in the soup pot. Cover with cold
   water. Quickly bring to a boil and blanch for 5 minutes. Drain and rinse
   under cold water.

2. Return the meats to the soup pot. Cover again with cold water. Slowly bring
   to a boil. Add all the vegetables and aromatics and simmer for 2 hours or
   so or until tasty. When approximately 6 cups of broth are left, the soup base
   should be ready. Strain it into a clean pot; reduce it to 5 cups or so.

3. With butter and flour, prepare a white roux, cooking it only a few minutes.
   Bind it with the hot broth. Simmer for 15 minutes, removing the worst of
   the flour scum from the surface of the velouté. Add the creams and correct
   seasoning.

4. To serve, bring to the boiling point. Turn the heat off. Add the saffron
   threads and the peas. Serve while the threads are losing their bright orange
   color through the velouté.

LA MULARDE {A Duck Consommé}

This consommé has been composed so as to use all the duck carcasses available
after roasting several ducks or preparing *confit* (see pp. 315–17). The con-

sommé should ideally be prepared with Secondary Stock (p. 23), but is also good if started with water. The presence of a carcass or several carcasses of any type of smoked birds (chicken, pheasant, ducks, or quails) is the key to its wonderful taste.

SERVES 6

CONSOMME:

1 veal bone

About 1 pound carcass(es) of smoked bird(s)

Necks and carcasses of 2 or 3 ducks, plain, raw, or already roasted

Duck hearts and gizzards if available

2 small carrots

3 large onions

10 cloves garlic, unpeeled

3 leeks (white and green parts only), cut into 1-inch chunks

About 2 quarts Secondary Stock (p. 23) or water

2 small white turnips, cut up

1 tablespoon tomato paste

Large bouquet garni (see p. 82)

1 teaspoon Quatre-Epices (p. 35)

Salt and pepper

GARNISH:

1 pound white turnips

1½ tablespoons butter or confit (rendered duck) fat

1 teaspoon sugar

1 tablespoon vinegar of your choice

Salt and pepper

1 very small red pepper

3 tablespoons fine-scissored scallion rings

1. Preheat the oven to 400°F. Wash the veal bone and place it in a large stockpot. Add the smoked carcass(es). Meanwhile, brown the duck carcasses (if used), hearts, and gizzards as well as the carrots, onions, garlic cloves, and leeks in the oven until dark golden. Transfer to the soup pot.

2. Add some of the stock or water to the roasting pan. Deglaze it well. Add this deglazing to the soup pot together with the remaining stock, the turnips, tomato paste, bouquet garni, *quatre-épices*, salt, and pepper. Bring to a boil, turn down to a simmer and cook gently for 2 hours. If the volume of the stock reduces too much, add enough salted water to maintain the liquid at all times level with the solid ingredients.

3. When the stock is finished cooking, clarify it if you wish (see p. 92), but that is not a necessity since the garnish will make it somewhat cloudy again.

4. To make the garnish, peel the turnips and turn them into small olive shapes; blanch them. Heat the butter or *confit* fat in a sauté pan and brown the turnips. Add the sugar and let it caramelize around the turnips. Add the vinegar. Ladle just enough duck consommé over the turnips to cover them and cook in the stock until dark brown and glazed. Correct the seasoning with salt and pepper.

5. Meanwhile peel the raw pepper and cut 36 confetti squares ⅓ inch in diameter from its pulp. Toss the red pepper confetti into the hot glazed turnips and pour the consommé over this garnish. Ladle into soup plates and top each portion with scallion rings.

CREME DE CHOUX AU BEURRE DE ROQUEFORT {Cream of Cabbage Soup with Roquefort Butter}

This is a refinement of a country soup that was prepared for me by an old farm woman of the Millau area when, as a child, I spent a summer in the area of Langeac. The soup became a meal, served with a heavy bread crumb omelet known as a "*rouzole*" and a piece of *confit* of goose or duck. *Pancetta* is essential to the original taste of the soup. If you cannot locate it, use salt pork as rancid tasting and smelling as possible.

SERVES 6

SOUP:

5 *ounces* pancetta, *bought in 1 piece and diced carefully into ⅛-inch cubes*

2 *tablespoons* confit *(rendered duck)* fat *(see p. 315) or butter*

4 *cloves garlic, chopped coarse*

2 *potatoes, diced*

1 *head of white cabbage, shredded*

Salt and pepper

1½–2 *quarts water*

2 *tablespoons walnut oil*

GARNISH:

½ *cup unsalted butter*

3 *ounces* Roquefort, *without the slightest trace of a greenish tinge in its paste*

Coarsely cracked black pepper

1. Place the *pancetta* and fat or butter in a very large sauté pan over medium heat. Cook until the *pancetta* starts taking on a bit of color. Add the garlic and potatoes and continue cooking until the potatoes start turning golden. Add the cabbage, salt moderately and pepper generously, toss into the *pancetta* and garlic mixture, cover and let the cabbage mellow slowly. Add the water, bring to a boil. Turn down to a simmer and cook until the cabbage falls apart.

2. Purée the cabbage and potato soup in the blender, adding the walnut oil as you blend. The soup will turn creamy and whitish. Strain back into a soup tureen.

3. To prepare the garnish, put the butter, Roquefort, and pepper in the food processor container and process until smooth. Float a large tablespoon of butter onto each plate of soup.

CREME D'ARTICHAUTS AU BEURRE DE NOISETTES GRILLEES
{Cream of Artichoke Soup with Hazelnut Butter}

The only problem with this soup is its price, but it's well worth the "investment" once in a while. In France this is prepared with the huge *"Prince de Bretagne"* artichokes. In the United States, use the largest specimens grown in California.

SERVES 6

SOUP:

1 lemon	*6 tablespoons butter*
8 extra-large artichokes or 12 smaller ones	*Pepper*
2 tablespoons flour	*1 quart Secondary Stock (p. 23)*
2 quarts cold water	*1 cup heavy cream*
2 tablespoons ordinary corn oil	*⅓ cup sour cream*
Salt	*1 tablespoon fine-chopped tarragon*

GARNISH:

¼ cup hazelnuts
½ cup butter
Salt and pepper

1. Remove a strip 1 inch by ⅓ inch from the rind of the lemon; set aside.
2. Peel the artichokes to obtain 8 large artichoke bottoms (hearts) and rub them immediately with the lemon.
3. Prepare a *blanc* by mixing the flour with the cold water, the juice of the lemon, and the corn oil. Add very little salt and bring to a boil. Add the artichoke bottoms and blanch them in this mixture until a needle penetrates the bottoms but does not come out easily.
4. Cook the butter to the dark "noisette" stage. Clarify it to remove all traces of dark cooked whey. In this butter, cut the artichoke bottoms into slivers, salt and pepper them, cover the pot, and finish cooking them until they fall apart.
5. Add the stock and the reserved lemon rind and bring to a boil. Simmer until the artichoke taste has blended very well with the stock, approximately 30 minutes. Put in the blender container and purée. Strain back into a clean saucepan. Add both creams, correct the salt and pepper, and, just before serving, add the tarragon.
6. To make the garnish, toast the hazelnuts to a medium golden brown in a 400°F. oven. Rub the hot hazelnuts in a towel until all the skins have rubbed off. Put the hazelnuts into the food processor and chop them. Add the butter, salt and pepper, and process into a smooth butter. Top each plate of soup with a tablespoon of hazelnut butter.

CREME DE POIVRONS AU BEURRE DE SAFRAN *{Cream of Red Pepper Soup with Saffron Butter}*

Those who hate to peel peppers will be happy to know that no peeling is needed here.

SERVES 6

SOUP:

8 very ripe large red bell peppers
2 tablespoons olive oil
3 large onions, chopped
Stems of 1 bunch of basil
Salt and pepper
1½ quarts Secondary Stock (p. 23) or water

2 tomatoes, peeled, seeded, and chopped
2 cloves garlic, crushed
1 cup heavy cream
⅓ cup sour cream
Fino (dry) sherry as needed

GARNISH:

2 zucchini
½ cup butter
1 tiny package of powdered saffron

1. Cut each of the peppers into 6 wedges. Remove all traces of seeds and carefully cut off the "cotton" lining the internal ribs.
2. Heat the olive oil in a soup pot, add the onions and basil stems and toss them into the oil until the onions are golden. Add all the pepper wedges and toss until well coated with oil. Season with salt and pepper, cover, and let the peppers lose all their juices. Add the stock, bring to a boil, add the tomato pulp and garlic cloves, turn down to a simmer and cook gently, uncovered, until the broth is reduced to approximately 4½ cups.
3. Blend the soup in the blender and strain through a very fine *chinois* or "China cap" strainer to discard all traces of puréed skins. Add the creams, correct the seasoning, and add sherry to your taste.
4. To make the garnish, peel the zucchini so the skins are no more than ⅖–⅘ inch thick. Cut the skins into "angel hair" strips ⅕ inch wide; it will look like green spaghetti. Blanch them for 1 minute by plunging them into boiling salted water. Add them to the soup.
5. Cream the butter and add the saffron. Float a large dollop of saffron butter on top of each plate of soup.

A Few Terrines with a New Twist, Two Saucissons and a Versatile Galantine

---

PÂTÉS AND TERRINES seem to have survived the Cuisine Revolution of the last ten years very well; there is not one household or restaurant in the United States that is not proud of its terrine. Very often the courtesy gift one receives when visiting a colleague's restaurant is a most pleasant sampling of what the establishment has to offer in this line.

The following small collection of recipes represents approximately one-tenth of the collection we presented to our guests through the years at Chez la Mère Madeleine. The use of electric implements has made the preparation of terrines and pâtés considerably easier than it was when we had to hand operate meat grinders. Before one starts grinding, however, it is good to remember to clean the meats of gristle and connective tissues. As with all techniques one learns, the first try will be time-consuming and seem difficult; by the second try, things will already be easier, and by the third it will be routine.

Read the following techniques very carefully. They will allow you to fully understand the short recipes given in the pages that follow.

A. TABLE OF APPROXIMATE YIELDS OF MEAT FROM DIVERSE ANIMALS USED TO PREPARE TERRINES AND PATES

In order to know at the onset of your terrine work how much meat you should purchase, here is a list of the average yield of pure meat provided by a few of the most commonly used animals:

Animal	*Yield*
Rabbit; total carcass weight 2 to 2¼ pounds	1 generous pound
Hare; total carcass weight 6 to 7 pounds	2 generous pounds
Duck; total carcass weight 4 to 5 pounds	1½ to 1⅔ pounds
Small turkey; capon, or fowl total carcass weight 5 to 6 pounds	1¾ to 2 pounds
Pheasant; total carcass weight 3½ pounds	1½ pounds

The weight of the other meats included in the terrine depends on the yield of the main animal, which gives its name to the terrine or pâté.

B. COMPOSITION OF A TERRINE, PATE, SAUCISSON, OR GALANTINE

All of these preparations are made of two elements: the forcemeat and the garnish.

- A *terrine* is a kind of fancy meat loaf cooked in an earthenware dish.
- A *pâté* is a terrine mixture baked in a pastry. Pâtés remain striking looking, but are difficult to keep tasting fresh, either at home or in a restaurant. Also, they are extremely heavy and difficult to digest.
- A *saucisson* is a terrine mixture shaped into a large sausage and stuffed into natural skin or a plastic cook-in bag.

• A *galantine* is a very large sausage in which the forcemeat is held together by the skin of the bird used to prepare the mixture.

I. Composition of the forcemeat:

a. The *main meat*, which gives the terrine or pâté its name: the main meat of a hare terrine is obviously a hare, that of a duck terrine is duck, etc. Bone the animal, clean the meat of all gristle or "nerves" and weigh it. Restaurant operators must weigh rather than measure by volume. At home, if a scale is not available, one can measure by volume.

b. The *secondary meats*, which are generally veal and semifat/semilean pork. Divide the weight of the main meat by one-half (or measure it by volume and divide it by one-half). The amount obtained will represent the combined weight of the veal and pork meat to be used.

Example: You have boned two ducks. Set aside the 2 filets of duck to use as garnish (see p. 103). Weigh the remainder of the duck meat, including the diced liver and, if you have no scale, pack it into a large measuring cup. If the total weight of duck meat is 1 pound, or its volume 2 cups, you will need ¼ pound each of veal and pork or, by volume, ½ cup each of veal and pork.

At this point, your forcemeat consists of:

1 pound duck meat	*or*	*2 cups duck meat*
¼ pound veal meat		*½ cup veal meat*
¼ pound pork meat		*½ cup pork meat*
Total: 1½ pounds of mixture of main and secondary meats		*Total: 3 cups of mixture of main and secondary meats*

Note that the weight system of measuring is more accurate and therefore superior. The volume system is practical, but not truly accurate since the density of meats varies. The worst that can happen is that a terrine or pâté made by the volume method will not be consistent in taste or texture each time one prepares it. *Use whichever system is the most convenient for you.* I prefer the weight system, but have worked for years with the volume system quite successfully.

c. You must now calculate the amount of *fatback* you need. Fatback is pure unsalted fresh pork fat from the back of the animal. The amount of fatback needed is exactly one-half of the total weight of the meats. Since our present example contains a total of 1½ pounds of meats, you need ¾ pound of fresh fatback, or, in the volume system, 1½ cups.

Very important note: It is essential that the fat you use be white, fresh, solid, and compact and *never salted or cured as salt pork or bacon are*. As salt pork and bacon age, their water content is captured by the salt that comes to rest in crystals on the surface of the meat as the water evaporates. Since the water locked in adipose tissues is what gives a terrine its "slip" (moist feeling on the tongue), you defeat your own purpose if you use salt pork or bacon, which has been deprived of 95 percent of its natural moisture by its preserving salt.

d.   Having gathered main meat, secondary meats, and fatback into a bowl, you now have 2¼ pounds of forcemeat to process into an even mixture. The forcemeat will have to be bound and seasoned; the *binders* used to help the forcemeat hold together are usually part egg/part bread crumbs and cream in liver terrines and plain egg in pure meat terrines (a liver terrine contains 90 percent liver, a plain meat terrine may contain 1 or 2 fowl livers).

Minimum amount of binders and seasonings to use per pound of forcemeat:

Eggs: Minimum 2 eggs per pound of meat
Salt: Minimum 1½ teaspoons salt per pound of meat
Pepper: Minimum 35 turns of the mill of aromatic pepper per pound of
             meat
Spices: Minimum ⅓ teaspoon per pound of meat

Note: Terrines and pâtés are served cold and must be salted more heavily than foods that are served warm, since the cold blunts the perception of salt by the taste buds.

Varying the amount of fat in a terrine or pâté forcemeat:
If you are of the very modern school of cooking that tries to remove a lot of fat out of everything, you may substitute additional eggs for some of the fatback in the pâté. *Never* remove the total amount of fatback or the terrine will be too dry, but instead of using the whole amount recommended here, use only one-

half to two-thirds of it. Every time you remove ½ pound of fatback, you must replace it by 2 eggs. The two possible formulae for the quantities indicated above would then read as follows:

Full-fat formula	*Lean formula*
1 pound duck meat	1 pound duck meat
¼ pound veal meat	¼ pound veal meat
¼ pound pork meat	¼ pound pork meat
¾ pound fatback	⅓–½ pound fatback
5 eggs	7–8 eggs
3–4 teaspoons salt	3–4 teaspoons salt
1¼ teaspoons pepper from the mill	1¼ teaspoons pepper from mill
1 teaspoon *Quatre-Epices* (p. 35)	1 teaspoon *Quatre-Epices* (p. 35)

Final amount of eggs as binders in a terrine:
As indicated above, the amount of egg is 2 per each pound of meat (plus 2 for each ½ pound of fatback replaced in low-fat terrines). As it happens, the more egg there is in a forcemeat, the better its consistency will be, so do not hesitate to toss in an additional egg "for the mixing bowl." It will take care of any egg lost by splattering on bowl, beaters, and spatulas.

II. Composition of the garnish:
The garnish of a terrine or pâté will consist of whatever meat or vegetable, diced or sliced or otherwise cut, you add to the forcemeat. You must remember that the more garnish there is in a terrine or pâté, the drier it will feel to the palate when eaten. The quantity of garnish can be varied according to your personal taste, and you can vary the patterns of presentation and look of the sliced or diced garnish according to the time you have at your disposal or the final cost of the terrine. If you have to sacrifice either look or taste, do by all means sacrifice complicated garnish patterns and make sure that you concentrate on the taste of the terrine or pâté. Here, as in every other facet of food, good looks are not always commensurate with taste. Super looks are certainly wonderful, but super taste is always better. I personally like the garnish to be, by weight or volume, equal to approximately one-third of the terrine forcemeat. You can use more if you desire, but I do not recommend you use less.

For example, in the formula for full-fat forcemeat we've been using, there should be not more than approximately ¾ pound of garnish for the 2¼ pounds of total weight of the forcemeat. (In this particular case, it would be the 2 reserved filets of duck and approximately 3 ounces of diced fresh fatback.)

B. PREPARATION OF A TERRINE OR PATE

In no other preparation is the marriage of wines and liqueur(s) with foods more important than in the making of forcemeats. The degree of marination in wine or spirits, or a combination of both, is of great importance to the final taste of the forcemeat and, ultimately, of the terrine.

I. Marination:

Marination gives the forcemeat and terrine or pâté its personality and character. You can make the marination last for as long or short a time as you care to and choose the liqueur or wine that you like. The following combinations are usually quite successful:

WHITE WINE:	Rabbit
RED WINE:	Fowl, duck, squab, quail
SHERRY:	Duck, especially when Chinese spices are used, and also fowl, turkey
MADEIRA:	Rabbit, fowl, duck, squab, quail, pork, and veal
PORT:	Duck, squab, quail, fowl

All these wines must be used in their driest form (fino for sherry, Sercial for Madeira, and white port). They can be used alone or in combination with a strong spirit such as Cognac, Armagnac, Scotch, or bourbon.

You may also use any liqueur you like. But you will then have to compensate for the sugar content with other elements. Chartreuse Verte, for example, can give a sweetness that is not to everyone's taste; in this case it may be good to use the vegetal extract of Chartreuse, which is sugarless. Sweet Grand Marnier can be compensated for with a dash of bitters or orange bitters.

If you cannot get venison or game birds, which was my experience on the East Coast of the United States, marinate any meat for 4 full days in a mixture of equal amounts of white port, Sercial Madeira, fino sherry, and Armagnac. The finished terrine will have a definite taste of the wild after being baked.

Note: Always marinate the elements of the forcemeat and the garnish an equal amount of time.

II. *Processing and/or grinding the forcemeat:*

a. If you use the *food processor*, mix all the elements of the forcemeat well. Divide the forcemeat into 2 batches of equal weight or volume. Process the first half until it is almost so smooth that it could be used for a quenelle. Add half of the eggs needed and process again until they have been incorporated. Remove to a bowl. Process the second half of the forcemeat and the remainder of the eggs, keeping the mixture rather coarse this time. Remove to the same bowl and mix both batches of forcemeat very well. Correct the seasoning. The forcemeat is ready.

b. If you use the *meat grinder*, mix all the elements of the forcemeat very well together. Divide the total bulk of the meats into 2 equal batches. Using the fine grinding blade, grind the first batch *twice*, gathering the ground meat into the large electric mixer bowl. Then grind the second batch only once, adding it also to the mixer bowl. To clean up the grinder, grind 1 onion through the machine and let it fall into the bowl.

Note: Meats that are to be ground must be extremely well cleaned of all tendons, all superficial white fibrous sheaths, etc., or they will block against the grinder blade and impede its proper functioning.

III. *Seasoning the forcemeat:*

The seasonings consist of aromatics (onions, herbs, spices), salt and pepper, and a good spirit or fortified wine, or a mixture of a spirit and a fortified wine. A meat essence is sometimes used to strengthen the taste of the finished terrine.

a. *The aromatics*: The aromatics vary with the general theme of the terrine, but it is always good to make sure that they include *1 large onion* and *2 large shallots* for each 2 pounds of forcemeat. Onion may be replaced by chopped leek, and garlic may also be added. The spices always consist of a certain amount of *Quatre-Epices* as indicated before, but any other spices of your choice and in character with the nature of the terrine may also be used.

b. *Salt and pepper*: The amount of salt is in the vicinity of 1½ teaspoons (¼ ounce) per pound of meat (see p. 102).

c. *Spirits and fortified wines*: Adapt the spirit, wine, or liqueur to the type of meat (see p. 104); 2–3 tablespoons of either per pound of meat is a reasonable amount.

   d. *Meat essence*: The forcemeat can be reinforced by a meat essence from the bones of the bird(s) used in making the forcemeat. Chop the bones, brown them well, then cover them with stock to make an essence (see the definition and techniques on p. 268). This essence, thick as meat glaze, can replace part of the salt very advantageously and constitute what in the generalities on sauces on page 173 I call a "body" salt. Not only does it add salt to the forcemeat but it also contributes a wonderful depth of taste. This type of essence can be added to the raw forcemeat before baking or after the terrine has been baked (see the example on p. 267).

IV. *Homogenizing forcemeats prepared in a grinder:*
Forcemeats prepared in a food processor need not be homogenized, since the processor takes care of intimately mixing all ingredients. It is essential, however, that a forcemeat made in the grinder be beaten heavily with the electric mixer at the same time the seasonings and the eggs used as binder are added one by one.

   Beating the forcemeat blends all the meats into a paste, and you can see the fatback change texture and almost form an emulsion in the long strands of meat held together like a pudding by the eggs.

V. *Testing the forcemeat for seasoning and texture:*
To test the seasoning and texture of the forcemeat, cook 1 small patty of it in butter without browning it too much.

   Refrigerate the patty and taste it for salt, pepper, and liquor aroma as well as for texture. Check whether it is nice and smooth or whether it is crumbly. Add whatever is missing in the way of seasoning and, if the texture appears crumbly to you, do not hesitate to add 1 or 2 more eggs.

   Note: Remember to taste the forcemeat only when deeply chilled so as to have a true appreciation of the taste it will have once it has been baked and refrigerated.

D. BUILDING AND BAKING A TERRINE

Terrines are to be built with alternate layers of forcemeat and garnish.

I. Lining the terrine with fatback strips or buttering it:
The old-fashioned technique of lining the terrine with strips of fresh pork fatback can be safely abandoned. It is sufficient to butter the terrine heavily.

II. Preparing the garnish:
If the garnish consists of large pieces (strips of filets, for example), either dip those in lightly beaten and seasoned egg white or in seasoned flour. *Start the terrine or pâté with a layer of forcemeat and make sure that its top layer is also a layer of forcemeat.*

If the garnish is cut into dice, dip your hand in cold water and mix the cubes thoroughly into the forcemeat.

III. Baking the terrine:
Preheat the oven to 350°F. Bake the terrine in a hot water bath in the oven, keeping it covered until the fat runs clear; then remove the lid and bake until the top has nicely browned.

Cool for 30 minutes in the water bath after removing from the oven, then apply a moderate weight on the top of the terrine to pack the forcemeat. Let cool completely under weight.

E. BUILDING AND BAKING OR POACHING A GALANTINE

I. Preparing the galantine:
You generally need 1 very large bird or, if ducks are used, 2 birds. Make sure when you bone the birds and separate the meat from the skin that the skins or at least 1 of the skins remains completely free of holes and tears. Gently remove any blobs of fat present on the skin. Salt and pepper the skin and brush it with egg wash. Arrange the forcemeat and garnish in layers and close the skin over the filling. *Sewing the skin around the filling is most helpful.*

Brush a large piece of cheesecloth with oil. Align the edge of the cheesecloth nearest to you with the seam of the skin and roll the filled skin into the cheesecloth.

Although this is very feasible for one person, it ends up being easier if done by two: one person tightens the center while the other tightens both ends of the roll that forms as one rolls the galantine into the cheesecloth.

When rolled, the galantine looks like a very messy, blobby sausage. Turn that formless sausage so that the ends of the cheesecloth face you at one end and your working partner at the other. Each of you should now start to turn your end of the cheesecloth clockwise as tightly as possible. The galantine will shape into a huge sausage as you twist. Tie each end of the cheesecloth with many turns of string, constantly passing each tie above the already existing ones. The galantine is now ready for baking or poaching.

II. Baking the galantine:

You may bake the galantine by the roasting method of dry baking or by the braising method (see p. 355). If roasting, preheat the oven to 400°F. and put the galantine on a rack; if braising, the oven temperature should be 325°F. In both cases the cheesecloth remains around the galantine during the cooking. The cooking time will vary from 1¾ hours to 2½ hours, depending on the size of the galantine. It is done when an instant meat thermometer reads 170°F.

III. Poaching the galantine:

To poach the galantine, bring a large container of salted water or light broth to a boil (the best vessel for poaching a galantine is a fish poacher), add a bouquet garni and any spice you desire. Immerse the galantine in the boiling stock, reduce to a simmer as soon as the broth has reboiled, and poach for 1½ hours. When the poached galantine is done, let it cool in its cooking bath, and when it is cold, unwrap it from its cheesecloth. Then, to pack its center well, wrap it very, very tightly into several layers of aluminum foil. Refrigerate for at least 48 hours.

F. MAKING A SAUCISSON THE MODERN WAY: POACHING IT

I. Preparing the saucisson:

You will use a large "cook-in" plastic bag for roasting turkey. Open it on the right side and again on the bottom so you obtain a large single flat sheet of plastic.

Lay that sheet flat on the table or counter top. Add the forcemeat to it— no more than 1½ pounds of it. Roll the forcemeat into the plastic and, asking another person to help you, twist the plastic sheet clockwise at each end of the saucisson. You will see the saucisson shape by itself. Tie it very carefully with many turns of string, passing each new tie above the already existing ones. Wrap the saucisson in a triple layer of cheesecloth.

II. Poaching the saucisson:

Bring a pot of water to a boil, reduce it to a simmer, and add the saucisson. Let it poach for approximately 45–60 minutes. Let it cool in its cooking water; when cold, refrigerate it for at least 48 hours.

G. PRESENTATION OF TERRINES AND SAUCISSONS

Terrines and saucissons will be sliced. A portion of terrine will be 2 slices, one of saucisson will be 3 slices cut ¼ inch thick. The slices of each are served on a bed of lettuce and accompanied by a sparkling little salad, which, in its composition, is related to the components of the terrine forcemeat and garnish.

H. RIPENING TERRINES AND SAUCISSONS; THEIR SHELF LIFE

Terrines and saucissons need to ripen several days to be at peak of flavor. They must be kept refrigerated between servings, but must not be served ice cold. Give the slices time to mellow before serving them. The shelf life of a terrine properly refrigerated between the cutting of portions is 2 weeks. A saucisson keeps 7–10 days.

A FEW TERRINES AND SAUCISSONS SERVED
AT CHEZ LA MERE MADELEINE

A word of caution before you start to make a terrine or saucisson. Gather all your implements: food processor or grinder, terrine or plastic bag, etc., or whatever else applies to your chosen formula.

Before you purchase the meats you need, be sure to read the preceding sections carefully. All the technical details are given in the generalities pages that immediately precede this section. The recipes as they are given here represent a sequence of steps.

Note: The little salads will serve only 6 people; extend the recipe if you need to.

PASTE DE MALARS AU LART, PERSIL,
ET SALETTE DE POIS ET CLOCHE
{Duck, Bacon, and Parsley Terrine}

This recipe was devised after I spent several weeks reading and rereading *Le Ménagier de Paris* and prepared a medieval menu for our dining room, hence the funny spelling of mallard and bacon. A *"salette"* was then what we now know as a salad, *"pois"* were snow peas, and *"cloche"* the medieval word for gingerroot. The recipe can be divided exactly by half.

SERVES 16–20

PURCHASING:

1 pound chicken and/or duck livers	1/2 pound slab bacon
One 5-pound duck	1 dozen eggs
1/2 pound pork meat	2 heads of garlic
1 pound fresh fatback	Parsley

FORCEMEAT:

12 ounces chicken and duck livers, mixed

12 ounces duck meat

6 ounces pork meat, semilean and semifat

15 ounces fresh fatback

1 onion

3 shallots

6–8 eggs

GARNISH:

8 ounces smoked bacon

24 cloves garlic

1 cup very coarse-chopped parsley

SEASONING MIXTURE:

Salt as needed

Aromatic pepper as needed

2 teaspoons Quatre-Epices *(p. 35)*

2 teaspoons whole coriander seeds

3 tablespoons whole green Madagascar peppercorns, rinsed

½ cup Sercial Madeira

½ cup Armagnac

2 bay leaves

1. *To prepare the forcemeat*: Bone and clean all the meats to obtain the correct quantities. No marination is necessary for this formula. Mix forcemeat ingredients.
2. *To prepare the garnish*: Cut the smoked bacon into ⅓-inch cubes and blanch it for 2 minutes. Blanch and peel the garlic cloves.
3. Process or grind the forcemeat with the implements you own. Mix the forcemeat and garnish. Season to your taste with the seasoning mixture (except the bay leaves).
4. Preheat the oven to 350°F. Test the taste and texture of the forcemeat by making and cooking a small patty of it, according to the directions on page 106. Pack the terrine with the forcemeat. Top the forcemeat with the 2 bay leaves and bake, covered, in a hot water bath until the fat runs clear; remove the lid and bake until the top has browned. Cool and ripen.

PRESENTATION:

Present the terrine in slices placed on soft lettuce leaves with a small salad.

SALAD:

½ pound snow peas	3 tablespoons corn oil
1 small fresh gingerroot	1 tablespoon sesame oil
1 tablespoon sherry vinegar	Salt
1½ teaspoons Worcestershire sauce	2 carrots, sliced into curls
½ teaspoon powdered Szechuan pepper, untoasted	

Cut both the snow peas and the gingerroot into ⅛-inch julienne and blanch. Season the salad with a dressing made of sherry vinegar, Worcestershire sauce, Szechuan pepper, both oils, and salt.

On the plate, separate the salad and slices of terrine with a few carrot curls crisped in cold water in the refrigerator.

TERRINE DE LAPIN ET POIREAUX RABASSES {Rabbit Terrine with Truffled Leeks}

This was inspired by my first trip to Tricastin many years ago, when with still wondrous eyes I saw my first truffle being dug up. In this area of France the truffles lie relatively close to the surface of the soil, and an experienced gatherer can show you how they occasionally peak just a bit below the surface of the ground; if the day is a still one—a rarity in a country well aerated by its mistral —one may even see a cloud of "Helomiza" flies rising over a nest of truffles, on which they like to feed. The truffled leeks were the showpiece in this composition.

SERVES 12–16

PURCHASING:

One 4-pound rabbit or 2 smaller rabbits, liver or livers attached
½ pound shoulder of veal without skin or bone
½ pound shoulder of pork (Boston butt)
¾ pound fresh fatback
8 eggs

FORCEMEAT:

1 pound rabbit meat
¼ pound veal meat
¼ pound pork meat
¾ pound fresh fatback

2 onions
1 shallot
6–8 eggs

SEASONING AND MARINATING MIXTURE:

Aromatic pepper
1 teaspoon Quatre-Epices *(p. 35)*
½ cup dry white wine
½ cup marc (Provence, Bourgogne)
* or grappa*
1 teaspoon thyme leaves

½ teaspoon rosemary
½ teaspoon oregano
½ teaspoon savory
2 teaspoons fennel seeds
Salt as needed

GARNISH:

30 cloves garlic
3 tablespoons olive oil
5 thin slices of prosciutto each cut into 6 small sheets
2 bay leaves

1. *To prepare the forcemeat*: Bone the meats to obtain the correct quantities. Marinate for 24 hours in the seasoning mixture, using all ingredients listed except the salt.
2. Process the forcemeat with the implements at your disposal; season to your taste with salt and more marc, spices, and pepper if needed.
3. Test the taste and texture of the forcemeat as directed on page 106; *under-salting* may be useful here because of the prosciutto in the garnish.
4. *To prepare the garnish*: Peel the garlic cloves and brown them very slowly and evenly in the olive oil. Cool and wrap each clove in a small sheet of prosciutto.
5. Pack alternate layers of forcemeat and garnish into a buttered terrine, starting and ending with a layer of forcemeat. Top with the 2 bay leaves.
6. Preheat the oven to 350°F. and bake, covered, in a hot water bath for 60 minutes. Uncover and finish baking until the fat runs clear. Cool for 30 minutes in the water bath, then place under moderate weight until cold.
7. Refrigerate and ripen for several days.

PRESENTATION:

Present the terrine on a plate with a large bouquet of parsley and a truffled (or not truffled) leek. Count 1 leek and 3 slices of fresh truffles per serving. You will find the recipe for braising the leeks on page 411 in the vegetable chapter.

TERRINE DE BASSE-COUR EN FAISANDAGE BEAUJOLAIS
{Barnyard Terrine in Beaujolais Marinade}

The meats used here can be found anywhere in the United States, but do not hesitate to use anything wild you can put your hands on, from hare to pheasant.

SERVES AT LEAST 16

PURCHASING:

6 medium or 5 large chicken legs
One rabbit
One 4-pound duck, less the filets
1½ pounds fatback
1 dozen eggs

FORCEMEAT:

Meat from 6 medium or 5 large chicken legs, diced coarse
Meat from 1 rabbit, diced coarse
Meat from one 4-pound duck, less the filets, diced coarse
1¼ pounds fatback, diced coarse
8–10 eggs

GARNISH:

The duck filets, cut into strips
¼ pound fatback, cut into strips
1 egg white
3 cloves garlic, chopped
⅓ cup chopped parsley
2 tablespoons butter

Gizzards, neck, and wing tips, lower leg and shoulder shanks of the duck and of the rabbit
1 cup excellent Beaujolais
3 cups heavy Golden Veal Stock (p. 20)

SEASONING AND MARINATING MIXTURE:

2 teaspoons Quatre-Epices *(p. 35)*   *⅓ cup Marc de Bourgogne or other*
2 onions   *equivalent spirit*
6 shallots   *¼ cup fino (dry) sherry*
¼ cup Sercial Madeira   *1 cup excellent Beaujolais*
¼ cup white port

1. Put the meats and fatback for the forcemeat in 1 dish and those for the garnish in another.

2. Mix all the elements of the marinade and pour half of the mixture into each of the 2 dishes. Marinate a full 4 days.

3. *To prepare the garnish*: Dip the strips of marinated duck filets and fatback first in lightly beaten egg white, then in chopped garlic and parsley, mixed.

4. Brown very well in butter the necks, gizzards, and wing tips of duck together with legs and shoulder shanks of duck and rabbit. Add 1 cup Beaujolais and reduce to a glaze. Then add 1 cup heavy veal stock three times, reducing to a glaze each time. You will obtain approximately ½–⅓ cup of essence. Set aside.

5. Process the forcemeat. Preheat the oven to 350°F. Build the terrine by packing alternating layers of forcemeat and garnish in a buttered terrine. Bake in a hot water bath for about 1½ hours.

6. When done, drain off half the liquid fat around the terrine. Punch 20 holes into the surface of the terrine and pour the essence (you may have to reheat it) into these holes. Cool for 30 minutes, then put under moderate weight.

7. Ripen for at least 2 days.

PRESENTATION:

Present the terrine on a lettuce leaf with a small salad of zucchini and carrot julienne.

SALAD DRESSING:

1 tablespoon red wine vinegar
1 teaspoon Dijon mustard
4 tablespoons corn oil
3 rashers of crisp bacon, crumbled

SAUCISSON SAVOYARD {Savoie Saucisson}

SERVES 6–8

PURCHASING:

1⅓ pounds pork shoulder (Boston butt)
½ pound fresh pork fatback
1 small head of cabbage

FORCEMEAT:

1 pound meat from a shoulder of
   pork
½ pound fresh pork fatback
3 cloves garlic, chopped coarse
1 onion, chopped

½ teaspoon fennel seeds
1 ounce marc or grappa
2 eggs
Salt
Pepper from the mill

GARNISH:

½ packed cup blanched and well-drained cabbage leaves, cut into julienne
¼ pound prosciutto, cut into ⅛-inch cubes
2 tablespoons prosciutto fat, cut into ⅛-inch cubes

1. Cut the pork and fatback into ⅓-inch cubes; mix them with the garlic, onion, and fennel seeds and marinate in the marc for 24 hours.
2. Divide the forcemeat into 2 equal parts: process half of it extremely fine and the other half coarse. Mix very well, adding the eggs as well as the cabbage julienne and both prosciutto meat and fat.
3. Store as is in its mixing bowl overnight in a cold refrigerator, then test the seasoning of the forcemeat as directed on page 106 and add salt and pepper as needed.
4. Roll into a plastic sheet as described in detail on page 109. Poach 1½ hours in salted simmering water and cool completely in its water bath. Refrigerate for 2 days before serving.

PRESENTATION:

Present the slices of saucisson on a lettuce leaf with a small salad.

SALAD:

> 1 rutabaga (yellow turnip), cut into ¼-inch julienne and
> blanched until almost well done

DRESSING:

> 1 tablespoon red wine vinegar
> 1 shallot, chopped fine
> 1 teaspoon Dijon mustard
> 4 tablespoons walnut oil
> 2 tablespoons fine-chopped chervil

SAUCISSON DU LARZAC
{Saucisson from the Roquefort Area}

SERVES 6–8

PURCHASING:

¾ pound shoulder of pork (Boston butt)	Saffron
½ pound fresh fatback	1 ounce dried Eduli (Porcini, Cèpes)
1 large lamb shank or 2 smaller ones	One ¼-pound slice boiled ham

FORCEMEAT:

> ½ pound meat from a shoulder of pork (Boston butt)
> ½ pound fresh fatback of pork
> ½ pound meat from 1 large or 2 small lamb shanks, without fat or gristle
> 2 eggs

SEASONING AND MARINATING MIXTURE:

> 3 cloves garlic, chopped fine
> 1 onion, grated
> ⅛ teaspoon powdered saffron
> 1 teaspoon dried basil
> ¼ teaspoon fine-ground dried orange rind

GARNISH:

> 1 teaspoon dried Boleti Eduli, chopped in their dried state
> One ¼-pound slice boiled ham, recut into ¼-inch cubes
> Salt and pepper

1. Cut all the meat elements of the forcemeat into ⅓-inch cubes. Dry marinate them overnight in the seasoning mixture.
2. Divide the forcemeat into 2 equal parts; process one very fine and process the other one coarse. Mix very well, adding the crumbled Boleti Eduli, the boiled ham, salt, and pepper.
3. Store as is overnight, then test the forcemeat as directed on page 106. Correct the seasoning with salt and pepper.
4. Roll into a plastic sheet as described in detail on page 109. Poach 1½ hours in salted simmering water and cool completely in its water bath. Refrigerate for 2 days before serving.

PRESENTATION:

> Present 3 slices of saucisson on a chilled plate with a small salad.

SALAD:

> 1 head of curly chicory
> 2 tablespoons crumbled walnut meats
> 2 tablespoons crumbled Roquefort cheese

DRESSING:

½ tablespoon Armagnac   1 tablespoon heavy cream
1 teaspoon Dijon mustard   3 tablespoons walnut oil
2 teaspoons wine vinegar   Salt and pepper

GELEE DE LAPIN AUX PETITS LEGUMES CROQUANTS {Jellied Rabbit and Vegetables}

From the kitchen of my Aunt Claire who was a restaurateur in Touraine. This is more a jellied rabbit stew than it is a terrine, but it unmolds and looks like a terrine when presented at the table. If serving in a restaurant, oil individual round terrines of approximately 3-ounce capacity and unmold onto a plate side by side with the little tomato salad.

SERVES 8 AT HOME, 7 AT A RESTAURANT

RABBIT STEW:

1 tablespoon oil of your choice
One 3-pound rabbit, cut into 8 pieces
1 large carrot, sliced thick
1 onion, sliced thick
6 cloves garlic, peeled
Salt and pepper

Bouquet garni (see p. 82)
2 tablespoons chopped tarragon
1 ounce Cognac or Armagnac
3 cups Golden Veal Stock (p. 20)
1 gelatinous veal bone, blanched and
    chopped, or 1 envelope gelatin

GARNISH:

12 tiny white onions
12 carrot pieces, 1 inch long by 1/3
    inch wide
12 turnip pieces, 1 inch long by 1/3
    inch wide
12 rutabaga pieces, 1 inch long by 1/3
    inch wide
1 zucchini, cut into pieces 1 inch by
    1/3 inch
2 tablespoons oil of your choice
    (hazelnut is best)

2 beets, cut into pieces 1 inch by 1/3
    inch
1 cup very strong Golden Veal Stock
    (p. 20)
2 tablespoons chopped tarragon
2 tablespoons chopped parsley
2 tablespoons chopped chives
2 tablespoons chopped chervil
1–2 tablespoons wine vinegar to your
    personal taste
Salt and pepper

1. Rub a braising pot with the oil; in it mix the rabbit, carrot, onion, and garlic cloves. Season with salt and pepper. Brown in a 350°F. oven until golden.

2. Remove the pot from the oven and lower the oven temperature to 325°F. To the stew add the bouquet garni, chopped tarragon, Armagnac or Cognac, and the veal stock. Bring to a boil. Add the veal bone or gelatin. Cover with a piece of aluminum foil fit flush over the meat and broth, then top with the pot lid and braise in the oven until tender.

3. Meanwhile, blanch the baby onions, carrots, turnips, and rutabagas, keeping them slightly crunchy. Sauté the zucchini pieces in a drop or so of oil, keep-

ing them slightly crunchy, and blanch the pieces of beet in vinegar water until thoroughly cooked. Set the beets aside.

4. In a large saucepan, mix all the root vegetables *except the beets* with the veal stock. Reduce the mixture over high heat until you have a glaze. Add the zucchini to the pot.

5. Add all the herbs to the vegetable pot. In another little dish mix the beets with the vinegar. Keep separated until the last minute.

6. When the rabbit is done, remove all the meat from the bones and cut the meat into pieces approximately the size of the vegetables. Strain the cooking juices through a fine "China cap" sieve. Cool them; they will quickly turn extremely thick. *Make sure that the juices are free of all traces of fat.* At this time mix the vegetables in with the rabbit meat and its defatted juices.

7. Brush the chosen molding vessel or vessels with oil; drip upside down onto a paper towel. Just before molding the mixture, mix in the beets and correct the final seasoning for salt and pepper. Spoon the mixture into the mold(s) and refrigerate overnight.

PRESENTATION:

Unmold the stew and present it on a small luncheon plate on a lettuce leaf with 3 slices of peeled tomato. Finish the plate with a bouquet of chervil or parsley. Season the tomatoes with the following dressing.

SALAD DRESSING:

> *2 tablespoons* Verjus *(p. 44) or* Aceto Balsamico *(p. 45) or*
>   *vinegar of your choice*
> *¼ teaspoon honey*
> *Salt and pepper*
> *3 tablespoons hazelnut oil*

GALANTINE EN CHINOISERIE
{Galantine of Duck with Chinese Seasonings}

This galantine can be served either warm or cold.

SERVES 10–12

GALANTINE:

One 4–5-pound duck
½ pound shoulder of pork (Boston
   butt)
¾ pound fresh fatback
1 tablespoon fresh blanched green
   Madagascar peppercorns (if
   unavailable, use canned
   peppercorns, drained)
1 teaspoon ground ginger

1 teaspoon powdered Szechuan
   pepper, untoasted
1 teaspoon Quatre-Epices (p. 35)
4–5 eggs
Pepper from the mill
¼ cup fino (dry) sherry
Strong soy sauce, as needed
Salt
Oil as needed

SAUCE:

1 carrot, sliced thick
1 onion, sliced thick
2 tablespoons butter
3 cups heavy Golden Veal Stock
   (p. 20)
Bouquet garni (see p. 82)

¼ cup extremely fine julienne of
   gingerroot
½ cup scallion rings, cut ⅛ inch thick
   (green part only)
Dark strong soy sauce, as needed
Sherry, as needed
Powdered Szechuan pepper, as needed

1. Bone the duck completely to obtain 1–1¼ pounds meat; dice the meat small and reserve the skin. Dice both the pork shoulder and the fatback small. Mix all the meats with half the green peppercorns, the ground ginger, the Szechuan pepper, and the *quatre-épices* and marinate overnight.

2. Process the mixture to obtain a very fine forcemeat. Place it in the large electric mixer bowl and beat well, adding eggs, pepper, sherry, and soy sauce as needed to salt the mixture. *Do not salt exclusively with soy sauce*; use part soy sauce and part regular salt. When the forcemeat is smooth, blend in the second half of the green peppercorns. Test the forcemeat for texture and seasoning as directed on page 106.

3. Roll into the skin of the duck and do not hesitate to sew the skin closed around the forcemeat to make the rolling in cheesecloth easier.

4. Brush a large piece of cheesecloth very well with oil. Roll the galantine in it and tie carefully according to instructions on page 108.

5. Sauté the carrot and onion in the butter until golden. Meanwhile sear the cheesecloth-wrapped galantine in a 400°F. oven. If you're worried about

burning the ends of the cloth, wrap each of them into a piece of foil. The galantine will sear very well through the cloth.

6. Transfer the galantine to a braising pot. Lower the oven temperature to 325°F. Add the veal stock to the pot, bring to a boil, and add the bouquet garni. Cover the meat with a sheet of foil placed flush over it and the braising stock. Close the pot with its lid and braise 1½–2 hours in the oven. (If you are hesitant about braising methods, read p. 355 or *The Making of a Cook*, pp. 193–94.)

WARM PRESENTATION:

1. As soon as the galantine is cooked, remove the cheesecloth carefully and pull out the sewing thread if there is one. Let stand for 15 minutes before slicing.

2. Skim and reduce the cooking juices well. Add the julienned gingerroot and the scallion rings. Correct the final seasoning with soy sauce, sherry, and Szechuan pepper.

3. As a vegetable, you may want to prepare a julienne of bell peppers of all colors—peeled or not peeled, depending on your taste—mixed with a julienne of zucchini and flowerets of broccoli and cauliflower. Stir fry the mixture quickly before surrounding the galantine with it.

COLD PRESENTATION:

1. Let the galantine cool completely after unwrapping it. Roll it tightly into a long sheet of aluminum foil and refrigerate for at least 12 hours. Strain the cooking juices and reserve them.

2. Defat the cooking juices completely.

3. When ready to decorate the galantine, place it on a rack over a jelly roll pan. Remelt the cooking juices and correct their final seasoning with soy sauce, sherry, and Szechuan pepper.

4. Place one-quarter of the cooking juices at a time into a bowl placed into another larger bowl containing ice cubes in salted water. As soon as the juices turn to a thickish oily mixture, brush them over the surface of the galantine. Repeat until all the juices have been used and the galantine is fully coated with the chaudfroid, then immediately sprinkle with the julienne of gingerroot and the scallion rings mixed.

5. Keep refrigerated until ready to serve; the galantine must be served within

6 hours or the chaudfroid coating will dehydrate badly. Cover with a tent of foil to minimize dehydration.

6. Present on a platter lined with Italian parsley or cilantro and with a salad of bell peppers of all colors, cauliflowerets and broccoli flowerets well seasoned with your favorite vinaigrette dressing.

Versatile Noodle Dishes

The invention of multiple types of noodle-making machines has brought the pleasure of fresh noodle dishes to many homes and restaurants. As much as I want to be tolerant, modern, and accepting of machines, which definitely make life easier, I feel compelled to say that the best noodles are always handmade.

The best noodle makers are and will always be women who have practiced the art for many years and who have an incomparable *"tour de main."* As a restaurateur, I had to think of many ways of presenting noodles, so I combined the techniques taught me by my great-aunts in Alsace, my good acquaintance Anna-Maria Santegrini of Emilia, and a few German and Austrian cooks whose names I do not even know, but who have in one way or another contributed to my "pasta" hands.

The following pages contain first the techniques, then a few recipes for side dishes and main dishes that, accompanied by a green salad, provide both family and restaurant guests with a royal meal. I will explain here only the hand techniques; those who prefer to use machines certainly can do so, following the manufacturer's directions.

SIMPLE EGG DOUGH

3 eggs
3 egg yolks
2½ cups unsifted all-purpose flour
½ teaspoon salt

In a small bowl beat well the eggs and egg yolks. Place ¼ cup of the flour in another bowl, so you can rub your hands with it if need be.

Place the remaining 2¼ cups of flour on the counter, or, even better, a wooden table top. Make a well in the flour, add three-quarters of the total volume of the eggs to the well, and add the salt. Beat with a fork, gradually bringing the flour from the sides into the well, until the paste has thickened enough so the liquid will not run out onto the counter. Switch from your fork to your hands. Gather all the flour into the already wet part and knead until the dough is smooth and elastic and does not show any more air bubbles when cut through its center.

This kneading takes a bit of time; you will, in the process, see the dough pass through diverse stages. It may be stiff and refuse to bend. Remedy that by taking a bit of the remaining egg mixture on your hands and kneading it in; continue doing this until the dough becomes more manageable. Do not in any case pour egg on the counter or you will see your dough "squish-squash" all over the place and stubbornly refuse to accept the additional egg. It may happen, on the contrary, that during the first stage you have added a bit too much egg so that your dough feels too soft and tacky. In this case, reach for the small bowl of flour and rub your hands with it while you continue kneading. You will see the dough stiffen and dry to the correct texture.

So the solutions are easy:

- Too dry a dough: rub your hands in egg while continuing the kneading.
- Too wet a dough: rub your hands with a veil of the remaining flour while continuing the kneading.

It takes a little bit of time for the dough to reach that "bubble-free" stage that you are looking for, and you may get tired, but all the while you are kneading you are building the gluten strands in the dough. As the kneading goes on, these will break down from long strands into smaller ones; this breaking down is what will allow you to stretch your dough without difficulty if you roll it out by hand. You can reach a compromise and do half the kneading by hand and half by machine.

If you choose the latter method, as soon as the dough is homogeneous, cut it in half and pass each piece of dough several times through the rollers of the noodle machine.

In any case, let the dough rest a good 30 minutes under an inverted mixing bowl before you start the final stretching and cutting.

Machine stretching requires no special care; simply feed the pieces of dough through the roller, gradually going from number 8 to number 2.

Hand stretching is an art, a true *"tour de main"* that, once mastered, gives you the very best noodles in the world and leaves you, by the time you have kneaded and rolled out a recipe, effectively 1 pound lighter in body weight, allowing you consequently to eat that dish of noodles without qualms. Isn't that nice!

So try to stretch it by hand. Roll it with a solid rolling pin with tapered ends until it is first ¼ inch thick, then ⅛ inch thick. Now it is ready to stretch.

To stretch away from you:
Work from the center of the dough away from you: place both hands at the center of the rolling pin, apply pressure only from the hand cushions below your thumb and index and middle fingers; let both your hands travel in opposite directions from the center of the pin toward each of its ends. You will see the dough advance forward a good inch, even more.

To stretch toward you:
Reverse the process, working from the center of the dough toward yourself to cover the yet unstretched part of the dough. Place your hands at opposite ends of the rolling pin and apply pressure, letting your hands travel from the ends of the rolling pin toward its center until they meet there; you will see the dough advance and stretch a good inch or more toward you.

To stretch the dough evenly:
Keep turning the dough by 90 degrees during the stretchings. Your work will also be easier if you keep turning the sheet over and over again to make use of the moisture constantly brought to the surface of the dough by your stretching. Avoid flouring the sheet; the flour would absorb that moisture and

prevent rather than help stretching. Use flour only if the dough is tacky, and then only the thinnest veil.

To cut the noodles:

Why not use the machine for this, so as to obtain a very regular size and also save a bit of time? Cut the sheet into strips of a size that will fit through the rollers. Let the cut sheets dry a few minutes, then roll them through to obtain ribbon noodles. Loosely roll these in "nests" and let them dry as long as you want on a lightly floured paper or a cookie sheet. Once the noodles are dry, they can be stored in canisters and used later. Cooking time will depend on their state of dryness. See cooking directions on page 128.

MACARONI DOUGH

Macaroni, or eggless noodle dough, is made with only flour and water. I like to blend the flour with a proportion of fine semolina for better and more interesting texture.

> *2 cups unsifted all-purpose flour*
> *½ cup semolina*
> *Cold water, as needed*
> *½ teaspoon salt*

Proceed exactly as you would for egg noodle dough (preceding recipe). It is extremely difficult to state exactly how much water is to be used, since each and every flour absorbs water differently. Start with ½ cup and gradually add as much as will be needed to prepare a macaroni dough of the proper consistency, always rubbing your hands with water rather than pouring it onto the counter.

VEGETABLE-FLAVORED DOUGHS

All kinds of flavored doughs can be made by using vegetable purées as part of the liquid ingredients instead of water or eggs. I have given some interesting ideas on the following pages. Notice that when the purée contains quite a bit of moisture, that moisture is first evaporated by cooking the vegetables in oil or butter. Also, the volume of egg white is diminished, since some of its moisture is replaced by that of the vegetable purée; the amount of egg yolk is slightly increased.

NOODLE DOUGHS MADE WITH DIVERSE FLOURS

Buckwheat flour or corn flour can be blended with all-purpose flour to prepare a noodle dough with a different taste and texture. It is essential always to use at least one-half to two-thirds regular all-purpose flour with a high protein content (11–12.5 percent) to compensate for the relative lack of body-building proteins in the weaker flours. The amount of egg yolk can be slightly increased to give a better texture to the dough.

COMMERCIAL NOODLES AND MACARONI

Obviously some brands are quite good, and your favorite ones can be used with any of the sauces and garnishes proposed in this chapter. Even lowly down-to-earth orzo can be turned into excellent "starch" dishes for dinners or lunches if treated as a pilaf, exactly like rice; see page 140 for a few ideas.

COOKING NOODLES

All noodles are cooked in a large amount of wildly boiling water. Bring a gallon of water to a boil in a large stainless steel pot. Of course you can also use one of those noodle cookers that are fitted with a special strainer—on the one hand, they are nice because all one has to do is lift the upper part of the pot to remove the noodles from the water; on the other hand, they do not cook the noodles quite as fast because they are not as wide as a regular pot.

Whichever you choose, bring the water to a boil first, add the salt to it only a few seconds before you add the noodles, and use at least 1½ teaspoons salt per quart of water. You may or may not also add a dash of oil; I do only for ravioli or tortellini.

Cook at a rolling boil to the consistency you like, taking care not to overcook. Italian cooks are supreme at cooking pasta, while even the greatest restaurants in France overcook it royally.

Make sure that a little crunch remains to keep your palate interested and to preserve the taste of the noodle. As soon as the noodles are cooked, drain them and shake the colander immediately to discard excess water. Rinse them under *warm* water (not cold, not hot) *only* if the noodles have been floured a bit excessively while stretching or if they are to be used cold in a salad. Add the noodles to the sauce or seasoning.

NOODLES WITHOUT KNEADING (SPAETZLE)

For cooks who cannot knead and do not own a pasta machine, as well as for restaurateurs whose budget will not allow for so time-consuming a process, the obvious solution is to prepare those wonderful "liquid" noodles offered by all the cuisines of Europe under different names and with a variety of seasonings. In the Germanic countries, they are called spaetzle; in Lorraine they are *totelots* where one speaks French and *knepfs* where one speaks German.

The batter may be flavored with any spice or herb available. The noodles take the same sauces as other pasta, and, simply buttered, they keep in the warming oven of a restaurant for the many hours of a dinner service.

> *3 cups unsifted flour (11–12 percent protein)*
> *9 eggs*
> *¾–1 cup milk*
> *1 teaspoon salt*
> *Flavoring to your taste*

Mix the flour and eggs gradually; add the milk, then the salt. Let stand for 30 minutes.

Bring a large pot of water to a boil. Salt well. Pour some of the batter onto a small chopping board or the bottom of a cake pan and, with a long, narrow metal spatula, push ¼-inch-wide strips of batter into the water. The noodles come floating to the top of the water as soon as they are cooked; remove them with a large slotted spoon and transfer them to a large buttered baking dish. Dry them for 15–20 minutes in a 275°F. oven before saucing them.

MARIE BECKER'S KNEPFS AUX ECHALOTES
{Spaetzle with Shallot Cream}

From the German-speaking part of Lorraine. If serving as a main dish, follow it with a salad.

SERVES 6–8 AS A MAIN DISH, 10–12 AS A SIDE DISH

1 recipe Spaetzle (p. 129)   *⅓ cup Secondary Stock (p. 23)*
6 tablespoons butter   *2 cups heavy cream*
1½ pounds small shallots   *¼ cup chopped parsley*
Salt and pepper

1. Cook the spaetzle and put them to dry in a 275°F. oven in a dish buttered with 1 tablespoon of the butter.
2. Peel the shallots and cut a cross in their root ends to prevent their falling apart while cooking. Heat 2 tablespoons of the butter in a large skillet and sauté the shallots in it until light golden. Salt and pepper; cover the skillet and cook until tender. Add a tablespoon or so of stock every so often to build a bit of glaze.
3. Remove the shallots to the dish containing the spaetzle; mix well.
4. To the pan in which the shallots were cooked add the cream, scraping well to deglaze all the juices. Reduce the cream a bit, until it starts to thicken.
5. Heat the remaining 3 tablespoons of butter in a small pan and cook it to the russet brown "noisette" stage (see p. 48). Add the butter to the reduced cream and mix well. Season to your taste. Add the chopped parsley and mix into the spaetzle and shallots.

Variation: Instead of shallots, you may add to the cream ½ cup chopped chervil leaves, well dried, and 1–2 tablespoons Meaux mustard (with seeds).

NOUILLES AU CAMEMBERT
{Noodles, Camembert, and Walnuts}

From my mother's kitchen, where this dish was prepared with all the ends of Camembert and Brie a household can accumulate; I applied the same method in the restaurant. Serve with any red or white meat; it does not go well with lamb or pork.

SERVES 6–8 AS A SIDE DISH

1 recipe Simple Egg Dough (p. 125)
6 ounces Camembert or Brie (net weight with rind removed)
4 tablespoons butter

⅓ cup chopped walnuts
Salt
Pepper from the mill
1 tablespoon chopped parsley

1. Prepare the noodle dough. Cut it into ¼-inch-wide strips and cook in salted water.
2. Cut the Camembert or Brie into ⅓-inch cubes. Heat the butter well in a large skillet and in it sauté the walnuts until they toast lightly.
3. Add the cooked noodles to this butter, toss well, and remove to a heated dish. Toss the cheese through the noodles; correct the seasoning with salt and pepper. Sprinkle with chopped parsley.

Variation: Replace the walnuts with 1½ teaspoons aniseeds. The dish will then become a side dish for pork but will still not be appropriate to serve with lamb.

PATES A LA CREME D'OIGNONS ET AUX CHAMPIGNONS {Noodles with Onion Cream and Mushrooms}

A note on the choice of mushrooms: The best is a huge truffle, cut into slivers and heated slowly in the cream, but any butter-sautéed wild mushroom or dried and revived morels will do handsomely. Fresh morels are too delicate, but fresh chanterelles are a perfect happy medium.

This dish is so distinctive in flavor that it should be served alone in the Italian manner.

SERVES 6–8

1 recipe Simple Egg Dough (p. 125)
1 pound white onions
4–6 tablespoons butter
Salt
Pepper from the mill
1 quart heavy cream

1 large or 2 smaller truffles, cut into ⅛-inch julienne or 1 pound any good wild or cultivated mushrooms, sliced thin
1 clove garlic, mashed
Chopped parsley

1. Prepare the noodles.
2. While the noodles dry a bit, slice the onions paper thin, by hand or in a processor. Sauté in 4 tablespoons of the butter. Season with salt and pepper and let cook until the onions have lost three-quarters of their volume and have turned uniformly golden. Add the cream and cook until it has reduced by one-third. Strain only if desired.
3. If you use the truffles, add them to the onion cream. Reheat well and let stand 10 minutes. Do not add garlic and parsley.
4. If using mushrooms, sauté in 2 tablespoons butter. Season with salt and pepper and cover to extract their juices, then raise the heat, uncover, and let brown; add garlic and parsley.
5. Cook the noodles; as soon as they are done to your taste, add them to the onion cream and toss well. Correct the seasoning and transfer to a serving platter. If using mushrooms, sprinkle them over the noodles.

LES PATES EN CHINOISERIE
{Pilaf of Noodles with Chinese Spices}

An excellent accompaniment to pork or any warm smoked meat.

SERVES 6

1 recipe Simple Egg Dough (p. 125)
  cut in ribbons ⅛ inch wide by
  ¹⁄₁₆ inch thick, or store-bought
  noodles of the same size
2 cups Secondary Stock (p. 23)
1½ teaspoons Lapsang Souchong
  tea (the best is Hu-Kwa)
¼ teaspoon very fine-powdered
  Szechuan pepper, untoasted
2 cloves garlic, mashed

4 scallions
1 large (3 inches by 1½ inches)
  gingerroot, rather young
½ a red pepper, peeled and seeded
2 tablespoons vegetable oil
Salt
2 tablespoons sunflower seeds
Dark soy sauce
Pepper from the mill

1. Make sure that the noodles, if homemade, have been dried for several days.
2. Bring the stock to a boil and add the tea. Remove from the heat and let steep for 10 minutes. Strain and reheat without boiling.

3. Prepare on a plate the Szechuan pepper; the garlic; the white part of the scallions cut into ⅛-inch slivers, the green part cut into elongated rings obtained by holding the knife at a very wide angle; the gingerroot peeled, cut into ⅛-inch julienne and blanched; the red pepper cut in ⅛-inch julienne.

4. Heat the vegetable oil. Add the Szechuan pepper, garlic, and the white part of scallions and toss well. Add the noodles and the hot broth. Stir once with the tines of a fork to mix well; add salt to your taste. Cover the pot with a triple layer of paper towels and the pot lid and cook over medium-low heat until the pasta has completely absorbed the liquid.

5. Toss into the noodles the gingerroot and the sunflower seeds. Correct the seasoning with either plain salt or dark soy sauce and pepper from the mill.

6. To serve, empty onto a round platter and sprinkle well with a mixture of scallion greens and red pepper julienne.

MACARONI AU KARVI ET GORGONZOLA
{Caraway-flavored Macaroni with Gorgonzola Cream}

Serve by itself in the Italian manner.

SERVES 6

2 dozen tiny California artichokes
3 cups heavy cream
1 recipe Marcaroni Dough (p. 127), made with 1 teaspoon finely powdered caraway seeds included in the dough, or 1 pound store-bought macaroni

1 teaspoon caraway seeds (if using store-bought macaroni)
3–4 ounces very ripe Gorgonzola cheese
Freshly grated Parmigiano-Reggiano cheese
Salt
Coarsely cracked pepper from the mill

1. Bring a large pot of water to a boil. Trim the small artichokes of all leaves until only a ¾-inch core is left. Cut the tip off. Cook the artichokes in quickly boiling salted water until tender.

2. Mix the heavy cream and the artichokes. Slowly heat together until the cream simmers. Keep warm.

3. Cook the macroni until done to your taste. Add to the cream and artichokes. Add also the caraway seeds if using store-bought macaroni and the Gorgonzola and toss well together, until the Gorgonzola has melted. Correct the final seasoning with salt.

4. Empty onto a platter. Dust liberally with Parmigiano-Reggiano and sprinkle with coarsely cracked pepper.

PATES AU KARI, PIGNONS DE PIN ET CORINTHES {Curry-flavored Pasta with Pignoli and Currants}

A perfect side dish for a plain, well-done, and crisp American roast duck or for quails; also good as a bed of noodles for chicken breasts.

SERVES 6

¼ cup currants
2 tablespoons Cognac or Armagnac
¼ cup pignoli nuts
6–8 tablespoons butter
¼ teaspoon strong, fresh curry powder

1 recipe Simple Egg Dough (p. 125) made with 2 teaspoons strong, fresh curry powder added to the flour before mixing
Salt and pepper

1. Soak the currants in the Cognac or Armagnac.
2. Sauté the pignoli nuts in the butter. Add the ¼ teaspoon curry and reserve.
3. Cook the noodles in boiling salted water. Add them to the pan containing the pignoli and curry butter and toss well. Add the currants and whatever liqueur may be left and correct the final seasoning with salt and pepper.

TAILLERINS AUX FRUITS DE MER {Basil and Saffron Pasta with Shellfish Stew}

This is a main course that should be followed by a wonderful salad with a dressing extremely light in acid. A friend helping you to cook one of the batches of noodles will be a joy!

SERVES 6–8

SAFFRON NOODLES:

1 recipe Simple Egg Dough (p. 125) flavored with ⅓ teaspoon powdered saffron beaten into the egg mixture prior to making the dough

BASIL PASTA:

1 packed cup basil leaves
2 eggs
3 egg yolks
1 teaspoon salt
2½ cups sifted all-purpose flour

SHELLFISH STEW:

2 dozen medium shrimp in their shells
2 tablespoons olive oil
1 pound deep sea scallops
1 cup Fish Fumet (p. 28)
1 cup clam juice
3 shallots, chopped fine
2 onions, chopped fine
3 tablespoons cut-up basil stems
1 piece of orange rind, the size of a quarter
Bouquet garni (see p. 82)
1 pound mussels, well scrubbed

1 cup dry white wine
1 quart heavy cream
Salt
Coarsely cracked pepper from the mill
½ cup butter
1 large pinch of saffron threads
2 tablespoons fine-cut julienne of basil leaves
½ tablespoon superfine julienne of orange rind, blanched
2 tablespoons freshly grated Parmigiano-Reggiano cheese

1. Prepare the saffron pasta. Stretch, cut, and dry.
2. To prepare the basil pasta, put basil leaves, eggs, and egg yolks in a blender and whirl until homogenized. Mix salt and flour together. Make a well in the flour. Add four-fifths of the basil-egg mixture and work into a pasta dough as described on page 125; reserve the last one-fifth of the egg-basil mixture in case you need to moisten the dough as you work. Cut and dry the noodles. This noodle dough *must* be prepared and cooked on the same day or it will turn brown.
3. To prepare the stew, devein the shrimp but do not remove their shells. Heat the olive oil in a large sauté pan and stir fry the shrimp until they turn color. Remove to a plate and shell.

4. Separate the "feet," or tough side tendons, from the scallops.

5. Return the shrimp shells to the skillet, add the fish fumet, clam juice, chopped shallots and onions, basil stems, orange rind, bouquet garni, mussels, white wine, and the scallop "feet." Steam the mussels open in this mixture.

6. Shell the mussels and reserve them on the same plate as the shrimp. Slice the scallops into ¼-inch slices.

7. Reduce the juices in the sauté pan by two-thirds.

8. While the shellfish juices reduce, in another pot reduce the cream to 3 cups.

9. Add the reduced cream to the reduced shellfish juices and simmer together for 10 minutes. Correct the seasoning.

10. Meanwhile cook the 2 types of noodles in a different pot of salted water.

11. Heat 7 tablespoons of the butter in a large pan and add the noodles to the butter as soon as each is cooked; mix the noodles well and season them well.

12. Quickly stir fry the scallops for 1 minute in the remaining tablespoon of butter. Add shrimp and mussels to reheat.

13. Toss the shellfish into the noodles and, using a "China cap" strainer, strain the finished shellfish sauce into the mixture. Toss well again. Serve on a large platter dotted with saffron threads, basil leaves, orange rind, and a fine spray of Parmigiano-Reggiano.

PATES A L'ANETH, AUX ASPERGES ET AU SAUMON FUME
{Dill Noodles with Asparagus and Smoked Salmon Butter}

Serve by itself in the Italian manner.

SERVES 6-8

NOODLES:

1 pound medium-size asparagus, peeled and blanched

2 eggs

4 egg yolks

¾ cup chopped fresh dill weed

2½ cups sifted all-purpose flour

1 teaspoon salt

GARNISH:

4 slices of smoked Nova Scotia
   salmon
½ cup butter
3 cups heavy cream

Salt
Pepper from the mill
¼ cup chopped fresh dill weed

1. Remove the asparagus tips and cut two-thirds of the stems into 1-inch pieces; set aside. Chop the remainder of the stems very fine; place in the blender container with the eggs and egg yolks and the dill weed and process until smooth.

2. Make a well in the flour, add the asparagus-egg-dill mixture and the salt and work into a nice pale green pasta dough. Let rest for 30 minutes under an inverted bowl before stretching and cutting.

3. Roll out, stretch, and cut the dough into band noodles (see pp. 126–27).

4. Put 2 slices smoked salmon in the food processor container, add the butter, and process until smooth. Chop the remaining 2 salmon slices into ¼-inch-wide strips. Reserve butter and salmon strips.

5. Heat the cream to a good boil and reduce it lightly. Cook the noodles. Meanwhile, whisk the salmon butter into the reduced cream. Reheat the asparagus segments. Correct seasoning with salt and pepper.

6. As soon as the noodles are cooked, add them and the asparagus segments to the salmon cream. Add the dill.

7. Serve dotted with the smoked salmon strips.

CROZETS TARENTAIS
{Buckwheat Noodles from the Isère Valley}

A small buckwheat or rye noodle with origins in the ancestrally Ligurian areas of the Savoie, the *crozets* have a first cousin in the Italian Ligurian Alps, the *corzetti*. That could be another argument against Marco Polo and his noodle mission to the Orient. The mass of cooked shallots is called a *cerfuse*.

SERVES 6

CROZETS:

> 2 cups sifted all-purpose flour
> 1 cup unsifted buckwheat flour
> 3 eggs
> 3 egg yolks
> ½ teaspoon salt

CERFUSE:

2 pounds shallots, peeled and sliced ¼ inch thick

½ cup hot melted butter, or more if needed

Salt

Pepper from the mill

⅓ cup fresh chervil

Grated Beaufort or Gruyère cheese to taste

1. Mix the 2 flours and make a well in the center. Beat together the eggs, egg yolks, and salt and add three-quarters of the mixture to the well. Prepare a noodle dough as indicated on page 125. Let rest for 30 minutes before stretching.
2. Stretch the noodle dough ¹⁄₁₆ inch thick, and, with a pizza wheel, cut the sheets into 1-inch squares. Dry well before cooking in boiling salted water for no more than 2–3 minutes.
3. While the dough rests, cook the shallots slowly in the hot butter; season well with salt and pepper. The shallots will lose two-thirds of their volume. They may caramelize a bit, but do not let them burn, or the dish will be bitter.
4. Add the cooked noodles to the *cerfuse*, correct seasoning, add butter if necessary, and serve heavily sprinkled with fresh chopped chervil and grated cheese.

CROZETS A LA FARINE JAUNE {Cornmeal Noodles}

A personal interpretation of *crozets*, made with the delicious cornmeal of the Savoie and, in this area, served as a special side dish with all marinated rabbit, lamb, or wild birds (see pp. 350 and 353).

SERVES 6

¼ cup currants

2–3 tablespoons dry Chambery or
  other vermouth

1 cup very fine cornmeal

1 cup unsifted all-purpose flour

3 eggs, well beaten

1 teaspoon salt

½ teaspoon powdered sage

6 juniper berries, crushed

½ cup butter

Salt and pepper

1. Rinse the currants under hot water and cover with vermouth. Let stand as long as possible.
2. Mix the cornmeal and flour; make a well in the center and add the beaten eggs, salt, and sage. Work into a homogeneous dough. This will require only a few minutes. Cut into 4 small pieces and set to rest under an inverted bowl.
3. Flour the table to roll out the sheets of dough and cut with a pizza wheel into either band noodles or squares. Let dry for 15 minutes before cooking. Cook in boiling salted water for 4–5 minutes.
4. Put the crushed juniper berries in the food processor container together with the butter and salt and pepper. Process until smooth; do not strain.
5. Toss together the juniper butter, noodles, and currants soaked in vermouth. Correct seasoning and serve.

Note: These noodles taste best when cooked 10–15 minutes after cutting. If you dry them, separate them well and dry flat on a lightly floured tray or sheet of paper.

LES PATES AU FER {Iron Noodles}

The result of an improvised demonstration in the Annecy kitchen, this is a solid remedy for iron deficiencies. Serve by itself in the Italian manner.

SERVES 6–8

2 pounds red or green Swiss chard,
with leaves on
2 tablespoons olive oil
2½ cups sifted all-purpose flour
2 eggs
3 egg yolks
Salt
Pepper from the mill

2 large cloves garlic
2 tablespoons vinegar
3 cups heavy cream
⅓ pound fresh goat cheese
½ teaspoon grated lemon rind
¼ teaspoon grated orange rind
1 anchovy fillet
2 tablespoons butter

1. Remove the leaves from the ribs of the Swiss chard. Reserve the ribs. Wash the leaves very well, dry and chop extremely fine. Heat olive oil in a large sauté pan; add chopped chard, reserving only 1 tablespoon for decoration. Let the chard ooze all its moisture, raise the heat, and stir until all water has evaporated and the chard has changed color and appears coated with oil. Cool completely.

2. Following the instructions on page 125, prepare a noodle dough using the cooled cooked chard, the flour, the eggs and egg yolks well beaten together, salt, pepper from the mill, and 1 clove garlic, peeled and mashed. Knead well and rest under an inverted bowl until ready to stretch.

3. Peel, pare, and cut the Swiss chard ribs into 1-inch by ½-inch chunks. Cook until tender in boiling salted water acidulated with the vinegar. Drain well.

4. Stretch and cut the noodles. Reduce the cream a bit. Dice the goat cheese on a plate. Mix together the lemon rind, orange rind, the remaining garlic clove, peeled and well mashed, and the anchovy fillet.

5. Cook the pasta. Add it to the slightly reduced cream together with the Swiss chard ribs, the diced goat cheese, and all the aromatics. Reheat well together and serve dotted with flecks of butter and the reserved raw Swiss chard leaves.

ORZO PILAFS

Adapt the garnish to the meat served. For example, lemon and orange rind mixed with olives will go well with lamb, while toasted cashews, coconut flakes, and currants will do better with white poultry. This pilaf keeps very well in a warming oven.

SERVES 6

BASIC RECIPE:

6 tablespoons butter or oil, or a
   mixture of both
1 onion, chopped fine

2 cups orzo (soup pasta as bought in
   supermarket)
2 cups hot Secondary Stock (p. 23)
Salt
Pepper from the mill

POSSIBLE GARNISHES:

⅓ cup slivered almonds, toasted
¼ cup pignoli nuts, toasted, mixed
   with 3 tablespoons currants
3 tablespoons chopped walnuts
   mixed with ⅓ cup diced
   Camembert
¼ teaspoon each grated lemon and
   orange rinds mixed with ¼ cup
   chopped black olives
¼ teaspoon grated orange rind plus
   a pinch of saffron mixed with 2
   tablespoons scissored fresh basil

2 tablespoons each toasted cashew
   nuts, unsweetened crumbled
   coconut flakes, and currants
2 tablespoons each chopped toasted
   almonds or hazelnuts and chervil
1½ teaspoons fennel seeds or aniseeds
2 tablespoons chopped parsley mixed
   with 1 large clove garlic, peeled
   and mashed
2 tablespoons julienne of gingerroot,
   blanched, mixed with ¼ teaspoon
   powdered Szechuan pepper
2 tablespoons scallion rings

1. Heat the butter, add the onion, and cook until translucent. Add the orzo
   and toss in the hot butter until the pasta turns whitish and hard.
2. Add the hot stock and bring to a boil. Add salt and pepper from the mill
   and cover with several layers of paper towels and the pot lid. Cook on low
   heat until all the stock has been absorbed.
3. Correct the seasoning and add any of the garnishes indicated in the list
   of ingredients.

Salads and Their Dressings

I T LOOKS AS IF MANKIND'S APPETITE for raw greens has found again in the last thirty years the impetus it must have had at the time our hominid ancestors roamed the African savanna.

Salads are probably our most ancient food and can be traced back all the way to Greco-Roman days. *"Salettes,"* as they were called in the sixteenth and seventeenth centuries, were not, however, plentiful in cookbooks until the great classic works of the beginning of the twentieth century. In both Escoffier and Montagné's books, a distinction is made between the green salads that accompanied hot and cold roasts at that time and the *salades composées* served as a first course and with a dressing of mayonnaise or some other related sauce.

Nowadays, we seem to be more or less abandoning the midmeal green salad to the profit of the *salade composée* served at the onset of a meal. This could easily be explained by our concentration on good nutrition, but good nutrition is not the only reason. A salad, well dressed with a delicious oil, is a comfortable food that will satiate a restaurant guest and leave only enough stomach capacity for meat portions kept at reasonable levels. The American "salad bar" is partly responsible for the now rapidly developing French passion for more and more *salades composées*. However "amusante" my French colleagues may say they find the American salad bar habit, they have not disdained adapting it to our French mentality by extending considerably the French repertoire of *salades composées*.

Whether I'm considered a gastronomic "plouf" or not, I happen to enjoy "that good ole gooky American salad bar" with all its paraphernalia of jars, bowls, lousy Bacos, dried-out cheeses, canned chickpeas, and pseudo-Indian-style red beans and onions. If nothing else, it is fun, and it is not necessarily always bad; a lot of restaurants do serve true bacon and true cheese.

The best salads in America are to be found in California. My frustration at the greens arriving in the Boston area was often great; trips to farm stands were made necessary by the average quality of whatever was distributed even by the best greengrocers.

In France, I am always as happy as a fish in water, for the European Economic Community distributes good greens and vegetables year round, and then there are those farm greens all over the market from March through October. What fun and what pleasure.

Most of the following recipes have been adapted so they can be served all over America. The ingredients needed are always indicated first and their American replacements second. Each dressing is given with its particular salad, as a second list of ingredients. The best uses of the salad are given at the start of the recipe.

For the sake of avoiding monotony, I have alternated down-to-earth little salads with opulent ones that can be either the first course of a great dinner or the main course of a wonderful lunch.

The old rules of salad preparation have not changed. The greens must be washed and dried carefully—spun if you use that crazy but so useful salad spinner—and kept refrigerated, rolled in towels. No cutting of leaves with carbon steel knives ever, only tearing gently by hand. The dressing should be prepared early enough to develop all its flavor, but not so early that its acid balance is upset by the onions or shallots absorbing all the vinegar.

Chilled plates are of necessity, unless the salad has one or more warm elements.

A salad is a low-calorie food that helps in weight control only if the dressing used on its components is prepared with low-calorie ingredients. For a prototype low-calorie dressing, see page 164.

All dressings can be made either in the blender or by hand using a bowl and a small whisk. Blended dressings are smoother and stay well emulsified longer. Or, if you like, use a jar with a good lid and continue to shake these dressings as your grandmother did.

Those dressings containing chopped aromatics such as onions and fresh herbs can be made in the blender if the aromatics are added last. Onions and shallots can be blended with the basic components of the dressing, but nuts and herbs should be added later to keep their texture and individual taste.

SALADE DE PETITS OISEAUX AU CHOCOLAT AMER ET A L'ORANGE
{Small Birds Salad with Chocolate and Orange Dressing}

This salad is excellent in a restaurant to utilize small braised birds such as quails and pigeons that remain unsold. At home, the cook will have to braise the birds first, then use the reduced cooking juices to build the dressing—see braising on page 355. Serve as the first course of a dinner or the main course of a luncheon. In the latter case, double the proportions.

SERVES 6

SALAD COMPONENTS:

2 braised pigeons or 6 braised quail   *Salt and pepper*
1 head of curly endive   *¼ ounce unsweetened chocolate,*
3 Valencia oranges   *chopped*
6 large red-tipped lettuce leaves   *Chopped parsley*

DRESSING:

1 teaspoon cocoa powder   *1½ tablespoons* Aceto Balsamico
3 tablespoons heavy cream   *(p. 45)*
Salt   *1 tablespoon orange juice*
Pepper from the mill   *3 tablespoons hazelnut oil*
2 teaspoons Mandarine Napoléon or
   Grand Marnier

1. Skin and bone the birds. Separate the meat into large shreds and set it on a plate.

2. Prepare the curly endive, removing all heavy and tough ribs and using all the pale green and only the semidark green. All dark green leaves should be kept for a soup.

3. Remove, cut into ⅟₁₆-inch julienne, and blanch the rind of 1 orange. Grate ½ teaspoon rind from a second orange (for the dressing), bruising it as little as possible, and peel all 3 oranges to the blood. Slice the oranges into sections, gathering the dripping juice into a bowl as you do so.

4. To prepare the dressing, mix the cocoa and cream and thicken over medium-low heat. Add salt, pepper from the mill, the chosen liqueur, the grated orange rind, *aceto balsamico*, orange juice, and hazelnut oil. Let stand for 30 minutes. Correct the final seasoning.

5. Line a round 12-inch platter with the red-tipped lettuce leaves. Toss endive and meat together, seasoning lightly with salt and pepper and approximately one-third of the dressing. Mound it at the center of the platter and separate the red leaf lettuce from the mound of salad with a border of tastefully arranged orange sections. Spoon the remainder of the dressing over the whole salad. Serve sprinkled with chopped chocolate and parsley and the julienne of orange rind.

Variation: The same recipe can be executed with a roasted duck.

SALADE DE COQUILLES SAINT-JACQUES, COURGETTES ET POIVRONS ROUGES
{*A Provençal Salad of Scallops, Zucchini, and Peppers*}

This is a delicious first course at dinner or a main course for a luncheon.

SERVES 6

SALAD COMPONENTS:

2 tablespoons olive oil
1 pound deep sea scallops, cut into
   ¼-inch slices
Salt
Pepper from the mill

3 large zucchini
3 large red peppers
6 large romaine lettuce leaves
Basil leaves

DRESSING:

1½ tablespoons lemon juice

2 tablespoons orange juice

½ cup Fish Fumet (p. 28) or ¼
  cup clam juice

½ clove garlic, mashed

½ teaspoon fine-grated orange rind

¼ teaspoon saffron powder

Salt

Pepper from the mill

3 cups olive oil

3 tablespoons fine-scissored basil leaves

1. Heat 1 tablespoon of the olive oil in a large skillet, add the sliced scallops, and stir fry for 2 minutes. Season with salt and pepper and turn into a colander placed over a bowl to collect the dripping juices. Refrigerate until ready to use.

2. Remove the skins and ⅛ inch of zucchini flesh by paring the zucchini to obtain 12 strips of vegetable, as long as each zucchini and approximately 1½ inches wide. Discard the remaining flesh and seeds. Out of these strips cut as many ¾-inch-round pieces as can be obtained using a round aspic cutter. Stir fry these "confetti" for 1 minute in ½ tablespoon of the oil in the same skillet you used for the scallops. Season with salt and pepper.

3. Peel the peppers, cut them into 1-inch-wide strips, and from those strips stamp out ¾-inch-wide circles, using the same round cutter as for the zucchini. Stir fry in the remaining ½ tablespoon of oil, using the same skillet as for the scallops and zucchini. Season with salt and pepper.

4. Make sure to keep the scallops, zucchini, and pepper "confetti" in 3 different bowls to prevent the pepper from losing its color on the white scallops and zucchini.

5. To the same skillet in which you cooked all 3 elements of the salad add the lemon and orange juices, the juices dripped from the scallops, the fish fumet or clam juice, the mashed garlic, and the orange rind. Reduce together to no more than 3½ tablespoons.

6. Cool slightly, add the saffron, let stand until cold. Whisk in salt and pepper as well as the olive oil and mix until completely homogenized. Just before serving, add the scissored basil leaves to the dressing.

7. Line a 10-inch platter with the romaine lettuce leaves. Toss the scallops and vegetables with the dressing and pile the salad at the center of the plate. Arrange dark green basil leaves at the edge of the platter to contrast with the green of the lettuce and serve immediately.

TROIS MELONS A L'HUILE D'AVOCAT
{Three Melon Salad in Avocado Oil Dressing}

Use as a first course for a dinner or a luncheon.

SERVES 6

SALAD COMPONENTS:

12 salad bowl lettuce leaves

Twelve 1/3-inch-thick wedges of cantaloupe, cut lengthwise

Twelve 1/3-inch-thick wedges of honeydew melon, cut crosswise

Twelve 1/3-inch-thick wedges of cranshaw melon, cut crosswise

2 tablespoons tawny port

6 macadamia nuts, chopped

1 bouquet of mint leaves

DRESSING:

2 tablespoons pineapple vinegar

1/3 teaspoon honey

1 clove garlic, mashed

1/2 teaspoon pure vanilla extract

Salt and pepper

6 tablespoons avocado oil* or corn oil

1. Line a round platter with salad bowl lettuce leaves and arrange wedges of melon, alternating the colors for eye appeal. Sprinkle the melons with the tawny port. Let stand at room temperature covered with plastic wrap for 30 minutes.

2. Immediately prepare the first part of the dressing. Mix the vinegar, honey, and mashed garlic clove. Let stand for 20 minutes.

3. After 20 minutes, add vanilla, salt, and pepper and whisk in the oil. Correct the seasoning. Strain.

4. Sprinkle a pinch each of salt and pepper over the melon and spoon the dressing onto the fruit. Sprinkle with the macadamia nuts and arrange the mint bouquet at the center of the plate.

Note: For full flavor do not serve ice cold but do serve it without delay.

* Avocado oil is available under several labels in health food stores.

ASSIETTE DE JAMBON CRU AUX FRUITS ET LEGUMES FRAIS
{*A Plate of Hams with Melons, Strawberries, and Cucumbers*}

I have given here a list of mostly Italian meats, but all types of raw hams may be used; Smithfield as well as German Lachsschinken would be equally excellent. Use as a first course only.

SERVES 6

SALAD COMPONENTS:

6 Boston lettuce leaves
6 slices of prosciutto
6 slices of braseola
6 slices of coppa
6 slices of Genoa salami
2 cucumbers

1 pint large ripe strawberries
½ a cantaloupe
¼ of a honeydew melon
6 watercress bouquets
Coarsely cracked pepper

DRESSING:

3 tablespoons sour cream
3 tablespoons plain natural yogurt
Salt

Pepper from the mill
6 tablespoons virgin olive oil
¼ cup chopped watercress

1. Clean, wash, and dry the lettuce leaves; keep refrigerated in a towel.
2. Roll the slices of cured meats into cornucopias or curls. Cover with plastic wrap and keep refrigerated.
3. Peel the cucumbers, slice in half lengthwise, seed them well using a melon baller, and slice into ⅛-inch half moons. Wash, dry well, and slice the strawberries. Peel the melons, cut them into ¼-inch slices, and out of each slice, recut 1½-inch-long pieces using a half-moon–shaped aspic cutter. Mix the fruit and vegetables.
4. Mix the sour cream, yogurt, salt, pepper, and oil. Just before using the dressing, add the chopped watercress.
5. To serve, line each of 6 plates with a lettuce leaf. Arrange the meats in a fanlike pattern at the top of the plate. Place a watercress bouquet where they meet at the center of the plate. Toss the fruit and vegetables in the

watercress dressing and tastefully arrange on the remaining free space on the plate. Dot the whole salad with coarsely cracked pepper and serve promptly.

SALADE DE CHOUX DE BRUXELLES ET DE TREVISE {Brussels Sprouts and Red Trévise Chicory}

Use as a first course at dinner.

SERVES 6

SALAD COMPONENTS:

1 head of curly endive
3 small heads of red "trévise" chicory (radicchio)
½ pound baby Brussels sprouts cooked al dente

DRESSING:

¼ cup olive oil	*Salt and pepper*
2 cloves garlic, sliced	*1 small semidry goat cheese such as*
¼ cup chopped walnut meats	*Crottin de Chavignol, cut into*
1 teaspoon Dijon mustard	*¼-inch cubes*
2 tablespoons cider vinegar	*Chopped parsley*

1. Clean the curly endive and the red trévise chicory and dry well.
2. Cut the cooked Brussels sprouts into halves lengthwise.
3. Heat the olive oil in a skillet, add the garlic slices, and let cook until the slivers turn light golden. Remove and set aside the garlic chips; cool the oil completely.
4. To the garlic-flavored oil add the chopped walnuts, mustard, cider vinegar, salt, and pepper and mix thoroughly.
5. Alternate layers of endive and chicory with layers of Brussels sprouts and goat cheese in a large salad bowl. Sprinkle with chopped parsley and the crumbled garlic chips.
6. Just before serving, toss all the elements of the salad with the dressing.

SALADE DE DINDE FUMEE
ET AVOCATS SAUCE ABRICOT
{Smoked Turkey and Avocado Salad with Apricot Dressing}

For Brad Golenski, who passed on to me his apricot and avocado combination. Start 48 hours ahead of serving time. Enjoy this as the first course of a formal dinner or, by doubling the proportions, as the main course of a luncheon.

SERVES 6

SALAD COMPONENTS:

6 large red-tipped lettuce leaves
3 ripe avocados
18 slices of smoked turkey
Chopped chives

DRESSING:

30 dark orange dried apricot halves	*1 teaspoon honey*
2–3 tablespoons Aceto Balsamico *(p. 45)*	*⅓ teaspoon cardamom powder*
	Salt
6 tablespoons light cream	*Pepper from the mill*

1. Soak the apricots for 2 days in just enough water to rehydrate them. Drain and rinse. Select 6 very pretty apricot halves and reserve them for decoration.
2. Put ¼ cup fresh water, the remaining apricots, the *aceto balsamico*, cream, honey, cardamom, salt, and pepper in the blender container and process until smooth. Strain through a fine conical strainer to discard any trace of apricot skins. Carefully correct the seasoning with vinegar, salt, and pepper. The dressing tastes better if prepared 24 hours ahead of time.
3. Cut the leaves of red-tipped lettuce into a fine, ⅛-inch-wide chiffonade and arrange them on a round 9–10-inch platter. Cut the avocados into slices. Arrange avocado and turkey slices alternately in a pinwheel pattern, nestling the slices of turkey into the hole left by the pit of the avocado. Arrange the 6 apricot halves to cover the tips of the avocado slices at the center of the plate.
4. Taste the seasoning and correct its taste and texture with vinegar, salt, cream, or water.

5. Carefully pour some of the dressing through the center of the avocado and turkey pinwheel. Sprinkle with freshly chopped chives and serve quickly. Pass the remainder of the dressing in a small bowl.

SALADE DE HOMARD ET DE CREVETTES SAUCE MANGUE
{Salad of Lobster and Shrimp in Mango and Rum Dressing}

This is a wonderful salad for a summer luncheon. Keep the dressing refrigerated at all times; the mango ferments easily.

SERVES 6

SALAD COMPONENTS:

Two 1½-pound Maine lobsters, boiled, drained, and cooled

18 medium shrimp in their shells

2 tablespoons olive oil

Salt and pepper

1 head of Boston lettuce

2 papayas

3 kiwi fruit

Chopped parsley

DRESSING:

The meat of ½ a very ripe mango

2 tablespoons dark rum

1 tablespoon pure vanilla extract

2 tablespoons lime juice

1 teaspoon fine-grated lime rind

2 tablespoons lemon juice

1½ teaspoons dried mint, powdered

1 small clove garlic, mashed

Salt as needed

½–⅔ cup olive oil

⅛ teaspoon cayenne pepper

1. Shell the lobsters, cut the 4 claws in half lengthwise, and cut the tails into 6 slices each, carefully removing all traces of the vein. Refrigerate.

2. Gently pull the vein out of the raw shrimp before cooking them. It will come out easily. Heat olive oil in a large skillet and stir fry the shrimp until the shells turn red. Cool and shell. Refrigerate.

3. To prepare the dressing, cut the mango meat in small chunks, place in the blender container, add rum, vanilla, lime juice, and rind, lemon juice, powdered mint, mashed garlic, salt, and olive oil; blend to a smooth dressing.

Correct the salt and add the cayenne. Blend again and strain into a bowl. Let stand, refrigerated, for 1 hour before using.

4. Wash and trim the Boston lettuce leaves of all ribs. Pat dry. Roll several leaves into one another and cut into a ⅛-inch chiffonade. Garnish the bottom of a large round platter or 6 luncheon plates with the chiffonade.

5. Peel the papayas, cut each one into 12 slices lengthwise. Peel the kiwi fruit and cut it crosswise into ⅛-inch-thick slices. Arrange the papaya and kiwi slices on the platter or plates in a pinwheel pattern, leaving a 1-inch border of lettuce chiffonade all around the edge of the plate. Brush the fruit lightly with the dressing so it appears only lightly glazed.

6. Toss the shellfish with the remaining dressing; arrange the shellfish at the center of the platter or plates and sprinkle with chopped parsley.

LA DOUCETTE COMME A ANNECY
{Lamb's Lettuce in the Annecy Manner}

A simple accompaniment to a plain piece of grilled poultry or red meat.

SERVES 6

*½ pound lamb's lettuce or Bibb
  lettuce
1 ounce slab bacon, cut into ¼-inch
  dice
1½ tablespoons wine vinegar
1 teaspoon Dijon mustard
Salt*

*Pepper from the mill
6½ tablespoons corn oil
2 cloves garlic
½ a red onion, chopped fine
½ cup lightly toasted croutons, made
  from the center of a French bread
½ cup diced semidry goat cheese*

1. Trim, wash, spin, and dry the lettuce. Keep refrigerated.
2. Render the cut slab bacon in its own fat until golden, but not brittle. Discard the fat. In the same frying pan, slightly cooled, add the vinegar, mustard, salt, pepper, and 4½ tablespoons of the oil and emulsify well by scraping and whisking.
3. Crush 1 garlic clove and rub your salad bowl with it.
4. Place the red onion in a small bowl. Salt it and let it render the worst of its

juices. Pat dry with paper towel and add to the salad bowl. Mix in the dressing.

5. In the same pan that you used to prepare the dressing, heat the remaining 2 tablespoons of corn oil. Add the second garlic clove, chopped fine, and the croutons. Cook until both are golden. Drain on paper towels.

6. Toss together greens, croutons, and dressing and top with the diced goat cheese. Serve immediately.

SALADE D'ASPERGES A LA VINAIGRETTE DE FRAMBOISES {Green Asparagus in Raspberry Vinaigrette}

Use as a first course for luncheon or dinner.

SERVES 6

SALAD COMPONENTS:

30 young spinach leaves
30 jumbo asparagus spears

DRESSING:

One 10-ounce package frozen
*   raspberries, drained until dry*
2 tablespoons sherry vinegar
Salt

Pepper from the mill
6 tablespoons olive oil
½ cup heavy cream
1 teaspoon chopped chives

1. Wash and stem the spinach leaves, pat dry with paper towel. Keep refrigerated.

2. Blanch the asparagus in boiling salted water until cooked crisp-tender.

3. Place the berries in the blender container, add the vinegar, salt, pepper from the mill, olive oil, and cream and process until well blended. Strain through a "China cap" strainer to discard all seeds.

4. Arrange the spinach leaves on 6 salad plates. Place 5 asparagus spears on each plate and add a large spoonful of dressing across the spears. Sprinkle each plate with chopped chives and coarsely cracked pepper from the mill.

JARDINIERE DE POISSONS FUMES
AU RAIFORT *{Smoked Fish and Vegetable Salad}*

Serve as a first course for dinner.

SERVES 6

SALAD COMPONENTS:

30 spinach leaves　　　　　　　*12 slices of Nova Scotia salmon*
2 large carrots　　　　　　　　*12 slices of smoked sable fish*
2 zucchini　　　　　　　　　　*Scallion rings*
1 bunch of radishes

DRESSING FOR VEGETABLES:

1 large shallot, chopped fine　　*Pepper from the mill*
2 tablespoons vinegar　　　　　*6 tablespoons corn oil*
Salt　　　　　　　　　　　　*⅓ cup chopped fresh dill weed*

HORSERADISH CREAM:

½ cup mayonnaise, preferably homemade
2 tablespoons sour cream
2 tablespoons heavy cream, whipped
Drained prepared horseradish to taste
Salt and pepper

1. Stem the spinach leaves, wash them, and blot them dry in a towel. Keep refrigerated. Cut the carrots, zucchini, and radishes into ⅛-inch-wide julienne. Mix these vegetables and keep refrigerated in a covered bowl.

2. Prepare the light dressing for the vegetables. Squeeze the chopped shallot in the corner of a towel to extract the aggressive juices. Add vinegar, salt, and pepper and whisk in the corn oil. Let stand for 30 minutes at room temperature. Just before using, add the chopped dill weed.

3. Mix the mayonnaise, sour cream, and whipped heavy cream, add the drained prepared horseradish and salt and pepper to your taste. Let stand for 30 minutes at room temperature. Correct seasoning before using.

4. To present, arrange the salad on 6 plates. Prepare a crown of spinach leaves on each plate, brush these with some dill dressing, arrange 2 slices each of

salmon and sable on top so the tips of the spinach leaves show well. Inside the ring of fish, add a ring of julienne of carrots, zucchini, and radishes tossed in dill dressing at the last minute. Place a large tablespoonful of horseradish cream at the center of each plate and top it with a few scallion rings. Serve immediately.

SALADE DE RIS DE VEAU AUX ASPERGES
{Sweetbreads and Asparagus Salad}

The longest work in this recipe is braising the sweetbreads. The texture of sweetbreads is a matter of personal taste; if you prefer them crunchy, simply blanch them and dice them. Make sure in any case that no traces of blood remain. For best timing both at home and in the restaurant kitchen, soak the sweetbreads the day before cooking them. Soaking is essential whether you are going to braise or not. Use the salad as the first course of a dinner.

SERVES 6

SALAD COMPONENTS:

1 whole sweetbread
1 large onion, sliced thick
1 small carrot, sliced thick
Bouquet garni (see p. 82)
2 tablespoons butter
2–3 cups Golden Veal Stock (p. 20)
⅓ cup Sercial or Rainwater Madeira

Salt and pepper
1 pound asparagus
6 large leaves of soft leaf lettuce,
    Boston or Bibb
24 orange wedges
1 scallion (green part only), cut in
    elongated rings

DRESSING:

¼ cup reduced braising juices of the
    sweetbreads
¼ teaspoon lemon rind
⅓ teaspoon cardamom powder
2 tablespoons orange juice
2 tablespoons lemon juice, or more to
    taste

1 tablespoon Sercial or Rainwater
    Madeira
1 teaspoon Dijon mustard
⅓ cup olive oil
⅓ cup heavy cream
Salt if needed
Pepper from the mill

1. Soak the sweetbreads in cold water for 2 hours. Put them in a pot, cover them with cold water, and bring to a boil; simmer for 5 minutes. Drain and refresh under cold water. Remove the large pieces of cartilage and sinew. Place between 2 plates and weight with a heavy object to flatten and extract all blood.

2. Sauté the onion, carrot, and bouquet garni in butter. Add the sweetbreads, stock, Madeira, a dash each of salt and pepper, and bring to a boil. Preheat the oven to 325°F. Cover the pot with a piece of foil put flush on the surface of the sweetbreads to form an upside-down lid. Put the pot lid on and bake for 45 minutes. Open the pot lid and cool completely. Reserve the cooking juices.

3. Clean the sweetbreads of all membranes and separate them into small nuggets; keep these in a bowl, well covered with plastic wrap, so they do not dry out.

4. Peel and boil the asparagus until cooked al dente, about 7 minutes. Drain, reserving ½ cup of the cooking water. Cool the asparagus under cold water, then cut into ¾–1-inch-long pieces. Mix with the prepared sweetbreads.

5. To prepare the dressing, quickly reduce the cooking juices of the sweetbreads to ¼ cup. Add the lemon rind, cardamom, orange and lemon juices, Madeira, Dijon mustard, and olive oil. Process in the blender to obtain a mayonnaiselike sauce. Taste and add enough heavy cream (approximately ¼ cup) to rebalance the salt. If the dressing is too salty, add more lemon juice, and if it is too sour, add salt. If the texture is too thick, loosen it up with some of the reserved asparagus cooking water. Add pepper to your taste.

6. Salt again both asparagus and sweetbreads before tossing them with the dressing. Line the salad plates or serving platter with lettuce leaves. Pile the salad onto the leaves and decorate with orange wedges placed around the edge of the plates or platter. Sprinkle with sliced scallions and serve.

JOLI MESCLUN AUX FLEURS
{A Pretty Green Salad with Edible Flowers}

The younger the greens, the better the salad. Use the leaves and the first flowers of any edible herb such as sage, borage, chives, and only very young tender shoots or hearts of lettuce, spinach, asparagus tips, etc.; outer leaves make good soups. This is a midmeal salad for dinner or a luncheon salad to serve with a plate of cold meats.

SERVES 6

SALAD COMPONENTS:

1 cup very young, small, and tender spinach leaves

The hearts of 4 small Belgian endives

The yellow part of 1 heart of curly chicory

The heart of 1 head of romaine lettuce

1 head of red-tipped lettuce

6–8 small nasturtium leaves

1 cup arugula leaves

1 cup watercress bouquets

¼ cup chive flowers

1 cup nasturtium flowers

DRESSING:

1 large clove garlic

1 shallot, chopped very fine

1 sour apple, peeled, seeded, and cut into ¼-inch julienne

1 tablespoon lemon juice

1 tablespoon Aceto Balsamico *(p. 45)*

Salt and pepper

6 tablespoons virgin olive oil

1. Clean, wipe dry, and store in towels the spinach leaves, hearts of endives, chicory, romaine and red-tipped lettuce, the nasturtium leaves, arugula, and watercress.

2. Examine the flowers of the chives and nasturtiums for bees or other insects; brush with a pastry brush to discard any sand and keep refrigerated on a plate.

3. To prepare the dressing, rub a crystal salad bowl with a large clove of garlic, expressing as much juice as possible as you rub. Squeeze the chopped shallot vigorously in the corner of a towel.

4. Place the shallots and apple in another bowl. Add lemon juice, *aceto bal-samico*, salt, pepper, and oil. Mix gently so the fruit does not break. The fruit will absorb most of the acid.

5. Arrange alternate layers of light and dark greens and the chive flowers in the prepared crystal bowl. Surround the top of the salad with a border of nasturtium flowers. Just before serving, toss with the dressing.

SALADE DE GESIERS A LA POITEVINE
{Salad of Chicken Gizzard in the Poitou Manner}

This is my version of a salad that my great-grandmother used to serve as part of her *cuisine de misère*. Serve as a luncheon salad.

SERVES 6

SALAD COMPONENTS:

1 pound fresh chicken or duck gizzards

1 onion, peeled and stuck with 2 cloves

Small bouquet garni (see p. 82)

2 leeks (green parts only), chopped; white and pale green parts reserved

1 bunch of fresh radishes

2 small fresh goat cheeses or 2 ounces any semifresh goat cheese

3 slices of French bread

¼ cup corn oil

2 cloves garlic, chopped fine

1 head of escarole

2 tablespoons chopped parsley

DRESSING:

Broth from the cooking of the gizzards

2 tablespoons vinegar of your choice

Pepper from the mill

1½–2 teaspoons Dijon mustard

6 tablespoons walnut oil

1 large shallot, chopped fine

2 tablespoons chopped walnuts

3 tablespoons heavy cream

Salt

1. Wash the gizzards and put them in a large saucepan. Add the onion, bouquet garni, and the chopped green part of both leeks. Add just enough water to cover the gizzards and bring to a boil. Skim, turn down to a simmer, and cook, covered, until the gizzards are tender. Strain, discarding all vegetables and carefully reserving the gizzards and broth.

2. Trim the gizzards of all traces of skin and gristle, then slice into ⅛-inch-thick slices. Set aside. Slice the white and light green parts of the leeks into ¼-inch-thick slices. Blanch them in the gizzards' cooking broth for 3 minutes. Drain, reserving the broth, and set sliced leeks aside on a plate. Slice the red radishes.

3. Dice the goat cheese and set aside on a service plate. Remove the crust from the French bread slices and cut the center into ⅓-inch cubes.

4. Heat the corn oil in a frying pan and sauté the garlic in it for 1 minute. Immediately add the croutons and toss them until they are golden. Drain on paper towels. Set aside.

5. Prepare the escarole greens: wash and pat dry; roll in a towel and keep refrigerated.

6. To prepare the dressing, reduce the cooking juices of the gizzards to a nice glaze. Transfer to a mixing bowl and add the vinegar, pepper, Dijon mustard, walnut oil, shallots, and walnuts. Mix well. Correct the seasoning. Add heavy cream to balance the taste or texture only if you think it is necessary. Toss all the salad elements, except the parsley and garlic croutons, with the dressing. Arrange on a platter, correct the seasoning, and top with the chopped parsley and the garlic croutons.

SALADE DE TOMATES ET ASPERGES SAUCE CONCOMBRE
{Salad of Tomatoes and Asparagus in Cucumber Dressing}

Use as a midmeal salad.

SERVES 6

SALAD COMPONENTS:
> 1 pound green asparagus
> 9 Italian plum tomatoes
> 6 Boston lettuce leaves

DRESSING:

1 small cucumber	1 tablespoon ground coriander seeds
1 very small onion, chopped	1 teaspoon green herb mustard or
Salt	Dijon mustard
Pepper from the mill	3 tablespoons corn oil
1½ tablespoons vinegar	3 tablespoons hazelnut oil
1 tablespoon sour cream	3 tablespoons chopped dill

1. Clean and pare the asparagus. Cook al dente in boiling salted water. Rinse under cold water. Chill. Cut into 1½-inch chunks.

2. Peel the tomatoes. Cut into halves and remove all seeds. Cut each tomato half into ⅓-inch-wide strips. Keep chilled until ready to use. Wash, trim and dry the Boston lettuce leaves.

3. To prepare the dressing, peel the cucumber and seed it completely using a melon baller. Chop the cucumber, mix it with the onion, and salt liberally. Let stand for 1 hour. Drain all the juices that have exuded from the onion and cucumber and rinse under cold water. Put the mixture in the blender container. Add salt, pepper, vinegar, sour cream, coriander, mustard, and corn and hazelnut oils and blend until a smooth dressing results; correct the seasoning and add 2 tablespoons of the dill.

4. Line each of 6 plates with a Boston lettuce leaf. Toss the mixture of asparagus and tomato strips in the dressing and arrange a mound of the mixture on each plate. Sprinkle each with a pinch of the remaining tablespoon of the dill.

SALADE MARIE-GALANTE
{A Creole Salad of Avocados, Papayas, Pineapple, and Bananas}

For Thomas Connors. Use as a first course salad.

SERVES 6

SALAD COMPONENTS:

6 Boston lettuce leaves

2 large ripe avocados

2 large ripe papayas

Juice of 1 lemon

½ a ripe pineapple

2 ripe bananas

DRESSING:

1 tablespoon lime juice

2 tablespoons lemon juice

½ teaspoon grated lemon rind

6 tablespoons olive oil

⅓ teaspoon very fresh curry powder

1 large clove garlic

Salt

Pepper from the mill

1. Clean, trim, and dry the lettuce leaves. Peel the avocados and papayas and cut them first into halves lengthwise, then cut each half crosswise into ¼-inch-thick slices. Sprinkle with lemon juice; let macerate while you

prepare the pineapple. Peel it, core it, and cut it into slices ¼ inch thick. Peel bananas and slice them into ¼-inch-thick elongated ovals.

2. To prepare the dressing, put lime and lemon juices with the lemon rind into the blender container. Heat the olive oil and curry well together and let cool completely. Then add to the blender as well as the garlic, salt, and pepper. Process until a smooth dressing results. Let stand for 10 minutes, then correct the seasoning.

3. Arrange lettuce leaves on 6 plates. Arrange the slices of fruit in a pleasing design of various shapes and colors. Spoon the dressing over the salad. Serve promptly.

UNE DAUSSADE PAS ORDINAIRE
{A Daussade *in a Different Manner*}

The *daussade* is the cream, vinegar, and scallion dressing that the cooks of the northern provinces of France (Artois and Picardie) like to use as a dressing for their green salads. Having extended the idea considerably in a tongue and Roquefort salad, my *daussade* was declared *"pas ordinaire"* (unusual) by an older aunt, who is considered quite a cook. Use as a first course salad.

SERVES 6

SALAD COMPONENTS:
2 heads of Boston lettuce
5 ounces smoked tongue, in 1 piece
2 ounces crumbled Roquefort cheese

DRESSING:
⅔ cup heavy cream
3 tablespoons cider vinegar
Salt
Pepper from the mill
⅓ cup sliced scallions (white and green parts only)

1. Clean and dry the lettuce leaves. Dice the tongue into ⅓-inch cubes and coarsely crumble the Roquefort cheese. Alternate lettuce and garnishes in a glass bowl.

3. Mix the heavy cream, vinegar, salt, and pepper from the mill; the cream will thicken immediately. At serving time, add the scallions. Let stand for only 5 minutes.

3. Toss the salad at the table by pouring the dressing over the greens and mixing well. Serve immediately; any waiting provokes excessive wilting of the lettuce.

SALADE DE FAISAN FUME DU VERMONT
{Smoked Pheasant Salad with Apples and Cheddar Cheese}

Smoked chicken or turkey can be substituted for the pheasant in this salad. All these birds are available at the best delicatessen stores anywhere in the United States. This is a good way to use home-smoked products. Use as the first course of a November-through-February dinner or as a main course for an Indian summer luncheon.

SERVES 6

SALAD COMPONENTS:

1 smoked pheasant or chicken or the equivalent in smoked turkey
3 ounces mild Vermont or New Hampshire Cheddar
3 green Granny Smith apples or 3 small fennel bulbs

1 tablespoon lemon juice
2 tablespoons corn oil
¼ cup walnut halves
1 head of escarole
1 head of curly chicory
Chopped parsley

DRESSING:

1 shallot, chopped fine
1 egg yolk
1 teaspoon Meaux mustard (with seeds)
2 tablespoons cider vinegar
1 tablespoon fino (dry) sherry

¼ teaspoon Quatre-Epices (p. 35)
6 tablespoons walnut oil
3–4 tablespoons heavy cream
Salt
Coarsely cracked pepper from the mill

1. Cut the meat from the chosen bird(s) into 2-inch by ½-inch chunks. Cover and refrigerate.

2. Cut the Cheddar into ¼-inch by 1½-inch sticks. Peel and slice the apples and julienne them into ¼-inch by 1½-inch sticks. Toss in the lemon juice to prevent excessive browning. If using the fennel, slice it thin across each bulb.

3. Heat the corn oil in a skillet and in it sauté the walnut halves until lightly toasted. Pat very dry on paper towels.

4. Prepare the escarole and chicory without soaking them at length in water to prevent bitterness. Dry well and keep refrigerated rolled in a towel. Use only the light green and white leaves, keeping the dark green ones for a soup or the dish of polenta on p. 434.

5. To prepare the dressing, squeeze the finely chopped shallot in the corner of a towel to extract all strong juices. Put the shallot, egg yolk, "seedy" mustard, cider vinegar, sherry, and *quatre-épices* in a bowl. Mix well. Gradually whisk in the walnut oil and heavy cream. Correct the seasoning with salt and pepper.

6. Present this salad in a large crystal bowl, alternating layers of greens, meat, cheese, and apples, and topping with walnut halves, coarsely cracked pepper, and chopped parsley. Present the dressing in a small bowl and toss the salad at the table.

SALADE DE HARICOTS ET DE TOMATES A LA CREME DE CRESSON
{Salad of Green and White Beans and Tomatoes in Watercress Cream Dressing}

A Brittany version of a salad that is most popular all over France. Serve as a luncheon salad.

SERVES 6

SALAD COMPONENTS:
½ pound navy beans, soaked overnight
¾ pound fine green beans (¼ inch wide only)
1 small red onion

Salt and pepper
3 sun-ripened tomatoes
6 Boston lettuce leaves
Watercress bouquets

DRESSING:

1 teaspoon mustard of your choice

3 tablespoons cider vinegar

Salt

Pepper from the mill

3 tablespoons oil of your choice

¼ cup heavy cream, whipped

⅓ cup chopped watercress leaves

1. Cook the navy beans in boiling salted water until tender; drain and cool at room temperature.

2. Clean and string the green beans. Cook them in boiling salted water until crisp-tender and still bright green. Drain, rinse under cold water, and refrigerate.

3. Cut the onion in half, peel it, and cut each half into paper-thin slivers. Salt the slivers so they render their bitter juices and let stand for 45 minutes. Rinse and pat dry.

4. Mix the white beans, green beans, and onions and season lightly with salt and pepper.

5. To prepare the dressing, mix mustard, cider vinegar, salt, pepper, and oil until homogeneous. Fold in the whipped cream and all but 1 tablespoon of the chopped watercress.

6. Peel the tomatoes, quarter them, and seed them delicately so as not to crush the quarters. Line a large platter with the lettuce leaves. Add a border of tomato quarters alternating with watercress bouquets. Finally toss together the beans, onions, and watercress dressing and pile at the center of the plate. Sprinkle the mound of salad with the reserved tablespoon of chopped watercress.

SALADE DES PERDEURS DE POIDS
{A Salad for Dieters}

The dressing for this salad intends to be a prototype for all low-calorie salad dressings. The seasonings here are in the Arabic style, but they can be changed to any other combination. Use as a first course as is; to transform it into a main course, add 6 ounces tuna or 6 hard-boiled eggs.

SERVES 6

SALAD COMPONENTS:

2 yellow peppers   *2 small zucchini*
2 red peppers   *1 hothouse cucumber*
2 green peppers   *Salt*
2 tomatoes   *1 head of Boston lettuce*

DRESSING:

2 tablespoons vinegar   *½ teaspoon cumin powder*
⅔ cup water   *A dash of cayenne pepper*
1 teaspoon cornstarch   *½ teaspoon grated orange rind*
2 teaspoons olive or corn oil   *¼ teaspoon paprika*
Salt   *1 clove garlic, mashed*
Pepper from the mill   *1 small red onion*
½ teaspoon dried mint, crumbled   *Fresh chopped mint leaves*

1. Roast the peppers. Peel them and cut each one into 6 wedges. Set the peppers to drip on the bottom of an upside-down bowl placed on a large round platter, which will collect the juice.
2. Peel and slice the tomatoes. Cut the zucchini and the cucumber into thin slices; salt them to extract their excess moisture. Trim the Boston lettuce, wash and dry it carefully.
3. To prepare the dressing, mix the vinegar, water, and cornstarch. Bring to a boil, stirring constantly. As soon as this base for the dressing boils, add oil, salt, pepper, dried mint, cumin, cayenne, orange rind, paprika, and garlic. Remove from the heat. Let stand until cold.
4. Chop the red onion very fine. Salt it a bit. Let stand. Drain excess moisture and add onion to the dressing.
5. Drain the water accumulated around the zucchini and cucumbers, and pat the vegetables dry.
6. Line a large round platter with the leaves of the Boston lettuce; arrange the vegetables in concentric circles of alternating colors; spoon the dressing over the salad just before serving, and sprinkle with fresh chopped mint.

SALADE DE ZUCCHINI ET KOHLRABI A LA MOUTARDE DE FRAMBOISE
{Salad of Zucchini and Kohlrabi in Raspberry Mustard Dressing}

If you have no raspberry mustard, you can either make it, according to the recipe on page 38, or strain a few crushed raspberries into plain Dijon mustard and add a dab of tomato paste. Use as a first course salad for a plain dinner or luncheon.

SERVES 6

SALAD COMPONENTS:

6 Boston lettuce leaves
3 small zucchini, cut into ¼-inch by
  1½-inch julienne
Salt

4 kohlrabi, peeled and cut into
  ¼-inch by 1½-inch julienne
18 raspberries
1½ teaspoons each fresh chopped
  chervil and chives

DRESSING:

1 chopped shallot
2 tablespoons red wine vinegar
Salt
Pepper from the mill

1½–2 teaspoons Raspberry Mustard
  (p. 38)
6 tablespoons corn or sunflower oil
2 tablespoons heavy cream

1. Wash and dry the Boston lettuce leaves, wrap them in a towel, and keep them refrigerated.
2. Place the cut zucchini sticks on a plate. Salt them lightly, toss, and let stand for 30 minutes; then rinse and pat dry.
3. Blanch the kohlrabi sticks in boiling salted water until crisp-tender. Drain, refresh under cold running water, and mix with the zucchini.
4. To prepare the dressing, mix the shallot, vinegar, salt, pepper, and raspberry mustard, and let stand for 5 minutes. Add the oil and heavy cream, whisking well. Toss with the zucchini and kohlrabi.
5. Arrange 1 lettuce leaf on each of 6 small plates. Divide the zucchini with kohlrabi salad evenly and dot each salad with 3 raspberries. Sprinkle with chervil and chives.

SALADE DE POULET FUME
AUX POIVRONS MULTICOLORES
{Salad of Smoked Chicken with Multicolored Peppers}

This salad is excellent with either smoked chicken or turkey, but best with smoked lamb, if you do your own smoking. Use as a first course for a Mediterranean dinner or as a main course for a late summer luncheon.

SERVES 6

SALAD COMPONENTS:

1 head of salad bowl lettuce   *3 yellow peppers*
3 red peppers   *1 smoked chicken*
3 green peppers   *1 tablespoon chopped parsley*

DRESSING:

1 small red onion, chopped fine   *¼ cup hazelnut oil*
3 tablespoons cider vinegar   *¼ cup sunflower or corn oil*
2 teaspoons Red Bell Pepper Mustard   *¼ cup fine-chopped parsley*
*   (p. 38) or Dijon mustard*   *1 tiny clove garlic, mashed*
Salt and pepper

1. Clean, wash, and dry the salad bowl lettuce. Roll in a towel and keep refrigerated.
2. Place the peppers on a jelly roll pan 4 inches away from the broiler element of your oven. Broil, turning at regular intervals, until the whole surface of each pepper is evenly blistered. Remove from the oven, cover with a tea towel, and peel, cutting each pepper as you do so into 6 strips. Pile all pepper strips on top of a bowl placed upside down on a large plate and let drip for 30 minutes.
3. Skin and cut the chicken into 2-inch by ½-inch chunks.
4. To prepare the dressing, mix the red onion, vinegar, mustard of your choice, salt, and pepper. Dilute with the oils and add parsley and mashed garlic. Let stand for 20–30 minutes.
5. Arrange the leaves of salad bowl lettuce on a large round platter. Roll the pepper strips into curls. Arrange the curls on the lettuce to form a second

border, leaving 1½ inches of lettuce clearly visible at the edge of the platter. Spoon one-third of the dressing onto the peppers.

6. Toss the smoked chicken chunks with the remainder of the dressing, pile the chicken at the center of the plate inside of the border of pepper curls, and sprinkle it evenly with the tablespoon of chopped parsley. Serve promptly.

Generalities on Sauces in Modern French Cuisine

TYING MODERN SAUCES TO CLASSIC SAUCES

In MODERN FRENCH CUISINE, the sauces remain plentiful and varied. They are easier to prepare than the classic sauces, take considerably less time, and are lighter in texture and often more attractive in appearance.

The few classic sauces still used have undergone modifications of one sort or another. It is safe to say that the disappearance of the classic espagnole and demiglace sauces is an accepted fact. The velouté seems restricted to the making of soups. Béchamel, the all-purpose, centuries-old milk and white roux compound, is rapidly disappearing as a sauce or sauce base and now subsists mostly as the thick base for soufflés and timbales. The hollandaise and béarnaise type sauces are still used quite often, although their textures have lightened considerably and they now appear more often in combination with a stock or wine reduction than alone.

The bulk of fish saucery in the modern cuisine has come to rest on the principle of an emulsion of butter in an acid base. The best example of this is the *beurre blanc* of the Angevin countryside, which has been adopted with such gusto by the whole French nation that the great majority of dishes nowadays are served under a *beurre blanc* of one sort or another. The names may vary, but the components remain the same, even if one cook in the Alps calls it *"beurre de neige,"* while another in Brittany rebaptizes it *"beurre de la vierge."* I became so tired of the sempiternal *beurre blanc* in the late sixties that when I wrote *The Making of a Cook*, I decided to bring a number of variations to the basic formula. I have kept the habit during the last ten years, preparing many fish sauces with components other than reduced vinegar, shallots, and butter while still following the principle of using an emulsion of butter in an acid base. You will find these outlined in the next chapter, "Fish and Shellfish and Their Sauces."

The principle used nowadays in the making of meat sauces is the capacity of thick, reduced stocks to retain a rather large amount of butter in emulsion. The simplest application of this principle is found in the plain deglazing of a frying pan with stock and the whisking of some butter into that somewhat reduced stock; this method produces an excellent gravy for any meat one has panfried or roasted.

Following the same principle, but using reduced meat stock and/or essences (see p. 268), one obtains excellent sauces adapted to every type of meat, with better strength, taste, and texture than results from simple deglazing.

In the classic cuisine, flour-bound sauces were categorized as either mother sauces or small sauces, each sauce description in the manuals being followed by an indication of which type of meat it could accompany. Sauces for beef tended to be prepared with brown beef stock as were those for veal and lamb, while those for poultry were prepared with chicken stock containing some veal. The decadent classic cuisine of the fifties and sixties replaced all brown, flour-bound sauces with a uniform brown veal stock reduced and bound with a bit of potato starch. It lacked body, strength, and personality.

There is no uniform way to make sauces in modern French cuisine. Some cooks reduce stocks made with the trimmings of beef for beef dishes, veal and lamb for veal and lamb dishes, poultry for poultry dishes.

I have preferred to use Golden Veal Stock (p. 20) for all meat sauces, but, as I already mentioned in *The Making of a Cook*, I utilize the capacity of the veal stock to take on the taste of any meat stronger than itself in order to prepare essences of various meats. These essences are the base for each and every one of my sauces. So, instead of listing sauces in one chapter in this book, they will be listed together with the meats they complement; the chapter on meats is called "Meats and Their Sauces" as that on fish sauces is called "Fish and Shellfish and Their Sauces."

On pages 144 and 145 of *The Making of a Cook*, I explained the thickening of sauces with pure egg yolks diluted into the cooking juices of meats or fish. These sauces, in which the thickening took place in only a matter of minutes, were the direct precursors of the flourless sauces of the present French cuisine.

These "custard" sauces will keep the name of custard sauces in this book. Other cookbook writers have made use of them under the name sabayon sauces, because they started by foaming the egg yolks very well before blending them with the reduced stocks and/or clear vegetable purées. The similarity to a true sabayon—a dessert sauce made with foamed egg yolks, sugar, and a liquid—is not significant enough to cause me to change my nomenclature. Custard sauces will remain the term for savory meat or fish sauces made with a liaison of egg yolks whether those are foamed or not. Custards will remain sweet egg and sugar sauces that will include sabayon, crème anglaise, and pastry cream.

In the realm of cold sauces, our good old delicious mayonnaise is not yet ready to disappear. It still accompanies a lot of salads and other cold food items. I have also introduced in this book new types of cold salad dressings built on fruit purées and reduced gelatinous meat-cooking juices rather than on egg yolks. They can be found in the chapter called "Salads and Their Dressings."

GENERALITIES ON THE TASTE AND TEXTURE OF SAUCES IN MODERN CUISINE

Those cooks who will use the recipe ideas given in this book should know that they are absolutely free to correct the final taste and texture of a sauce until it answers to the demand of their own taste buds.

Too many elements will differ from one location to the other for a sauce to work out exactly as described on paper. Variations of taste and texture are normal, and the cook must know that such variations are the rule rather than the exception, for no one will use exactly the same stock, the same butter—or the same taste buds.

Here are some important pointers on correcting the texture and taste of sauces.

The glass of water:

Keep a glass of water at hand to refresh your palate while balancing a sauce. It is necessary to drink to break the salt buildup on the palate. All sauces based on essences and reductions are very concentrated and are best tasted if one refreshes the palate with neutral water.

Tasting the sauce on the food rather than by itself:

If you taste a sauce alone, using a teaspoon dipped into it, you will not have quite the proper appreciation of it. It is better to taste it on a bit of the meat or food it will complement. You will immediately have a more precise perception of what must be corrected in its basic taste.

Salting the sauced item before saucing it:

Salting the meat or fish or any other food before saucing it provides an essential "taste bridge" between the sauced food and the sauce. Forgetting to salt the item to be sauced creates a gap between two entities which, to satisfy the eater completely, should blend well with one another. Almost all clashes between food and sauce come from cooks having forgotten to salt the item to be sauced.

The difference between a taste or texture modifier and a taste or texture corrector:

A modifier is an ingredient added to the sauce while it is cooking to change its taste or texture. Sweet spices added while a sauce cooks can be considered taste *modifiers*; butter added to a sauce at the end of its cooking is both a taste modifier and a texture modifier.

A taste or texture *corrector* will repair errors committed unwittingly and is added to the sauce after it has been finished according to the directions in a recipe. For example, stock added to a finished sauce to lighten it is a texture corrector, while meat extract added to a sauce to correct its lack of strength on the palate will be a taste corrector.

THE FINAL SEASONING OF SAUCES

This section lists taste correctors for the various problems liable to occur at the time of final seasoning.

1. Correcting lack of salt:

Lack of plain salt is easily corrected by gradually adding salt as needed. The final tasting of the sauce is made on a piece of food properly salted before being sauced.

2. Correcting lack of depth and body:

Some sauces, due to too light a stock or some other obscure reason, will lack not only salt but also depth and body. The sauce will be perceived as "flat" on the palate and described as "needing help." The salt corrector in this case will have to be one of the following "body" salts:

  a. *Meat glaze* if you have some.

  b. *Meat extract* of the semisolid type. The meat extract will give the sauce the rounded body you are looking for, but *meat extract should be added only in minute amounts* until the sauce has acquired the required depth. One should not be able to detect it in the final taste. *Meat extract is always a corrector; it cannot ever be used as a base for a sauce.*

  c. *Anchovy paste* is an excellent corrector for fish sauces. As with meat extracts, it should give body but not be detectable. Obviously, the only time one should be able to discern the presence of anchovy is when one prepares an anchovy sauce.

  d. *Soy sauce*, sign of the times and witness to the melding of civilizations, can be used as a salt body corrector, especially in those sauces with an Oriental character and containing ginger and scallions. Again, do not use so much that it would be detectable in the final taste of the sauce.

3. Correcting too much salt:

a. *Lemon juice.* Use a few drops to cut the sauce. If this does not work, increase the dose of lemon juice gradually. In sauces made with vinegar, do not hesitate to reduce some more vinegar and whisk it gradually into the sauce until the taste has been corrected.

  b. *Sour cream or crème fraîche* can be used in both meat and fish sauces to cut salt concentration.

  c. *Heavy cream and sour cream* can be used if the acid cream alone fails to correct your salt problem. Reduce the heavy cream in combination with sour cream; the concentration of lactose may be helpful.

4. *Correction of too much acid:*

Sauces made by reducing acid ingredients such as wine, vinegar, or citrus fruit juices are often perceived as too acid when finished. The basic corrector for acid is salt in any of its forms (plain salt or meat extract). Try plain salt first.

A bit more butter will also help; for fish and shellfish sauces, reduced heavy cream is infallible.

Reduced heavy cream deserves a special paragraph, for it is one of the most precious ingredients for the cook in modern cuisine. Should one add plain cream to a sauce already too acid, the cream would immediately turn sour and proceed to reinforce the already existing sour taste. By reducing the cream, one changes its chemical composition. Water evaporates, protein and milk sugars (lactose) concentrate, and the dominant taste in the cream is then that of the lactose, the element that will counteract the acidity of any sauce. One should proceed gradually, adding the reduced cream in small amounts until the taste is corrected.

5. *Correction of too little acid:*

Add a drop or so of lemon juice or a tablespoon or so of sour cream or crème fraîche if the nature of the sauce allows it. Also try prepared Dijon mustard added very gradually, in minute amounts.

6. *Correction of too much sweetness:*

Too much sweetness will occur in sauces containing fruit juices and fruit purées. The correctors are: lemon juice, sour cream, or prepared Dijon mustard —each and any added very gradually until the sweetness disappears.

7. *Correction of an edge of bitterness:*

An "edge" of bitterness will occur in sauces containing burned shallots or garlic, citrus rinds, chocolate, and sometimes a cooked purée of garlic (in this case because the green bud inside older cloves has not been removed before the garlic is cooked). To correct this problem, try adding reduced heavy cream or a dab of honey in minute amounts.

THE FINAL TEXTURE OF SAUCES

Most of the sauces in modern cuisine are, as already stated, based on emulsions of butter in reduced stocks or other liquids such as wine and vinegar. A few texture problems may occur. They will be examined in detail in each category of sauce, but here are a few of the major problems that might arise and the way to correct them quickly.

1. The sauce is overreduced:

Add stock, fish fumet, or plain water. Notice that an overreduced sauce will often need a taste corrector as well because it is likely to be oversalted.

2. The sauce breaks butter:

If the butter goes out of emulsion and "separates," as the expression goes, add stock, fish fumet, or any adequate liquid to reform the emulsion.

3. The sauce is too thin:

a. *Continue reducing.* If the sauce is too thin and can stand further correction as far as the taste is concerned, bring the sauce back to a full boil and continue reducing.

b. *Process with butter.* If you do not mind lightening the color of the sauce considerably, put the sauce in the blender, add a tablespoon of butter, and process. The thickening that results will be somewhat artificial due to all the air churned into the sauce. Serve promptly before the air reintegrates the atmosphere, which will be within 20 minutes after the blending.

c. *Thicken with starch.* If the sauce is too thin, but cannot take any more reduction because it tastes just right as is, do not hesitate to stabilize (lightly thicken) the sauce with a slurry of pure starch, proceeding this way: Dissolve the pure starch (potato starch, arrowroot, or cornstarch) in a bit of cold stock. Turn the sauce down to a simmer and stir the slurry into the sauce until the latter thickens; *simmer, do not boil,* and *stir gently, do not whisk violently.* Any wild movement cuts through the starch molecules and thins the gel again. Pure starches are very variable in their thickening powers and very fickle in their reaction to heat.

Do not even measure the starch; take a tablespoon or so of it and prepare a slurry with it. Add minute amounts of the slurry to the sauce until you reach the texture you are looking for. Discard the remainder of the slurry.

A word of caution on the stability of starches: Often pure starches react wildly to very high heat or whisking and simply and stubbornly refuse to thicken. A chemist probably could identify the exact reason; the cook always works too fast to take time to ponder such an erratic reaction. If this happens to you, do not try to reinforce the thickening by adding more of the same starch, for nothing will happen and the sauce will remain forever thin as some wild chain reaction seems to take place in the pot. Instead, *change your starch*: If you were using cornstarch, switch to potato starch or vice versa; you will see your sauce thicken instantly.

THE FINAL COLOR OF SAUCES

There is a general fetish among modern cooks against anything "not natural." More than one flat-tasting sauce has been served because the cook did not want to use meat extract or, even worse, did not want to use a color corrector if the sauce was not of a very good color.

Being a cook, a cooking teacher, and a restaurateur all in one, I look at the effect of food on the eyes, and consequently on the mind and the palate. An unappealing, gray-looking sauce will destroy appetite in the diner by provoking the reaction: "That looks awful." Can anything that looks awful be totally gastronomically satisfying? Probably not.

Hostesses and restaurateurs must put all the guarantees on their side and know that the psychology of taste passes through the eyes and the brain as well as the taste buds. One should make certain that every dish not only tastes eminently good but also looks eminently edible; never underestimate the value of a drop of food coloring or caramel coloring.

Choosing coloring agents that are chemically safe and gastronomically acceptable is, of course, essential. The choice of coloring agent remains a personal one. Watch for off tastes such as sweetness or bitterness that could upset the final taste of the sauce.

The best way to prevent the need for coloring agents is to use good techniques at the outset of cooking the sauce. Brown sauces may become gray looking when the initial browning of the meat has not been done properly. In all brown sauces you can avoid this color problem by deep browning the meats.

See the chapter on meats and their sauces. The most common problem of color in white sauces occurs when the wrong pot is used to whisk the emulsion. Use good stainless steel, double bottom pots, not enameled cast-iron saucepans in which the scraping of the whisk on the bottom of the pot will release a small amount of iron oxide and turn a white sauce gray or an egg emulsion of the hollandaise type greenish gray.

Fish and Shellfish and Their Sauces

THE BASIC BEURRE BLANC

ALL CLASSIC SAUCES FOR FISH rested on the use of a good fish fumet; they were made either into veloutés bound with a white roux or into "white wine sauce for fish," bound (as was hollandaise) with egg yolks fluffed up into a reduction of fish fumet and lemon juice; sometimes béchamel was blended with the fish fumet. All these classics could be quite pretty if well prepared, or downright ugly if techniques fell short and skimming or proper whisking were neglected.

In the fifties, the plain *beurre blanc* that traditionally had been the fish sauce of the Nantes to Saumur areas came into the culinary limelight and suddenly conquered the whole of the French territory. Various food writers submitted all kinds of theories about its origin: for some, a cook would have made a mistake and forgotten to add the egg yolk to her béarnaise; for another a "genial" cook would have "invented" it. No one knows for sure, but part of my family is from the Saumur area, and I can attest to the way their fish has always been cooked, either whole or in large fillets: It was put in a buttered dish, generously sprinkled with finely chopped shallots and a couple of glasses of white wine, and also sometimes a tablespoon or so of vinegar. The whole was put to bake, and as the fish began to lose some of its juices into the wine and shallot mixture, the base of the fish sauce would build around the fish in the oven. Once the fish was cooked, the juices were drained, reduced further if necessary, and additional butter was fluffed into the reduced base. What is that if not a *beurre blanc?*

Pike, of course, or shad were the favorite fish of these areas; shad was always baked, but pike was always poached in a very flavorful court bouillon. In this case, the best cooks would reduce together shallots, part wine/part court bouillon, and a dash of excellent white wine vinegar, then fluff butter into the reduction and strain it over the skinned fish fillets. Every cook had her method, and women were "known" for the excellence of their *beurre blanc.* I was trained by a past master in the art.

In November 1924, a magazine known as *La Bretagne Touristique* was giving voice to its fear for the disappearance of traditional Breton foods and wines and wrote, among other things, "The disappearance of the *beurre blanc* of the Nantes countryside, of the 'Lard Nantais' [a dish of pork chops baked with pork rind and offal], and of the Muscadet wines would be an irreparable loss," a statement that for me clearly indicates the traditional value of all three items.

The *beurre blanc* has triumphed and survived and so has the Muscadet. The *beurre blanc* has, in fact, invaded the whole country. I think this is because in 1950 France was first emerging from the most somber years in its history, years during which the people literally starved, and such a sauce, silky with a half pound of the best Breton, Charentes, or Normandy butter, was in some way a balm to soothe all deprivations. This very rich and supremely delicious sauce also happens to be one of the quickest and easiest to prepare, ideal for a time when kitchen personnel were no longer plentiful.

BEURRE BLANC

By now *beurre blanc* has become the prototype of the modern fish sauce. So that the reader can understand the new modern sauces, I will review the basic techniques for making *beurre blanc* very quickly here. The sauce described below is eminently usable on all fillets of fish; plain scallops; plain shrimp and lobster, poached or broiled; and frogs' legs.

½ cup excellent Muscadet or other
    dry white wine (Mâcon, Entre-
    deux-Mers, Alsace Riesling,
    California Chenin Blanc or
    Chardonnay)
⅓ cup very mellow (5–6 percent
    acetic acid) vinegar
2 tablespoons extremely fine-chopped
    shallots

⅓ teaspoon salt
¼ teaspoon white pepper from the
    mill
½ pound best quality unsalted butter
    (93 score AA grade), at room
    temperature

Method "A":

Mix white wine, vinegar, shallots, and salt and reduce to 3 tablespoons of solids and liquids together. Cool the pot, add the pepper, keep on extremely low heat and, tablespoon by tablespoon, whisk in the butter until a semicreamy semi-foamy sauce has built. Strain into a warm (not hot) sauceboat.

Note: You are instructed here to keep the pot on low heat and to whisk the butter into the acid base:

a. To prevent evaporation of the very small amount of liquid at the bottom of the pot. Should this liquid completely evaporate, you will see the butter slowly start melting as it goes out of emulsion and breaks into an oily mess.

b. To constantly cool the mixture by introducing air into it and preventing it from coming to a boil.

Method "B":

Mix white wine, vinegar, shallots, and salt, reduce to ⅓ cup of liquid *plus* the solid shallots, or a total of approximately ½ cup altogether. In essence the reduction of your acid mixture is *not* finished and you can reduce it still farther. Bring this very acid mixture to a *full* boil and with your whisk add the butter, tablespoon by tablespoon, so that the hard boiling, supplemented by your whisking, will cause the butter to be broken down into millions of droplets and absorbed into the acid base. While you add the butter, the acid base will continue to reduce, concentrate, and evaporate, so *be careful*! If you boil the acid base off completely, your sauce will break and you will soon see your shallots floating in the melted butter. Stop cooking as soon as all the butter has been completely incorporated and the sauce leaves a thin coating on the back of a stainless steel spoon.

The two methods used here to prepare the *beurre blanc* are those used to prepare all fish sauces in the modern cuisine. You will find all possible variations outlined in this chapter. Please read these pages carefully before you start cooking any of the fish or shellfish dishes that follow so that you will recognize the method I have followed in each recipe.

GRANDES SAUCES POUR POISSONS
(Elaborate Sauces for Fish)

Liquid aromatic components of fish sauces:
These liquid components can be: a wine, always dry, white or red or fortified; fish fumet, clam juice, or other shellfish juice; court bouillon; vinegar or lemon juice. They are not all mixed together, of course. The most common combinations are:

> Wine + fish fumet or fresh clam juice
> Wine + fish fumet + vinegar
> Fish fumet + court bouillon
> Fish fumet + court bouillon + lemon juice

Every combination is possible. The various elements can be combined to your heart's content, but I find the fish fumet to be essential because it ties the fish to the sauce that covers it and eliminates that slight feeling of "unrelation" between fish and sauce existing in the *beurre blanc*. Its neutral taste also somewhat counteracts the acids of the wine, vinegar, or citrus fruit, and the slight viscosity it gets from gelatinous proteins is most helpful in forming the emulsion of butter into the sauce base.

Solid aromatic components of fish sauces:
The solid components will be the following, used alone or in combination, depending on your choice:

Chopped onions, chopped shallots, chopped leeks, bouquet garni, the chopped stems of herbs, crushed garlic cloves, chopped fresh herbs, fish bones, shellfish shells, pieces of skinless fish or shellfish, spices

Note: The smaller you chop the aromatics, the more flavor they will give to your sauce. You will have to distinguish between those aromatics used at the onset of cooking before the reduction starts and those aromatics added as garnish when the sauce is finished. Sometimes the reduction is also blended with a purée of vegetables or a purée of acid fruit (see taste modifications on p. 184).

The reduction, or sauce base, of a fish sauce:
The reduction, or sauce base, is obtained by mixing and reducing together the liquid and solid aromatic components of the fish sauce; the reduction must be by at least 50 percent. That means that if you start with 1 cup liquid altogether, you cannot use the reduction to finish the sauce until it is reduced to ½ cup.

The enriching elements of a fish sauce:
The enriching elements are mostly heavy cream and butter.

I. *Heavy cream as enrichment*: You can add heavy cream to a fish sauce two ways:

a. *By reduction* on a high heat. Having reduced the sauce base to only 50 percent of its original volume, add the cream bit by bit on high boil and stir constantly until the sauce leaves a thin coating on the back of a stainless steel spoon. Your base finishes reducing at the same time that the cream loses its water and concentrates its milk solids and fat content.

b. *By addition* of already reduced cream to a base that has been reduced by at least three-quarters. If at the onset of the cooking you had 1 cup liquid in the pan, and you have now only ¼ cup left, you can blend reduced heavy cream into that base and obtain an excellent fish sauce. The amount of reduced cream is up to you and depends on the basic taste of the sauce and its texture.

The second method is the one to use if you have inadvertently overreduced the base. It is less time consuming, since you can reduce both sauce base and cream at the same time on two different burners. Also, this type of sauce tends to be less acid than the first type.

II. *Butter as enrichment:*

a. If butter alone is used: Prepare your reduction or sauce base and use one of the two methods outlined on page 180 under Beurre Blanc.

b. If butter is used in combination with cream: Remember that when two fat ingredients such as heavy cream and butter are added to a sauce, the fattest of the two always comes last. If you are adding butter to a sauce already containing cream, remove the sauce from the heat and fluff in the butter *off* the heat. You will need only a small amount of butter, since you do not want to choke the sauce with too high a fat content.

Texture modifiers in fish sauces:

- Heavy cream and butter as enrichment are texture modifiers. So are sour cream and mustard, both of which add a tiny degree of thickening. Butter can be plain, but it also can be combined with other elements that are taste and texture modifiers, such as lobster or crayfish roe, to make a *compound butter.* Please follow the instructions in the recipes carefully, for boiling a fish sauce containing lobster or crayfish butter can have some dire consequences such as chalkiness and bitterness.
- Purées of fruit or vegetables can also be considered texture modifiers, as the sauce will either thin or thicken with their addition. For example: cucumbers will thin a sauce while rhubarb purée will thicken it by souring the cream.
- If butter is introduced into a sauce with the help of the blender, a sort of "mechanical" and temporary thickening will occur as a result of the rapid microscopic dispersion of millions of butter droplets into the sauce, and because of the amount of air being churned into the sauce by the blender blade. This thickening will last approximately 15–20 minutes and gradually disappear as the air in the sauce reintegrates the atmosphere. This "blender trick" is a good one to use if a sauce is hopelessly thin and you have no time to work on it further.
- If after it has completely reduced, a sauce base tastes just right but remains terribly thin, another quick way to give it body is to turn it down to a simmer and whisk into it a bit of cornstarch dissolved in a bit of water or fish fumet or cream. Do not even measure the starch; simply dilute a tablespoon of it into the liquid and add a little bit at a time, stirring until your sauce reaches the desired thickness.

Taste modifiers in fish sauces:
- The aromatics combined for the reduction of the sauce base (see pp. 181–82).
- The aromatic elements added to a semifinished or fully finished sauce; they can be chopped herbs, fortified wines—especially dry sherry, a mustard of any type, a shellfish butter, a purée of vegetable or acid fruit, and occasionally very tart berries such as red currants.
- The very final taste modifiers that can be added to "save" a finished sauce that just does not taste right, remains thin tasting, or lacks "body salt": anchovy paste and meat extract used in tiny, tiny amounts and added until the sauce takes a turn for the better. Quantities cannot be indicated here as they have to be tasted and appreciated by the cook.

Methods of production of elaborate fish sauces at home and in the restaurant:

At home, working on small quantities, one can use any method one wishes to prepare fish sauces: long reductions, quick reductions, addition of cream and butter on low or high heat. It does not matter, and I would like to suggest that the cook experiment with the various possibilities suggested here until she or he achieves fluency in all methods.

In the restaurant operation 1 quart reduced base will need 2–2½ cups heavy cream already prereduced. After blending the 2 elements, bring to a high boil and add ½ pound butter, plain or compound. This "long sauce" will serve 24–30 persons. Reheat and slightly reduce the sauce in batches of ¼ cup per portion and add a final dose of either plain or compound butter at the ratio of a small tablespoon per person.

Shelf life of elaborate fish sauces:

The shelf life of an elaborate fish sauce full of fish fumet and perishable butter and cream is 48 hours in an excellent refrigerator. In consequence, prepare only what you need or very little more; in any case, these sauces taste best if prepared fresh on a regular basis. If necessary, they freeze well and keep several weeks if well sealed.

To reheat elaborate fish sauces—the problem of separation:

Put a small amount of sauce in a saucepan and quickly bring it to a boil, whisking. Whisk the remainder of the leftover sauce, tablespoon by tablespoon, into the boiling portion of sauce until the whole is reheated. Add 1–2 tablespoons fish fumet or clam juice. Correct the seasoning.

Note: Remember at all times that if a sauce separates, the way to repair it is to whisk tepid (not hot) liquid into it. The liquid to use for fish sauces is obviously fish fumet or, in its absence, clam juice artfully cut with water, to reduce its saltiness.

PETITES SAUCES RAPIDES POUR POISSONS
(Quick Sauces for Fish)

I used these quick sauces for the dinners of the *cuisine de misère.* They usually accompanied quickly panfried and pansteamed fish. Their methods of preparation are the essence of simplicity and consist of both classic elements and new quick methods.

The classic elements:
- The plain old-fashioned "noisette" butter (see p. 48), blended with lemon juice and poured over quickly fried fillets of fish.
- The "vinaigrette" type dressing poured over a bright hot fish and served either hot or after a few hours' marination in the refrigerator.
- The plain thickening of a sauce made of part clam juice and part light cream with a bit of cornstarch. This method, used in several of the recipes that follow, is most useful, because of its simplicity and speed of execution and also because it can be used in landlocked areas where the preparation of a fish fumet is virtually impossible.

This type of sauce, which we call "universal" sauce, can be served on anything from fillets of trout from a local brook to frozen and artfully defrosted scallops.

The more modern elements:
- The use of reduced heavy cream combined with aromatic vegetables and blended with clam juice.
- The use of vegetable purées such as a plain little fondue of tomato blended with butter and flavored with fresh herbs.

MOUSSELINES AND QUENELLES-MOUSSELINE

If only for the making of mousselines, the food processor is worth its price. Thanks to its existence, I was able one day to prepare a mousseline from start to finish in seven minutes—and using, at that, my favorite method, which employs the electric mixer as well as the food processor. I have no nostalgia for the days of old when mousselines and quenelles were prepared in mortars, especially since I cannot completely forget those days: they left me with a chronic case of bursitis in the right shoulder!

Before I describe the two procedures I use to make mousseline paste, I would like to explain in some detail the ingredients used to prepare them so that we establish first and foremost what should and should not be included. Mousselines are nothing more than small molded fish puddings prepared with fish meat, eggs, heavy cream, butter, fish fumet, and sometimes a garnish. Let us look at each of these elements in succession.

Elements of mousseline:
I. *Solid ingredients.*
   a. *Fish or shellfish meat.* It is essential that the meat be extremely fresh, *raw*, and free of skin, "brown tissues," and bones.
   Taste: The cleanest, most agreeable taste is always best obtained by using a fish that has literally just jumped out of the ocean, lake, or river. You can immediately see that people who live on the seacoast or by a lake or major river will have a privileged situation.
   Texture: A mousseline, as we shall see a little later, is made by using the principle that the collagen (the liquid gelatinous tissue that binds the fish fibers together) has the capacity to retain butter and heavy cream in a state of suspension or emulsion. If the collagen is fresh and still stiff, it will retain butter and cream better, and a smooth, even emulsion will form. This will result in a firmer and airier texture.
   In fish fillets that are not so fresh and that have been waiting to be sold in the fish store, dehydration takes place at the same time as a certain liquefaction of the collagen. A mousseline paste made with such fish will lack firmness and will not hold the cream as well. The final texture will be imperfect and will look semicurdled.

Fish fillets that are very fresh never have the slightest tinge of grayness; they are firm and always have a pinkish or solidly white hue to their color.

The best fish to use is a superfresh one that you fillet yourself or ask the fish store to fillet before your eyes. The most desirable fish are, in order of preference: Pike, salmon, lake trout, sweetwater trout, healthy gray sole, petrale sole, winter flounder, red snapper, large halibut.

The most desirable shellfish are: Maine lobster, deep sea scallops, Louisiana crayfish—as large as possible and caught early in the season before the water warms up too much, rock lobster (clawless lobster), large shrimp or prawns. Lobsters from cold water will always be far superior to lobsters from warm water, and shrimp caught in the winter will be superior to shrimp caught in the warmer months.

It is entirely possible to make a mousseline with a fish the natural texture of which is not as firm as all the species mentioned above provided one adds, at the same time one adds the heavy cream, 3–4 tablespoons double-strength fish fumet (see p. 189) enriched with 1 tablespoon gelatin per pound of fish meat. This reinforcement method will also allow you to use a fish that is not quite as fresh as you would like. The same results can be obtained if one binds the same amount of double-strength fish fumet with ½ teaspoon cornstarch. Of course, the double-strength fumet stabilized either with gelatin or starch must be melted or cooked respectively, then cooled before being added to the fish, and it is best added alternately with the heavy cream.

This method is in fact so efficient that I have been able, as an experiment (only for the sake of it and to know whether it would help), to prepare a mousseline with fish that had been flash frozen and then defrosted in the refrigerator. I am giving this information only as a pointer for those who have only frozen fish at their disposal. Mousselines made with frozen fish usually show a slight grain if the fish is not of top quality when flash frozen and/or if it is defrosted out of the refrigerator so that the natural juices (collagen) are lost. Frozen large shrimp have such tough fibers that they can be made into a mousseline without any help.

Although this is not a subject I like to write about, I urge the cook to inspect his/her fish fillets for traces of the parasites that feed by sucking the liquid collagen from the fish. Parasite-infested fish make a poor mousseline, with an unsteady, slightly granular texture. As a matter of fact, I discovered the problem of parasites after making several batches of less than satisfactory mousselines. I became so impatient, and at the same time so intrigued that I had the fish store deliver the fish (gray sole) whole instead of filleted. After filleting the fish myself, I discovered what my problem was; after a long, disheartening meeting with a health inspector and a food scientist, I struck gray sole off my list forever. Of course, there are still some specimens of gray sole that are unpolluted, but you will never know whether you have the right kind unless you fillet the fish yourself, and you are always taking a chance when you buy the whole fish. Your only chance is a wonderful fish purveyor who will sort the fillets for you after he has filleted a number of fish.

b. *Butter.* I was trained to prepare mousselines according to the Escoffier method that uses no butter at all. Adding butter to a mousseline paste was my first act of culinary independence some twenty years ago. I decided that the master was wonderful but that his mousselines were all too basic, and I started to add butter in varying quantities, from 3 to 4 ounces for each pound of fish. Even more can be added, all the way up to 8 ounces, but there is a point at which the mousseline loses its fish or shellfish taste and turns into bland baby pap, so I use 3 ounces for Atlantic salmon and 4 ounces for Pacific salmon, due to their different fat contents, and 4 ounces with tough shellfish such as lobster and deep sea scallops. Use whatever amount of butter you prefer; if you like your mousselines softer, do not hesitate to increase the quantity of butter. Always use Grade AA 93 Score unsalted butter.

II. *Liquid ingredients.*

a. *Eggs.* Egg whites were added to the fish meat in most classic recipes, probably to secure a perfect white color. A wonderful conversation with André Soltner twenty years ago put me on the way to using part egg white/part whole egg. Mr. Soltner felt that the color was better, and I wholeheartedly adopted his point of view. I would, however, like to warn of a possible problem resulting from the use of egg yolks with deep sea scallops, shrimp, and lobster. Once in a while the yolk will provoke a massive syneresis (erratic separation of an apparently perfect mousseline batter upon baking, and not because of overcooking). This—probably enzymatic—reaction does not always occur, but it has happened enough that while I had the restaurant I stopped preparing shellfish mousselines with egg yolks. I prepare scallop mousselines with a proportion of their own roe plus egg whites. Obviously the eggs will add quite a degree of solidity to a mousseline batter, besides being a determinant of its final color.

b. *Heavy cream.* I have made mousselines with many types of cream, from light cream to thick French crème fraîche, and these are my conclusions.

Light cream may be used by those who would enjoy having a mousseline without automatically clogging their arteries. The resulting mousseline is not bad, but it lacks "slip" on the tongue and is by no means as good as it should be; it is only an acceptable product.

The best mousselines are made with pasteurized heavy cream containing 38 percent butterfat—sterilized cream may be used, but pasteurized is better. The American heavy cream is perfect and gives by far the best results.

However, the crème fraîche craze is such that I feel compelled to say a word about it. Yes, you may use some crème fraîche if you think the taste "does something" for the finished product, but if you are smart, you will limit your use of crème fraîche to no more than one-third the total volume of cream, and before using it you will dilute the crème fraîche with one-fifth of its volume in cold milk to return it to a more liquid texture. For example, were you to use a total of 2 cups cream to prepare a mousseline, you would use first 1⅓ cups regular American heavy cream, then dilute ½ cup crème fraîche with 2½ tablespoons cold milk. This way, you will be able to add the crème fraîche without running the risk of seeing your whole batch of mousselines come out with a slightly uneven texture.

When I was growing up, we made mousselines with the only cream there was at the time: double crème fraîche. We always cut our crème fraîche with milk and then folded it into the fish purée to prevent making that new breed of food "fish cheese." Mousselines are much more difficult to do in France than they are in the United States because of endless variations in the texture and sourness of the creams.

III. *Double-strength fish fumet, or fish essence to reinforce mousselines.*

If, as I explained above, the quality of your fish necessitates the use of a mixture of gelatin or starch with double-strength fish fumet, prepare the fumet as follows:

Mix approximately ½ pound fish bones (heads are best) with ⅔ cup fish fumet that has been combined with ⅓ cup dry white wine. Cook for 35 minutes as you would a regular fumet (see p. 28).

Why not take simple fish fumet and reduce it until thick? Try it if you have the time and an excess of fish fumet at your disposal. The result is not the best smelling or best tasting mixture, for as the gelatinous texture thickens, so do the taste and smell, and not in the most attractive manner. The simple "fish essence" I recommend here is better—Escoffier thinks so and taught me that fact on page 14 of *Le Guide Culinaire* (Crown Publishers, American edition).

IV. *Seasonings and spices, garnishes.*

The most frequently used seasonings are:

> 1½ teaspoons salt and
> 35 turns of the pepper mill

per pound of fish meat. However, scallops often require up to 3 teaspoons salt to the pound. The seasonings are mixed into the fish purée at the onset of the processing. If more salt is needed when the mousseline is "finished," dilute it into a tablespoon or so of cream and fold the mixture into the paste. A pinch of nutmeg is often used, and chopped fresh herbs can be added to the paste. See the different techniques for making mousselines on pages 190–92.

A garnish of cooked fish, shellfish, or diced vegetables can be enclosed in the center of the mousseline; these garnishes should all be cooked and tossed with a bit of sauce first, so that they just reheat as one bakes the mousseline.

Small dices of raw shellfish can also be added to a mousseline paste; these should be tossed into a bit of egg white before being folded into the finished paste.

Mousseline mixing techniques:

A. *The quick one-step food processor way*: If you have never made mousselines, start this way; the result is nice and pleasant and the work minimal.

Process the ice-cold fish meat combined with the chosen egg mixture until completely puréed. As soon as this is done, remove from the processor and strain the purée if you wish (remember that deep sea scallops never need straining). Put the entire quantity of butter—at room temperature—into the processor along with the salt and pepper and any other spices you are using, and process to cream the butter. Then gradually return the fish meat to the food processor, processing until fish and butter are homogeneous. Now add the ice-cold cream in a steady stream, leaving the machine on all the time you are doing so and stopping as soon as the cream has been completely incorporated. Total required time approximately 8 minutes.

B. *The food processor–electric mixer combination*: This is the method I use all the time; I prefer it to any other.

1. Process the meat and the egg mixture in the food processor until completely smooth. Strain the purée into a stainless steel bowl. Deep chill it for 2 hours. If your refrigerator is not superefficient, put the bowl containing the purée into another one containing ice cubes in *salted* water. The fish must get ice cold.

2. With an electric mixer, cream the butter combined with the salt, pepper, and any other spice used until smooth. The butter must be at room temperature, but not oversoft or oily! Keeping the mixer on medium creaming speed, add the ice-cold fish purée, tablespoon by tablespoon, until all has been added. Continue beating until the mixture develops elasticity: this happens as the liquid collagen and the broken fish fibers rehomogenize. The development of elasticity is to be compared to the development of gluten in bread; it happens under the mechnical action of the mixer whip. Do *not* overwhip and overdevelop the elasticity, or you will have to add more cream than is called for to soften the paste, and you will lose the fish taste in the mass of cream. As soon as you see the fish purée stick in blocks to the mixer whip, you are ready to add the cream.

3. Reduce the speed of the mixer to slow (speed 2)—your goal is to whip the cream into the fish purée without making it break and separate. Your cream must be as ice cold as it would be if you were whipping it by itself; if it is soft, it will not take on any volume, and you will be left with liquid cream containing islands of fish purée. Add the cream in a steady 1/4-inch-thick stream, until all the cream has been incorporated.

Note: Your mixer must be well adjusted so that the base of the whip scrapes lightly against the bottom of the bowl, or 1/2–1 inch of mixture at the bottom of the bowl will not mix evenly with the cream. To prevent this, slide a taste-free rubber spatula between the side of the bowl and the mixer blades— and be careful not to let the spatula get caught in the blades.

4. Now make a test: prepare a small ball (quenelle) of dough with two teaspoons and poach it in a bath of salted *simmering* water until when tested with the finger it feels springy under slight pressure. Cut the quenelle in half, taste it, and check for these possible problems:
   a. If the quenelle is good and homogeneous but a bit too "solid": add more cream.
   b. If the quenelle is somewhat granular and the fish can still be perceived in tiny particles on the tongue and between the teeth: add more cream.

Your next question is: How much cream? Well, I do not know; you are on your own there. Add as much as needed until a new test gives you that wonderfully airy texture of the perfect quenelle. Trust yourself. You will know. You cannot miss it—all of a sudden it is there. To help you, I have given the amounts of cream in 2 measurements—for example, 2½–3 cups heavy cream. Test after adding the lesser amount and go to the higher amount only if necessary. How much is truly needed depends on the quality of your fish, and that will vary every time you prepare a new batch.

As you taste the first test, also check the salt and pepper, and if more are needed dissolve and add them in your last addition of cream. If you use chopped herbs, do the same: mix them into your last addition of cream and beat them or fold them into the fish paste. If you use diced shellfish dipped in egg white, fold it extremely quickly into the finished mousseline.

Mousseline baking techniques:

Pack the paste, without leaving any air holes, into heavily buttered ramekins or paper cups 1–3 ounces in capacity. Two 1-ounce mousselines make a lovely first course. One 3-ounce mousseline, well garnished, constitutes a main course in America only; in France it can be only a first course even to this day.

Preheat the oven to 325°F. Bake in a hot water bath, setting the bath on the oven rack and pouring the *boiling* water into it *after* the mousselines have been put in. If you fill the bath before putting it in the oven, you may slosh some water into the mousseline batter. The mousselines must be covered with parchment paper to prevent a dry skin from forming on the top. The cooking time varies from 12 minutes for the 2-ounce cups to 17 minutes for the 3-ounce ramekins. The mousselines are usually done when the parchment can be lifted off. Invert them onto individual plates to serve—and do not forget to remove the cup or ramekin before you sauce them!

Shelf life of mousselines:

The shelf life for a mousseline paste prepared ahead of time is 24 hours, to be absolutely safe. It is good to know that mousselines can be made and kept in a very cold refrigerator a whole day ahead of time, so one can do them and stop worrying about them. After baking, their shelf life increases another 48 hours, and you can serve them cold with a very lightened mayonnaise-derived sauce.

Mousselines and mousses of salmon:

Nowadays, when good fish has become so scarce, one is always pleased to use any salmon at hand, provided it is absolutely fresh and glistening with collagen when cut and prepared. You will find yourself more or less locked into the season: the Eastern season is from late June to mid-July, while the Western lasts way into the fall. Since I love smoked Nova Scotia, I used it quite a bit in combination with fresh salmon, either in a sauce or in the mousseline paste. All sauces indicated later for salmon medallions (pp. 226–29) are also usable on any of these mousselines.

TERRINES CHAUDES DE SAUMON A LA RHUBARBE ET AUX ECORCES
{Mousselines of Salmon with Rhubarb and Citrus Rind Sauce}

Atlantic salmon is preferable, but any Pacific breed will do very well. Use the lesser amounts of butter and cream for the Atlantic fish and the larger ones for the Pacific breeds. This sauce looks deceptively easy on paper. There is absolutely no way to tell exactly how much rhubarb purée to add, since no two rhubarbs have the same degree of acidity. Observe carefully the order of mixing of the ingredients; finish the sauce with reduction, cream, and butter, then add the rhubarb until you reach a degree of acidity that is pleasant to your palate.

SERVES 6 AS A MAIN COURSE; 12 AS A FIRST COURSE

MOUSSELINES:

1 pound salmon meat, without skin, bones, and brown tissues
1 egg
1 egg white
6–8 tablespoons unsalted butter
3 gratings of fresh nutmeg
1½ teaspoons salt
35 turns of the pepper mill
2–2½ cups heavy cream

SAUCE:

2¼ cups Fish Fumet (p. 28)	2 ribs of young fresh rhubarb,
1 cup heavy cream	unpeeled
¾ teaspoon each fine-julienned	8 tablespoons butter
lemon, lime, orange, and grape-	Salt
fruit rinds, each blanched for 3	Pepper from the mill
minutes	

1. To prepare the mousseline, process the salmon meat with the eggs. Strain through a tamis sieve and deep chill for 2 hours. In an electric mixer, cream the butter with the nutmeg, the salt, and the pepper; gradually add the salmon meat and beat until elastic. Turn the mixer down to low speed and add the heavy cream. Keep chilled until ready to use.

2. To prepare the sauce, mix 2 cups of the fish fumet with the heavy cream; reduce slowly to 1 cup. Add ¼ teaspoon of each of the blanched rinds and continue reducing until 2 more tablespoons have evaporated.

3. While the sauce reduces, wash the rhubarb and cut it into slivers. Cover and cook slowly with a drop of water until it completely collapses into approximately ¼–⅓ cup rhubarb purée. Stir well with a wooden spoon to mix the water and fibers into an even-textured compote.

4. Empty the reduced fish fumet, cream, and rinds reduction into the blender and purée until smooth. Add 6 tablespoons of the butter while the sauce is hot; blend to emulsify the butter well into the mixture. Then add the rhubarb purée very gradually, alternating with salt and pepper until you reach the balance of acidity and salt you personally enjoy. Keep the sauce in the blender container while you cook the mousselines.

5. Preheat the oven to 325°F. Use the remaining 2 tablespoons of the butter to grease the ramekins or timbales in which you will poach the mousselines. Pack the mousseline into the timbales, cover with nonstick parchment paper, and bake in a hot water bath for 12–17 minutes. Unmold onto warm plates as soon as done.

6. Taste the sauce; add a bit more rhubarb or salt as needed. Reblend for 15 seconds and strain the sauce into a small saucepan with the remaining blanched citrus rinds. Reheat well together, stirring with a wooden spoon. Correct the final texture with a bit more fish fumet from the remaining ¼ cup, if needed to lighten the texture. Spoon over the mousselines.

MOUSSELINES DE SAUMON FUME
A LA COTE-ROTIE
{Mousselines of Smoked Salmon in Red Wine}

Excellent for the late salmon season when only the deep red species of Pacific fish is available; the rich smoked salmon and opulent sauce are successful at hiding the slightly dry texture of Pacific salmons.

SERVES 6 AS A MAIN COURSE; 12 AS A FIRST COURSE

MOUSSELINES:

¾ pound deep red Pacific salmon, without skin, bones, or brown tissues

¼ pound Nova Scotia smoked salmon, cut into small pieces

2 eggs

10 tablespoons unsalted butter

¾–1 teaspoon salt

35 turns of the pepper mill

2¼–2½ cups heavy cream

2 tablespoons chopped parsley

SAUCE:

½ pound tiny mushrooms

12 tablespoons butter

1 zucchini, cut into 1-inch by ½-inch "olives" (see p. 368)

1½ cups Fish Fumet (p. 28)

1 cup Côte-Rôtie or other good Côtes-du-Rhône or Zinfandel wine

2 tablespoons chopped carrot

6 shallots, chopped

1 small onion, chopped

Small bouquet garni (see p. 82)

Salt

½ cup heavy cream

Pepper from the mill

1. Place the fresh and smoked salmon in the food processor container. Add the eggs and process until smooth. Strain through a tamis sieve and refrigerate for 2 hours.

2. Cream 8 tablespoons of the butter in the electric mixer; add salt and pepper and gradually add the salmon to this mixture. Beat until stiff, turn the mixer down to low speed, and add 2¼ cups of the cream in a thin, steady stream. Test for taste and texture and add more salt or cream if needed.

3. Butter ramekins or timbales with the remaining 2 tablespoons of butter and fill the containers with the mousselines. Keep refrigerated until ready to

use. When ready, preheat the oven to 325°F. and bake the mousselines for 15–17 minutes in a hot water bath.

4. To prepare the sauce, clean and pare the mushrooms. Sauté them in 1 tablespoon of the butter for 1–2 minutes, then cover them to extract their juices. Strain and reserve the juices. Sauté the zucchini in another tablespoon of the butter. Set mushrooms and zucchini aside.

5. Mix the fish fumet, red wine, carrot, shallots, onion, bouquet garni, and a pinch of salt. Reduce to approximately 1 cup and blend with the mushroom juices. Simmer the mixture for 5 minutes at the same time you reduce the cream to ¼ cup. Blend the reduction and the reduced cream; bring to a high boil and whisk in the remaining butter, tablespoon by tablespoon. Strain into a clean pot, add the mushrooms and zucchini, and reheat well. Correct the final seasoning.

6. Unmold the cooked mousselines onto warmed plates. Spoon the sauce around the mousselines, not on top, and sprinkle the top of each mousseline with chopped parsley.

AN IDEA FOR SALMON AND GOOSEBERRIES

If you own a gooseberry bush, prepare a gooseberry sauce, making and using the gooseberry purée exactly as I did the rhubarb purée on page 193.

I use this idea when, in July, our Annecy market is suddenly flooded with gooseberries. At the same time, the seaweed known as "Passepierre" arrives from the Atlantic Ocean, and it is a lovely sight on the plate surrounding the pale pink salmon steak or mousseline floating in a bath of darker pink gooseberry sauce. This is just in case you live on the ocean and also grow gooseberries.

Mousselines and mousses of pike:
Pike is in some areas difficult to find and in others daily fare. In the areas where the supply is limited, you may want to prepare mousselines and dishes made with pike at the times of the Jewish holidays both in the spring and fall, when fish markets stock it for the traditional gefilte fish.

Good fresh pike is extremely collagenous, and you will notice that the amount of cream used per pound of fish is closer to 3 cups than it is to the customary 2 cups recommended by Escoffier in *Le Guide Culinaire.* Watch the electric mixer as you beat the fish; if you overbeat, you will find in your bowl a stiff mass requiring much more cream than you wish to use to soften it again to a pleasant, edible texture. As soon as you have added all the fish to the butter, check the texture; if it is already elastic, start adding the cream immediately.

The following sauce recipe can also be used with mousselines made with brook trout, brown trout, rainbow trout, or large lake trout (*omble chevalier, ouananiche* in Canada), gray or petrale sole. Also look in the section on "quick fish" recipes, where you will find many very quick sauces that can be served on a pike mousseline.

When preparing the fish fumet for the sauce, be sure to include, in addition to the necessary poundage of fish fumet bones, all the pike bones, well cleaned, that your fish market will possibly give you.

MOUSSELINES DE BROCHET AU VIN JAUNE
{Pike Mousselines with Sherry-flavored Sauce}

In the original recipe, prepared in France, I used a Jura Vin Jaune and walnuts gathered on a road around Arbois. In America I used instead of the Vin Jaune a mixture of ordinary Entre-deux-Mers and amontillado sherry. Have the fish market give you the bones and head of the pike to include in your fish sauce.

SERVES 6 AS A MAIN COURSE; 12 AS A FIRST COURSE

MOUSSELINES:

1 pound pike fillets, without skin or bones	*35 turns of the pepper mill*
2 egg whites	*8 tablespoons unsalted butter*
2 tablespoons light cream or milk	*2⅔–3 cups heavy cream, chilled*
1¾–2 teaspoons salt	*6 parsley bouquets*

S A U C E :

1½ cups Fish Fumet (p. 28)

1 cup Entre-deux-Mers white wine

The head and bones of the pike, chopped

1 onion, chopped fine

1 shallot, chopped fine

1 tablespoon coarse-chopped carrot

3 scallions (white part only), sliced thin

Small bouquet garni (see p. 82)

¼ cup amontillado sherry

⅔ cup heavy cream, reduced by half

8 tablespoons butter

Salt

Pepper from the mill

1 tablespoon walnut oil

3 tablespoons coarse-chopped walnut halves

1½ tablespoons chopped parsley

1. Process the pike, the egg whites, and the light cream in the food processor until perfectly smooth. Strain through a tamis sieve and deep chill for 2 hours. After that time, put salt, pepper, and butter in the electric mixer bowl and cream until fluffy and white. Add the pike meat in 4 equal additions; beat until stiff—no more than a minute or two. Turn the mixer to low speed and add the heavy cream. Test the mousseline after adding 2½ cups and add the remainder if needed. Deep chill until ready to use.

2. To prepare the sauce, put the fish fumet, white wine, pike bones, onion, shallot, carrot, scallions, and bouquet garni in a saucepan. Bring to a boil, reduce to ½ cup liquids and solids combined, and strain through a fine "China cap" sieve to obtain ⅓ cup of reduction. Add the sherry to the reduction and simmer together for 5 minutes. Add the reduced cream; bring to a high boil and whisk in 6 tablespoons of the butter. Season carefully with salt and pepper.

3. Heat the walnut oil in a skillet, and in it lightly toast the chopped walnuts to minimize the tannic taste of their skins. Gather the walnuts in a slotted spoon and, without patting them dry, set them aside on a plate.

4. Preheat the oven to 325°F. With the remaining 2 tablespoons of butter, grease the chosen ramekins and cook the mousselines for 15 minutes in a hot water bath, covered with buttered parchment paper.

5. Unmold the mousselines onto individual plates. At the last minute add the walnuts to the hot sauce without patting them dry and whisk well to homogenize the walnut oil into the sauce. Add parsley, correct the final

seasoning, and spoon over the mousselines. Decorate each plate with a small bouquet of parsley.

Mousselines of trouts of all types:

One word of caution as far as trout is concerned: it must be "freshness personified": the eyes must be like black diamonds and slightly bloodshot, the gills bright red, and the natural covering of algae that trout gather when floating in any clean body of water detectable on the fish. The trout will slip out of the hand and try to escape somewhere on the kitchen counter. Do not try to wash away the slippery stuff; it simply will not be washed. Instead, hold the trout by the tail and wipe it off with paper towels.

When you prepare the fish fumet for the sauce, make sure that in addition to the necessary poundage of fish fumet bones you also add all the trout heads and bones your fish market can give you.

If salmon trout cannot be found, use any sweetwater trout or lake trout. Lake trout, as found in the cold northern New England lakes by family fishermen, are the very best, quickly followed by brown trout.

All the sauces given for the preceding salmon and pike recipes will also be excellent with any trout.

MOUSSELINES DE TRUITE A LA SAVOYARDE
{Mousselines of Trout with Chervil and Hazelnuts}

This is the dish I cooked for the first company to visit my new Annecy dwelling. It was made with the wealth of fresh hazelnut and chervil I found on the market. The sauce is also excellent on sole or halibut mousseline. To prepare it I used our local Crepy, a happy, "spritzig" mountain wine.

MOUSSELINES:

1 pound trout meat, preferably brook or brown, without skin or bones
2 eggs
10 tablespoons butter

1 ½ teaspoons salt
35 turns of the pepper mill
4 gratings of nutmeg
2½ cups heavy cream, well chilled

SAUCE:

1½ cups Fish Fumet, preferably
    prepared with trout heads and
    bones (p. 28)
⅔ cup dry white wine (Mâcon,
    Entre-deux-Mers, Alsace Riesling)
6 very fine-chopped shallots
2 tablespoons chopped chervil stems
Small bouquet garni (see p. 82)
3 tablespoons unsalted butter

1 tablespoon hazelnut oil
4 tablespoons "noisette" butter, well
    clarified (see p. 48)*
3 tablespoons fine-chopped toasted
    hazelnuts
¼ cup fine-chopped chervil
Salt
Pepper from the mill

1. Process the trout meat and the eggs in the food processor until a smooth purée results. Strain through a tamis sieve and deep chill for 2 hours. Cream 8 tablespoons of the butter with the salt, pepper, and nutmeg, and gradually add the fish meat, then the heavy cream. Keep refrigerated until ready to use.

2. To prepare the sauce, mix the fish fumet, white wine, shallots, and chervil stems and reduce to ½ cup of solids and liquids combined. Strain to obtain approximately ⅓ cup of reduction. Place the reduction in a small pot over low heat; whisk in the butter, then the hazelnut oil, and the clarified "noisette" butter. Keep warm until ready to use.

3. Preheat the oven to 325°F. Butter the ramekins or timbales with the remaining 2 tablespoons of butter; pack the trout mousseline into the ramekins. Cover each ramekin with buttered parchment paper and bake for 14–17 minutes in a hot water bath. Unmold onto warm plates as soon as done.

4. Whisk the sauce energetically for a minute or so, then add the chopped hazelnuts and chervil and correct the final seasoning with salt and pepper. Spoon the sauce over the mousselines.

* Sauces made with "noisette" butter have a tendency to "break" because the butter had been melted before being added to the reduction. If indeed the sauce should separate, do not worry; simply mix ¼ teaspoon cornstarch into 2 tablespoons heavy cream, mix into the broken sauce, and gently bring to a boil, stirring. The sauce will rehomogenize immediately. In the restaurant, where a larger quantity will be prepared, do not hesitate to stabilize the base with a slurry of cream and cornstarch before adding both butters.

Shellfish mousselines:

I have included here a scallop, a shrimp, and a lobster mousseline. Notice several points that are extremely important:

- The scallops used for mousseline paste are always large deep sea scallops, never the delicious tiny bay scallops that are in season during the late winter months. Large scallops are more collagenous than those tiny sweet things and the best for mousselines; you will find them hungry for cream and liable to absorb a good 3 cups to the pound.

- As already mentioned, even frozen shrimp will make a good mousseline, but, since all frozen fish and shellfish are difficult to handle when making mousselines, you will see me blend ¼ pound fresh scallop with ¾ pound shrimp. You can also use 50 percent of each shellfish if you like. The fish and shellfish add solidity and firmness to the mousseline. Devein the shrimp in the raw state by pulling the black vein out gently so it does not break.

- The recipe for lobster mousseline on page 205 follows basically the proportions of the classic cuisine, but I have added that bit of raw tomalley to the lobster butter that makes a bit of difference in the final taste. You may, in Louisiana and Texas, replace the lobster meat by that wonderful "crawfish," as they say in the Bayou.

- Notice that all sauces prepared for shellfish mousselines contain, as will the sauces for stir-fried and steamed shellfish, a certain amount of clam juice to tie the sauce to the shellfish.

- These shellfish mousselines also make a handsome cold presentation with a small salad and a light mayonnaise-style sauce.

- Good news: the straining of scallop and shrimp mousseline paste is not necessary. Bad news: the straining of lobster is mandatory!

- When I write about the "feet" of the scallop, I mean the tough little muscle attached to the side of each scallop. Remove them, but do not discard them; always add them to your sauce ingredients to tie the sauce and the scallops together, for the "feet" are as flavorful as they are tough.

MOUSSELINE DE GAMBAS A LA TOMATE
{Mousseline of Shrimp with Tomato Saffron Sauce}

In Europe, I use the Mediterranean Gambas, in the U.S.A., those wonderful Louisiana jumbo shrimp. If you can find shrimp with their heads on, as in Louisiana and Texas, use them. In other areas, buy large shrimp and use the tail shell.

SERVES 6–8 AS A MAIN COURSE;
14–16 AS A FIRST COURSE

MOUSSELINES:

1/4 pound deep sea scallops without "feet" (see p. 201)
3/4 pound raw, deveined shrimp, net weight without shells (reserve shells)
2 egg whites

8 tablespoons butter
1 3/4 teaspoons salt
40 turns of the pepper mill
A pinch of cayenne pepper
5 gratings of nutmeg
2 1/2 cups heavy cream

SAUCE:

2 onions, chopped fine
1 clove garlic, crushed
1 tablespoon olive oil
1 pound sun-ripened tomatoes, unpeeled, seeded, and cut up
1 teaspoon each fresh chopped basil, tarragon, chives, and fennel seeds
1/4 teaspoon each dried rosemary, oregano, and thyme
1/2 a Turkish bay leaf
A tiny pinch of sugar

Salt
Pepper
1 1/4 cups Fish Fumet (p. 28)
1/4 cup clam juice
1/2 cup dry vermouth
3 shallots, chopped fine
The reserved shrimp shells
8 tablespoons butter
10 saffron threads
3 tablespoons scallion rings, cut slantwise

1. Cut up the scallops and shrimp and put them in the food processor. Add the egg whites and process until very, very smooth. There is no need to strain. Chill the mixture for 2 hours. Cream 6 tablespoons of the butter with the salt, pepper, cayenne, and nutmeg. Gradually add the shellfish paste and beat until elastic. Turn the mixer down to low speed and gradually add the

heavy cream. Test the dough by poaching a quenelle (see p. 191), and do not hesitate to add a bit more cream if the mousseline paste is too sturdy when cooked. Keep chilled until ready to use.

2. To prepare the sauce, brown the onion and garlic in the olive oil; add the tomatoes and all the herbs, fresh and dried, plus the bay leaf, the sugar, and a bit of salt and pepper. Cook until approximately ⅔ cup of thin, very fluid tomato purée is left. Strain it through a very fine strainer and set it aside.

3. Mix the fish fumet, clam juice, dry vermouth, chopped shallots, and shrimp shells and reduce to ⅔ cup of liquid. Strain into the pot containing the tomato purée and simmer together until 1 cup of good sauce is left. Bring it to a high boil and, tablespoon by tablespoon, whisk in the butter. Correct the seasoning with salt and pepper. Keep warm.

4. Preheat the oven to 325°F. Butter the chosen ramekins with the remaining 2 tablespoons butter and pack the mousseline paste into them. Cover them with buttered parchment paper and bake in a hot water bath. Remove from the oven as soon as done and invert onto warm plates.

5. Just before serving the sauce, reheat it very well and add the saffron threads and 2 tablespoons of the scallion rings. Spoon the sauce around the mousselines and dot the top of each with 2 or 3 scattered scallion rings.

PETITES MOUSSES DE COQUILLES SAINT-JACQUES AU CURRY ET AUX AVOCATS
{Mousselines of Scallops with Curry and Avocados}

You need very fresh curry. Its taste should be a hint rather than a statement. Use this for a first course—it's too rich to be a main course.

SERVES 8 AS A FIRST COURSE

MOUSSELINES:
½ pound deep sea scallops, net weight without "feet" (reserve feet)
1 egg white
½ teaspoon salt
½ a mashed anchovy
16 turns of the pepper mill
A pinch of cayenne pepper
4 tablespoons butter
1½ cups heavy cream
32 parsley sprigs
32 macadamia nuts

S A U C E :

The reserved scallop "feet"　　　　　*2 tablespoons heavy cream*
1⅓ cups Fish Fumet (p. 28)　　　　*½ teaspoon cornstarch*
⅓ cup clam juice　　　　　　　　*½–¾ teaspoon fresh curry powder*
½ cup dry white wine　　　　　　*8 tablespoons unsalted butter*
1 large onion, chopped fine　　　　*2 tablespoons sour cream*
2 shallots, chopped fine　　　　　*32 thin avocado slices*
Small bouquet garni (see p. 82)

1. Put the scallops and egg white in the food processor and process until smooth. Deep chill for 2 hours. Mix the salt, anchovy, pepper, and cayenne pepper with the butter, and cream together until homogeneous. Add the scallop purée very gradually; as soon as well homogenized, add the heavy cream. You must use all that cream or the texture will not be airy enough. Keep chilled until ready to bake.

2. To prepare the sauce, put the "feet" of the scallops, the fumet, clam juice, white wine, onion, shallots, and bouquet garni into a saucepan and reduce to approximately ¾ cup. Strain well through a "China cap" sieve. Mix the heavy cream and the starch. Bring the sauce base to a boil, turn it down to a simmer, and stir in the cream-and-cornstarch slurry. Keep hot. Heat the curry powder and 6 tablespoons of the butter together in a small saucepan and cook the curry a few minutes. Bring the sauce back to a boil and add the curry butter. Turn down to a simmer and add the sour cream, whisking well to homogenize. Keep warm.

3. Preheat the oven to 325°F. Grease sixteen 1-ounce timbales with the 2 remaining tablespoons of the butter from the sauce ingredients. Pack the mousseline into the small timbales, cover them with buttered parchment paper, and bake in a hot water bath for 11–12 minutes.

4. Heat the avocado slices extremely quickly in the 2 remaining tablespoons of the butter from the sauce ingredients.

5. Unmold 2 small mousselines onto each plate. Arrange 1 slice of avocado around each, placing the mousse where the avocado pit was and with the tips of each avocado slice going in opposite directions. Spoon a bit of sauce over each mousseline and top with a tiny sprig of parsley and 1 macadamia nut.

MOUSSELINES DE HOMARD A LA MEMOIRE DE PROSPER MONTAGNE
{Mousselines of Lobster in Memory of Prosper Montagné}

Monsieur Montagné is for me the true genius of the classic cuisine between 1900 and 1935. His food presentations were already infinitely more modern than those of Escoffier, and his sauces *thickened with only emulsified butter* already plentiful when everyone else was still using flour all over the place.

Buy the additional lobster claws needed already cooked from your fish market. A large female lobster is an imperative for the mousseline.

SERVES 8 AS A MAIN COURSE

MOUSSELINES:

1 pound lobster meat from a female lobster (use the tail of one large 2½-pound specimen)

½ tablespoon each tomalley and coral (reserve remainder for sauce)

2 egg whites

¾–1 teaspoon salt

35 turns of the pepper mill

⅛ teaspoon cayenne pepper

2 cups heavy cream

2 tablespoons butter

SAUCES AND GARNISHES:

2½ cups Fish Fumet (p. 28)

½ cup clam juice

1 cup Champagne Brut or excellent Chablis or Meursault, or California Chardonnay

The lobster head, crushed

6 shallots, chopped very fine

1 tablespoon chopped parsley stems

1 tablespoon each chopped tarragon and chervil

1 clove garlic, mashed

¼ cup tomato purée

1½ cups heavy cream, reduced to ¾ cup

Reserved lobster tomalley and coral

10 tablespoons unsalted butter

2 zucchini, cut into ¼-inch by ½-inch beads

4 tablespoons clarified butter

1 pound finished Puff Pastry (p. 461)

1 egg yolk

3 tablespoons milk

1 ounce Cognac or Armagnac

1 ounce beluga caviar (optional)

14 cooked lobster claws

1. Place the lobster meat, tomalley, and coral in the food processor with the egg whites. Process until as smooth as possible. The mixture will look downright awful, semiliquid and unsteady. Don't worry. Strain it through a tamis sieve directly into the bowl of your electric mixer and deep chill for 2 hours. Add ¾ teaspoon salt, the pepper, and cayenne to the heavy cream, and chill this in the refrigerator, then in the freezer for 20 minutes before using it. Beat the chilled seasoned cream on low speed into the puréed lobster meat until it has been completely absorbed. Taste for seasoning and add more salt if necessary. I have never used more than a scant teaspoon. Keep chilled until ready to use.

2. To prepare the sauce, mix the fish fumet, clam juice, white wine, the crushed lobster head (well cleaned of its bag, which is found just behind the eyes), the shallots, parsley, tarragon, chervil, garlic, and tomato purée and reduce to ⅔ cup liquid. Strain into a clean pot, mix with the reduced cream, and simmer together a few minutes.

3. Process the remainder of the raw coral and tomalley and the butter to obtain lobster butter. Strain through a stainless steel strainer. Set aside.

4. Sauté the zucchini beads in 2 tablespoons of the clarified butter until they turn bright green. Keep in the skillet.

5. Preheat the oven to 425°F. Roll out the puff pastry into a rectangle ⅛ inch thick and as large as possible. Cut 8 large triangles. Cut through the edges of the triangles with a paring knife to make a decorative border. Brush them with a mixture of the egg yolk and milk and "score" with a fork. Bake for 25 minutes until nicely puffed. Keep lukewarm. Lower the oven temperature to 325°F.

6. Butter the ramekins of your choice with the 2 tablespoons butter. Fill them to within ½ inch of the top with the mousseline batter. Bake, covered with buttered parchment paper, in a hot water bath for 14–17 minutes. Remove from oven and keep warm in the water bath until you finish the sauce.

7. Bring the sauce to a boil, remove it from the heat, and whisk in the lobster butter. Reheat without boiling. Heat the Cognac or Armagnac, light it, and whisk it while flaming into the sauce. Strain into a clean pot in which you have placed the caviar, if used, and the zucchini. Keep hot. Cook the 2 raw lobster claws by steaming them for 8 minutes. Shell them, add them to the 14 cooked lobster claws.

8. Gently reheat all the cooked lobster claws in the remaining 2 tablespoons

clarified butter. Slice the pastry triangles in half crosswise to obtain a bottom and a top. Unmold each mousseline onto the bottom of a triangle. Sauce the mousselines, place the upper part of the triangle askew on top, and put a lobster claw on either side of each triangle, so that the arrangement looks like a crab. Sprinkle a few zucchini beads between the claws and serve promptly.

Timing notes:
- Prepare the puff pastry as long as a week ahead of time. Cut triangles and freeze them. Preheat the oven to 425°F. Brush triangles with egg mixture. Reduce the oven to 400°F. and bake triangles still frozen just before you bake the mousselines.
- Prepare the mousseline paste and the zucchini beads the day before. Keep chilled.
- Prepare the sauce base either the day before or in the morning. Keep chilled.
- Prepare the lobster butter the day before. Keep chilled.

Cold mousselines and mousses:
Although I very much prefer them served hot, all the mousselines and mousses in this section can be served cold to make a very handsome first course. For this purpose, you can bake them in small individual containers or in larger glass loaf pans lined with parchment paper and cut them into slices for serving.

The best way to serve a cold mousse is with a little salad that will blend well with the fish used and a very fluid and flowing mayonnaise well flavored with herbs and aromatics. All mousselines can be served cold, but salmon and scallop mousses taste better than pike or trout mousselines.

A. *For cold salmon mousse, use:*
- An asparagus garnish and coriander and dill mayonnaise.
- A garnish of spinach and lightly blanched carrot curls with a fluid mayonnaise strongly flavored with scallions.
- A garnish of fine julienne of zucchini and yellow squash and a basil mayonnaise
- A fine cucumber garnish with a very lightly minted mayonnaise.

B. *For cold scallop mousse, use*:
- A small garnish of red, yellow, and green pepper with a plain anchovy, basil, olive oil, and vinegar dressing.
- A zucchini and radish garnish with a fluid fine herb mayonnaise flavored with shallot.
- A tomato and green bean garnish with a lightly tomatoed mayonnaise garnished with extremely fine-scissored basil.
- A mixed, blanched julienne of vegetables with a lightly curried mayonnaise.
- A papaya and avocado garnish with a lime, garlic, olive oil, and vinegar dressing.

QUICK FISH-COOKING TECHNIQUES IN MODERN FRENCH CUISINE

Here is a collection of recipes for simple, quickly executed fish dishes. You will find the recipes grouped by techniques of cookery, and I have listed at the beginning of each recipe all the other fish that can be used throughout the United States.

1. Poissons à la vapeur (steaming in a steamer):

Steaming is becoming very popular in France, although it took our people quite a few years to catch up with the Chinese, who have cooked according to the "jing" (steaming) method for several centuries. French people became aware of the value of steamers in the kitchen when the Pieds-Noirs came back from Algeria with their couscoussiers. A few very serious chefs who traveled to the Far East have adopted the method and obtained some wonderfully simple and delicious fish dishes. Steaming is deceptively easy, so much so that it is not easy at all and requires the complete attention of the cook. Here are a few guidelines:

- Although steamed scallops are universally praised, scallops should not be steamed, because they develop that tiny little film of overcooked fibers on their outside, which contrasts unpleasantly with their tender inside. In this book we shall only stir fry scallops, and you can find the recipes on pages 238–44.

- Fish steaks are easily and quickly steamed. However, they, like scallops, can become overcooked on the outside. If you steam fish steaks, you will want to protect them with a layer of vegetable leaves, a buttered parchment, or even a wrapping of clear plastic, which will prevent the steam from damaging the texture of the outside tissues.
- The best fish to steam are whole small ones such as red mullet, butterfish, or trout, which are protected from the steam by their skins. When the skins crack open you know the fish is ready.

Be extremely attentive when you steam fish; steaming it for 30 seconds too long will result in your dinner's turning into an irretrievably tough and fibrous disaster.

The following average cooking times apply:

- Trout, whole: 12 minutes
- Red mullet (*rouget barbet, triglia, barbouni*), whole: 7 minutes
- Salmon steaks: 7 minutes, ¾ inch thick
                    8 minutes, 1 inch thick
- Haddock steaks: 7 minutes, ¾ inch thick
- Cod steaks: 8 minutes, ¾ inch thick
- Mackerel, whole: 15 minutes. Fillets: 5 minutes.
- Snapper, whole: 30 minutes. Fillets: 8 minutes.

Steamed fish requires only a small pat of compound butter or a few tablespoons of cream to sauce it. It is excellent for people on low-fat diets, who can skip the fat but still find full flavor.

It is recommended that you flavor the steaming water to add delicate flavor to the fish.

MARINADE DE DORADE DES PIEDS-NOIRS
{Red Snapper Fillets Marinated in an Arabic Dressing}

This recipe is also good with Gulf red fish, mackerel, haddock, or striped bass fillets.

SERVES 6

1 tablespoon lemon juice
3 tablespoons wine vinegar
1 tablespoon Dijon mustard
1 small red onion, chopped fine
1 teaspoon sweet paprika
A pinch of cayenne pepper
1 teaspoon ground coriander
½ teaspoon cumin powder

⅓ teaspoon each grated orange and
  lemon rind
1 teaspoon salt
Pepper from the mill
1 cup excellent virgin olive oil
2 lemons
Several large bouquets of fresh
  coriander
12 fillets of red snapper

1. Put lemon juice, vinegar, Dijon mustard, chopped red onion, paprika, cayenne, coriander, cumin, citrus rind, salt, and pepper in a bowl. Mix well and whisk in the olive oil. Let stand for 2 hours.

2. Cut the lemons in paper-thin slices, place them on a plate, and sprinkle them generously with salt. Let steep for 2 hours and pat dry.

3. Cut the stems from the coriander bouquets and chop them. Reserve the coriander leaves. Pour one-third of the dressing into a ½-quart baking dish. Pour ½ inch of water into the bottom container of the steamer, add the chopped stems of the fresh coriander, and bring to a boil.

4. Line the steamer basket with some fresh coriander leaves, place the snapper, 3 fillets at a time, seasoned with salt and pepper, in the steamer basket and cover them with more coriander leaves. Cover with the steamer lid and set to steam over the boiling coriander water for 5 minutes. Remove from the heat and transfer to the baking dish. Repeat the same operation until all the fillets are used. Pour the rest of the marinade over the fillets. Dot the fillets with the lemon slices and refrigerate for 24 hours.

FILETS DE HADDOCK A LA CREME
ET AU LARD {Finnan Haddie Fillets with Bacon Cream}

The steam here will soften the smoke-hardened outside of the finnan haddie, and the tea will sustain its smoky flavor. Plain Haddock can also be used; steam them 4–5 minutes.

SERVES 6

3 rashers of bacon	2 tablespoons chopped parsley
1 cup heavy cream	2 fillets of finnan haddie
Salt	1 leek (green part only), chopped
Pepper from the mill	1 teaspoon Lapsang Souchong tea

1. Render the bacon in a skillet until golden. Crumble it; discard the fat from the frying pan, deglaze with the cream, and reduce to ⅔ cup. Add salt if needed, pepper from the mill, and chopped parsley.
2. Place the fillets of finnan haddie in the steamer basket. Bring 2 inches of water to a boil in the bottom container of the steamer, add the leeks and tea. Simmer for 5 minutes.
3. Put the steamer basket over the simmering water and close its lid. Steam the fillets for approximately 6 minutes (check every minute after the first 5) and serve topped with the bacon and parsley cream.

FILETS DE CABILLAUD AU BEURRE D'AULX
{Fillets of Scrod Steamed with Garlic Butter}

Red snapper, red fish from the Gulf, or fillets of striped bass can also be used.

SERVES 6

25 cloves garlic	Pepper from the mill
½ cup Secondary Stock (p. 23) or water	6 tablespoons butter, creamed
	1½ pounds scrod or young cod fillets
1½ tablespoons chopped parsley	6 Boston lettuce leaves
Salt	1 teaspoon garlic powder

1. Peel and cook 12 of the garlic cloves in the secondary stock or water until you have 1½ tablespoons heavily reduced garlic purée. Cool. Mash another garlic clove and add it to the purée with the parsley. Mash all together well with salt and pepper. Add to the creamed butter. Mix well and set aside.
2. Season the pieces of scrod with salt and pepper. Peel the remaining 12 cloves of garlic, cut into slivers, and apply regularly over the top and bottom surfaces of scrod. Wrap each piece in a lettuce leaf.

3. Bring 1½ inches of water to a boil in the bottom of the steamer. Add the garlic powder. Arrange the 6 packages of fish in the basket of the steamer. Fit over the boiling water, cover with the lid, and steam for 8 minutes.

4. Remove each lettuce leaf and all the garlic slivers from the pieces of fish and top each with a tablespoon of the garlic butter.

2. "Pansteaming" in a heavy, covered skillet:

This is a personal method I have used more and more during the last few years; it is quick and produces a wonderful, moist fish.

The method consists of brushing the skillet with melted clarified butter or with oil, heating it well, quickly sealing one side of the fish, turning it over, quickly sealing the second side, seasoning with salt and pepper, covering the pan, and letting the fish steam off the heat in its own juices until done. It takes a minimum amount of time; the fish is buttered with plain or compound butter or sauced with a very quickly prepared sauce or dressing.

FILETS DE TASSERGAL AU BEURRE DE SAUMON FUME (Bluefish with Smoked Salmon Butter)

Also good with salmon, salmon trout, or fillets of any sweetwater trout.

SERVES 6

6 tablespoons butter
2 slices of Nova Scotia smoked
    salmon
Salt
Pepper from the mill

1½ tablespoons clarified butter
Six 4-ounce fillets of bluefish
2 tablespoons chopped fresh parsley
Lemon wedges

1. Mash together the butter and the Nova Scotia salmon until perfectly smooth. Add as much salt as needed and pepper from the mill.

2. Brush the skillet with clarified butter. Heat it until hot but not smoking. Sear the first side of each bluefish fillet, turn over, salt and pepper and sear the second side. Cover the skillet, remove it from the heat and let stand for 7–8 minutes, until the fish has poached all the way to its center.

3. Top each piece of fish with a tablespoon or so of smoked salmon butter and a sprinkling of parsley. Serve with a lemon wedge on each plate.

TRANCHES DE SAUMON TIEDES A LA VINAIGRETTE DE NOIX OU DE NOISETTES
{Salmon Slices with Walnut or Hazelnut Vinaigrette}

Use either walnut or hazelnut oil, depending on which nuts you have chosen. You can cut either one with corn oil, if you wish to save expense.

SERVES 6

7 tablespoons walnut or hazelnut oil
6 salmon medallions, ¾ inch thick
  (see p. 225)
Salt
Pepper from the mill
2 shallots, chopped very fine
2 tablespoons fine-chopped walnuts
  or chopped toasted hazelnuts

1½ tablespoons Aceto Balsamico
  (p. 45) or 1 tablespoon sherry
  mixed with ½ tablespoon cider
  vinegar
2 tablespoons chopped parsley

1. Brush the skillet with 1 tablespoon of the oil. Heat it well. Sear the salmon pieces on one side. Turn over, season with salt and pepper, and sear on the second side. Cover and let the fish cook in the hot pan, in its own juices and off the heat, for 6–8 minutes. Remove to a dish.
2. To the skillet add the remaining 6 tablespoons of the oil. Squeeze the shallots in the corner of a towel and add them. Add the walnuts or hazelnuts, depending upon which oil you have used, the vinegar, and salt and pepper. Whisk well to homogenize and pour evenly over the pieces of fish. Sprinkle with parsley. Serve lukewarm or marinate overnight to serve cold the next day.

3. Poissons en papillotes (steaming fish in foil):
This method of cooking allows you to prepare fish without fats if you desire. For maximum taste you can add, in the foil, all the possible herbs you desire,

as well as tomato slices or a tomato fondue. If you have no diet problems, do not hesitate to add a dose of cream to your foil package; you will find that a wonderful sauce builds during the baking, which lasts 10–12 minutes.

You can steam by putting your foil packages in a jelly roll pan and baking in a 375°F. oven, or, if you prefer to save the energy, you can put a small, square cake rack into an electric frying pan filled with ½ inch of water and tightly close the lid of the frying pan. The baking lasts 10 minutes for a steak and 10–14 minutes for a whole small fish, depending on size.

TRUITES A L'AUTRICHIENNE
{Fillets of Trout the Austrian Way}

This dish can also be done with fillets of ocean perch or whole trout. For the fat-controlled version, use the corn oil; for the regular version, use the butter.

SERVES 6

12 fillets of trout	*Pepper from the mill*
1 carrot	*2 tablespoons chopped fresh dill weed*
1 leek	*2 tablespoons cider vinegar*
1 large purple top turnip	*6 tablespoons heavy cream (optional)*
6 gherkins, preserved without sugar	*3 tablespoons sour cream (optional)*
1 tablespoon corn oil or 2 tablespoons	*6 parsley sprigs*
butter	*6 scalloped lemon slices*
Salt	

1. Put the fillets of trout, two by two, on a plastic chopping board.
2. Cut carrot, leek, turnip, and gherkins into a very fine julienne. Heat the oil or butter in a skillet and sauté the julienne until semitender. Season with salt and pepper and add 1 tablespoon dill. Cool. As soon as cooled, sandwich equal portions of the mixture between 2 fillets.
3. Preheat the oven to 375°F. Place each trout sandwich on a large square of foil set dull side down. Top it, only if you want, with 1 tablespoon heavy cream mixed with ½ tablespoon sour cream; in any case, season with salt and pepper and sprinkle with the remaining tablespoon of the dill. Fold

the foil, seal tightly, and bake for 10 minutes in a jelly roll pan in the oven or in a well-sealed electric frying pan as indicated in the generalities on page 214.

4. To serve, slide the contents of each package onto a warm plate and add a sprig of parsley and a lemon slice.

LOTTE AUX POIREAUX ET AU VIN ROUGE
{Monkfish with Leeks and Red Wine}

Halibut, striped bass, black bass, or carp can also be used.

SERVES 6

10 leeks (white and light green part only), sliced thin
2 tablespoons butter
1 cup Secondary Stock (p. 23)
1 cup red Médoc wine (or any red wine that will not turn blue while cooking)
1½ tablespoons light raisins

1 tablespoon red wine vinegar
Salt
Pepper from the mill
6 fillets of monkfish, each 4 ounces and ¾ inch thick, cleaned of all fibrous tissues
6 tablespoons heavy cream (optional)
Chopped parsley

1. Blanch the leeks for 2–3 minutes in boiling water. Drain well. Heat the butter in a skillet, add the leeks, and cook until translucent. Add stock and wine. Cook until a "compote" of very overcooked leeks results. Meanwhile soak the raisins in the vinegar. When the compote is ready, mix in the soured raisins. Add salt and pepper and cool.

2. Place 6 squares of foil dull side down on the kitchen counter. Put one-twelfth of the leek mixture on each piece of foil. Top with a piece of monkfish seasoned with salt and pepper; top each piece of fish with another twelfth of the compote and, if you use it, 1 tablespoon cream. Close the foil by folding it over to seal it.

3. Preheat the oven to 375°F. Place the foil packages on a jelly roll pan and bake for no more than 10 minutes. Slide the contents of each foil package onto a warm plate and sprinkle with chopped parsley.

STEAKS DE SAUMON AUX CORNICHONS FRAIS {Salmon Steaks with Fresh Pickles}

This can also be made with fillets of larger salmon trout.

SERVES 6

6 salmon steaks, preferably shaped into medallions (see p. 225) ¾ inch thick	2 tablespoons butter
Salt	6 teaspoons fresh chopped tarragon
Pepper from the mill	6 tablespoons heavy cream, reduced to 3 tablespoons
6 smallish fresh pickling cucumbers	3 tablespoons sour cream

1. Place 6 squares of foil dull side down on the counter.
2. Season the salmon pieces with salt and pepper. Cut the cucumbers into paper-thin slices and stir fry them for 1 minute in the butter. Season with salt and pepper. Cool. Add the tarragon.
3. Preheat the oven to 375°F. Place the salmon pieces on the prepared pieces of foil and top each with some of the cucumber mixture. Mix the 2 creams and spoon equal amounts onto each piece of fish.
4. Close the foil packages hermetically and bake for 10 minutes in the oven or in a tightly closed electric frying pan, as suggested on page 214. To serve, slide the contents of each package onto a warm plate.

4. Poissons grillés (grilled fish):

Le "Grill" has become the most beloved little implement of the modern French kitchen; there are old-fashioned iron grills, cast iron grills, Teflonized grills, and even double electric grills allowing cooks to prepare very attractive-looking fillets or steaks of fish that are as succulent as they are appetizing. All you need at home is one of those grill pans with a ribbed surface: the ribs sear the fish and brown it attractively while any fat dribbling into the small canals between the ribbing can be poured out. It is essential that the fish be brushed with either plain excellent olive (or corn) oil or with a mixture of oil and clarified butter, so it does not stick to the pan.

It is preferable to use fish with a very rich texture such as monkfish, tuna, bluefish, swordfish, or salmon. The thickness of the fillets or steaks should not be less than ¾ inch and no more than 1 inch.

People on a diet can simply enjoy the steaks with lemon juice and fresh herbs, while those without dietary problems can prepare some lovely compound butter. A few examples follow.

Note that all recipes given here for the grill can also be executed in a broiler, placing the fish 4 inches away from the radiating heat element, be it electricity or charcoal.

FILET DE THON AU BEURRE DE GIGONDAS
{Tuna Fillet with Gigondas Butter}

SERVES 4

GIGONDAS BUTTER:

1½ cups Gigondas or excellent Côtes-du-Rhône	1 tablespoon chopped parsley stems
5 cloves garlic, mashed	8 tablespoons unsalted butter
2 anchovies, mashed	2 tablespoons chopped parsley
A pinch of thyme	Salt, only if needed
½ a bay leaf	Pepper from the mill

FISH:

1 large fillet of tuna, 1½–2 pounds, or two 1-inch-thick slices of bonito	Pepper from the mill
2 tablespoons olive or corn oil	6 parsley bouquets
Salt	6 scalloped lemon slices

1. Reduce the wine, garlic, anchovies, thyme, bay leaf, and chopped parsley stems to approximately 2 tablespoons good glaze. Cream the butter and whisk into it the wine glaze, adding the 2 tablespoons chopped parsley. Correct the seasoning with salt and pepper and store in a little bowl.
2. Brush the fish and the grill with oil. Heat the grill over medium-high heat. Sear both sides of the fish well, seasoning the seared side each time. If the fish is thickish, you may put a lid over the grill during the last 3–4 minutes

of cooking to force the heat to the center of the piece of fish. Remove from the grill, let stand a few minutes, and slice across into ⅙-inch-thick slices that should look bright pink. Any dark-looking meat is undercooked; any "gray"-looking meat is overcooked.

3. Serve several slices of fillet per portion. Spread each serving with a large tablespoon of Gigondas butter and garnish with a parsley bouquet and a slice of scalloped lemon.

ESPADON AU BEURRE BEAUNOIS
{Swordfish and Mustard Butter}

This is also good made with ¾-inch-thick halibut steaks, thick lemon sole fillets or ¾-inch-thick monkfish steaks. Serve half a swordfish steak per person.

SERVES 6

3 swordfish steaks 1 inch thick,
    4 inches wide, and 6–7 inches long
2 tablespoons olive or corn oil
Salt
Pepper from the mill
8 tablespoons unsalted butter

1½–2 tablespoons extra-strong
    Dijon mustard
1 large clove garlic, mashed
1½ tablespoons chopped parsley
¼ teaspoon freshly grated nutmeg
6 parsley bouquets
6 lemon wedges

1. Brush the fish steaks and the grill with oil and heat the grill over medium-high heat. Sear the steaks for 2 minutes on the first side. Season the seared side with salt and pepper, turn, and sear for 2 minutes on the second side. Turn the heat down and cook for another 2 minutes on each side. Put a lid on the grill for the last 2 minutes of cooking.

2. Meanwhile, cream the butter, add the Dijon mustard, garlic, chopped parsley, nutmeg, salt to your taste, and pepper from the mill and pack into a small bowl.

3. Serve the swordfish portions boned and skinned on warm plates, topping each serving with a portion of compound butter. Add a small parsley bouquet and a lemon wedge.

TRANCHES DE SAUMON GRILLEES
AU BEURRE D'EAU DE MER
{Grilled Salmon Steak with Seawater Butter}

If you live at the seashore (an unpolluted shore!) do not hesitate to use ½ cup seawater. The recipe can be used also for swordfish, halibut, or lobster tails.

SERVES 6

6 salmon steaks	*10 tablespoons butter*
2 tablespoons olive or corn oil	*A large pinch each of grated lime*
Salt	*and lemon rinds*
Pepper from the mill	*½ teaspoon very coarsely cracked*
½ cup water	*black pepper*
⅓ teaspoon salt	*6 parsley bouquets*
The pulp of ½ a lemon, diced fine	

1. Brush the salmon and the grill with the oil. Sear the salmon steaks for 2 minutes on one side, season with salt and pepper, turn over, and sear on the second side for 2 minutes. Season again. Turn the heat down and finish cooking for another 2–3 minutes, covering the steaks with a lid during the last minute to force the heat to the center.
2. Put water, the ⅓ teaspoon salt, and the lemon pulp into a small saucepan and reduce to 2 tablespoons liquid. Turn the heat to very low, whisk the butter into the saucepan, tablespoon by tablespoon, and strain into a warm bowl. Add lemon and lime rinds and cracked pepper. You probably will not need any more salt.
3. Serve the steaks skinned on warm plates. Spoon equal portions of butter onto each steak and garnish with a parsley bouquet.

5. *Poissons cuits à la poële (panfried fish):*
To prepare these, you might want to have one of those wonderfully quick-cooking frying pans made of stainless steel with a reinforced cast aluminum bottom. Use one or even two 10-inch pans.

The best medium to use for panfrying fish is clarified butter or oil (corn or olive) or a fifty-fifty mixture of each. The clarification of the butter is a must for the final look of panfried items. The food to be panfried must be coated with the thinnest veil of seasoned flour. The choice of fish must be such that it will cook almost as it sears, so thin fillets or thin whole fish are recommended. I have simply stated fish fillets, then listed those that are applicable to each recipe. If you use whole fish, they must be small so that they will cook in no more than 6–8 minutes. Fish steaks can also be done this way, but they should be no more than ¾ inch thick. I have included here two recipes for soft-shell crabs, since the panfrying technique is the very best for them.

TRUITES DE L'AVEYRON {Panfried Trout with Pancetta}

This recipe can be made with whole trout or fillets of trout. The whole trout is more in character with the mountain origin of the recipe, which comes from the area of Millau and Roquefort.

SERVES 6

6 trout, cleaned but heads left on for
   presentation
3 tablespoons flour, seasoned with
   salt and pepper
2 tablespoons each clarified butter
   and olive oil

3 ounces pancetta, diced into ¼-inch
   cubes
2 cloves garlic, chopped very fine
2 tablespoons chopped parsley

1. Roll the fish into the seasoned flour. Heat the clarified butter and oil over medium-high heat. Sear the fish on both sides, turn the heat down to medium, and finish cooking 2 minutes more on each side. Remove the fish to a platter and keep warm.
2. In the same pan (if the fat is too brown, discard and replace it), cook the *pancetta* until light golden, then add the garlic and parsley. As soon as these have browned, pour the mixture over the trout. The skin is so good and crisp that one should be able to eat it, as the Aveyron people do.

Note: The *pancetta* should not be crisp. Italian and southern French people like their *pancetta* and bacon just golden, still mellow inside.

FILETS DE POISSON A LA NORMANDE
{Fillets of Fish the Old Normandy Way}

Normandy is fond of its apple cider, shallots, chives, and cream. The sauce used here goes back at least to the seventeenth century. Use fillets of trout, perch, gray sole, any flounder, large sand dabs, sole petrale, mackerel, or even mussels and shrimp.

SERVES 6

2 tablespoons butter	*1 ¼ cups heavy cream*
6 shallots, chopped fine	*¼ cup corn oil or clarified butter*
⅓ cup cider vinegar (5 percent	*2 tablespoons flour, seasoned with*
* acetic acid)*	* salt and pepper*
Salt	*12 fillets of fish of your choice*
Pepper from the mill	*Chopped parsley*

1. Heat the butter in a skillet. Add the shallots and sauté them until they take on a golden color. Add the vinegar and let it reduce slowly until no liquid is left. Add salt, pepper, and heavy cream and let reduce until approximately ¾ cups well-bound cream results. Correct the seasoning and set aside. *Do not strain.*
2. Heat the oil or clarified butter in 1 or 2 skillets. Flour the fillets quickly with the seasoned flour and cook in the very hot fat for 2 minutes on each side. Drain on paper towels. Remove to warm plates, sauce with the shallot-and-vinegar reduction, and sprinkle with chopped parsley.

Panfried soft-shell crabs:
Of the 2 recipes for crab that follow, the quickest one is that from Martinique. It requires no sauce—only fruit, curry, and crab. The other recipe will demand a little more of your time and of your funds, but it is a wonderful main course for the spring months. Note that, although they can be prepared with small frozen crabs, thrown *solidly frozen* into the frying pan, the two dishes reach peak flavor only if you use live crabs. Sorry, crab lovers, this is a fact of life, and if your butter is nice and hot, the poor beasts are dispatched instantly.

CRABES MOUS EN COLOMBO MARTINIQUAIS
{Soft-Shell Crabs with Avocado, Papaya, Lime, and Curry}

Proportions given here are for a first course. If you wish to make the dish a main course, double the papaya and avocado and use 3 crabs per person. A tropical dish to be served warm, never hot.

SERVES 6

8 tablespoons clarified butter
1 tablespoon extremely fresh curry powder
1 large clove garlic, chopped
1 avocado, peeled and cut into 12 slices
1 ripe papaya, peeled, seeded, and cut into 12 slices

3 tablespoons flour
6 live soft-shell crabs
Salt
Pepper from the mill
Lime juice as needed
6 scalloped lime slices

1. Heat the clarified butter and in it cook the curry for 2–3 minutes. Remove from the heat, immediately add the garlic, and let steep while you prepare the remainder of the ingredients.
2. Arrange the avocado and papaya slices on a large plate. Flour the soft-shell crabs and set them in a deep dish.
3. Line up 6 warm luncheon plates on the kitchen counter.
4. Strain half the curry butter into a large skillet and sear the avocado and papaya slices in it. Season with salt and pepper and sprinkle with lime juice. Transfer 2 slices each of avocado and papaya to each warm plate.
5. In another skillet, strain the remainder of the curry butter and panfry the crabs for 2 minutes on each side. Arrange each crab over the fan of fruit slices. Mix the butter in the fruit skillet into the crab cooking butter and add lime juice, salt, and pepper. Mix well and spoon an equal amount over each crab. Garnish with lime slices.

CRABES MOUS A LA VIERGE NOIRE
{Soft-Shell Crabs in Black Virgin Butter}

This is a main course. As garnish, choose a pilaf of wheat (p. 424), grilled or panfried tomatoes, the happy spring jardinière on page 387, and a large parsley bouquet.

SERVES 6

1 cup Fish Fumet (p. 28)
½ cup dry white wine (Muscadet or Mâcon)
4 shallots, chopped fine
1 large onion, chopped fine
⅔ cup heavy cream, reduced to ⅓ cup
1 tablespoon sour cream
8 tablespoons clarified "noisette" butter (see p. 48)

Lemon juice as needed
Salt and pepper
⅓ cup flour
18 soft-shell crabs
6 tablespoons clarified butter or oil of your choice
18 medium asparagus tips, blanched and warm
1 ounce beluga caviar (optional)

1. To prepare the sauce, put the fish fumet, wine, shallots, and onion in a saucepan and reduce to approximately ½ cup. Blend this reduction with the ⅓ cup reduced heavy cream and the sour cream. Bring to a full boil and whisk in the strained "noisette" butter. Add lemon juice and salt and pepper to your taste. Set aside and keep warm.
2. Flour the soft-shell crabs and pat them smartly to discard any excess flour. Heat the clarified butter in 2 skillets and fry the crabs for 2 minutes on each side.
3. Put 3 crabs on each of 6 warm plates, arranging them along one side, overlapping slightly. Place 1 asparagus tip at the center of each crab on the diagonal. Add the caviar to the sauce, if desired, and spoon the sauce over the soft-shell crabs.

Note: As I have already explained (see footnote, p. 200), sauces made with "noisette" butter have a tendency to separate on standing. If you want to prevent this, mix ⅓ teaspoon cornstarch with the reduced cream and whisk it into the simmering reduction before you add the butter.

6. Poissons pochés au court bouillon
(fish poached in court bouillon):

At the very beginning of this book, on page 31, you will find a recipe for an all-purpose court bouillon, the very flavorful mixture of water, wine, and aromatics in which one poaches fish. A good court bouillon is always very flavorful so as to give the fish it cooks a tasty outside surface. If you have no time to prepare a court bouillon, you may use salted water. Add a generous teaspoon of salt to each quart of water.

The instrument used to poach in a court bouillon is a long fish poacher fitted with a rack.

Techniques of cooking in court bouillon
in the modern French cuisine:

A. *For fish steaks and medallions:* Bring the court bouillon to a rolling boil. Butter the rack. Set the fish steaks or medallions on the rack and brush their surface with soft butter. If, for dietary purposes, you prefer not to use butter at all, wrap the fish steaks or medallions in a piece of "food quality" plastic wrap, such as a small "cook-in" plastic bag opened flat. Both the butter and the plastic wrap protect the surface of the fish from hardening when submitted to the extreme high heat of the court bouillon. If you use the plastic wrap, you need not butter the rack, but you will lose the flavor the court bouillon imparts to the fish, so consider using only salted water.

Immerse the rack in the wildly boiling court bouillon; the liquid will, within a minute or so, come back to a rolling boil. Cover the poacher, remove it from the heat, and let it stand for 7 minutes for steaks and 8 minutes for medallions. This method is a variation on the English "crimping," and I give the credit for it to my English friend Ann Heitman, who learned it in Essex from her mother. It beats all other techniques for poaching in the old-fashioned French manner. The fish remains translucent and extremely moist—not "rare," as so many devotees of nouvelle cuisine want to have it, but cooked just enough so the fibers do not shrink and completely retain all their natural collagenic juices.

B. *For small fish:* Small fish such as trout, red mullet, and larger butterfish should be immersed in the boiling court bouillon exactly as described above and left to stand in it for 12–14 minutes after it comes to a second boil. This method is particularly well adapted to stuffed trout, for which you will find 2 recipes later on in this chapter (pp. 231, 233).

Making salmon steaks into medallions:

It is preferable to use salmon steaks ¾ inch thick—in any case, never more than 1 inch thick. With a small parer, separate the meat from the bone on either side (keep the bone). (Illus. 1) Leaving the 2 sides of the steak flat on the cutting board, pass your index finger over their surface to feel the large bones that are at the thickest part of the meat. Gently pull them off; they will slide out without difficulty. Slide your knife blade between skin and meat to remove the skin and brown tissues completely.

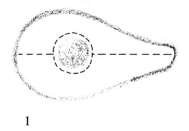

1

The 2 salmon steak halves should face each other, thick part against thick part and with the "belly flap" of the upper one pointing to the right, while the "belly flap" of the lower one now faces to the left, or vice versa. Push the two halves together so as to seal the thick parts together. (Illus. 2) Now wrap the belly flap of the upper part around the bottom half and the belly flap of the bottom part around the upper part, or vice versa. You now have a well-shaped

2   3

oval medallion. (Illus. 3) Using your sharpest parer, gently cut off any remaining brown tissues. Push 4 wooden toothpicks into the medallion so they crisscross at its center and prevent the medallion from falling apart while cooking. Leave ¼ inch of each toothpick peaking out of the salmon meat, so as to be able to pull it easily once the fish has cooked. Always *count* your toothpicks when you remove them to be sure you've got them all.

You may want to use medallions in any of the recipes for salmon steaks. If for a first course a two-sided medallion is too large, make a small one by wrapping each "darne" (each side of the salmon steak) around itself. Toothpicks secure these easily.

Les médaillons de saumon comme chez la mère Madeleine Medallions of Salmon (as presented in my restaurant):

I prefer using Atlantic salmon when the season allows, but the various breeds of Pacific salmon can be used as well.

In addition to the sauces indicated below, you can use any of the sauces or compound butters found in the recipes for salmon steaks and salmon mousses in previous sections of this chapter. The Rhubarb and Citrus Rind Sauce on page 193 is most attractive with medallions.

MEDAILLONS DE SAUMON DU MENAGIER DE PARIS {Medieval Salmon Steak}

I created this recipe after reading the ten or so lines the author of *Le Ménagier de Paris* dedicated in 1392 to the cooking of salmon.

SERVES 6

6 salmon steaks
9 leeks
10 tablespoons butter
2 cups Fish Fumet (p. 28)
4 quarts White Wine and Vinegar
   Court Bouillon (p. 31), ready to
   use
Salt
Pepper from the mill

1 large onion, chopped fine
2 shallots, chopped fine
1 generous tablespoon heavy cream
1 generous tablespoon sour cream
3 slices of bacon, cooked, patted dry,
   and crumbled
6 slices of Nova Scotia smoked
   salmon

1. Skin and bone the salmon steaks and set aside in the refrigerator. Reserve the bones, discard the skins.

2. Cut the white parts of 8 of the leeks at an angle into ¼-inch-thick slices. Blanch them in boiling water for 1 minute. Set 18 slices of leek aside. Sauté the remainder gently in 1 tablespoon of the butter. As soon as they are translucent, add 1 cup of the fish fumet and cook over low heat until a thick purée results. Set aside.

3. Chop the green part of the remaining leek fine. Place the remaining cup of the fish fumet, 1 cup of the court bouillon, the onion, shallots, chopped leek, and the reserved salmon bones into a large saucepan and bring to a boil. Reduce to ½ cup liquid. Strain into the leek purée. Reheat well and strain again into a clean saucepan. Bring to a high boil, whisk in the heavy cream and 6 tablespoons of the butter. Remove from the heat and add the sour cream and the crumbled bacon. Correct the seasoning with salt and pepper and keep warm.

4. Sauté the reserved slices of leeks in 1 tablespoon of the butter until golden.

5. Place a slice of Nova Scotia between the 2 halves of each boned salmon steak and shape them into medallions (see p. 225). Secure with toothpicks (see instructions, p. 226). Butter the poaching rack and the top of the medallions with the remaining 2 tablespoons of butter. Poach in the remaining court bouillon for 7–8 minutes.

6. To serve, place 1 medallion on each warm plate; sauce well, so the sauce covers the bottom of the whole plate, and top each salmon steak with 3 slices of leek arranged in a fleur-de-lis pattern.

MEDAILLONS DE SAUMON PARIS-MILAN
{Medallions of Salmon in Barolo and Gremolata Sauce}

SERVES 6

6 salmon steaks
10 tablespoons butter
4 quarts White Wine and Vinegar
   Court Bouillon (p. 31)
1 ¼ cups excellent old Barolo, Côte-
   Rôtie, Hermitage, or
   Côtes-du-Rhône
¼ cup dry white wine
1 cup Fish Fumet (p. 28)
2 onions, chopped fine
2 shallots, chopped fine
1 leek (white and light green parts
   only), chopped fine

Small bouquet garni (see p. 82)
10 white peppercorns
Salt
Pepper from the mill
⅔ cup heavy cream, reduced to ⅓ cup
2 tablespoons chopped parsley
¼ teaspoon grated orange rind
Grated rind of 1 lemon
1 clove garlic, mashed
1 large anchovy fillet, mashed
1 large zucchini

1. Skin and bone the salmon steaks. Reserve the bones, discard the skins. Shape the steaks into medallions (see p. 225). With 2 tablespoons of the butter, grease the poaching rack and the tops of the salmon steaks.

2. Place ¼ cup of the court bouillon, the red wine, white wine, fish fumet, onions, shallots, leek, and bouquet garni in a saucepan and reduce by one-half. Add the peppercorns and continue reducing the liquid to two-thirds its original volume. Strain into a clean saucepan. Add salt and pepper. Add reduced cream and set aside.

3. On a small plate mix together the parsley, orange rind, lemon rind, mashed garlic, and anchovy. Set aside. Bring the remaining court bouillon to a boil. Peel the zucchini and cut the peels into a julienne as fine as angel hair. Sauté the zucchini peels in 1 tablespoon of the butter for just a few seconds.

4. Poach the salmon medallions in the remaining court bouillon for 7–8 minutes (see instructions, p. 224). While the salmon poaches, bring the sauce base to a high boil and add the remaining 7 tablespoons of the butter. At the very last minute add the parsley-anchovy mixture. Serve the medallions on warmed plates, spoon some of the sauce over them, and top each steak with a small nest of julienned zucchini peels.

ASSIETTE LEGERE DE SAUMON POUR LE PRINTEMPS {Salmon Medallions for the Spring}

For those who desire their sauce a bit lighter and "on the side."

SERVES 6

6 salmon steaks
8 tablespoons butter
4 quarts plus 1 cup White Wine and
   Vinegar Court Bouillon (p. 31)
1 cup Fish Fumet (p. 28)
1 onion, chopped fine
2 shallots, chopped fine
1 leek, chopped fine
Small bouquet garni (see p. 82)
2 tablespoons each chopped chervil,
   tarragon, chives, parsley, dill

⅓ cup sour cream
Salt
Pepper from the mill
Lemon juice
1 pound leaf spinach, cleaned and
   stemmed
18 baby onions, blanched
18 jumbo asparagus, blanched
3 teaspoons red keta caviar

1. Bone the salmon steaks and shape them into medallions (see instructions, p. 225). Reserve the salmon bones. Brush the poaching rack and the top of the salmon medallions with 2 tablespoons of the butter.
2. Put the salmon bones, 1 cup of the court bouillon, the fish fumet, onion, shallots, leek, bouquet garni, and 1 tablespoon of each of the herbs into a saucepan and reduce to ½ cup. Strain into a saucepan, bring to a boil, add the sour cream and simmer for 5 more minutes, stirring with a spatula. Whisk in 3 tablespoons of the butter; correct the salt and pepper and add lemon juice to taste and the remaining herbs.
3. Poach the salmon medallions in the remaining court bouillon for 7–8 minutes (see p. 224). Meanwhile, toss the spinach leaves quickly in 1 tablespoon of the butter, just to wilt them. Sauté the baby onions in ½ tablespoon of the butter until golden. Toss the jumbo asparagus spears in the remaining 1½ tablespoons of the butter. Arrange the vegetables on 6 plates.
4. Put each salmon steak on a bed of spinach and top it with the red keta caviar. Serve the sauce on the side in a small sauceboat.

Variation: If you have access to them, instead of the green jumbo asparagus, you can, of course, use any of the delicious white jumbo French asparagus. (Fresh only, please, or not worth the expense.)

RAIE POCHEE A LA CREME D'ECHALOTES
{*Poached Skate with Shallot Cream*}

SERVES 6

4 quarts White Wine and Vinegar
  Court Bouillon (p. 31)
2 large "wings" of skate, ¾–1 pound
  each
2 tablespoons butter
½ pound shallots, sliced thin
1 cup heavy cream
Salt

Pepper from the mill
1 ounce capers with their brine or
  vinegar
2 tablespoons "noisette" butter (see
  p. 48)
Lemon juice to taste
Chopped parsley

1. Have the court bouillon ready and cut each of the "wings" of skate into 3 portions.
2. Heat the butter in a skillet and add the sliced shallots. Sauté until the vegetables take on a golden "candied" look, keeping the heat medium low to prevent the shallots from burning and tasting bitter. As soon as the shallots are ready, add the cream and reduce to ⅓ cup. Add salt, pepper, the capers with their brine or vinegar, and the "noisette" butter. Also add lemon juice to your taste and correct the final seasoning.
3. Poach the pieces of skate in the court bouillon for no more than 5 minutes for ¾-inch thickness and 7 minutes for 1-inch thickness (see p. 224). Slide a spatula between the bone and the meat and discard the bone. Put both halves of each piece of fish on a warm plate. Season lightly with salt and pepper, spoon an equal amount of sauce over each portion, and dot with chopped parsley.

TRUITES FARCIES SAINTE-ODILE
{Trout Stuffed with Mousse of Frogs' Legs}

This recipe uses the best the Alsace has to offer: trout from the torrents of the Vosges, frogs from the Ried and Riesling. The bread crumbs–milk mixture, known as a *"panade,"* is used on the frog mousse, so that one can use previously frozen frogs' legs if one has no fresh ones.

SERVES 6

TROUT AND MOUSSE:

6 small salmon or brook trout, uncleaned
3 pounds frogs' legs
1 slice of white bread, crust removed
1/3 cup milk
1 egg

8 tablespoons butter
1 2/3 teaspoons salt
35 turns of the pepper mill
2 cups heavy cream
4 quarts White Wine and Vinegar Court Bouillon (p. 31)

SAUCE:

1 cup each Fish Fumet (p. 28) and Alsace Riesling
1 onion, chopped fine
1 leek (white and light green parts only), chopped fine

2 shallots, chopped fine
18 frogs' leg bones, chopped
1 cup heavy cream, reduced to 1/2 cup
8 tablespoons butter

GARNISH:

3 leeks (white and light green parts), cut into julienne 2 inches by 1/8 inch and blanched
The "foreleg" muscles of the frogs' legs

3 tablespoons butter
1 1/2 tablespoons chopped chives
6 scalloped lemon slices
6 parsley bouquets

1. Cut the trout open through the back, flush all insides away, and rinse well. Pat dry and set aside in the refrigerator.
2. Bone all the frogs' legs, separating the back leg muscles (thighs) from the foreleg muscles (drumsticks). Weigh 1 pound exact weight of the muscles,

using all the thighs and some of the drumsticks. Reserve the remaining drumsticks for the garnish. Reserve 18 bones for the sauce.

3. Crumble the white bread very fine; bring the milk to a boil. Place the crumbs in the food processor container, add the milk and process until smooth. Cool completely. Add the weighed pound of frog meat and the egg and process until smooth. Strain through a tamis or conical strainer. Chill for 2 hours.

4. After that time, cream the butter with the salt and pepper in the food processor container; gradually add the chilled frog purée and process until smooth. Then gradually add the heavy cream in a steady stream.

5. Salt and pepper the cavities of the trout, stuff them with the frog mousse, and sew the backs closed.

6. To prepare the sauce, reduce the fish fumet, Riesling, onion, leek, shallots, and chopped frogs' leg bones together to ¾ cup very flavorful liquid. Add the reduced heavy cream, bring to a high boil and add the butter, whisking well.

7. To prepare the garnish, quickly sauté the julienne of leeks and the frog drumsticks in 1½ tablespoons butter each. As soon as both are ready, strain the sauce over them and correct the final seasoning. Add the chives.

8. Bring the court bouillon to a boil, add the trout, bring back to a rolling boil, cover, remove from the heat, and let stand for 12–14 minutes.

9. To serve, skin the trout and spoon an equal amount of the prepared sauce over each portion. Garnish each plate with a lemon slice and a parsley bouquet.

Timing notes:
- Prepare trout and mousse 24 hours ahead of time, as well as sauce base and sauce garnish.
- On the day you serve, you should stuff, sew, and poach the trout; cook the sauce garnish; finish the sauce.

TRUITES FARCIES MADAME STEPHANIE
{Trout Stuffed with Smoked Salmon Mousse}

SERVES 6

TROUT AND MOUSSE:

> *6 trout*
> *Salt and pepper*
> *1 recipe Mousselines of Smoked Salmon (p. 195)*
> *4 quarts White Wine and Vinegar Court Bouillon (p. 31)*

SAUCE AND GARNISH:

1 cup each Fish Fumet (p. 28) and
Pinot Rouge d'Alsace wine
1 onion, chopped fine
1 leek (white and light green part),
chopped fine
2 shallots, chopped fine

Small bouquet garni (see p. 82)
1 cup heavy cream, reduced to ½ cup
9 tablespoons butter
4 pickling cucumbers, scrubbed
1 tablespoon each scissored chives and
dill

1. Cut the trout through the back, flush all insides away, rinse well, and pat dry.
2. Salt and pepper the cavities of the trout and fill them with the smoked salmon mousse. Sew them closed and set trout aside in the refrigerator.
3. To prepare the sauce, mix the fish fumet, wine, onion, leek, and shallots. Add the bouquet garni and reduce to ½ cup liquid. Blend with the reduced heavy cream. Bring to a high boil and add 8 tablespoons of the butter. Strain into a clean saucepan.
4. Score the length of each pickling cucumber with a zester and cut each into ⅙-inch slices that will look "crinkle-cut." Sauté the pickling cucumbers quickly in the remaining tablespoon of butter and add the chives and dill. Add to the sauce.
5. Bring the court bouillon to a rolling boil, add the trout, and bring to a second rolling boil. Remove from the heat, cover and let stand for 12–14 minutes. Skin the trout and serve covered with the sauce.

Timing notes:
- Prepare the trout and mousse 24 hours ahead of time, as well as the sauce base and garnish.
- On the day you serve, you should stuff and poach the trout, cook the sauce garnish, and finish the sauce.

Variations:
A. In areas where sweetwater crayfish are available, add 1 dozen of these little critters to the list of ingredients, use their crushed heads in the preparation of the sauce base, and add their tails to the sauce.
B. The same sauce can be made with Riesling instead of Pinot Rouge d'Alsace.

SHELLFISH DISHES

Homard et langouste (lobsters of all types):

The classic lobster dishes were nothing short of a true disaster: overcooked lobster meat so clogged by overrich sauces that one could not find the taste of the lobster. There are a few ways of cooking lobster in the modern cuisine that leave the lobster meat absolutely succulent with its own natural juices and a true pleasure to eat. One, indicated to me by my friend and graduate Ethel Goralnick, consists in cooking the live lobster for 6 minutes in the microwave oven. The second method is to poach it for 8 minutes in a court bouillon, and the third is to shell it raw and sauté it gently in butter until it turns translucent pink. Here are 3 recipes using each of these techniques. The steaming and broiling and grilling of lobsters being a great American sport, I have not discussed these subjects further.

HOMARD A LA VIERGE A LA MEMOIRE DE DOM PERIGNON
{Lobster in Champagne Butter in Memory of Dom Pérignon}

Every time I make this recipe, I regret that Dom Pérignon could not taste what the results of his seventeenth-century efforts do to lobsters as cooked in the twentieth century. Massively expensive but worth its price.

SERVES 6

15 quarts water

5 full tablespoons salt

1 bottle brut champagne (French only, please)

6 shallots, chopped very fine

12 tablespoons unsalted butter

2 tablespoons heavy cream, whipped

Salt

Pepper from the mill

Six 1¼–1½-pound lobsters, live and heartily kicking

1 teaspoon each chopped chervil, chives, tarragon, and parsley

1. Bring the water to a full boil. Add the salt and bring to a second boil.
2. While the water heats, reduce the champagne and shallots together over low heat until only ½ cup solids and liquids are left. Turn the heat off, let cool to lukewarm.
3. Put the saucepan on a very low burner and whisk in the butter, tablespoon by tablespoon, to obtain a very white emulsion. The more butter you add, the more you will increase the heat, but progress very slowly and do not go over 175°F., or N°3 on European burners.
4. Season the whipped cream with salt and pepper, and whisk into the sauce base. Strain into a clean pot. Keep warm, but do not allow the sauce to overheat or it will break.
5. Immerse the lobsters in wildly boiling water, bring back to a second boil, cover, remove from the heat, and let stand for 7–9 minutes.
6. Shell the lobsters to extract the tail and claw meat. Cut off the tip of each head with the antennae and the eyes. Arrange the claw and tail meat around the decorative head shell in each of 6 small oval dishes and sprinkle with the chopped fresh herbs. Serve the sauce on the side in small ramekins. Guests can dip the meat into the sauce.

Technical note: If the sauce thickens while cooking, do not reheat it on the flame; gradually whisk into it a few teaspoons of hot court bouillon.

Variation: For a less expensive but equally tasty variation, replace the champagne with 1 bottle of Côteaux de Champagne plus 1½ tablespoons *Aceto Balsamico* (p. 45). This dish tastes just as wonderful, as the sweetness of the vinegar underlines that of the lobster. Côteaux de Champagne is the unbubbly champagne as nature makes it.

HOMARD AU CAVIAR
{Microwaved Lobster with Caviar Sauce}

The cooking technique for the lobster is that of Ethel Goralnick and is used here with her permission.

SERVES 6

*1 bottle Côteaux de Champagne or
  other Pinot Chardonnay*
6 shallots, chopped extremely fine
Salt
Pepper from the mill
12 tablespoons unsalted butter
3 tablespoons sour cream

*1 ounce best available caviar (beluga
  is perfect)*
Lemon juice as needed
Six 1½-pound lobsters
6 parsley bouquets
6 scalloped lemon slices

1. Empty the bottle of wine into a saucepan. Add the shallots and reduce over medium-low heat to ½ cup solids and liquids. Add salt and pepper to your taste. Whisk in the butter, tablespoon by tablespoon, increasing the heat to no higher than 160°F., or N°3 on European burners. Strain. Just before serving, add the sour cream and the caviar and reheat, keeping the temperature low at all times. Correct the seasoning with salt, pepper, and lemon juice. Keep warm.

2. Rub the lobster heads until the shellfish stiffens. Put each lobster in a plastic bag. Tie it closed with a knot, not a tie, because of the metal wire in it. Pierce 3 holes in each bag and place 2 or 3 bags on a plastic tray. Turn the microwave oven on for 6 minutes. Keep the already cooked lobsters in their bags while the second and eventually the third batches cook.

3. Shell the lobsters to extract the tail and claw meat. Present on 6 individual porcelain dishes with a small parsley bouquet and a slice of lemon nicely scalloped. Spoon an equal amount of the caviar sauce over each lobster.

CASSEROLE DE HOMARD AUX ASPERGES
{Casserole of Lobster and Asparagus}

If possible, use 2 female and 2 male lobsters. The best month to cook this dish is June, when asparagus is still around and female lobsters carry eggs (coral).

SERVES 6

Four 1½-pound live lobsters, or
　6 lobster tails
24 jumbo asparagus spears
½ teaspoon dried orange rind
The shell of 1 lobster, head crushed
　fine
The coral and tomalley of 1 lobster
1 cup freshly squeezed orange juice
1½ teaspoons lemon juice

8 tablespoons unsalted butter
2 tablespoons each heavy and sour
　cream
Salt
Pepper from the mill
4 tablespoons clarified butter
1 piece of fresh orange rind, 2 inches
　by ¾ inch
Chopped parsley

1. Kill the lobsters by severing the spinal canal at the place where the head shows a ½-inch-long transversal line. Shell the lobster tails and claws raw. Set aside on a tray and cover with plastic wrap. Discard the lobster "blood" or thin translucent liquid coagulated on the chopping board—it clutters and clouds sauces rather than giving them taste.

2. Peel and blanch the asparagus. Reserve 1 cup blanching water. Drain asparagus, refresh under cold running water, and cut into ½-inch chunks. Set aside.

3. In a saucepan mix the blanching water, the dried orange rind, the crushed lobster shell, coral, and tomalley, the orange and lemon juices, and reduce over medium-low heat to ½ cup liquid. Strain it into a clean saucepan, bring to a boil, and immediately whisk in the butter. Add the 2 creams, season with salt and pepper, and keep warm.

4. Heat the clarified butter in 1 large or 2 smaller skillets. Cook the lobster meat in it over medium-low heat. Transfer to a large serving dish or 6 individual dishes and keep warm. In the same butter, add at once the asparagus pieces and the fresh orange rind and reheat, stir frying over very high heat. Discard the orange rind and mix the asparagus into the lobster meat. Pour the sauce over the mixture of asparagus and lobster and serve promptly, dotted with chopped parsley.

Coquilles Saint-Jacques et gambas (scallops and shrimp):

I have over the last ten years begun to stir fry bay and sea scallops as well as shrimp, simply because it seems to be the culinary treatment that best agrees with them.

Before they are stir fried, sea scallops should be either diced into 4-inch cubes or, better, sliced into ¼-inch slices. The scallop "feet"—the tough, inedible little muscle attached to each scallop—must be discarded. It does, however, communicate a nice scallop flavor to all sauces and should be used in their bases. Tiny bay scallops are cleaned of their tiny feet and left whole.

The cooking of scallops is almost instantaneous and is "done" before one even has the time to think about it. If you are hesitant, undercook rather than overcook—the scallops will finish cooking in their final sauce.

Shrimp is also a fast "cooker." Purchase them in their shells. Pull out the vein while the shrimp are raw, but do not shell them. Stir fry shrimp in the shell, which acts as a protective layer so the shrimp cook to that wonderful translucent look and an ever so lightly crunchy and juicy texture. The shape of a shrimp is a good indicator of its state of cooking: when raw, the shrimp in its shell is limp and can be pulled to stay in a straight line; a slight oval curve is characteristic of a perfectly cooked shrimp; a curled up shrimp is always over-cooked and tough.

Scallops and shrimp can be sauced quickly or elaborately. The quick sauces are always made with some clam juice—which tastes very much like the juice of the scallop, unfortunately lost when the shellfish is cleaned—and light cream thickened with a wee bit of cornstarch. Most quick sauces will barely coat the shellfish and will not be very abundant.

The elaborate sauces follow the regular pattern of reduction of fish fumet, wine, and always a certain proportion of clam juice, blended with reduced heavy cream and butter in emulsion. They require a bit more time and care but make a dish of scallops or shrimp pass into the realm of truly *grande cuisine*.

When shrimp and scallops are a main course, it is a good idea to serve a small portion of rice with them.

COQUILLES SAINT-JACQUES
AU VINAIGRE DE XERES
{Scallops in Sherry Vinegar Glaze}

Use as a main course.

SERVES 6

1 large red pepper	2/3 cup light cream
1 ripe avocado	1/2 teaspoon cornstarch
1 pound deep sea scallops	Salt
2 tablespoons butter	Pepper from the mill
1/4 cup clam juice	2 cups cooked rice pilaf (p. 424)
2 tablespoons sherry vinegar	Chopped parsley

1. Peel the pepper and cut it lengthwise into 8 wedges. Also peel the avocado and slice it, but keep the slices close against the pit until ready to use.
2. Clean the scallops and cut them into 1/4-inch-thick slices.
3. Heat the butter in a large skillet. Sauté the peppers for 2 minutes, or until they become ever so slightly limp. Remove to a plate. In the same skillet stir fry the scallops for 1 minute, just to heat them through; remove them to a stainless steel strainer placed over a bowl to collect their drippings.
4. To the skillet add the clam juice and vinegar. Reduce to approximately 2 tablespoons of very pungent base. Mix the light cream and starch and thicken over medium heat. Add the scallop juices and correct the seasoning.
5. Finally, toss scallops, peppers, and avocado slices together in the sauce until well heated through. The sauce will be virtually nonexistent. It is just a superficial coating for all ingredients. Correct salt and pepper extremely carefully.
6. Serve each portion over cooked rice and dab generously with chopped parsley.

COQUILLES ET GAMBAS A LA ROMAINE
{Shrimp and Scallop the Antique Roman Way}

Use as a main course.

SERVES 6

2 pounds fava beans, in their shells
1 dozen large shrimp, in their shells
½ pound deep sea scallops
3 tablespoons olive oil
1 clove garlic, sliced
Salt

Pepper from the mill
Lemon juice to taste
1 sage leaf, powdered
6 slices of French bread, fried in olive
 oil

1. Shell the fava beans, peel them, and separate each bean into 2 sides. Blanch them for 2–3 minutes. Drain and set aside.
2. Devein the raw shrimp and clean the "feet" off the scallops. Slice the scallops ¼ inch thick.
3. Heat the olive oil in a large skillet and quickly stir fry the shrimp until they bend into an oval curve. Cool slightly and peel off their shells. In the same skillet, quickly brown the slivers of garlic. Remove them with a slotted spoon and discard.
4. Reheat the oil and quickly stir fry the scallops for 1 minute, add the shelled shrimp and the fava beans, season well with salt and pepper, and cook for another minute. Squeeze as much lemon juice over the shellfish as you like, and sprinkle with the powdered sage. Serve promptly over croutons fried in olive oil.

COQUILLES SAINT-JACQUES AUX ARTICHAUTS {Scallops with Artichokes and Lemon Rind}

Use a a main course.

SERVES 6

2 dozen baby artichokes	*½ teaspoon cornstarch*
1 lemon, cut into halves	*⅔ cup light cream*
Salt	*1½ tablespoons chopped tarragon*
1 pound deep sea scallops	*1 tablespoon fine-julienned lemon rind,*
2 tablespoons butter	*blanched*
Pepper from the mill	*2 tablespoons chopped parsley*
⅓ cup clam juice	

1. Remove the stems and the leaves of the artichokes until 2 dozen little cork-like (½ inch by ¾ inch) hearts are left. Bring 2 quarts water to the boil, add the 2 lemon halves and 3 teaspoons salt to the pot. Boil the artichokes until tender (a needle inserted in the bottom of an artichoke will come out easily). Drain and set aside.

2. Clean the scallops and cut them into ¼-inch slices. Heat the butter in a large skillet. Quickly stir fry the scallops in the hot butter. Season with salt and pepper and remove them to a conical strainer placed over a bowl to catch their juices. To the skillet add the clam juice and reduce to 2 table-spoons. Mix the cornstarch and light cream and blend into the reduced clam juice along with the juice dripped from the scallops. Now add the artichokes, reheat them well, and at the last minute blend in the scallops, tarragon, and lemon rind. Serve promptly, dotted with chopped parsley, in true scallop shells or porcelain shells.

COQUILLES SAINT-JACQUES A LA MEUNIERE TOMATEE
{Scallops in Tomato Noisette Butter}

Prepare this dish as a first course with September sun-ripened tomatoes.

SERVES 6–8

1 pound deep sea scallops	*Pepper from the mill*
2 pounds fresh tomatoes	*8 tablespoons "noisette" butter (see*
1 onion, chopped	*p. 48)*
3 tablespoons olive oil	*½ ounce Cognac*
⅔ cup Fish Fumet (p. 28)	*1½ teaspoons each chopped chervil,*
¼ cup dry white wine	*chives, tarragon, and parsley*
⅓ cup clam juice	*6 pastry shells of your choice, or 2 cups*
Small bouquet garni (see p. 82)	*cooked rice*
Salt	

1. Remove and reserve the scallop "feet." Cut the scallops into ¼-inch-thick slices and set aside.
2. Cut the tomatoes, squeeze the seeds and water out, and chop them coarsely. Heat 2 tablespoons of the olive oil and cook the onion in it; add the tomatoes and cook over very low heat until approximately 1½ cups tomatoes are left. Strain through a fine conical strainer to retain only the tomato pulp.
3. Mix 1 cup tomato pulp with the fumet, white wine, and clam juice. Add the scallop "feet" and the bouquet garni and cook until reduced to 1½ cups. Correct the seasoning with salt and pepper.
4. Bring the sauce to a high boil, add the "noisette" butter, and, at the very last minute, the Cognac and the herbs.
5. Stir fry the scallops very quickly in a large skillet heated with the remaining tablespoon of the olive oil and blend them with the sauce. Serve either in small pastry shells or on rice.

PÉTONCLES AU PERNOD
{Bay Scallops with Fennel and Pernod}

Pétoncles is the French name for bay scallops. Use as a first course.

SERVES 6–8

1 pound small bay scallops	*¼ teaspoon cornstarch*
2 tablespoons butter	*⅔ cup heavy cream*
½ ounce Pernod	*1 tiny clove garlic, mashed*
¼ teaspoon fennel seeds	*1½ tablespoons chopped parsley*
¼ cup clam juice	*6 small parsley bouquets*

1. Check that all the scallops have been well cleaned of their small, often barely visible "feet." Discard them if you find any.
2. Heat the butter in a large sauté pan. Add the scallops, stir fry them for 1 minute, and remove them to a conical strainer placed over a bowl to catch the scallop drippings.
3. Drain all the scallop juices into the pan in which you stir fried the scallops and cook them down to a thick, almost brown glaze. Add the Pernod, fennel seeds, and clam juice and reduce again to 3–4 tablespoons. Mix the cornstarch with the heavy cream and blend with the pan juices until lightly thickened. Cook for a few minutes.
4. Put the scallops back into a sauté pan. Strain the sauce over them and reheat well together without allowing a trace of boiling. Add the garlic and chopped parsley and spoon the scallops into 6 or 8 true scallop shells or porcelain shells. Add a tiny parsley bouquet for color.

COQUILLES SAINT-JACQUES
AUX TRUFFES ET AUX PISTACHES
{Coquilles Saint-Jacques with Truffles and Pistachios}

I hesitated to publish this recipe because the truffles are so expensive, but I've found it such a successful first course that I finally succumbed. Première cuisson truffles are canned raw without precooking and taste very close to fresh truffles.

SERVES 6–8

1 pound bay scallops, cleaned of their "feet"	⅓ cup clam juice
	⅓ cup Fish Fumet (p. 28)
2 truffles, 1½ inches in diameter, fresh or "première cuisson"	Salt
	Pepper from the mill
1½ cups heavy cream	¼ cup coarse-chopped pistachio nuts
4 tablespoons butter	1–1½ teaspoons kirschwasser
1 teaspoon sherry vinegar	6–8 tartlet shells, hot (p. 67)

1. Have the scallops cleaned and ready on a plate. Keep covered with plastic wrap at room temperature for 15 minutes before cooking.
2. Peel the truffles and chop the peels extremely small. Bring the cream to a boil, add the truffle peels, and reduce to 1 cup. Strain and keep ready to use.
3. Chop the truffles rather coarsely.
4. Heat the butter almost to the "noisette" stage (see p. 48) in a large sauté pan. Quickly stir fry the scallops in it and remove them to a strainer placed over a large bowl to catch their juices.
5. Heat the sauté pan until the bit of scallop juice on the bottom turns golden; add the dripped scallop juices and reduce well; then add the vinegar, clam juices, and fish fumet and reduce slowly to ⅓ cup. Strain the already reduced truffle-flavored cream into the reduction. Mix well and let stand on the turned-off burner. Season well with salt and pepper.
6. Return the scallops to a large sauté pan and strain the sauce over them. Blend well and reheat without allowing a trace of boiling. Add the chopped truffles and pistachios and, at the very last minute, a teaspoon of kirsch. There should be no more than a tiny hint of kirsch; no statement, please. Correct the final seasoning and serve in tartlet shells.

Other ideas for scallops or shrimp:
- Coquilles Saint-Jacques with bacon chips and mushrooms.
- Coquilles Saint-Jacques with toasted almonds and "noisette" butter.
- Coquilles Saint-Jacques and jumbo shrimp in the Oriental manner, with water chestnuts, scallions, and Worcestershire sauce.
- Coquilles Saint-Jacques with smoked salmon butter and dill.
- Shrimp with candied shallots and reduced cream.
- Shrimp or scallops or a medley of both with cucumber, lime, and mint.

All serve 6 as a main course.

Huîtres et moules (oysters and mussels):

The dilemma is growing: should one or should one not eat raw oysters? I remember some passionate discussion on the subject with a copy editor when I published one of my earlier books. The answer is simple: do not buy any oysters unless you know where they came from and who raised them and always, unless they will be boiled in a soup base, use oysters that you shuck open yourself so that you can be sure the mollusk is alive. Ascertain this by touching the "beard" all around the oyster with the tip of your knife blade; it will recede instantly if the shellfish is alive. Discard systematically any dead oyster. You owe it to yourself—it is too dangerous to take a chance.

You will have to go on a systematic chase for excellent oysters. Each and every area has its good mollusk producers; I know of some excellent ones on Cape Cod, in Virginia, in Louisiana, in Washington and California, as well as around the whole of Quebec; so investigate. And always remember that, if you use oysters already shelled in those mean little cartons, they must be unmercifully cooked. I use them exclusively for making broth.

There are two basic types of oyster: the flat-lidded one, Ostrea Edulis, is by far the best and most luxurious and the one to be used for broiling whenever one can afford and find it. The other type, Crassostrea, has that long, very curly shell, and its size on American shores can reach gigantic proportions. Crassostrea is used for all oyster broths, for sauces, and for stews because of its very tasty, briny juice. The basic taste of oysters varies from sweetish and flat to briny and slightly salty. I prefer the saltier ones.

To open an oyster without damaging your hand, first choose your knife properly. A good oyster knife has a round handle 3 inches long and 1 inch in diameter. The blade is 1 inch shorter than the handle and a little more than ⅓ inch wide, with a tip that curves slightly upward. That upward slant does not always exist, so look for it; it is the one feature that makes opening oysters easier.

Wrap the oyster in a kitchen towel so that only 1 inch of the tip of the shell shows. Hold the oyster fast onto the counter. Engage the tip of the blade ⅛–⅙ inch into the oyster opening valve. It is clearly visible at the thin end of the shell—it is not on the rounded end, nor on either side. Push forward at the same time as you twist to the right; you will hear the shell click open. Pass the blade between the 2 halves of the shell, scraping upward against the lid. The oyster is opened. Now gently pass the blade between the bottom shell and the oyster to cut the mollusk away from its shell by severing the "scallop" that controls the opening of the shell.

If the oysters are to be consumed on the half shell, leave them in their shell "as is." If they are to be broiled or poached, gently remove the "scallop" and add it to your sauce base; its flavor is excellent. Drain oysters to be cooked on a stainless steel tamis or in a strainer placed over a bowl to collect all the precious juices.

As with oysters, one must take great care when selecting one's mussels. Mussels must soak in water salted with 1½ teaspoons salt per quart of water before scrubbing. Scrub mussels with a plastic scouring pad to remove small barnacles and pull the beard off. They are opened by steaming, as has been done through the centuries. Only one word of caution: start in cold wine or water over medium-high heat so that the steam develops gradually and pries the shells open. Boiling liquids cook shut those mussels bathing directly in them.

GALIMAFREE DE MOULES AU SAFRAN ET AU COGNAC {Mussels in Cream with Saffron and Cognac}

From my great-grandmother's repertoire of recipes from the Angoulême area. Use as a first course.

SERVES 6

MUSSELS:
4 pounds mussels
1 onion, chopped fine
1 shallot, chopped fine
1 clove garlic, mashed

1 teaspoon peppercorns
2 tablespoons chopped parsley stems
1 cup Muscadet or other dry white wine
1 ounce Cognac

SAUCE:
3 tablespoons butter
1 onion, chopped extremely fine
1 clove garlic, mashed
1 tablespoon flour
1 cup heavy cream
½ teaspoon saffron threads

Salt if needed
A large pinch of cayenne pepper
Very coarsely cracked pepper from
   the mill
2 tablespoons chopped parsley

1. Scrub the mussels, put them into a large kettle, add the onion, shallot, garlic, peppercorns, parsley stems, wine, and Cognac, cover and steam for 5–6 minutes over medium-high heat to open. During the cooking, grab the lid and both handles of the pot and toss well twice to bring the mussels already open to the surface and vice versa. As soon as the mussels are opened, drain them in a colander placed over a bowl to catch the juices. Discard any mussels that have not opened.

2. Discard the top shell of each mussel and place the shells containing the mollusks into 6 small oval baking dishes. Filter the collected mussel juices through a coffee filter.

3. To prepare the sauce, heat the butter well and in it sauté the onion and garlic until translucent. The smell will develop considerably. Add the flour and cook for 2–3 minutes. Whisk in the filtered mussel juices and bring to a boil, stirring. Simmer until the taste of raw wine has disappeared, approximately 10 minutes. Blend in the heavy cream, the saffron, cayenne, salt if needed, and pepper from the mill. Reheat to the boiling point and ladle over the mussels. The heat of the sauce is sufficient to reheat the mussels. Serve immediately dotted with parsley.

Note: Each guest will need a "finger bowl" of lemon water since this is finger, fork, and soup spoon food, all in one.

PETITS CHAUSSONS DE MOULES A LA FONDUE DE POIREAUX
{Mussels on a Bed of Leeks}

Do not forget the teaspoon of Pernod or Pastis: it is the key to the dish! Born on a day we intended to prepare Fernand Point's Vol au Vent de Moules aux Épinards, this dish has leeks for lack of spinach in the winter market. Use as a first course.

SERVES 8

1 recipe Puff Pastry (p. 461)

1 egg yolk

2 tablespoons milk

8 large leeks (white and light green
    parts only), sliced thin

Butter as needed

Salt

Pepper from the mill

1 quart mussels, scrubbed

½ cup dry white wine

2 shallots, chopped

2 tablespoons chopped parsley stems

1 clove garlic, chopped

1 cup heavy cream

1–1½ teaspoons Pernod or Pastis

1. Roll out the puff pastry ¼ inch thick. Cut it out with a semicircular cutter
    6 inches by 3 inches or cut 6-inch circles and cut each circle in half. Set
    on a buttered pastry sheet. Preheat the oven to 425°F. Mix egg yolk and
    milk and brush lightly on pastry. Refrigerate for 1 hour, then bake until
    nicely puffed and browned, approximately 15–20 minutes.

2. Blanch the leeks and drain them well. Heat 4 tablespoons butter in a sauté
    pan and add the leeks; toss into the butter, add salt and pepper, and cover.
    Let cook until a mellow "fondue" of leeks results; the vegetable should
    be as tender as a purée and present no crunchiness. Season well with salt
    and pepper. Set aside.

3. Mix the mussels, wine, shallots, parsley, and garlic in a large kettle. Add
    pepper to taste and toss well together. Steam the mussels open. Shell them
    and set them aside.

4. Strain the mussel cooking juices into a sauté pan and reduce them by
    one-third. Add 3–4 tablespoons of the reduced juices to the leek purée.
    Reheat well together. Correct seasoning.

5. Reduce the heavy cream by two-thirds. Thin the cream with ¼–⅓ cup
    mussel juice. Reduce 5 more minutes together. Add the mussels and the
    chosen liqueur.

6. Cut the baked pastry semicircles in half horizontally so as to obtain a lid
    and a bottom. Remove excess dough from the bottom shell if any, fill
    it with leek purée and top with creamed mussels. Put the lid on top of the
    mussels and serve.

Variation: Following the same recipe you can substitute 36 excellent
oysters for the mussels. Omit the Pastis or Pernod.

RAMEKINS D'HUITRES DE BELON
AU GEWÜRZTRAMINER
{An Oyster Stew Prepared with Gewürztraminer}

The most delicious little oyster stew ever. This can be made with any good oyster but tastes best with Belon oysters.

SERVES 6

36 Belon oysters
½ pint regular oysters, chopped (can be bought shelled in small containers)
1 bottle Gewürztraminer from Alsace
1–1¼ cups Fish Fumet (p. 28)
2 shallots, chopped fine
1½ tablespoons freshly chopped tarragon leaves or 1¼ teaspoons dried

⅔ cup crème fraîche or ½ cup reduced heavy cream and ¼ cup sour cream, mixed as needed
Salt if needed
Pepper from the mill
Chopped parsley
A dash of Tabasco sauce

1. Shuck the Belon oysters. Remove and keep the "scallop" that attaches each oyster to its shell. Drain the oysters in a stainless steel drum sieve placed over a bowl to collect their liquid. Set aside.

2. Place the pint of regular chopped oysters in a large saucepan. Add the reserved Belon oyster "scallops." Measure the amount of oyster liquor dripped from the Belon oysters; add an equal amount of Gewürztraminer and of fish fumet (to triple the quantity). Add the shallots and tarragon leaves and cook, reducing together by two-thirds. Strain into a clean saucepan and discard the contents of the strainer, overcooked oysters and all.

3. Blend the obtained liquor with the crème fraîche or the reduced heavy cream mixed with the sour cream. Bring to a boil. Add the Belon oysters to the boiling mixture. Immediately remove from the heat. Correct the seasoning with salt and pepper from the mill. Add the parsley and Tabasco sauce and serve promptly in large ramekins.

HUITRES A LA POINTE D'ARMAGNAC
{Broiled Oysters with a Pinch of Armagnac}

This recipe is without doubt best with Belon oysters, but I have also prepared it very successfully with ordinary oysters from California, Massachusetts, and Louisiana.

SERVES 6

36 Belon or other first-class oysters

1 pint ordinary oysters, chopped (can be bought shelled in small containers)

1 cup Fish Fumet (p. 28)

1 cup champagne brut (French only, please) or excellent dry white wine

2 shallots, chopped fine

Very small bouquet garni (see p. 82)

12 tablespoons unsalted butter

Salt

Pepper from the mill

A dash of Armagnac

1. Shuck the oysters. Remove and reserve their "scallops." Reserve the shells. Put the Belon oysters in a stainless steel strainer or tamis placed over a bowl to collect their liquor.

2. In a saucepan, mix the chopped ordinary oysters with their own juices, the "scallops" from the Belon oysters, the fish fumet, champagne, shallots, and bouquet garni and reduce to 1 cup liquids and solids mixed. Strain into a clean saucepan, squeezing well all the solids to extract approximately ½ cup of pure liquid reduction.

3. Bring the reduction to a boil and whisk in the butter, tablespoon by tablespoon. Correct the salt and pepper and add the Armagnac.

4. Rinse and dry the Belon oyster shells. Add a teaspoon of sauce and an oyster to each shell, then top each oyster with an equal amount of the remaining sauce. Broil the oysters for 2–3 minutes, or until the sauce browns to a lovely gold. Serve piping hot.

Escargots et grenouilles (snails and frogs):
These are two foods not always to be found in the best condition in the United States. The first comes from various countries in cans, and the second comes frozen from who knows where.

The truth is, the snails imported from France and from China are quite good, even canned, but the frogs or rather the bullfrogs one buys frozen can be disheartening in looks and taste. Here and there one can find a bunch of nice little frogs that have been properly frozen. So look first for small size and check the color. While frozen, the legs should be whitish but never gray, and when defrosted slowly in the refrigerator, they should regain their slight pinkishness. On the contrary, when they are of poor quality, because of having partially defrosted then refrozen again, they are a terrible noncommittal yellow-beige and the leg fibers appear clearly visible and somewhat separated instead of forming a compact solid muscle.

Season frogs' legs well—very well—both before and during cooking, for they have, living in water, the most watery-tasting flesh ever. They can use a good dry marinade of fresh herbs and aromatics. Cook them fast over high heat only if they are young and fresh; mature defrosted frogs must be cooked longer over medium heat.

Remember that snails that come in cans have already cooked at length and that recooking or resimmering them will do very little for their texture. Rather than simmering, one should always marinate snails, pouring the boiling marinade over them and letting them steep in it overnight.

CASSEROLE DE GRENOUILLES ET D'ESCARGOTS A LA BEAUNOISE
{Casserole of Frogs and Snails in the Burgundy Style}

Use the strong Dijon mustard, not the extra-strong. Serve as a first course only.

SERVES 6

1 tablespoon each tarragon, chervil, and parsley leaves
1 tablespoon chopped chives
12 frogs' legs
3 dozen canned snails, from France
1 cup clam juice
1 cup excellent Golden Veal Stock (p. 20)
2 cups Pinot Noir from California or any of the Chambertins or Pommards from France
2 onions, chopped fine

3 shallots, chopped fine
6 cloves garlic, mashed
Bouquet garni (see p. 82)
1/2 pound button mushrooms
1/2 pound unsalted butter
1/2 pound silverskin onions, peeled
Salt
Pepper from the mill
Dijon mustard to taste
1/4 cup heavy cream
Meat extract if needed

1. Chop the terragon, chervil, and parsley leaves. Mix with the chives. Bone the frogs' legs and put the bones in a large saucepan. Set the frog meat in a small dish and mix it with one-third of the chopped herbs.

2. Drain the snails into a strainer placed over the pan containing the frogs' bones. Put the snails to marinate in a glass dish with the remainder of the chopped herbs.

3. To the saucepan, add the clam juice, stock, red wine, chopped herb stems, onions, shallots, garlic, and bouquet garni. Chop the stems of the mushrooms and add these to the mixture. Bring to a boil, turn down to a simmer, and reduce to 1¼ cups liquids.

4. Meanwhile, heat 1 tablespoon of the butter in a skillet and sauté the silverskin onions until golden brown. Remove them to a plate. To the same skillet add the mushroom caps. Season with salt and pepper and add a tablespoon or so of the butter. Toss the mushrooms in the butter. Cover the skillet, turn down the heat, and let the mushrooms steam until they have released their juices. Pour the mushroom juices into the reducing sauce base. Add 1 more tablespoon of the butter to the pan and brown the mushroom caps well. When ready, put on the same plate as the onions.

5. When the reduction is ready, strain it into a clean saucepan. Bring it to a high boil and add ¾ cup of the butter, whisking well. Correct the seasoning with salt and pepper from the mill. Add the snails to the sauce; heat them well and slowly. Heat the last tablespoon or so of the butter in a skillet and in it toss the frog meat for a few minutes. Remove from the heat, mix the mustard and heavy cream together and pour over the meat. Add this mixture to the snails and mix very well. Add the mushrooms and onions. Reheat very well together, correct the final seasoning with salt, pepper from the mill, and, if needed, meat extract added with discretion so as not to be detected in the final taste. Serve in small gratin dishes.

ROTIES AUX LUMAS EN COLERE
{Hot Snails on Buttered Toast}

From the Poitou region and the repertoire of my great-grandmother. Rough but delicious. Use as a first course.

SERVES 6

6 dozen canned snails, from France

1½ tablespoons chopped parsley

1 large clove garlic, mashed

12 tablespoons unsalted butter

5 cloves garlic, chopped fine

2 onions, chopped fine

3 shallots, chopped fine

½ teaspoon Quatre-Epices (p. 35)

½ teaspoon cumin powder

½ teaspoon ground coriander

½ pound mushrooms, preferably
   wild (Boleti or death trumpets),
   chopped coarse

2 cups tomato sauce

¾ cup clam juice

2 cups dry white wine

Bouquet garni (see p. 82)

1 dried chili pepper, chopped

Salt

Pepper from the mill

6 slices of French bread

1 ounce Cognac

6 parsley bouquets

1. Drain the snails in a strainer placed over a bowl to collect their juices. Refrigerate the juices. Mix the snails with the chopped parsley and the mashed garlic clove. Let them dry marinate with these aromatics for 12 hours in the refrigerator.

2. Melt 2 tablespoons of the butter in a skillet. In it brown the chopped garlic, the onions, and the shallots. Add the *quatre-épices*, the cumin powder, the coriander, and the mushrooms. Toss until the mushroom juices have evaporated.

3. Add the reserved snail canning juices, the tomato sauce, clam juice, white wine, bouquet garni, and chili pepper. Bring to a boil, then turn down to a simmer. Season lightly and cook until reduced by half and very hot and tasty. *Do not strain.* Add the snails with all their aromatics and reheat well. While reheating, gradually add the remaining 10 tablespoons of the butter.

4. Toast the slices of French bread lightly. Heat the Cognac in a small saucepan, ignite it, and pour it into the snail pot. Correct the final seasoning with salt and pepper. Place the bread slices on small plates, spoon equal amounts of snails and sauce on each plate. Add a bouquet of parsley.

SOUPES DE POISSONS, CRUSTACES ET GASTEROPODES
(Fish Soups, Shellfish Soups, Snail Soups)

Nothing can ever be more satisfying and delicious than a good Mediterranean fish soup, and often I have felt: This is the best; why try another style? Though other shores have also produced delicious whole meal fish soups, it is those of Italy, Greece, and the Atlantic coast of France that deserve attention.

Everywhere, the quality of a fish or shellfish soup depends on the skills of the cook and on the time and care brought to the basic preparations. There is no good fish soup that does not rest on the principle of the Double Strength Fish Fumet (see p. 189). That means that the liquid used to cook the fish cannot be plain water and wine, but must be a fish fumet already well reduced and completely defatted after one has recooked it with the fish bones or the shellfish to give the soup its character. The aromatics are also important, and you will notice that in all the following recipes they are used in rather large quantities. Also, notice that the fish and shellfish never boil but rather are put to poach in the wildly boiling soup base and removed from the heat immediately. The fish is then cooked just enough to preserve all its natural juices and succulent taste.

If you are not willing to start with a good fish fumet, consider another, easier fish dish. Fish soups have the advantage of being "one pot" dinners and are generally enjoyed by all.

POTAGE D'HUITRES FUMEES {Smoked Oyster Soup}

This is good with ordinary smoked oysters, but becomes great if you can find excellent freshly smoked oysters in your area.

SERVES 6

1 quart Fish Fumet (p. 28),
  defatted
2 cups clam juice, preferably fresh
2 pints fresh shucked oysters and
  their natural juices
4 tablespoons butter
3 large onions, chopped fine
2 shallots, chopped fine
6 cloves garlic, chopped fine
3 rashers of thick-sliced bacon, diced
  very fine

Bouquet garni (see p. 82)
1 tablespoon cornstarch
1 cup heavy cream
4 dozen smoked oysters
4 tablespoons butter, creamed
6 slices of French bread
1 whole clove garlic
Olive oil
⅓ cup scallion rings

1. Mix the fish fumet, clam juice, and oysters with their juices in the blender container and process until puréed.

2. Heat the butter in a large saucepan. Add the onions, shallots, and chopped garlic cloves and sauté until translucent. Add the bacon and cook until the bacon starts taking on some color. Add the blended purée of shellfish to these ingredients. Bring to a boil, turn down to a simmer, add the bouquet garni, and cook until tasty, at least 1 hour. When done, strain carefully into a clean pot.

3. Reheat very well and bring to a simmer. Mix the cornstarch and the heavy cream and thicken the soup base, stirring constantly. Add the smoked oysters and reheat without boiling. Add the creamed butter.

4. Lightly toast the French bread slices. Rub them with the whole clove of garlic and fry them in olive oil until golden.

5. Serve the soup topped with the scallion rings and pass the bread slices on a plate.

POTAGE DE CRUSTACES ET COQUILLAGES DES COTES DE L'OUEST
{Shellfish Soup from the Western Coasts of France}

This soup could come from any of the seaports of France, from the Basque country to Boulogne and Calais. It is a personal composition that borrows some ingredients from just about everywhere. It's a meal in itself—a salad, cheese, and fruit will handsomely round out the feast.

SERVES 6

SOUP BASE:

6 pounds fish "frames" (from sole, whiting, petrale sole, salmon, etc.) (see p. 27)

2 tablespoons butter

3 onions, sliced

2 shallots, sliced

2 leeks (white and light green parts), sliced

1 small carrot, sliced

6 cloves garlic, unpeeled and crushed

1 cup dry white wine

Medium large bouquet garni (see p. 82)

2 dozen live Atlantic green crabs or 4 small Pacific Dungeness crabs

36 raw shrimp in their shells, preferably with their heads on

1 quart Fish Fumet (p. 28)

Water as needed

GARNISH:

1 carrot, cut into ⅛-inch julienne

1 white turnip, cut into ⅛-inch julienne

2 leeks (white and light green parts), cut into ⅛-inch julienne

1 medium zucchini, cut into ⅛-inch julienne

6 large mushrooms, cut into ⅛-inch julienne

14 tablespoons butter

6 tablespoons flour

1 quart mussels

Pepper from the mill

1 pound deep sea scallops, diced into 4 parts each

1 cup heavy cream

Salt

The tomalley of the crabs

Tabasco to taste

Dijon mustard to taste

Lemon juice as needed

Chopped flat-leaf parsley

2 tablespoons scallion rings

French bread slices, toasted

1. Clean the fish bones as described on page 28. Heat the butter in a large sauté pan. Add the onions, shallots, leeks, carrots, and garlic cloves and sauté over medium heat until the onions are translucent. Add the white wine and bouquet garni.

2. Chop the live green crabs by putting them on their backs, holding them down with a towel, and chopping them in half with a large knife. Chop

larger crabs into 4 pieces. Collect the crab tomalley in a bowl and set it aside for the garnish; add the crabs to the sauté pan.

3. Shell and devein the shrimp. Put the shells in the pan and put the shrimp on a plate and set aside. Add the fish fumet plus enough water to the sauté pan to cover the fish and shellfish. Bring to a boil, turn down to a simmer, and cook for 35 minutes, pushing and crushing all the materials in the pan to release their flavor. Strain through a "China cap" sieve.

4. To prepare the garnish, blanch the julienned carrot and turnip for 2 minutes. Mix them with the leeks, zucchini, and mushrooms. In a sauté pan, toss the mixture for a few minutes in 2 tablespoons of the butter. Set aside.

5. In a small kettle heat 6 tablespoons of the butter and add the flour. Cook together for 3–4 minutes. Bind this roux with the strained soup base. Bring to a boil, stirring, and simmer for 15–20 minutes. Skim as you simmer.

6. Scrub the mussels. Put them in a sauté pan, add a bit of pepper and a ladleful of the cooking soup base and steam them open. As soon as the mussels are ready, shell them, putting the shellfish on a plate and straining the steaming juices into the simmering soup. Clean the scallops and add their "feet" to the soup.

7. Continue simmering the soup another 15 minutes, then strain through a "China cap" sieve over the julienne of vegetables. Add the heavy cream. Correct the salt and pepper.

8. Place the remaining 6 tablespoons of the butter and the crab tomalley, together with a few dashes of Tabasco, salt, and Dijon mustard, in the food processor. Process to a compound butter.

9. Bring the soup to a high boil and add the shrimp. Bring back to a boil, add the scallops and mussels, and remove from the heat immediately. Correct the final taste with whatever is needed: salt, pepper, Tabasco, lemon juice.

10. Serve in bowls, floating a dollop of compound butter on top of each portion and sprinkling chopped parsley and scallion rings on top. Pass the toasted French bread separately.

Variation: to transform this recipe into a Mediterranean-style formula, change the garnish to strips of red and green peppers and zucchini. Add a strip of orange rind and some basil to the soup base, and add a large pinch of crushed saffron threads just before serving.

BROUET DE HANNONS DU MENAGIER DE PARIS
{A Scallop Soup with Lobster and Fresh Vegetables}

I had the idea for this dish while reading the 1392 cookbook known as *Le Ménagier de Paris*. The Hannons of the recipe title are known as *pétoncles* in modern French, and *pétoncles* are bay scallops. This is an expensive main course for a celebration dinner.

SERVES 6

1½ cups dry white wine
1½ quarts excellent Fish Fumet
  (p. 28)
3 cups clam juice, preferably fresh
2 onions, chopped
6 shallots, chopped
Bouquet garni (see p. 82)
2 pounds bay scallops

One 1½-pound live lobster
3 egg yolks
1 cup heavy cream
1 cup packed small, young spinach
  leaves
⅛ teaspoon saffron threads, well
  crumbled
¼ cup scallion rings

1. Mix the white wine, fish fumet, and clam juice in a saucepan. Add the onions, shallots, and bouquet garni. Bring to a boil. Turn down to a simmer.
2. Clean the bay scallops and add their tiny "feet" to the reducing broth.
3. Put the lobster on a board. Hold the tail fast with a towel and plunge the tip of a heavy chef's knife into the head, where a horizontal line appears ¼ inch above the lower edge; this severs the spinal cord. Cut off the claws and the tail. Shell these carefully so as not to tear or damage the meat. Cut the tail meat into 6 equal slices and set them with the claw meat on a plate.
4. Cut the lobster head in half. Remove the tomalley to a small dish. Set it aside. Add the lobster head to the cooking broth. Continue simmering until the broth is reduced to 5½ cups. Add the lobster tomalley to the broth. Let cook together another 15 minutes. Strain through a "China cap" strainer lined with several layers of cheesecloth.

5. Mix the egg yolks with the cream. Set aside. Roll the spinach leaves into cigars, then recut them into a ⅛-inch-wide chiffonade.

6. Bring the soup back to a boil. Add at once the scallops, lobster pieces, and spinach. Remove from the heat. Add a ladleful of soup broth to the egg yolk–cream mixture. Add the saffron to it, then blend the mixture into the soup and reheat until very warm but not boiling. Serve immediately with scallion rings sprinkled over the surface of the soap.

DENNY'S SNAIL BOUILLABAISSE

For my friend Denny Cox. A good Mediterranean snail soup for a first course on a winter day.

SERVES 6

3 tablespoons butter
4 onions, chopped fine
11 cloves garlic, chopped
1 pound mushrooms, chopped fine
Salt
Pepper from the mill
2 cups each Fish Fumet (p. 28), clam juice, and Golden Veal Stock (p. 20)
Bouquet garni (see p. 82)
1½ teaspoons fennel seeds
1 tablespoon Provençal herbs

1 tablespoon fresh basil or 1 teaspoon dried
4 dozen canned snails, preferably French
2 tablespoons chopped parsley
1 yellow summer squash (yellow zucchini)
1 zucchini
1 large carrot, peeled
1 or 2 dashes of orange bitters
1½ teaspoons Pernod or Pastis

1. Heat 2 tablespoons of the butter in a skillet. Add the onions and 10 cloves of the garlic and sauté until the onions and garlic start to color. Add the mushrooms and season with salt and pepper. Cover the pot and steam the mushrooms to extract their natural juices.

2. Add the fish fumet, clam juice, and veal stock. Bring to a boil; add the bouquet garni, the fennel seeds, Provençal herbs, and the basil. Drain the snail juices into the pot. Turn down to a simmer and cook until reduced by half.

3. While the broth reduces, marinate the snails in the last chopped clove of garlic mixed with the chopped parsley.

4. Cut the yellow squash, the zucchini, and the carrot in half lengthwise. Remove the seeds from the squash with a melon baller. Slice the 2 different squashes into ⅛-inch-thick slices. Heat the remaining tablespoon of the butter in a skillet and stir fry the squash slices in it for 2 minutes. Season with salt and pepper. Slice the carrot into ⅛-inch slices cut on the slant and blanch them for 2 minutes.

5. Strain the finished broth into a clean pot. Add the vegetables and the snails with their marinating herbs. Reheat well. Correct the seasoning with salt, pepper from the mill, a dash or two of orange bitters, and the Pernod or Pastis. Serve in bowls with a loaf of crusty bread and a good slab of sweet butter. This is very short in broth and rich in vegetables and snails.

Meats and Their Sauces

THE PRESENTATION OF MEAT CUTS
IN MODERN FRENCH CUISINE

I N G O O D M O D E R N F R E N C H C U I S I N E , great care is taken to
trim and remove the fat from meats before cooking them. This results in
healthier foods both at home and in the restaurant, but it presents a small
problem in the restaurant: that of volume on the plate. There is no doubt that
a steak trimmed of all its fat and gristle will look considerably smaller than
one presented in the customary manner, or that a half duck properly cut into a
leg and a whole breast does not fill a plate as fully as if it were served in one
solid piece as was the custom up to ten years ago. But, generally speaking, the
public has become used to the new style of presentation.

The following are instructions for purchasing and trimming meats for
modern presentation.

Beef:
The most popular beef items are steaks and roast beef. To this day they outsell
any other item in a restaurant and remain the "pièce de résistance" for home
celebrations.

1. *Beef steaks:*
All the recipes you will find in this chapter are adaptable to expensive
and less expensive pieces of meat. Whatever the cut chosen, proceed as follows

to trim it of all its fat and gristle. Cut off or pull off the fat "finish" all around the steaks, then, with a parer, lift all traces of "silverskin" away, so that the bare muscle of the meat is visible on both sides as well as all around the edges.

Expensive cuts are:

a. Prime rib steaks

b. Sirloin strip steaks

c. Tenderloin steaks

Affordable pieces are:

a. Blade steaks, often called "chicken" steaks

Note: Cut steaks yourself out of the cuts described below. You can freeze any steak not used from a large cut and spend less by purchasing in bulk.

2. *Beef roasts*:

All roasts must be trimmed of their fat and silverskin until the bare muscle appears on the whole surface of the meat; rub the meat with olive oil before roasting.

Expensive cuts are:

a. Beef rib roast. This rib cut may be bought already boned at the butcher or supermarket. When one trims this piece of meat down to the bare muscle, one finds all around the beef rib eye roll at least 2 pounds of meat per cut with which one can prepare an essence (see p. 268). A whole rib roast serves 10–12 and yields twelve ¾-inch steaks.

b. Beef strip loin cut. Also in the best category, this beef loin cut is sold already boned by butchers and supermarkets. When trimmed, this piece of meat releases approximately 1½ pounds of meat per cut with which one can prepare an essence (see p. 268). A whole "strip" serves 10 persons as a roast and contains ten ¾-inch steaks.

c. Beef tenderloin, called beef tenderloin regular cut by butchers and in supermarkets. The "chain," or long stringy piece of meat that runs alongside the long muscle, and the "tail," which is too flat for utilization as steak or part of a roast, provide the meat for an essence (see p. 268). A tenderloin serves 8–10 both as a roast or cut into the steaks known as tournedos.

Less expensive cuts are:

a. Beef top sirloin butt

b. Beef bottom sirloin butt

c. Eye of round

d. Boneless chuck eye roast

All these cuts can be roasted when coming from prime or choice beef. Their sauces must be based on the deglazing of their roasting juices, for no "trimmings" are available to prepare an essence (see deglazing on p. 267).

Eye of round and boneless chuck eye roast are the least expensive of all and should properly be reserved for informal family dinners.

Veal:

Good veal raised by the PROVIMI (Protein, Vitamin, Minerals) Dutch process is now available on a daily basis in the United States. The price is high, but so is the quality. Buying large cuts is least expensive even for home use, as all parts of the cuts are usable.

1. Veal loin chops. Use this cut for veal steaks and veal roasts. One can purchase half the loin or the whole double loin. Once this piece of meat is trimmed, the bone can be used to prepare Golden Veal Stock (p. 20). Both the loin strip and the tenderloin can be used either whole for roasting or can be cut into steaks or grenadins (small tenderloin steaks), for panfrying. Also, a large quantity of meat can be found in the belly flap of the animal, below the fat covering. This can be used for the preparation of essences or ground for meatballs or veal patties.

2. Veal top. The whole leg of veal is not a good investment. The best piece to purchase from the leg is the smaller retail cut known as veal top, or top of the round of veal, which can be cut across the grain, *never with the grain*, into ⅓-inch-thick French-style escalopes, or ¼-inch-thick Italian-style scallopine. This is an expensive piece, but a good investment because of the very small amount of waste.

3. Veal chuck. For braising, I recommend buying this cut, square cut, clod out. Always buy it *boneless* and tied if you want to braise a whole piece. It can also be cubed for braising as a stew.

Lamb:

For the dishes of lamb offered in this chapter, you will need one of the following cuts:

1. Lamb back. To serve 12, purchase this cut, which is made of the whole length of the rack and the unsplit loin (both sides of the lamb along the whole length of its body from shoulder to leg). This back can be stripped of all fat and gristle and 2 strips of meat 12–14 inches long can be extracted from along the backbone. Each strip represents 5 portions, so there are 10 portions in 2

strips. Each strip can be cut into ½-inch-thick noisettes (small pieces of meat) for panfrying. The strips can also be panroasted (see p. 278) and sliced lengthwise and with the grain into ¼-inch slivers. Portions 11 and 12 will be found within the body cavity in the form of the tenderloins, each of which will serve 1 person.

2. Lamb leg. Buy bone in, or boneless. In addition to being roasted whole, it can be stripped, boned, and each muscle cut across into ⅓-inch-thick slices for *escalopes d'agneau* or *scallopine d'agnello*.

3. Lamb shoulder. For braising, buy it boned and tied. It remains very affordable and can be used either whole or cubed for stew.

Venison:

Since venison must be purchased from a meat wholesaler or from a butcher, use the *back* of a deer as you would a back of lamb (p. 263) and extract the loin strips and the tenderloins. You can then cut them into noisettes and panfry. The leg may be roasted as a leg of lamb.

Lamb or beef, marinated artfully and at length, are good substitutes for venison. In the following recipes, look for those bearing the mention "en chevreuil" or "en chamois" (deer or chamois style), meaning that they have been marinated to taste like deer or chamois.

Pork:

If you are going to roast a piece of pork, use the excellent *Boston butt*, boneless and tied. It is the best and the moistest roast ever.

For chops and "grilled" slices of Boston butt, either overcook them radically or freeze the chops for 12 days to avoid the risk of contamination by trichinae. You can then cook them medium rare, as I do in several recipes. Freezing is *a must*, however, if your pork is not to be overcooked.

Trim pork chops of absolutely all traces of fat and sinews for quick panfrying.

You can purchase a whole side of pork loin, extract the whole sirloin strip and tenderloin, and cut it into larger noisettes. Remember that freezing remains absolutely necessary.

Fresh ham, either with or without the bone, is an excellent winter dish. No need to freeze here, since the roasting must be slow and deep for best flavor. A whole ham will serve at least 25.

Chicken and turkey:

When purchasing whole chickens for roasting, the maximum weight should be 4½ pounds.

Chicken or turkey breasts are always the most popular part of the bird. They require little preparation but boning, trimming, and, if large, recutting into cutlets; chicken or turkey cutlets make pleasant light dinner fare. They are best quickly panfried if they are thin and panfried over medium heat if they are thick. The variety of sauces is unlimited.

Ducks:

Much more can be done with American ducks than simply to roast them. Right now, America is enamored of the legendary French duck. Well, I have, as usual, other views, and think that all that duck business is for the ducks . . .

France has ducks of all sizes and dimensions: babies that weigh 1½–2 pounds and roast in 25–30 minutes in a blasting hot oven, ducks weighing 4–5 pounds with succulent meat, and large old reproduction or "foie gras" birds with massive bodies and filets weighing almost 1 pound each that can be served as the famous—today unavoidable—*magrets*. The ducks in France, mostly of the Muscovy breed crossbred with Rouen or Nantes ducks, have fiercely dark red meat. Some in the southwest are known as "*Mulards*" and are a crossbreed, probably between Muscovy ducks and the plain white goose. These huge animals are used for the preparation of *confits* (see p. 311) and foie gras; like mules, they cannot reproduce, hence their name.

The truth of the matter is that there is not one single thing wrong with American ducks. We have both Peking ducks and Muscovy ducks, and we can take our pick of what we like best personally. Farms all over the United States are full of Muscovy ducks that often, by themselves and without force-feeding, develop heavy whitish livers much like the less successful fattened livers of the French southwest.

Peking duck, when roasted whole, should be slowly and deeply cooked and never served rare in the French manner. There are very large, 6½-pound American Peking ducks one can either roast or cut up for *confits* and *magrets*, so that all cooks can truly choose the method they like best. At this writing a new "Mullard" duck with huge *magrets* and a liver that can be fattened is just being marketed in the United States.

Pigeons:

When purchasing pigeons, use the North Carolina ones, and choose the 1-pound birds rather than the ¾-pound ones.

Pigeons in France are roasted rare, and I continue to prefer them that way, although Americans, generally, will like them better done.

Quails:

Quails, so popular in Europe, are all too neglected in America, though we do have some excellent quails coming from North Carolina. Quails are panroasted if whole or panfried if butterflied, and they can support some of the most delicious sauce ideas.

PANFRIED AND ROASTED MEATS AND THEIR BROWN SAUCES

The methods outlined below represent strictly my personal approach to sauces for panfried and roasted meats. Many other techniques may be and are used by other cooks.

The quickest methods of producing a brown sauce for meats are:

- Simple deglazing
- Combination deglazing and reduction

The following methods are more sophisticated and may produce a more satisfactory final taste and appearance:

- Simple essence method
- Multiple essence method

All methods use the principle of reduction of a stock or wine, or a combination of both, into which a certain quantity of butter can be emulsified.

Two very important points for the modern cook:

1. From the quickest to the most elaborate, all the methods outlined here for making a brown sauce are completely interchangeable in all cases, depending only on the amount of time and the ingredients available to you.

2. The enrichment of any brown sauce with butter is entirely optional. The cook can add *as much* or *as little* butter to the finished sauce as she or he wishes. This is an important point, since it makes the caloric and cholesterol

content of the sauce, and ultimately of the meat dish it accompanies, entirely controllable.

A. Producing the bases for brown sauces— deglazing and essences:

Stock, especially Golden Veal Stock as described on page 20, reduced until it coats a spoon by ⅛ inch, is the base in the modern cuisine for all brown sauces for red meats.

The most important goal for the cook making the base for a brown sauce is to *tie* the veal stock to the meat served either by deglazing the pan in which the meat cooked or by making an essence. The quickest method is simple deglazing.

1. Simple deglazing method (gravy method):

This method can be used for all panfried meats and all oven-roasted meats, which render a certain amount of juices as they cook. These juices precipitate at the bottom of the skillet or roasting pan and brown considerably.

An excellent totally natural sauce base can be obtained by:

- *First*, discarding any trace of fat from the skillet or roasting pan.
- *Second*, adding veal stock to the skillet or pan and, over medium heat, scraping well until all the brown meat juices have dissolved into the veal stock.
- *Third*, reducing that deglazing over high heat until it coats a spoon by ⅛ inch.

The sauce base is now ready for the addition of *however much* butter one cares to use.

Approximate volume and time involved:

The whole quantity of stock needed is approximately ¼ cup per person, added at once to the skillet and reduced until a sauce base is obtained.

The method is quick and the sauce can be finished in 5 minutes.

2. Combination deglazing and reduction:

When no stock is available, one can make a good sauce base by using an excellent red wine and any vegetable one cares to add to the pan.

Let us take an example. A cook is panfrying steaks that will be served in a red wine sauce with a garnish of mushrooms.

The steaks are first trimmed carefully of all fat and gristle, and the meat pieces found in what is commonly called "the tail" of the steaks are cut into ½-inch cubes. The mushroom stems are coarsely sliced and browned at the same time as the cubes of meat. The fat used for browning is now discarded, and a small amount of water is added to completely deglaze the pan. Still leaving the meat in the pan, one reduces this water well until the deglazing coats the meat and vegetables, then one adds, a small cup at a time, a bottle of wine, reducing well after each addition. Each time, a larger amount of liquid will be left, and by the time one has finished using the bottle of wine, one has approximately 1–1¼ cups extremely good red wine reduction, flavored with beef and mushrooms, which one can enrich with either butter or cream, and the taste of which one can further modify by the addition of herbs or mustard.

This method works best with full-bodied red wines such as Pinot Noir, Pauillac, Côtes-du-Rhône, Barolo, or Zinfandel. It is less successful with white wine in which the acidity increases with the reduction, or even with vermouth in which the bitterness will be accentuated by the reduction. When using these last two wines, start the reduction with plain water and continue it with a mixture of 50 percent water and 50 percent wine.

Approximate volume and time involved:
Besides mushrooms, you may use onions, leeks, shallots, garlic, and carrots, alone or in combination, to flavor this rather quickly prepared sauce. One bottle of wine produces enough sauce to serve 6 and takes about 30 minutes to make.

3. Simple essence method:
This method is well within the capacity of any cook, but is more time consuming and a bit more expensive than the simple deglazing method.

Trim the meat of all fat and gristle. Cut all available lean meat surrounding the trimmings into ½-inch cubes. Brown them well in fat, butter, or oil and discard the latter.

Add to the pan containing the browned trimmings 3–4 cups Golden Veal Stock (p. 20) and deglaze well. Reduce until the "essence" obtained coats a spoon by ⅛ inch. This essence constitutes a sauce base. One will soon realize that one has the equivalent of an espagnole sauce in the classic cuisine, less the roux and its binding effect.

This method is most effective with veal and beef trimmings.

Approximate volume and time involved:

The quantity of sauce obtained is 1–1¼ cups, and it will serve 8–10, depending on the amount of other garnishes and butter added to it.

The method is time consuming only in the 10 minutes it takes to brown the trimmings. The reduction of the stock to an essence happens by itself; it requires approximately 35–40 minutes for the proportions mentioned above. The time involved will be approximately 45 minutes if you double the recipe and 1 hour if you triple it.

4. Multiple essence method:

The method is directly derived from the old classic triple *tombage à glace* (see *The Making of a Cook*, p. 115). It works this way:

- As for the simple essence method, one browns the meat trimmings very well in fat, butter, or oil. The browning must be deep and intense.
- One then reheats a pot of stock and keeps it at hand, simmering on the stove.
- As soon as the fat has been discarded from the frying pan, add 2 ladles Golden Veal Stock (p. 20) and deglaze the pan well by scraping the bottom and without removing the cubes of meat. The stock is then left to reduce until it coats the cubes of meat well and no liquid can be seen at all on the bottom of the pan.
- As soon as this first glaze is reached, add 1 or 2 more ladles of stock and repeat the operation as many times as needed to build a sauce.

Approximate volume and time involved:

One uses approximately 4–5 cups Golden Veal Stock to obtain a sauce to serve 7–10, with each successive addition of stock measuring approximately 1 cup. The last cup added will be reduced only a little, and the texture of the sauce is tested by dipping a spoon into the multiple essence sauce base. The sauce base should coat the spoon by ⅛–⅙ inch. The time involved in producing this type of sauce base is approximately 50–60 minutes. It is essential to stay around the stove and take care that each successive glaze does not burn; the reduction time will depend very much on the quality of the stock used; the better and heavier the stock, the faster the sauce will be finished. The essence will not build very fast nor thicken very well if the stock does not contain enough proteins and gelatin.

The essence keeps for 3 weeks well refrigerated. Reboiled for 5 minutes, it is then good for another 3 weeks and is the equivalent to the classic demiglace sauce.

B. Producing small brown sauces from deglazings and essences:
Deglazings and essences replace in modern French cuisine the two mother sauces of the classic cuisine: espagnole and demiglace. As the basic taste of those sauces could be modified to obtain small brown sauces, the basic taste of meat essences can be modified in many different ways by the addition of the following flavor and taste modifiers.

1. Plain spices:
Add the spices chosen (peppercorns black, white, or green or ground allspice or juniper, for example) to the boiling sauce. Remove immediately from the heat and let stand to infuse the taste for a few minutes.

2. Herbs or pungent roots:
Add them to the boiling sauce. Remove immediately from the heat and let stand to infuse the taste for a few minutes. If the herbs are fresh, they go in just before serving. If the herbs were dried, they are first revived in just enough hot stock to resaturate them, then added to the sauce base a good 5 minutes before serving.

Ginger is a favorite and must be blanched before it is added to the sauce base.

3. Purée of vegetables:
You can add to an essence a cooked purée of any vegetable. The preferred ones, because of their fully aromatic flavors, are: leeks, garlic, shallots, or red peppers, but any other vegetable can be used. (For more ideas see the various recipes in this chapter.)

The vegetable purée must be:

    a. Extremely flavorful and concentrated.

    b. Very, very smooth; no particles of the vegetable should be detected in the sauce, only its basic taste and flavor.

    c. Approximately of the same texture and thickness as the essence, or the finished sauce will be too heavy. To obtain this result, the cook should not hesitate to dilute the purée with stock before adding it to the sauce base if necessary.

4. Purée of fruit or citrus fruit rind:

Especially in the cooking of ducks and other poultry, purées of berries or fruit are welcome additions to an essence. They provide through their acidity a taste bridge between the meat and the strong essence. In the recipes that follow, you will find raspberries, rhubarb, pears, and apples used as additions to sauce bases, as well as several examples of sauces containing finely julienned rinds of citrus fruit.

5. Condiments:

Mustards plain or flavored, fruit mustards in the old Italian manner, and chutneys can be welcome additions to a sauce base. Beware: all mustard-type condiments will bring an additional degree of thickening of the sauce base, and the finished sauce may have to be lightened again with a bit of good stock. It is preferable not to reboil a sauce after mustard has been added, to prevent further thickening and blunting of the characteristic sharp taste. Chutneys with a sweet taste will always necessitate the addition of lemon juice.

6. A good spirit:

The most common spirits are, of course, Cognac, Armagnac, and Calvados. But why not grappa, marc, Scotch or whiskey, aquavit, vodka, or gin?

    The old-fashioned method consisted in heating the spirit in a small pot, igniting it, and whisking it, flambéing, into the essence. Nowadays one prefers to use the spirit to deglaze the pan in which the meat has been panfried or roasted, which in effect burns off the alcohol just as efficiently. Some of the prepared essence is then blended into the deglazing, and the wonderful bouquet of the spirit modifies the taste of the essence for the better.

7. *A reduction of wine and/or vinegar and aromatics:*
I chose the term reduction to represent in this chapter any wine or vinegar mixture cooked down (reduced) with aromatics so that there would not be any confusion with an essence.

Since an essence is reduced stock, many people have a tendency to call an essence a reduction, which can be confusing. Bear in mind that all through this meat chapter:

- an *essence* will result from reducing stock
- a *reduction* will be the result of reducing a wine, a vinegar, or a mixture of both. It could also be a mixture of 2 wines, or the mixture of wine with an acid citrus fruit juice.

By blending an essence with an acid reduction, one can create an infinite number of small brown sauces. An acid reduction is always flavored with aromatics: chopped onions, shallots, herbs, bouquet garni, spices, and must always cook down by *one-half* to *three-quarters* of its volume before one can blend it with an essence.

To make 1–1¼ cups finished sauce, use:

1 cup essence

plus

⅓ cup reduced wine

The original quantity of raw wine must then be:

1 cup

For the final rounded taste of the sauce, it is absolutely necessary to simmer the mixture of essence and reduction. It will require 10–15 minutes to produce 1–1¼ cups finished sauce.

8. *Multiple taste givers and flavor modifiers:*
Why not blend several taste givers and flavor modifiers together? As you will see in the recipes that follow, mustard and herbs meet in saucepans as well as reduced wines and mustards or fruit purées.

Nothing is unfeasible as long as the affinities of taste are respected.

RECAPITULATION

Simple deglazing
Combination
deglazing
and reduction
Simple essence
Multiple essence

DEGLAZING

OR ESSENCE

$+$

TASTE

MODIFIERS

Spices and herbs
Purées of vegetables
Purées of acid fruit
Citrus rind
Condiments
A good spirit
A reduction of wine
or wine vinegar

$=$ **MODERN SMALL BROWN SAUCES**
FOR PANFRIED AND ROASTED MEATS

C. Stabilizers, texture modifiers, and texture correctors for modern small brown sauces:

These are the thickeners and the lighteners one adds to a small brown sauce to modify its texture. They vary from starches to stock, liver, butter and cream, or even the mechanical action of a blender.

1. Addition of a small amount of starch:

When a sauce based on a simple deglazing or essence is prepared in small quantity and used rather quickly, there is no need to stabilize it with any starch whatsoever.

In the production of sauces in larger quantities, where the finished product will stand in a hot kitchen before being finished in a number of smaller portions, as is the case in a restaurant, one can, if one desires, stabilize the sauce base with a bit of a pure starch. The best of all is cornstarch; potato starch can also be used, but it is more susceptible to breaking down (hydrolization).

The starch is introduced into the finished sauce in the form of a slurry—starch dissolved into a bit of cold stock and stirred into the simmering essence. A teaspoon or so of starch is enough to stabilize 2 quarts of sauce. The starch helps the sauce to retain the butter in emulsion. Sauces stabilized with starch rarely "break butter" on their surface after they have been finished (see p. 275 under Butter).

2. Plain stock:

An essence made of a large quantity of reduced stock will sometimes become too thick; when poured from a sauce spoon, instead of flowing in a tiny syruplike stream, it will form a thickish film that falls in irregular blobs; such an essence will also, as soon as spooned over a piece of meat, form a surface tension skin as it continues dehydrating on standing.

The addition of stock will immediately reintroduce the needed moisture into the sauce and return it to its normal texture.

3. Creams:

Light and medium creams can be used as thinners for an essence that has become too thick, while heavy cream, heavy cream mixed with sour cream, and "homemade" crème fraîche are used, on the contrary, as enrichers. They give the texture of the sauce an added degree of opulence that gives the impression that the sauce thickens, although it does not thicken that much. The true thickener in the way of creams is true crème fraîche—the naturally matured, slightly sour 40–42 percent butterfat cream that comes only from cream spooned off unpasteurized milks and is thus difficult to find in the United States. A few farmers produce it, but it is never sold on the open market because unpasteurized dairy products are not legal in all states.

Being personally very spoiled by the French crème fraîche, I do recommend not to bother with the "fabrication" of homemade crème fraîche—its taste and texture are radically different, and so are the results obtained. (See white sauces for white meats, p. 328, for more details.)

4. Butter, compound butters:

Modern sauces are said to be "finished" with an addition of butter, which, as it goes in emulsion into a deglazing or an essence, thickens it as well as changes its color to a lighter brown.

Any butter added to a deglazing or essence, be it plain butter or a compound butter, is always added last to the sauce according to one of the following techniques:

a. *"Low heat" method:*

Add the butter to the hot essence or deglazing over very low heat in tablespoon-size chunks, whisking well until the butter has been completely homogenized.

b. *"High heat" method:*

During the last few minutes of cooking of the essence or combination of essences plus reduction, bring the contents of the sauce to a high boil and add the butter at the center of the boil. The churning motion of the boil acts as a natural whisk, and the butter immediately finds itself dispersed in myriads of droplets into the sauce. If the sauce still needs reducing, do not hesitate to keep it on high boil and let it reduce to the taste and texture you desire—as long as you keep boiling hard, the emulsion will remain stable.

Note: A modern sauce is finished with butter either on very low heat or on high boil. Only these two ranges of temperature will allow the butterfat to remain in emulsion. A sauce finished with butter cannot simmer, or it will find itself in the range of temperature where the butter molecules will bond together, separate from the protein and moisture part of the sauce, and come floating to the top.

Should this type of separation occur, quickly bring the sauce to a high boil and try boiling hard. The butter may reintegrate into the body of the sauce. If the sauce is already well reduced, however, and stubbornly refuses to rehomogenize, your problem is lack of moisture; add stock, whisking very gradually at the center of the boil until the sauce has regained its original texture. Help the natural churning movement of the boil by adding to it that of your whisk or a blunt-ended wooden spatula, agitating the sauce in all directions—*do not stir* from the center, but cover the whole surface of the pan with the implement you are using, in a figure eight of sorts!

c. *Special blender method for smaller quantities:*

If you want, you can execute the buttering of the sauce by using your blender. Place the butter, plain or compound, in the blender container. Start the blender on medium-high speed, then, through the lid opening of the blender, pour the sauce over the butter. The emulsion occurs immediately and is good and stable. The color is very light and will darken again as the sauce stands and the air bubbles trapped in it by the speed of the blender reintegrate the atmosphere.

5. Blood or liver as thickeners or binders:

Traditionally, the blood of animals has been consumed as a source of protein; the many *boudins noirs* (black puddings) of France, as well as all the sausages and desserts made with pig's blood in Italy, are remnants of the old custom of using blood as a food. Latin Europeans do indeed like to use blood to thicken their sauces for birds and wild animals such as ducks, hare, wild rabbits, and even larger venison joints. Since blood is not available most of the time in the United States outside of Chinese neighborhoods and since the custom is not the most appealing to the Anglo-Saxon mind, one can substitute a small piece of fresh chicken or duck liver. Do not use too much liver—the liver must be "the dot on the i," not the "i" itself. It should bring added silkiness and a certain degree of thickness to the sauce, but it should remain pink, which means that it should be poached into the hot sauce, not cooked. Should it cook, it would immediately spoil the sauce with a greenish tinge and an irreversible graininess.

The best procedure to use is to place a small piece of liver (½ a small chicken liver, ¼ an average duck liver, ⅕ a rabbit liver) in the blender container, as well as the amount of butter you wish to use to "finish" the sauce. The butter will act as a damper between the liver and the heat of the sauce. Keep the plug of the blender lid open and start the blender on high speed. Immediately pour the hot sauce straight from the stove into the opening of the blender top. The thickening will occur as the liver poaches and the butter goes into emulsion in the sauce. The pink tinge comes from the liver poaching and the creamy hue from the butter going into emulsion, as well as from the air being churned into the sauce. Once strained back into its saucepan, the sauce must stand for approximately 10–15 minutes. It will darken slightly as the air comes to its surface in a fine blanket of bubbles that slowly reintegrate the atmosphere. A liver-bound sauce positively *cannot* boil or it will turn green and grainy.

It is very important not to confuse liver and foie gras. In both the classic and the modern cuisines, foie gras—the fattened liver of goose or duck—is used in small quantities as a binder or light thickener for brown or white meat sauces. Please bear in mind that absolutely nothing can replace fresh fois gras and that preparing a mock foie gras in the form of a mousse of chicken or duck livers cannot work. Since in this case the livers have already been poached in one way or another, any addition of heat would continue cooking them and would produce both the green color and the graininess that must be avoided at all costs.

Only those with access to true foie gras will be able to use this form of binding. Those who are part of the great majority of "foie gras-less" cooks could try this solution:

Use plain duck liver as described above, replacing a tablespoon of the butter normally used to finish the sauce by 1 tablespoon solid cold goose fat. Goose fat is kept in many Jewish homes of Hungarian or Central European origin or can be purchased in cans (imported from France). Don't worry about using only 1 tablespoon; anything left in the can may be used to fry the most delicious and gorgeous potatoes.

It is a good idea when preparing a sauce with a liver binding to choose livers that are as white as possible, such as those of stewing hens, which are almost as fat and pale as true foie gras.

Note: Liver from calf or pork is not usable to bind a sauce; it is too strong and too pungent.

6. Béarnaise sauce:

That wonderful old friend of mine, the classic béarnaise sauce, can be used as a binder as well as a taste modifier in a small brown sauce. Some of the results obtained are quite successful.

For the cooking techniques of béarnaise, see *The Making of a Cook*, page 132.

The cooking of panfried meat dishes:

1. Trim the meat of all fat and gristle
2. With any trimmings prepare an essence if you care to
3. Panfry the meat:

    Sear well on the first side. Turn over. Season the seared side. As soon as you see the blood or juices "bead" at the surface of the meat, the meat is cooked rare. If you want it medium rare, turn it over once more and cook 1 more minute after you season the second side. Discard the cooking fat.
4. Deglaze the frying pan with Golden Veal Stock (p. 20). If you prepare a simple deglazing, add the enrichment butter and chosen garnish and spoon over the meat.

5. If you use an essence, deglaze the pan with stock, add the essence, reduce together a bit, and add butter. Finally add the garnish and spoon over the meat.

Panfrying or panroasting:

If a piece of meat is ¾–1 inch thick, it will be simply panfried. If, however, it is thicker than that, it must be panroasted. There is little difference between the 2 methods except the time it takes to cook a piece of meat that is thickish.

To panroast either a thick steak or a piece of lamb loin 1½–2 inches thick, or even a quail, sear both sides well and season them well; keep turning them every 3 minutes or so, and during the last 3–5 minutes of cooking, cover the frying pan to force the heat through to the center of the piece of meat so that it does not remain too rare.

Panfried beef:

Steaks will obviously be the cuts of beef cooked by the panfrying method. You may use any steak of your choice: tenderloin, sirloin strip, prime rib, or chicken steak. In the recipes that follow, I have, for the sake of diversity and in order to illustrate various techniques, used a variety of methods for building sauces. Do remember that they are interchangeable and that you can at all times decide to switch to the simple or the more complicated way of preparing the sauce. Note that all essences can be prepared several days in advance and kept refrigerated.

TOURNEDOS A L'ESSENCE DE CEPES
{Beef Tenderloin Steaks with Wild Mushrooms and Pancetta}

This is not, in spite of the presence of the *pancettta* and the Boleti, an Italian-inspired recipe, but one coming from the part of Occitania that uses *ventrèche*, the old-fashioned salt pork that looks and smells exactly like *pancetta* and that was probably brought to the area during the Gallo-Roman period. The wild mushrooms can be replaced by ½ pound fresh ordinary mushrooms.

SERVES 6

6 tenderloin steaks, ¾–1 inch thick
½ cup butter
1¼ cups Golden Veal Stock (p. 20)
3 ounces pancetta, diced into ¼-inch
  cubes
2 cloves garlic, chopped fine
2 tablespoons chopped parsley
1 large fresh Boletus Edulis (Porcini)
  or 2 tablespoons dried Porcini
  chips

3 ounces fresh fairy ring mushrooms
  (Marasmius oreades) or 3
  tablespoons dried
Salt
Pepper from the mill
1 tablespoon olive oil

1. Trim the steaks of all traces of fat and gristle. Remove the "chain" to be found along one side. Cut each piece of "chain" in cubes.
2. Heat 1 tablespoon of the butter in a small skillet, brown the pieces of "chain" in it, cover them with 1 cup of the stock, scraping the bottom of the pan well, and reduce to ⅔ cup simple essence (see p. 268).
3. Heat another tablespoon of the butter in a large skillet and brown the pancetta lightly in it. Add the garlic and 1 tablespoon of the parsley during the last minute of cooking; empty into a small bowl. Do not wash the skillet. If you are cooking the steaks later in the day, you can use it—just cover it.
4. If using fresh mushrooms, clean them well, removing the "tubes" from under the large Boletus cap. Dice the Boletus and add it to the fairy ring mushrooms. Sauté in 1 tablespoon of the butter, season with salt and pepper, and cover for 1 minute to extract the natural juices. Add the mushrooms and their juices to the essence of beef. Simmer together for 5 minutes.
5. If you are using dried mushrooms, soak them in barely enough lukewarm water to cover and let them rehydrate well. Empty their soaking water into the prepared essence. Sauté the rehydrated mushrooms gently in 1 tablespoon hot butter. Add to the essence and simmer together for 10 minutes, until the sauce is reduced again to ⅔–¾ cup of solids and liquids.
6. When the time comes to prepare the steaks, panfry them in the olive oil and 1 tablespoon butter well heated together, to the degree of doneness you prefer.
7. When the steaks are done, keep them warm; deglaze the skillet with the remaining stock, glazing it a bit. Add the pancetta mixture, then the essence

and mushroom mixture, and the remainder of the butter. Correct the final seasoning and spoon over the steaks.

Recommended vegetables: A summer jardinière and a small, plain gratin of potatoes (pp. 382 and 399).

TOURNEDOS A L'OCCITANE
{Tenderloin Steaks the Occitanian Way}

There is a 24-hour marination period for this recipe!

SERVES 6

6 tenderloins steaks, ¾ inch thick	*9 tablespoons butter*
3 cups Cahors or Zinfandel wine	*2 tablespoons very fresh and white*
10 juniper berries, crushed	*Roquefort cheese, crumbled*
½ teaspoon each dried thyme, savory,	*2 tablespoons walnuts*
rosemary, and basil, well crushed	*Olive oil*
6 cloves garlic	*⅓ cup Golden Veal Stock (p. 20)*
1 large onion, chopped	*Salt*
2 shallots, chopped	*Coarsely cracked black pepper*
Chopped parsley stems	*Chopped parsley*

1. Trim the steaks of all fat and gristle. Reserve the "chain" pieces.
2. Mix the wine, juniper berries, thyme, savory, rosemary, basil, 6 crushed cloves of the garlic, the chopped onion and shallots, and the parsley stems. Bring to a boil, simmer for 2 minutes, and let cool completely.
3. Pour half the marinade into a glass baking dish. Add the steaks, cover them with the remainder of the marinade, and let marinate, covered, for 24 hours, in a cool place, but not in the refrigerator.
4. Cream 8 tablespoons of the butter and add the crumbled Roquefort. Sauté the walnuts in 1 tablespoon olive oil until golden; pat them dry, chop them, and add them to the Roquefort butter. Put the Roquefort butter in a piece of plastic wrap, shape it into a small sausage, and refrigerate it.
5. One hour before cooking the steaks, brown the reserved pieces of "chain" in the remaining tablespoon of the butter. Gather all the vegetables from

the marinade, pat them dry, add them to the skillet, and brown them with the meat already in the skillet.

6. Pour the marinade over the meat and vegetables and reduce until ½ cup of excellent reduction results. Strain into a saucepan.

7. Panfry the tenderloin steaks in olive oil to your preferred degree of doneness. Remove the fat, deglaze the pan with the stock, and reduce it well. Strain the deglazing into the marinade reduction. Bring to a high boil and add 2 tablespoons of the Roquefort and walnut butter. Correct salt and pepper.

8. To serve place 1 tournedos on a plate and spoon an equal amount of sauce over each tournedos. Top with 1 tablespoon of cold and solid Roquefort butter. Serve promptly, topped with cracked pepper and chopped parsley.

Recommended vegetables: The Occitanian Vegetable Plate on page 383 and the Italian Cabbage and Potato Purée page 412.

STEAKS DE CHASSEURS
{Steaks for Frustrated Hunters who cannot find a deer . . . }

It is essential, if one wants the meat to taste like true venison, to marinate it a full 3 days.

SERVES 6

6 sirloin strip steaks, ¾–1 inch thick
2 cups Châteauneuf-du-Pape or
   Petite Sirah from California
½ cup ruby port
½ cup Sercial Madeira
1 ounce Armagnac
10 cloves garlic, crushed
2 onions, chopped
2 shallots, chopped
½ a carrot, chopped
1 teaspoon thyme
1 bay leaf, crushed
1½ teaspoons dried basil

½ teaspoon majoram
12 juniper berries
2 tablespoons chopped parsley stems
3 ounces extra-lean hamburger meat
9 tablespoons butter
2½ cups Golden Veal Stock (p. 20)
3 tablespoons celery root, cut into
   ⅛-inch julienne and blanched
3 tablespoons smoked tongue, cut
   into ⅛-inch julienne
Coarsely cracked pepper
2 tablespoons chopped parsley

1. Trim the steaks of all fat and gristle. Set aside, keeping any trimmings of meat you can find from the "chain," which is very little. Place the steak in a large glass baking dish.

2. Bring the red wine, port, Maderia, and Armagnac to a boil. Add the garlic, onions, shallots, carrot, and all the aromatics including the chopped parsley stems. Simmer together for 15 minutes and cool completely. Pour over the steaks. Marinate for 3 days, turning over once a day.

3. On the fourth day, brown the pieces of "chain" and the hamburger meat in 1 tablespoon of the butter. Gather together and pat dry the vegetables from the marinade. Toss them with the hamburger meat until dry and starting to brown. Mix the liquid marinade with 2 cups of the veal stock, and gradually add it, ½ cup at a time, glazing each time to build a multiple essence. There should be approximately ½ cup of good essence by the time you have used all the stock (see p. 269 for the multiple essence technique). Strain into a small saucepan, bring to a boil, and add 6 tablespoons of the butter.

4. Panfry the steaks to your desired doneness in the 2 remaining tablespoons of the butter. Discard the cooking butter, deglaze with the remaining ½ cup veal stock, and reduce well. Mix with the buttered essence. Add the blanched celery root and the smoked tongue as well as cracked pepper.

5. Serve the steaks topped with the sauce and chopped parsley.

Recommended vegetables: Three purées, of squash, of zucchini, and of potatoes and artichokes, or a medley of celery root, onions, Brussels sprouts, and chestnuts (pp. 413–15 and 386).

Panfried pheasant and venison:

Only two recipes, because so little venison can be found. Remember that a whole back of lamb can be boned and marinated to be used exactly like a saddle of venison.

FAISANS DU BEGUINAGE {The Sister's Pheasants}

The presentation given here of cutlets cut out of the breasts of the pheasants and the cutlets called "pojarskis" prepared out of the legs, takes into consideration the fact that these running birds have tough muscles. Proceed over 2 days.

SERVES 6

MARINADE:

3 pheasants, if possible mature rather than young
¼ cup white port
¼ cup Sercial Madeira

2 tablespoons Calvados or applejack
24 juniper berries, crushed
⅓ teaspoon dried savory
½ teaspoon Quatre-Epices (p. 35)

CUTLETS AND SAUCE:

2 tablespoons olive oil
1 quart Golden Veal Stock (p. 20)
3 ounces bacon, blanched and diced
2 eggs
1⅓ cups fresh bread crumbs
Quatre-Epices (p. 35)
½ cup butter, at room temperature
2 tablespoons flour
1 teaspoon oil
1 teaspoon water
Salt
Pepper from the mill
½ cup Médoc or Cabernet Sauvignon wine

1½ cups dry cider (imported French or English)
2 shallots, chopped fine
1 teaspoon dried savory
12 juniper berries
1 pheasant liver
½ cup clarified butter
6 slices of apple, peeled, cored and cut into rounds
18 cooked chestnuts
1½ tablespoons chopped chives

DAY ONE:

1. Cut the pheasants into 2 breasts and 2 legs each. Remove the skin and bones from the legs and lift all the meat away, removing all sinews and nerves. Bone the breasts, keeping the breast meat whole and attached to the first joint of the wing. Reserve the wing tips and the bones.
2. Mix the port, Madeira, and Calvados with the juniper berries and savory. Brush some of this marinade on each side of the 6 breasts. Toss the leg meat with the remainder of the marinade. Store in a glass baking dish, covered with plastic wrap. Punch small holes in the plastic and marinate for 24 hours in the refrigerator.
3. Brown the wing tips of all 3 pheasants and the bones of 1 whole pheasant

in the olive oil. Discard the browning oil. Add 1 cup of the veal stock and reduce to a glaze. Add another cup of the stock and reduce again. Repeat with the remaining 2 cups of the stock; you should obtain approximately ⅔ cup excellent pheasant essence. Strain and store in the refrigerator.

DAY TWO:

1. Remove the 24 crushed juniper berries from the marinated meats. Place the leg meat only, the blanched bacon, 1 egg, ⅓ cup of the fresh bread crumbs, a dash of *quatre-épices*, 2 tablespoons of the butter, and any remaining marinade in the food processor and process into a smooth forcemeat. Correct the seasoning well. Shape into 6 cutlets. Flour the cutlets, brush them with a mixture of the remaining egg, the oil, and the water seasoned lightly with salt and pepper and coat them with the remaining cup of the bread crumbs. Dry on a rack.

2. To prepare the second part of the sauce; mix the red wine and cider, add the shallots, savory, and 12 juniper berries, and put the mixture in a saucepan. Reduce slowly to ⅔ cup solids and liquids. Reheat the essence of pheasant, strain the reduction into it, and simmer together for 10–15 minutes. Place ½ a pheasant liver and 5 tablespoons of the butter in the blender. Start the blender. Pour the sauce into it and blend well. Strain back into the saucepan. Let stand until ready to serve.

3. Heat the clarified butter in 2 large sauté pans. Brown the breaded cutlets on both sides until golden brown. Gently cook the breasts, turning them often until they do not give under finger pressure anymore.

4. Serve a breast and a breaded cutlet, topping these with 1 slice of apple browned in the remaining tablespoon of butter and 3 chestnuts. Reheat the sauce without boiling it and spoon it over the pheasant. Sprinkle with chopped chives.

Recommended vegetables: A winter purée of squash, artichoke, and a good pilaf of mixed white and wild rice (pp. 414–15, 425).

SELLE DE CHEVREUIL A L'AIGRE-DOUCE
{Saddle of Venison in Sweet and Sour Sauce}

SERVES 6–8

1 saddle of venison, as large as
   possible
1 quart Golden Veal Stock (p. 20)
1¼ cups excellent Pinot Noir–based
   wine, preferably from France
½ cup red port
6 tablespoons Cognac
1 onion, chopped
2 shallots, chopped
3 cloves garlic, chopped fine
2 tablespoons wine vinegar

⅓ teaspoon each dried thyme,
   marjoram, and savory
1 teaspoon dried basil
12 juniper berries, crushed
4 tablespoons butter, at room
   temperature
¼ cup currants
4 tablespoons clarified butter
¼ cup toasted pignoli nuts
Chopped parsley

1. Bone the saddle of venison. Chop the bones and brown them in a 400°F. oven. Deglaze the roasting pan with 1 cup of the stock. Transfer the bones to a sauté pan. Add the deglazing of the roasting pan and another cup of stock and reduce to 3–4 tablespoons; repeat with the remaining 2 cups of the stock to obtain approximately ⅔ cup venison essence. Set aside.

2. *Positively do not marinate the venison.* Strip it well of all fat and gristle and cut the loin strips into ⅔-inch-thick noisettes. Keep the 2 tenderloins whole.

3. Mix the Pinot Noir, the port, and 4 tablespoons of the Cognac. Add the onion, shallots, and garlic cloves, the vinegar, thyme, marjoram, savory, basil, and juniper berries. Reduce to ½ cup solids and liquids mixed. Strain into the venison essence. Simmer together for 10 minutes. Add the butter.

4. While the sauce cooks, steep the currants in the remaining Cognac.

5. Panfry the noisettes of venison to your desired doneness in the clarified butter. Also panfry the whole tenderloins, covering them for 2 minutes at the end of their cooking to force the heat to their center. Just before serving, mix the sauce, currants, and pignoli. Serve promptly topped with the sauce and sprinkled with chopped parsley.

Recommended vegetables: A medley of celery root, Brussels sprouts, baby onions, and chestnuts and a pilaf of coarse wheat (pp. 386 and 424).

Panfried lamb, pork, and veal:
All the recipes given below are applicable to:
  1. Rib chops of lamb, pork, or veal
  2. Loin chops of lamb, pork, or veal
  3. Rib or loin, boned and cut into ½-inch-thick noisettes or steaks
  4. Rib or loin, boned and cooked in one 2½–3-inch-long piece to be recut lengthwise into ⅙-inch-thin slices known as aiguillettes
  5. Top round of veal, cut into ⅓-inch escalopes
  6. Leg of lamb, boned and cut into ⅓-inch escalopes

To bone a loin of lamb, veal, pork, or venison:
The loin in all mammals is built as follows: under the fat covering you can see the 2 sirloin strips—they rest on the upper side of the backbone. Immediately under the sirloin strips are the 2 tenderloins, attached to the underside of the backbone. Inside the cavity is a lot of fat that can be discarded; lodged in this fat are the kidneys. These are usable in lamb and veal, but pork or venison kidneys would have to be overcooked to be safely consumed. On both sides of the saddle is a large belly flap that contains a lot of meat that can be cut out to prepare essences and sauces as well as veal patties.

When butchers cut loin chops, they start by splitting the loin into 2 halves, cutting through the middle of the backbone with their power saw or a cleaver; then they remove the belly flap and cut each side of the loin transversally into the chops that you buy in supermarkets. To make steaks or noisettes out of the chops, you simply remove the lean meat from the center, using a paring knife and making sure that there are no traces of fat or gristle left on the meat.

A better, more economical way is to purchase 1 whole side of the loin and lift out the whole sirloin strip and tenderloin to obtain 2 long pieces of meat.

For your safety, use a very sharp paring knife with as short a blade as possible, not one of those menacing boning knives. Hold the knife firmly *without extending your finger on the blade.*
  1. Lift the fat covering, called "finish" by butchers, from the top of the sirloin strip. You will see immediately under it the silverskin that covers the meat.
  2. Cut along the backbone, scraping down against it to leave as little meat

as possible on it, until you have completely separated the sirloin strip from the bone. You are now holding a piece of meat approximately 11–12 inches long. Remove the long stringy band known as the "chain" visible on one side of the strip; keep it to make essences.

3. Clean the piece of meat of all silverskin: pass your paring knife blade under it at the center of the piece of meat and slide your blade toward each end of the piece of meat lifting ½-inch-wide bands of silverskin at a time. This is best done by holding the blade at a 45 degree angle to the surface of the meat so as to leave as little flesh as possible attached to the membrane.

4. Once the silverskin has been removed, turn the piece over and remove any trace of additional thin silverskin visible where the muscle was originally attached to the bone.

The piece of meat you have just boned weighs approximately 2 pounds. If you want to roast it, see pages 298–311. If you want to use it in smaller pieces, cut it across into ½-inch-thick steaks for veal and pork (pork steaks are also called noisettes) or ½-inch-thick noisettes for lamb. Lamb can also be cut into 2½–3-inch-long pieces that can be cooked whole and recut lengthwise into ⅛-inch aiguillettes (see p. 286).

The tenderloin of all animals is too small to roast and is best cut into ½-inch grenadins for veal and in noisettes ⅛ inch thick for pork. In lamb, it is so small that it can only be panfried in 1 piece.

To panfry or panroast lamb, pork, and veal:

Sear chops on one side; turn over, season with salt and pepper. Sear on the second side until brown, turn over again; season with salt and pepper. Turn the heat down to finish cooking to the degree you prefer. The meat is rare when your finger sinks into it, medium rare when it gives in only a little, and well done when it resists and feels hard under the finger.

When you panroast a whole piece of loin 1½–2 inches thick, cover the pan a few minutes at the end of the cooking to force the heat to its center.

1. The optimum doneness in lamb is medium rare. The meat will be pink, not red.

2. The optimum doneness in pork is also pink, but *remember* that the meat must have been frozen for 12 solid days and defrosted before being cooked this way.

3. The optimum doneness in veal is also pink, but pink pink, not bluish pink. The juices must run out of the meat and the meat should under no

circumstances have turned white. If the idea of light pink veal is abhorrent to you, remember that veal is nothing more than miniature beef and just as unpalatable when well done as beef is.

About lamb essences:

Lamb essences are difficult to make taste frankly of lamb. Preparing a lamb stock can help, but I don't find it that useful in the long run, too time consuming and expensive. The best way to accentuate quickly the lamb flavor in an essence is to add some fennel seeds to it.

NOISETTES D'AGNEAU A LA VERVEINE ET AUX PIGNONS
{Noisettes of Lamb with Verbena Sauce and Pignoli}

SERVES 6

1 whole saddle of lamb with belly flaps (see p. 286)	2 tablespoons dried verbena, powdered fine
The trimmings of the lamb belly flap	½ teaspoon fennel seeds
6 tablespoons butter	1 tiny clove garlic, chopped
2¼ cups Golden Veal Stock (p. 20)	1 tablespoon chopped parsley
	2 tablespoons toasted pignoli nuts

1. Bone or have the butcher bone the saddle into sirloin strips and tenderloins totally free of fat and gristle. Cut the loin strips into 9 noisettes each ½ inch thick. Do not cut the tenderloins; they will cook in 1 piece. Set aside. Cube all pieces of lean meat to be found in the belly flap. (See p. 286 for more details.)

2. Gather the lamb trimmings found on the belly flap, brown them well in 1 tablespoon of the butter. Discard the butter. Add 2 cups of the stock and the verbena and fennel seeds and simmer down to 1 cup good single essence. When the essence is ready, strain it through a fine "China cap" sieve and add the garlic and parsley.

3. Panfry the noisettes and tenderloins in 2 tablespoons of the butter. When they are done, remove to a hot platter, discard the cooking butter, and

deglaze the pan with the remaining ¼ cup of the stock. Add the deglazing to the verbena essence. Enrich the essence with the remaining 3 tablespoons of the butter, then add the pignoli nuts.

4. Cut the tenderloins lengthwise into 3 pieces each. Put 1 slice of tenderloin on each plate and season it. Top each slice of tenderloin with 3 noisettes. Spoon the sauce over the noisettes.

Recommended vegetables: Using the techniques for stir frying vegetables p. 370, prepare a Provençal-style jardinière of julienned zucchini and peeled and julienned red and green bell peppers, plus a large watercress bouquet.

AIGUILLETTES D'AGNEAU A LA BATELIERE
{Aiguillettes of Lamb with Old-fashioned Remoulade}

This dish is inspired by the Grillade des "Bâteliers," a dish of beef slices prepared by the barge people who go up and down the Saône and the Rhône bringing goods north and south in their river barges. As quick as it is delicious.

SERVES 6

1 saddle of lamb, as large as possible	1½ tablespoons parsley
6 tablespoons butter	2 anchovy fillets, rinsed and mashed
Salt	¼ teaspoon fine-grated fresh lemon
1¼ cups Golden Veal Stock (p. 20)	rind
1–1½ teaspoons extra-strong Dijon	¼ teaspoon fine-grated fresh orange
mustard	rind
1 large clove garlic, chopped fine	Pepper from the mill

1. Bone or have the butcher bone the saddle into 2 sirloin strips and 2 tenderloins free of fat and gristle. Cut the sirloin strips into two 3½-inch pieces. Do not cut the tenderloins.

2. Heat 2 tablespoons of the butter in a large skillet, panroast the pieces of saddle and tenderloins, starting the tenderloins only after the sirloin strips have been cooked on one side. Salt the meat on both sides after each side has been seared. When the meat is done, remove it to a platter and keep it warm.

3. Deglaze the skillet with the veal stock, reducing it to approximately ¾ cup. In the hot deglazing, add the remaining 4 tablespoons of the butter,

still boiling hard; remove the pan from the heat and add the mustard, garlic, parsley, 1 anchovy, and the grated lemon and orange rind.

4. Taste the sauce. If more salt is needed, add the second anchovy and pepper from the mill.

5. Slice the pieces of loin and the tenderloins lengthwise into ⅛-inch-thin slices. Arrange in a fan pattern on 6 hot plates. Top with the sauce and serve promptly.

Recommended vegetables: A large watercress bouquet, a seasonal jardinière (p. 386), and any of the baked potatoes (pp. 393–95).

ESCALOPES D'AGNEAU A LA ROMAINE
{Escalope of Lamb the Roman Way}

Use the largest cuts (top, bottom, and true eye of the round) of a whole leg of lamb stripped of all fat first and cut into ⅓-inch escalopes. There will be just enough meat to prepare a dinner for 8 and make an excellent multiple essence out of the lesser pieces.

SERVES 8

One 4–4½-pound leg of lamb
½ cup butter
5¾ cups Golden Veal Stock (p. 20)
2 small artichokes
1 large clove garlic, chopped fine

1½–2 tablespoons chopped fresh
  mint leaves
Salt
Pepper from the mill

1. Bone the leg, removing all fat and gristle as you do so. Separate all the meat from the leg and cut against the grain into ⅓-inch escalopes. Remove all the lean meat you can find still attached to the bones of the leg (the whole shank will still be available).

2. Cut the shank and any other meat into ½-inch cubes. Brown very deeply in 2 tablespoons of the butter. Discard the butter and add 1 cup of the stock. Reduce to a glaze. Add a second cup of the stock and reduce to approximately 3–4 tablespoons essence. Repeat the process 3 more times, until a generous cup of essence is available. Strain the essence into a clean pot.

3. Remove the leaves of the artichokes (you can boil them for your lunch). Clean the artichoke bottoms very well. Sliver them fine and sauté them gently in 1–2 tablespoons of the butter; cover and cook them until tender and very soft. You may have to add a tablespoon or so of stock or water during the cooking.

4. Put artichokes and essence in the blender and purée well. Add 2 tablespoons of the butter and process to emulsify the butter. Strain the artichoke sauce into a saucepan. Add the garlic and the mint. Let stand until ready to use. It will be thickish, but its texture will lighten on standing.

5. Panfry the escalopes of lamb in the remaining 2 tablespoons of the butter. Season well with salt and pepper and keep warm. Deglaze the pan with the remaining ¾ cup stock and add the deglazing to the essence. Correct the seasoning with salt and pepper from the mill. Top the escalopes with the sauce.

Recommended vegetables: Zucchini and yellow squash beads mixed (p. 372), plus any baked tomato half (pp. 395–96) and a saffron rice pilaf with currants (p. 425), and, of course, a great big bouquet of watercress for each plate.

NOISETTES DE PORC AU CAMPARI
{Noisettes of Pork with Campari Sauce}

Have you frozen your pork chops for 12 days and defrosted them? If not, please choose another dish.

SERVES 6

12 loin pork chops, ⅔ inch thick
Dried orange rind
Salt
6 tablespoons butter
1¼ cups Golden Veal Stock (p. 20)
1 cup orange juice
½ cup Campari
5 teaspoons extremely fine-julienned
  orange rind

1 teaspoon extremely fine-julienned
  lime rind
1–2 teaspoons extra-strong Dijon
  mustard
Pepper from the mill
Angostura bitters
A few drops of lime juice (optional)
½ pound fresh spinach leaves
12 orange slices

1. Bone the pork chops. Trim the center muscle very well of all fat and gristle to obtain 12 noisettes. Sprinkle the noisettes on both sides with a tiny pinch of dried orange rind and salt. Let stand for 2 hours.

2. Cut small cubes of meat out of the trimmings of the chops, brown them in 1 tablespoon of the butter, discard the browning fat, and add 1 cup of the stock. Reduce to a glaze. Add the orange juice and Campari and simmer together until ½ cup mixture is left. Strain and set aside.

3. Blanch the julienned orange and lime rinds. Set aside.

4. Panfry the noisettes in 2 tablespoons of the butter. Do not over cook; they should remain juicy. Discard the fat in the skillet. Deglaze with the remainder of the stock and add the reduced orange juice mixture. Add mustard to your taste. Correct the salt and pepper. Strain into a clean saucepan and add the citrus rinds. Whisk in 2 tablespoons of the butter, add a dash of Angostura bitters and a few drops of lime juice if needed.

5. Wilt the spinach in the remaining tablespoon of the butter. Season with salt and pepper. On each plate set 2 noisettes on a bed of wilted spinach; top each noisette with 1 slice of orange and the sauce and serve promptly.

Recommended vegetables: Any dish of candied vegetables such as onions, shallots, or garlic or a combination of the three (p. 410).

NOISETTES DE PORC AUX RAISINS VINAIGRES *{Noisettes of Pork in Sweet and Sour Sauce}*

Have you frozen your pork for 12 days and defrosted it? If not, please choose another dish.

SERVES 6

½ cup raisins
3 tablespoons Aceto Balsamico
    (p. 45) or any other vinegar
1 side of a loin of pork
1 teaspoon ground coriander
Salt
Pepper from the mill

½ teaspoon cinnamon
½ cup butter
1 cup Golden Veal Stock (p. 20)
1½ teaspoons Red Bell Pepper
    Mustard (p. 38) or other mustard
2 tablespoons chopped parsley

1. Macerate the raisins in the *aceto balsamico* overnight.

2. Remove the whole side of pork loin from the backbone in one piece, then remove all of its fat and gristle. Cut the strip of fat-free meat obtained into 12 noisettes. Mix the ground coriander, ¼ teaspoon salt, ¼ teaspoon pepper from the mill, and the cinnamon to obtain 2 teaspoons of mixture. Sprinkle on the meat and let stand overnight in the refrigerator.

3. Panfry the meat in 2 large skillets, each containing 2 tablespoons hot butter. Remove the meat to a plate and keep warm. Deglaze the skillet with the veal stock and reduce by one-half. Add the raisins with their vinegar and as much mustard as you like. Correct the seasoning, add the chopped parsley and the remaining butter.

4. Serve the noisettes topped with the sauce and garnished with the following vegetables:

Recommended vegetables: Spaetzle and shallots (p. 130). Crisp blanched green beans, well buttered.

FOIE DE VEAU A LA PUREE DE FRAMBOISES VINAIGREES
{Calf's Liver with Vinegared Raspberries}

Use the best possible calf's liver cut into even ⅓-inch slices. A variation on a recipe from a bistro called Le Tire-Bouchon in Annecy.

SERVES 6

One 10-ounce package frozen raspberries in syrup	Pepper from the mill
2 tablespoons sherry vinegar or other vinegar	6 slices of calf's liver, ⅓ inch thick
	4 tablespoons butter
2 tablespoons flour	½ cup stock or broth of your choice
Salt	Lemon juice as needed
	Chopped parsley

1. Drain the syrup from the raspberries. Put them in a bowl and macerate them overnight in the vinegar. Then purée and strain into a bowl.

2. Mix flour, salt, and pepper.

3. Remove all traces of membranes inside and around the slices of calf's liver. This must be done with a parer for the large blood vessels visible in the slices of liver, but can be done by slipping the index finger between membrane and liver tissues for the outside membrane. Coat the cleaned liver slices with the seasoned flour.

4. Heat 2 tablespoons butter in each of two 10-inch skillets. Quickly panfry the slices of liver to medium rare. Set aside and keep warm. Discard the cooking butter.

5. Deglaze the pans with the stock, reducing well. Add half the vinegared raspberry purée to each pan. Correct the seasoning with salt, pepper, and lemon juice if needed. Add the chopped parsley and serve over the slices of liver.

Recommended vegetables: The salad of lamb's lettuce on p. 152, omitting the goat cheese.

STEAKS DE VEAU A LA CREME D'ENDIVES
{Veal Steaks with Endive Cream}

Excellent for a winter company dinner.

SERVES 6

3 rashers of thick-sliced bacon	Salt
Approximately 1 cup veal trimmings from the belly flap of the veal loin	Pepper from the mill
	Twelve ½-inch-thick sirloin veal steaks free of all fat and gristle
6 tablespoons butter	
2 cups Golden Veal Stock (p. 20)	½ cup heavy cream
3 Belgian endives	1 tablespoon chopped parsley

1. Remove the rind from the rashers of bacon. Cut them crosswise into ⅛-inch slivers. Render the bacon slowly in a frying pan until golden. Discard the fat and set aside the bacon.

2. Brown the veal trimmings in 2 tablespoons of the butter. Discard the browning fat and add the veal stock. Let the mixture reduce to 1 cup of essence. Strain it into a saucepan.

3. Meanwhile, wash, trim, and cut the Belgian endives into ⅛-inch slivers. Toss them in 2 tablespoons hot butter; season with salt and pepper. Cover the pan and cook until the vegetables fall into a few tablespoons of over-cooked purée. Put the endives and essence of veal into the blender container and purée well together. Set aside.

4. In the remaining 2 tablespoons of the butter, panfry the veal steaks for 2–3 minutes on each side. Without discarding the browning butter, deglaze the pan with the heavy cream; as soon as the cream thickens, strain it into the endive sauce. Add the bacon, adjust the seasoning, and spoon the sauce over the veal steaks. Sprinkle with chopped parsley.

Recommended vegetables: Blanched and stir-fried celery root and celery ribs mixed (p. 385) and a mixture of spinach and tomato pasta, well buttered.

STEAKS DE VEAU AUX NOISETTES ET A L'ORANGE {Veal Steaks with Hazelnuts and Orange}

When preparing this dish, remember that you are serving veal with orange sauce, not orange sauce with veal. The orange should be very understated or it will take over too strongly.

SERVES 6

½ cup toasted hazelnuts, chopped fine but not in powder

12 ½-inch veal steaks free of fat and gristle, from the loin, the rib, or the eye of the round

1 cup trimmings of veal from the boning of the veal loin

6 tablespoons butter

2 cups Golden Veal Stock (p. 20)

⅓ teaspoon dried orange rind

Grand Marnier as needed

½ teaspoon Dijon mustard

A dash of soy sauce

Pepper from the mill

12 slices of orange (preferably blood oranges)

1 tablespoon chopped chives

1. Sprinkle the toasted hazelnuts on a sheet of waxed paper. Press both sides of the veal steaks into the layer of nuts.

2. Brown the veal trimmings in 2 tablespoons of the butter. Discard the

browning butter, add the stock and the dried orange rind, and let reduce to 1 cup excellent veal essence. Strain into a saucepan.

3. Panfry the veal steaks in the remaining 4 tablespoons of the butter, using 2 large skillets. As soon as the meat is done, remove it to a plate; keep it warm.

4. Deglaze the 2 skillets with a dash of Grand Marnier in each. Strain the deglazing into the orange veal essence and reheat it well; add the Dijon mustard and a dash of soy sauce, using it as salt. Correct with the pepper.

5. Quickly heat the orange slices in the 2 skillets. To serve, top each steak with an orange slice and spoon the sauce over the steaks; sprinkle with chives.

Recommended vegetables: Using the techniques for stir frying vegetables on p. 370, prepare stir-fried Jerusalem artichokes and carrot julienne mixed and topped with scallion rings; plain rice pilaf with aniseeds (p. 425).

Panroasted quails:

These lovely little birds are at their best when quickly panroasted. The cooking time is even more reduced when the birds are opened through the back and "frogged." Remove the last 2 joints of the wings as well as the neck. Push the legs upward at the same time you fold them. Punch 2 small holes in the skin on either side of the tips of the breastbone and tuck in the end of each drumstick; the little quails are now nice and flat and almost uniformly thick on the breast and legs.

Season early, using only a bit of salt but quite a bit of pepper, and continue seasoning well all through the cooking.

The cooking is done by searing well on both sides first, seasoning well, then, during the last 2–3 minutes of cooking, pushing on the quails with a lid that is smaller than the skillet so that it just fits into the skillet and flattens the birds at the same time it forces the heat to their centers and finishes cooking them. The total cooking time of a panroasted quail is never more than 10 minutes.

The sauce is prepared by simple deglazing or with a small essence blended with a reduction of aromatics and the deglazing of the skillet.

CAILLES SAUTEES AU CHOCOLAT
{Sautéed Quails with Chocolate Sauce}

SERVES 6

12 "frogged" quails (see above)
Salt
Pepper from the mill
6 chicken wings, chopped
6 tablespoons butter
5⅓ cups Golden Veal Stock (p. 20)
1½ cups heavy cream
1 strip tangerine rind, 1½ inches by ½ inch

Mandarine Napoléon liqueur as needed
1 teaspoon grated unsweetened chocolate
2 tablespoons peeled and blanched pistachios
12 slices of tangerine, carefully peeled of all white membranes

1. Butterfly or have the butcher butterfly the quails, taking care to remove and keep the necks and the tiny wing tips. Salt the quails very lightly and pepper them quite a bit. Let stand, refrigerated, for 4 hours.

2. Brown the quail necks and wings as well as the chicken wings in 2 tablespoons of the butter. Discard the browning fat. Add 1 cup of the stock and reduce to a heavy glaze. Repeat with another cup of stock. Add a third cup of stock and reduce to approximately ¼ cup. Repeat with 2 more cups of stock until ¾–1 cup good essence is obtained; strain it into a clean saucepan.

3. Bring the cream to a boil. Add the strip of tangerine rind and simmer down to ¾ cup.

4. Strain the reduced cream into the essence, add a solid dash of Mandarine Napoléon and the bitter chocolate. Correct the salt and pepper and let stand for 15–20 minutes to blend the flavors well.

5. Panfry the quails in the remaining 4 tablespoons of the butter, seasoning them well with salt and pepper. Discard the fat in the frying pan and deglaze with the remaining ⅓ cup of the stock; strain the deglazing into the sauce.

6. Serve 2 quails per person, coating them well with the sauce and dotting each with a few pistachios and 1 slice of tangerine.

Recommended vegetables: A plain gratin of potatoes (p. 399) and a winter jardinière (p. 386).

ROASTED MEATS

Roasted beef:

Please refer to pages 262–63 for the choice of cuts to be roasted. I have given 3 recipes for either boned rolled rib or boned sirloin strip, but the recipes are applicable to other, less expensive cuts of beef.

Be careful, however: the loin and rib cuts may be completely stripped of their fat and gristle, all the way down to the bare muscle, because in grades prime and choice the tissues are quite nicely marbled. Other cuts of meat such as eye of the round or rump will not show this marbling and must retain their fat cover so as not to be too dry after roasting. Trim the meat after roasting in this case

In any case, deglaze the roasting pan well and add the deglazing to your prepared sauce.

All beef, especially when stripped and trimmed of all fat, must be roasted on a rack placed over a roasting pan at a quick 400°F., 20 minutes for the first pound and 15 minutes for each additional pound. Let any roast stand for at least 5 minutes before carving it.

ALOYAU DE BOEUF EN CHAMOIS
{Beef Sirloin Strip, Chamois Style}

Please refer to and follow the recipe for *Steaks de Chasseurs* on page 281, replacing the garnish of celery root and smoked tongue with 4 ounces of dried forest mushrooms of the type "Marasmius oreades" or "Boletus Edulis" and chopped parsley.

The mushrooms are soaked in just enough water to rehydrate them and chopped fine. Their soaking water is added to the wine reduction and the mushroom hash is sautéed lightly in butter and added to the finished sauce.

The marinating time for a large piece of meat like a rib, a tenderloin, or a sirloin strip is 4 full days.

FILET DE BOEUF EN CHINOISERIE
{Tenderloin of Beef with Chinese-style Sauce}

Use a very large tenderloin of beef with an eye at least 3½ inches wide.

SERVES ABOUT 8

1 whole tenderloin of beef, 6–7 pounds
Olive oil as needed
4½ cups Golden Veal Stock (p. 20)
1 piece gingerroot, 1 inch by 2 inches

Fine-ground Szechuan pepper, untoasted
1 tablespoon strong Dijon mustard
Dark soy sauce as needed
6 scallions (green part only), cut into elongated rings

1. Strip the tenderloin of all fat, gristle, and the large sheath of silverskin that surrounds it. Cut the flat part of the "tail" and the "chain" into cubes. Set the meat aside until ready to roast.

2. Rub your hands with approximately 2 teaspoons olive oil and massage it into the tenderloin.

3. Heat 2 tablespoons olive oil in a skillet and brown all the cubes of "chain" and "tail" until very dark. Discard the browning oil and gradually build a multiple essence with 4 cups of the veal stock, adding 1 cup stock at a time, to obtain approximately 1 cup excellent essence (see p. 269). Strain it into a saucepan.

4. While the essence cooks, peel and cut the gingerroot into a fine ⅛-inch-wide julienne; blanch it for a few minutes in boiling water. Sauté it in 2 teaspoons olive oil. Add it to the finished essence and let steep. Add approximately 1 teaspoon Szechuan pepper to the sauce.

5. Preheat the oven to 400°F. Mix the Dijon mustard with 2 tablespoons soy sauce. Roast the meat for 20 minutes. Brush it lightly all over with the mixture of mustard and soy sauce and continue roasting until a meat thermometer reads 135°F. Remove from the oven and let stand for 5–10 minutes while you finish the sauce.

6. Drain any fat collected in the roasting pan. Deglaze the roasting pan with the remaining ½ cup of the stock. Scrape well. Strain the deglazing into the ginger sauce. Correct the final seasoning of the sauce with soy sauce and Szechuan pepper.

7. When serving, slice and *salt* the slices of beef. Top them with the ginger sauce and the scallion rings.

Recommended vegetables: A pilaf of rice finished with toasted slivers of almonds (p. 425) and a julienne of peeled red, green, and, if possible, yellow peppers (p. 378).

COTE DE BOEUF A LA BIERE BRUNE
{Roasted Rib of Beef with Beer and Horseradish Sauce}

Use prepared horseradish; any freshly home-prepared horseradish would overpower the taste of the meat.

SERVES 10 TO 12

7-rib boneless roast of beef, about 8 pounds
Olive oil as needed
1 quart Golden Veal Stock (p. 20)
¼ cup heavy cream
2 tablespoons prepared horseradish

Salt
Pepper from the mill
½ cup dark beer
4 tablespoons butter
3 tablespoons scallion rings

1. Strip the rib of beef of all fat, gristle, and silverskin. Rub it with 2 teaspoons olive oil. Let stand at room temperature for 1 hour before cooking.
2. Cube the meat gathered from the trimmings ("chain," etc.) and brown it in 2 tablespoons olive oil. Discard the browning oil. Add the stock, cup by cup, reducing between each addition, to build approximately 1 cup excellent essence of beef. Strain the essence into a saucepan.
3. Preheat the oven to 400°F. Heat the heavy cream, reduce it to 2 tablespoons, and mix it with 2 tablespoons (more or less to your own taste) of prepared horseradish. Add the mixture to the prepared essence and let stand while the meat roasts.
4. Roast the meat for about 45–50 minutes. Season well with salt and pepper as soon as you take it out of the oven.
5. Deglaze the roasting pan with the dark beer, scraping and reducing well.

Strain this deglazing into the prepared horseradish sauce. Reheat to the boiling point, add the butter and remove from the heat.

6. Slice the meat paper thin and do not forget to salt the slices before you spoon the sauce and sprinkle the scallion rings over them.

Recommended vegetables: Red radishes sautéed in vinegar and butter, sliced plain sautéed zucchini, plus a gratin of celery root and potatoes (p. 379 and 400).

Roasted veal:

My personal philosophy on roasted veal is to use only the very best cut—sirloin strip—and to keep it for very special occasions.

Purchase 1 side of a loin of veal with belly flap attached. The belly flap provides cubes of meat for the essence and the loin provides that wonderful strip of meat roughly 11 inches by 3 inches that is the sirloin strip of veal. You will find, as I mentioned earlier, that the bones make a very good stock.

The loin, after cleaning and stripping, must be tied at regular ¾-inch intervals to insure an even size and thickness from one end of the piece to the other and, consequently, even roasting. The roasting temperature is 400°F. and the total duration of the roasting is no more than 20–25 minutes—smaller strips will take almost as long to cook as larger ones. Their mass being smaller, the heat does not penetrate as fast as it does the larger roasts.

The meat can be roasted plain, rubbed with 2 teaspoons olive oil, or coated with crumbs, nuts, aromatics, or herbs.

Panroasting in an electric frying pan is also very feasible. It is done relatively quickly in one of those "buffet" style rectangular electric frying pans. If you decide to panroast rather than oven roast, *do not tie* the meat; leave it flat, approximately 1¾ inches thick as it comes off the bone. Handle it like a thick beefsteak; it will panroast in approximately 15–20 minutes (see p. 278). Deglaze the frying pan as you would deglaze the roasting pan and add the deglazing to your essence.

Note that the meat should not be bluish but uniformly pink, and it should render a lot of good juices when sliced; these juices can be added to the finished sauce if you like. A normal portion is four ¼-inch slices per person.

Also, all the sauces given for panfried veal can be adapted to a piece of roast veal and vice versa.

ROTI DE VEAU ROSE A LA VERVEINE
{Quick Veal Roast with Verbena Coating}

SERVES 8

1 side of veal loin, bone in, with
   belly flap
About ¼ cup fine-powdered dried
   verbena
¼ cup chopped parsley
4 cloves garlic

½ teaspoon fine-grated lemon rind
2 tablespoons butter
4¼ cups Golden Veal Stock (p. 20)
3 tablespoons olive oil
Salt

1. Using a very sharp paring knife, separate the veal loin from the backbone to which it is attached to obtain 1 long roast; remove all traces of fat and silverskin from the surface of the meat. Tie it at ¾-inch intervals to equalize the thickness of the piece from one end to the other.
2. Mix together two-thirds of the powdered verbena, two-thirds of the parsley, and 1 garlic clove, chopped extremely fine. Add the grated lemon rind and mix well. Rub the piece of meat with 1 tablespoon very soft butter applied evenly over the whole surface of the roast and spread the herb mixture evenly on a piece of waxed paper. Roll the meat into it. Let stand at room temperature for 1 hour.
3. Cut approximately 2 cups fat-free meat cubes from the belly flap of the veal. Brown them in 1 tablespoon of the butter until dark golden brown. Discard the browning fat. Add 1 cup stock and reduce to a glaze. Repeat the same operation twice more with 2 more cups stock. Finally add 1 more cup of stock and simmer for 20 minutes or so to obtain a fine essence of veal. Strain it into a small saucepan. Add the remainder of the verbena and parsley. Let steep while you roast the meat.
4. Preheat oven to 400°F. Roast the meat for 20–25 minutes, or until an instant meat thermometer registers 130°F., no more. Remove from the oven and let rest for 5 minutes before carving.
5. During those 5 minutes, slice the remaining 3 garlic cloves lengthwise into paper-thin slivers and cook them in the olive oil until light golden. Drain on paper towel.
6. Deglaze the roasting pan with the remaining ¼ cup of the stock. Add the deglazing to the sauce.

7. Slice the meat into ⅛–¼-inch slices; salt the slices. If any juices run out of the meat while slicing, add them to the sauce. Spoon the sauce over the meat and dot with a few slivers of garlic.

Recommended vegetables: Separate the meat from the vegetables with a large bouquet of watercress. Serve a mixed julienne of zucchini and mushrooms and 2 croutons of fried polenta per person (pp. 373 and 432).

ROTI DE VEAU ROSE AUX GOUSSES D'AIL ET A LA FLEUR DE THYM
{Veal Roast with Garlic and Thyme}

SERVES 6–10

1 side of veal loin, bone in, with belly
    flap
2 tablespoons olive oil
7 cups Golden Veal Stock (p. 20)
3 heads of garlic, separated into
    single cloves
Dried thyme flowers or leaves as
    needed

4 tablespoons butter
¾ cup fresh bread crumbs
3 tablespoons fine-chopped parsley
1 clove garlic, mashed
Salt
Pepper from the mill

1. Using a very sharp paring knife, separate the veal loin from the backbone to which it is attached to obtain 1 long roast. Remove all traces of fat and silverskin from the surface of the meat. Cut approximately 2 cups veal cubes from the belly flap of the veal.
2. Brown the cubes of meat in the olive oil until nicely browned. Discard the browning oil. Add 1 quart stock and slowly reduce to 1 cup simple essence of veal (see p. 268).
3. Blanch the garlic cloves for 1 minute. Put them in a saucepan, cover them with the remaining 3 cups of the stock, and let them cook until they are tender. Add as much fine-crumbled thyme as you like. When the garlic cloves are cooked, add them and whatever stock is left around them to the veal essence. Let stand together.

4. Preheat the oven to 400°F. Tie the veal roast evenly all around. Rub it with 1 tablespoon soft butter. Spread the bread crumbs mixed with 2 tablespoons of the chopped parsley, the mashed garlic clove, and ⅓ teaspoon of very fine-crumbled thyme evenly over waxed paper. Roll the buttered roast into the mixture; pat well to impress the crumbs into the butter.

5. Roast for 20–30 minutes, depending on size and until a meat thermometer registers 135°F. Remove from the oven and let stand for 5 minutes before carving.

6. Reheat the garlic sauce well; add the remaining 3 tablespoons of the butter to it and correct its salt and pepper. Serve the meat sliced into ⅙-inch slivers, well seasoned and topped with the garlic and thyme sauce. Sprinkle with the remaining tablespoon of the fresh chopped parsley.

Recommended vegetables: A pilaf of saffron rice with basil and toasted pignoli nuts. A jardinière of peppers of all colors and zucchini cut into julienne strips (pages 378 and 425).

Les canards rôtis (roast ducks):

American ducks of the Peking breed look and taste best when roasted slowly at 325°F. for 2½ hours until well done. Of course, if you prefer your duck a bit more chewy and like much, much less gravy to prepare a good sauce, you can roast a 4½–5-pound duck for 1 hour at 400° F.

You will see that all the duck recipes presented here are for "whole duck" accompanied by sweet and sour fruit or berry sauce. You will notice that in 2 recipes coming originally from Normandy and Gascony, the filets of the duck and the legs are cooked separately. The *magret* or *maigret*—the name given to the filets by the Gascony and Landes people—is always panfried medium rare, while the legs roast slowly in the oven or cook in liquid duck fat as *confit. Remember* always that an acid sauce served on a rare or medium-rare *magret* does not truly represent the pinnacle of gastronomy, even if hundreds of French chefs prepare this kind of "heretic" dish every day. I have carefully avoided a very acid sauce on the *magrets* presented here, and the most acid ingredient I would allow any *magret* to come in contact with is a small amount of mustard used to finish and round off a good meaty sauce.

To roast a whole duck slowly, brush it first with ½ teaspoon honey mixed with 1 teaspoon dark soy sauce. This will give you an extremely good-looking and very crisp outside skin. Prick the skin on both sides of the bird, just below the filets, so the fat can escape. Syphon off the duck fat as it is released during cooking with a meat baster and accumulate it in a glass jar to prepare the *confit* on pages 315–17.

Muscovy ducks should not, in my opinion, be used for anything other than a duck forcemeat for terrines, but as stated before, this is a matter of personal taste, and if you like them better, by all means use them.

In addition to the recipes given below, here are a few more ideas for whole roast duck that I have found successful and that you can develop yourself.

- Roast duck with red pepper purée and vinegar
- Roast duck with pears and cassis
- Roast duck with assorted citrus rinds
- Roast duck with basil essence and persillade
- Roast duck with crushed mint
- Roast duck with green apples and green peppercorns
- Roast duck with pears, green peppercorns, and ginger
- Roast duck with wild mushrooms, *pancetta*, and candied shallots
- Roast duck with fresh figs and Pineau des Charentes sauce
- Roast duck with artichokes and lemon
- Roast duck with apricot purée and pistachios

CANARD AU CARAMEL VINAIGRE
{Whole Roast Duck with Caramel and Vinegared Currant Sauce}

SERVES 6–9

⅓ cup currants
2 tablespoons Aceto Balsamico
  (p. 45)
Three 5-pound Peking ducks
Salt
Pepper from the mill
Fine-ground Szechuan pepper
3 strips of orange rind, 2 inches by
  ¾ inch each

1 teaspoon honey
1 tablespoon dark soy sauce
2 tablespoons olive oil
4¼ cups Golden Veal Stock (p. 20)
2 tablespoons sugar
2 tablespoons toasted pignoli nuts
Chopped parsley

1. Macerate the currants overnight in the *aceto balsamico*. Toss every so often to mix well.

2. Remove the necks and the wing tips of the ducks, chop them into 1½-inch chunks, and set them aside.

3. Put salt, pepper, and fine-ground Szechuan pepper, plus a strip of orange rind into the cavity of each duck and truss all 3 birds. Mix the honey and soy sauce and brush lightly over the body of each duck.

4. Preheat the oven to 325°F. Roast the duck for 2½ hours. After 45 minutes of roasting, prick the sides well just below the breast to release the fat.

5. Remove the fat regularly with a baster, and after removing the fat each time tilt the ducks forward to let the juices run out of their cavities and build a good gravy at the bottom of the roasting pan.

6. Brown the reserved pieces of wings and necks well in olive oil; discard the oil and add a quart of the stock in 4 additions, reducing well after each addition to build a good multiple essence (see p. 269). Strain into a clean saucepan. Add the currants with their vinegar.

7. Cook the sugar to the dark (almost bitter) caramel stage, dissolve it with the remaining ¼ cup of veal stock, and set aside.

8. When the ducks are done, set them aside and keep them hot. Discard all traces of fat from the roasting pan. Deglaze the roasting pan with the caramel and stock mixture, scraping well and heating if necessary to dissolve all caramelized meat juices. Strain this deglazing into the prepared currant-vinegar-essence mixture and simmer together for 5 minutes to blend the flavors.

9. Serve the duck in portions of 1 leg and 1 breast topped with the sauce, toasted pignoli nuts, and chopped parsley.

Recommended vegetables: The three-grain pilaf on page 425. A very large bouquet of watercress and pears sautéed in butter and ginger (p. 422).

CANARDS ROTIS A LA MOUTARDE DE RHUBARBE ET FRAMBOISES
{Roast Ducks with Rhubarb and Raspberry Mustard Sauce}

Careful: this is—as all sauces based on rhubarb—very difficult to balance because of the infinitely varying acidities of the vegetable. Taste the rhubarb as soon as it is cooked, use little if it is very tart and more if its tartness is "civilized." Young shoots are too acid—wait for the larger, very red stalks. You must have frozen raspberries; you need their sugar content.

SERVES 6

3 stalks rhubarb 15 inches long and
¾ inch wide
2 boxes frozen raspberries (not fresh
raspberries)
2 tablespoons red wine vinegar
Three 5-pound ducks

Salt
Pepper from the mill
1 tablespoon olive oil
4¼ cups Golden Veal Stock (p. 20)
Dijon mustard as needed
A pinch of sugar if needed

1. Peel the stalks of rhubarb, cut them in chunks, put them in a saucepan, and let them cook until they fall into a purée; set aside.
2. Defrost the raspberries. Discard their juices. Choose 36 large raspberries, set them in a dish, and spoon the vinegar over them. Purée the remainder of the berries in the blender and strain through a fine strainer to discard all seeds. Set aside.
3. Cut off the wing tips and necks of the ducks. Cut them into chunks and reserve.
4. Season the cavities of the ducks with salt and pepper. Preheat the oven to 325°F. Truss the birds, prick their sides to release the fat, and roast for 2½ hours. Remove the liquid fat with a baster and, as the ducks cook, tilt them forward to release their juices and build a good gravy.
5. Brown the reserved wing tips and necks in the olive oil. Discard the fat and add 4 cups of the stock, 1 cup at a time, reducing well after each addition, to form a multiple essence (see p. 269). Strain into the blender container.
6. When the ducks are done, discard any trace of fat in the roasting pan, deglaze with the remaining ¼ cup of the stock, and add to the blender container.
7. To finish the sauce, add to the essence ¼ cup each rhubarb and raspberry purées, plus a large teaspoon Dijon mustard. Blend well together. Work with more of each purée and/or mustard and season with salt and pepper until you reach the taste you like best. Should you by mistake make the sauce overacid, correct it with a pinch of sugar.
8. Serve the duck in portions of 1 leg and 1 breast each, coated with the raspberry-rhubarb sauce and dotted with the vinegared raspberries.

Recommended vegetable: Prepare a plain lamb's lettuce and watercress salad with a raspberry vinegar and hazelnut oil dressing.

Le canard en Normandie (duck in the Normandy manner):

This is a modernized presentation, made without the famous blood sauce so special to the area of Rouen and Duclair and well adapted to American ducks. Notice that 2 recipes are included in this presentation—1 for the legs and 1 for the breasts, served medium rare as you would a steak. You can either make 2 light meals out of the roasted legs and 1 out of the filets, or you can serve a celebration meal, with both the roasted leg and the filet presented side by side.

CUISSES DE CANARD A LA MOUTARDE
{Duck Legs Roasted with Mustard Coating}

6 legs from three 5-pound ducks	*6 tablespoons dry bread crumbs*
Salt	*2 tablespoons butter, melted*
Pepper from the mill	*½ cup dry apple cider*
Dijon mustard, plain or flavored, to	*½ cup Golden Veal Stock (p. 20)*
taste	*Coarse-chopped parsley*

1. Preheat the oven to 325°F. Salt and pepper the legs on the meat side. Brush the skin side with a thin layer of mustard; sprinkle evenly with bread crumbs and dribble melted butter over the crumbing.
2. Roast the legs 1½–2 hours. When they are done, discard the fat from the roasting pan and deglaze well with a mixture of the cider and stock. Strain into a small saucepan and reduce to ½ cup. Spoon 1 tablespoon gravy over each leg and serve sprinkled with chopped parsley.

FILETS DE CANARD AU CRESSON CRU
{Filets of Duck with Raw Watercress Sauce}

In Normandy the whole duck is roasted and the 2 huge filets are lifted while the duck is still rare; they are then cut lengthwise into aiguillettes and served with a sauce made with port wine and a strong Bordeaux or Côtes-du-Rhône and all the blood of the duck extracted with a duck press. Since the duck press has become obsolete, if only because of the capital one must invest to purchase it, I have substituted for the blood a small piece of the liver. The raw watercress brings the dish into the realm of modern cuisine and is also my idea; its peppery freshness lightens the sumptuously rich sauce.

In the United States this method can be used very effectively with the breasts of any wild ducks.

6 filets cut from the breasts of three 5-pound ducks	*The necks, wing tips, and gizzards of the ducks*
1½ ounces each Calvados and Madeira	*1 tablespoon oil or melted duck fat*
	2 cups Golden Veal Stock (p. 20)
2 ounces red port	*⅓ of a duck liver*
1 onion, sliced paper thin	*4 tablespoons butter*
2 shallots, sliced paper thin	*Salt*
1½ cups excellent old Châteauneuf-du-Pape, Hermitage, Côte-Rôtie, or heavy Zinfandel	*Pepper from the mill*
	Quatre-Epices (p. 35)
	½ cup chopped raw watercress

1. Remove all traces of skin and sinew from the duck breasts. Place them in a baking dish. Add to the dish ½ ounce each of the Calvados and Madeira, as well as the port. Sprinkle the onion and shallots over the top of the meat. Cover with plastic wrap and keep refrigerated for 24 hours. Turn the meat once while marinating.

2. One hour before serving time, put the red wine in a small saucepan, add the vegetables from the marinade and any spirits still present in the dish. Reduce to ⅓ cup.

3. Chop the duck necks and wing tips and slice the gizzards. In another skillet brown them in the oil or duck fat. Discard the oil. Add the veal stock and reduce to 1 cup.

4. Strain the essence of duck into the wine reduction, mix well, and continue cooking together for 10 minutes. Strain into a clean pot and let simmer for 8–10 minutes.

5. Cut the liver into small pieces and put it into the blender with 2 tablespoons of the butter. Heat the remaining butter in a skillet and panfry the filets, keeping them rare. As you cook them, season with salt, pepper, and a dash of *quatre-épices*. Set aside and keep covered. The filets will continue cook-

ing to medium rare. Discard the browning fat and deglaze the frying pan with one-quarter of the sauce and the remaining ounce Madeira, reducing well. Start the blender, pour both the deglazing and remainder of the sauce into the working blender to poach the liver and emulsify the butter.

6. Strain the sauce back into its saucepan, heat the remaining ounce Calvados, ignite it, and whisk it, flaming, into the sauce. Add the raw watercress and any meat juices that escaped from the filets. Serve promptly topped with the watercress sauce.

Recommended vegetables: A small gratin of potatoes and celery, as on page 400, and a jardinière of baby onions and Brussels sprouts (p. 386).

Le canard en Gascogne (ducks as presented in Gascony):

As in Normandy, the breasts and the legs are cooked separately, following 2 very different methods. For both the cooking of the legs and the cooking of the breasts, I use here personal techniques based on the traditional methods of the Gascony but somewhat modernized.

MAGRETS DE CANARD
A L'ARMAGNAC ET AUX NOIX
{Panfried Duck Filets with Armagnac and Walnuts}

I have here removed the fatty skin and, once again, as in the Normandy presentation, cooked the *magrets* medium rare in a frying pan—to allow the true duck flavor to come through.

The wing tips and necks of 6 ducks
3 tablespoons rendered duck (confit) *fat or oil of your choice*
3 cups Golden Veal Stock (p. 20)
6 filets cut from the breasts of three 5-pound ducks
Salt
Pepper from the mill

1½ ounces Armagnac
2 tablespoons fine-chopped toasted walnuts
1 large clove garlic, chopped fine
2 tablespoons fine-chopped parsley
2 tablespoons butter
1½ teaspoons Dijon mustard
Lemon juice if needed

1. Chop the wing tips and necks into 1-inch chunks and brown them in 2 tablespoons of the chosen fat; discard the fat. Add the stock and reduce it to 1½ cups essence. Strain into a clean pot; set aside.

2. Panfry the duck filets to rare in the remaining tablespoon of fat as you would a steak; season with salt and pepper. Remove them to a plate and keep them warm. They will finish cooking in their own heat. Discard the fat in the frying pan and deglaze it with 1 ounce of the Armagnac, add the duck essence and reduce well; add the walnuts, garlic, parsley, the remaining ½ ounce of the Armagnac, the butter, and the Dijon mustard. Correct the seasoning with salt, pepper, and lemon juice as needed.

3. Serve the filets topped with the sauce.

Recommended vegetables: In addition to a large bouquet of watercress and a pilaf of three grains (p. 425), add the Occitanian Vegetable Plate, on page 383.

CONFITS
(Meats Preserved by Cooking Them in Fat)

Meat first salted, then cooked in its own or other rendered fat, is known as *confit*. The meat is often kept for months in large glass jars, sterilized or sealed with paper. Much has been written and said about *confits* and I have been forever haunted by the urge to find out who first thought of this method of cooking meats and preserving them in their own fat. After reading a lot and listening to many people over the last twenty years, I have come to the conclusion that several different civilizations and influences meet in this dish.

The cooking of the meat in its own melted fat seems to be universal, for in spite of the claims of several authorities that the southwest of France is the only place where one cooks meat in its own fat, it truly is not. It is done in the Peloponnesus, in Hungary, and even on the Loire where the local people salt their *rillons* and *rillauds* (short ribs of pork), then cook them in rendered pork fat. It does make sense; whenever one starts cooking chunks of fatty meat in water, the water will at some point evaporate and the meat will be left to cook in its own fat. The principle is used every time one renders fat, and Eskimos are experts at doing exactly this with large sea fish.

The rendering of fat and the cooking of meat in fat occurred very early in our history, probably at the time the caveman was still cooking out of large animal skins stretched like pouches over an open fire. Cro-Magnon man was probably cooking his version of *confit* in Périgord thirty thousand to seventy-five thousand years ago.

The salting of meat is also ancient and could possibly be traced to Semitic civilizations that "koshered" their meats before cooking them. This sort of koshering is still used nowadays in Morocco in the Khelea (beef that is salted, spiced, sun-dried, and cooked in mutton fat), as it is in Greece and Turkey and in all Jewish kosher families. On the other hand, why only Semitic populations? The Celts also salted their meats to preserve them and probably did not take the methods from the Semites with whom they had little or no contact. The Loire Valley, which was never invaded by the Arabs, also salts its *rillons* before cooking them in fat. Salting is a universal method for drawing the liquid collagen out of meats and making the meat fibers much less perishable.

The spicing of a *confit* is most probably Arab, for the diverse mixtures of spices used in the southwest of France are reminiscent of the favorite Arabic spices, and there is no doubt that the Saracens were present in Occitania well into the late 1300s; Leroy-Ladurie mentions the existence of Muslim cheese-makers in the Pyrenees in the early 1400s in his detailed history of Montaillou, the Cathar Languedocian village.

Simplified methods for making confits:
The ancient rules of the Occitania are involved and could be time consuming, if one let them. I have decided that matters could be decidedly simplified.

The first step to master is boning the duck (or goose, or turkey) and understanding what to do with each part of the bird. Since I prefer duck to any other bird, I have given complete instructions for making a *confit* of duck.

1. The boning of the bird:
Work on a cutting board. You need 2 knives, 1 large chef's knife and 1 parer, both extremely sharp; three 2-quart glass baking dishes, and 1 plate. You also need a 2-quart saucepan.

a. Remove all the fat in the cavity; cut it into small pieces and put it into the saucepan. Then cut off the neck skin and discard it (in the Périgord, it is not discarded but stuffed with a forcemeat to prepare the *Cou farci* or stuffed neck). Put the liver on a plate and keep it for a mousse, pâté, or salad, or even to bind a sauce.

b. Cut off the third and final joints of the wings and put them into one of the baking dishes together with the necks and the gizzards. (Illus. 1)

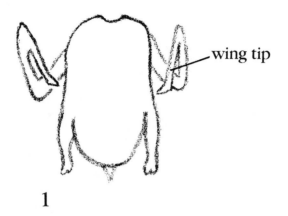

wing tip

1

c. Remove the wing joints still attached to the body. To do so, rotate your paring knife blade around each of the first joints where they are attached to the body and cut the skin as you do so. You will see the joint appear. Cut through it with your chef's knife. Put the wings into the second baking dish.

d. Remove both legs, including the "oysters": pull the leg away from the body and cut through the skin between breast and leg. The meat will appear; bend the leg backward and break the joint. Cut through the skin that still attaches the leg to the back side of the duck. Put the 2 legs into the third baking dish. (Illus. 2)

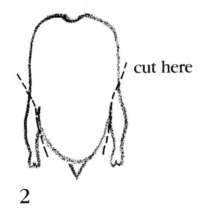

cut here

2

e. Now cut off the tail and discard it. Separate the skin covering the breast from the back of the bird by cutting in one straight line on both sides from leg to wing joints, working from what was the tail toward the neck. (Illus. 3)

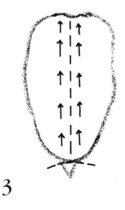

3

Switch to your paring knife to separate the skin from the whole breast of the bird. Wrap the skin around your left hand (the right hand if you are left-handed) as you snip away the thin membrane that keeps the fat layer of skin attached to the meat. As you progress, you will see the 2 filets appear. Continue snipping away until such time as the skin comes loose in your hand. Cut the skin into halves lengthwise, then cut each half into ¼-inch strips crosswise. Add these strips to the saucepan containing the fat.

f. Finally, lift out each filet (in French, *magrets*) one after the other (Illus. 4):

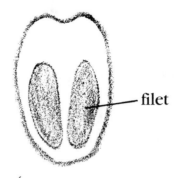

— filet

4

With the chef's knife, cut downward along the breastbone, scraping well and contouring the wishbone. Stay close to the bones so as not to lose any meat. When the filet is loose from one end of the carcass to the other, turn the carcass 90 degrees so that the cut you just made is facing you. Slide the knife blade with the point straight ahead into the cut, between bone and filet. Push ahead into the cut so the tip of the blade comes out at the center of the line marking the end of the filet along the rib cage.

Pass your left thumb between blade and meat; hold the filet firmly between thumb and index finger; give one stroke of the blade to the right, then one to the left. You will have cut the filet from the ribs and will be holding a *magret*. Repeat on the other side; put both filets in the third glass dish.

2. What to do with each of the ducks' parts:

a. Acquire a supply of fat to make *confits*: Cover the fat and slivers of skin with water to reach 2 inches above the solids. Add ½ a bay leaf, a pinch of dried thyme, and 2 cloves, and bring to a boil. Simmer until the fat has completely rendered, the water has totally evaporated, and the skin slivers are golden and crisp when removed from the fat. Salt them lightly and use them in the duck skin omelet on page 62.

To acquire more fat, never discard the fat melting from roasting ducks. Remove it from the roasting pan with a baster and accumulate it in jars. Should you be short of duck fat, do not hesitate to mix duck fat with goose fat or vice versa, or even to use some chicken fat or lard, both properly rendered. A supply of fat is a kitchen treasure and must be kept preciously in sealed jars, well refrigerated. One bath of fat will cook at least 4 *confits* and becomes better and more flavorful after each baking.

b. Using the giblets and the carcass: These can be used to prepare a good duck stock for soup (see the Duck Consommé on p. 93).

c. Using the wings and the legs to prepare a *confit*: I prefer to have only wings and legs in a *confit* made in the United States because the smaller duck breasts can become quite stringy. Should you prepare a *confit* with a goose, do not hesitate to use the breasts; they are large enough not to be a problem. With turkey use only the legs.

d. The filets are to be used and cooked as beefsteaks, either by panfrying or grilling (see recipes on pp. 278–81 and 322–23).

3. To prepare a confit to keep several months (traditional method):

You can use both the legs and breasts of at least 3 ducks, or only the legs, keeping the breasts to prepare as *magrets.* Weigh the meat and use exactly ⅓ ounce kosher salt per pound of meat. Marinate a total of 36 hours for duck and 48 hours for goose, and make sure that the meat is equally salted on all sides. When the time comes to cook the *confit*, drain all the pink juices that escaped to the bottom of the dish and blot off any excess salt from the surface of the meat. Pour duck fat, melted but not hot, over the meat. Put the meat to bake in a cold oven and gradually increase the oven temperature to a maximum of 325°F. This is the best temperature if you have a limited amount of time, but if you are in no hurry, keep it to 275°F.; the *confit* texture will be even better. When the *confit* is done, a skewer inserted into a thick piece of meat will come out freely. Remove the pieces of meat to a large glass jar with a tight-fitting lid. Strain the fat through a fine strainer to cover the pieces of meat with at least 1½ inches of fat. The goal is to seal the meat against any penetration of air; at this point the meat has been sterilized from its long cooking and its salting and will stay sterile for at least 6 months. The best true *confit* flavor develops after 6–8 weeks of storage. Store on the bottom shelf of the refrigerator or, better, in a cold cellar. This *confit* must be used to prepare a cassoulet and can be included in omelets and in salads.

After 6 months of preservation, it will be necessary to melt the *confit*, transfer it to a pan, and recook it for at least 20 minutes, with the fat temperature rising to 212°F. and kept there for the full 20 minutes. Use an instant thermometer to check the temperature of the bath. This is called *"renouveler"* in French and simply means resterilizing the *confit* to prevent spoilage.

4. To prepare a modern confit to keep a week to ten days (modernized method):

I so like *confit* that I prepare it rather often for my family and serve it to my guests in the restaurant, but I prefer a *confit* made only with the legs of ducks, salted with only ⅙ ounce salt to each pound of meat and marinated in salt and spices for only 24 hours. It does taste very different from a *confit* preserved for a long time—frankly less "ripe" and also much less salty. The reduced salt content draws less juice out of the meat, is less taxing on the human body and does not provoke thirst. It also allows older people with blood pressure problems to continue enjoying *confit*. However, it is essential to remember that this *confit* will not keep longer than 7–10 days. Still, it is a lovely dish; prepared and kept refrigerated ahead of time, it can be reheated easily for a happy dinner party.

5. The spice mixture:

The person from whom *confit* and all southwestern dishes came to our family —Marie-Antoinette Bourgain from Beynac in Périgord—used only thyme, bay leaf, cloves, and cinnamon. I added all the others out of personal taste. You may choose to use them or not. Mix them and keep any left over in a tiny box or tightly sealed jar:

1 teaspoon each ground cumin, ground coriander, and ground cinnamon
¾ teaspoon ground allspice
¼ teaspoon ground clove
½ teaspoon cardamom

½ teaspoon ground ginger
½ teaspoon ground nutmeg
1 Turkish bay leaf, crumbled
¾ teaspoon fine-powdered dried thyme leaf

Sprinkle this mixture sparingly on the meat, covering all surfaces before you add any salt. This will be sufficient for 2–3 *confits*.

6. The garlic cloves:

Some *confits* are prepared with and some without garlic cloves. Marie-Antoinette Bourgain, our *confit* mentor, used "a ton" of them, and I have kept the habit, for I love those golden nuggets that can also be used for a good salad. Use at least 36 garlic cloves for each 6 legs of duck, 20 for a goose, and 12 for each 2 turkey legs.

7. Recapitulation of the proper sequence for preparing a confit:

a. Cut the ducks into pieces.

b. Salt the meat with the proper amount of salt: ⅓ ounce for the long-keeping *confit* and ⅙ ounce for the short-lived *confit*.

c. Season the meat with as much of the spice mixture and as many garlic cloves as you like.

d. Let stand with the salt and spices: no less than 36 hours for a long-keeping *confit* or 24 hours for a rapid short-lived *confit*.

e. Drain carefully any red juices having escaped from the meat. Pat the meat dry. Transfer the meat and garlic cloves to a clean baking dish. Cover with liquid fat—goose, duck, chicken, or lard, mixed in any proportion you like.

f. Bake in a slow oven (275° to 325°F.) until a skewer inserted at the thickest part of the meat comes out without difficulty. Remove the cooked pieces and leave those not quite done to finish cooking.

g. Store the long-keeping *confit* in well-sealed glass jars and the short-lived *confit* in its baking dish.

8. *The* confit *garnishes:*

Many modern garnishes can be served with a *confit* to make it a wonderful, plentiful dinner.

All the garnishes described below will serve 6. Notice that all garnishes are either of an acid or lightly sweet character to offset the salty taste of the *confit*.

COMPOTE DE TOMATES FRAICHES
{Compote of Fresh Tomatoes}

12 Italian plum tomatoes, peeled and seeded
1 tablespoon butter or confit (rendered duck) fat
1 onion, chopped fine
1 tiny clove garlic, chopped fine

2 tablespoons chopped parsley
A dash of excellent Armagnac
A pinch of sugar
Salt
Pepper from the mill

Cut the tomatoes lengthwise into ½-inch pieces. Heat the butter or fat, add the onion and cook until it starts browning; add the garlic, chopped parsley, Armagnac, sugar, salt, and pepper and let cook for 5–10 minutes, until the tomatoes form a compote.

EPINARDS EN FEUILLES CITRONNES
{Lemon Spinach}

1 pound leaf spinach	*2 tablespoons lemon juice*
2 tablespoons butter or confit	*½ teaspoon grated lemon rind*
(rendered duck) fat	*Salt*
1 clove garlic, mashed	*Pepper from the mill*

Clean the spinach of all stems and wash it well. Heat the butter or fat and in it brown the garlic well. Add the spinach leaves and wilt them in the hot fat. Add lemon juice and rind. Season well with salt and pepper.

ABRICOTS ET GINGEMBRE *{Apricots and Ginger}*

1 pound apricots, fresh, or dried and revived in water
2 large gingerroots, 1 inch by 2½ inches each
1 tablespoon butter or confit *(rendered duck) fat*
Salt
Pepper from the mill

Cook the apricots—if fresh, until they fall apart; if revived, until they form a compote. Peel the gingerroot and cut it into a very fine ⅛-inch julienne; blanch the julienne and sauté it in butter or duck fat. Season lightly with salt and pepper. Serve the *confit* with apricot compote and ginger julienne.

CHAMPIGNONS ET MAIS *{Corn and Mushrooms}*

1 pound button mushrooms	*1 cup cooked corn niblets*
2 tablespoons butter	*1 large clove garlic, chopped*
Salt	*2 tablespoons chopped parsley*
Pepper from the mill	

Clean the mushrooms. Sauté them in butter until brown; add salt and pepper. Mix with the corn, garlic, and parsley. Heat well together. Correct the seasoning.

POMMES DE TERRE ET SALADE AMERE
{Potatoes and Bitter Salad}

½ pound potatoes, sliced	3 tablespoons walnut oil
Oil or confit (rendered duck) fat	Salt
1 head of escarole	Pepper from the mill
1 clove garlic	Confit-ed garlic cloves from the confit
1 teaspoon Dijon mustard	(see p. 317)
1 tablespoon wine vinegar	

Panfry the sliced potatoes in the oil or duck fat until nice and golden. Clean the escarole. Rub a salad bowl with the clove of garlic. Mix mustard, vinegar, walnut oil, salt, and pepper and whisk well to make a dressing. Toss the escarole with the dressing, add the confit-ed garlic cloves and the potatoes and toss again before serving.

LES VIANDES GRILLEES
(Grilled and Broiled Meats)

Here are some simple, lean recipes that, though delicious, will provide a pleasant respite from opulent brown and creamy white sauces.

Cooking meats by broiling or grilling:
You can use:
- Your oven broiler
- A top-of-the-stove cast-iron ribbed grill
- A barbecue
- A large restaurant-style vertical grill

The method of cooking is the same for all and follows this pattern:

1. First brush the meat with a thin layer of oil, preferably olive oil—no more than ½ teaspoon per steak or chicken cutlet is necessary.
2. *To broil*: Broil the first side of the meat unseasoned. Turn over, season the seared side; sear the second side and season it also. The searing is done 4 inches away from the source of heat in a broiler, and one continues cooking after searing only if the meat is more than 1 inch thick. In this case one brings the meat farther from the radiating element, approximately 6 inches, for another 2–3 minutes.
3. *To grill*: One sears exactly as described above, and all one has to do is lower the heat under the grill and continue cooking to the desired doneness after searing both sides.

It is essential to remember that white meats need a less intense degree of heat than red meats, so keep the grill on lower heat for veal and chicken than for steaks, and start any broiling 6 inches away from the source of heat.

Broiled and grilled meats are ideal for lean diets. They are delicious served absolutely plain, but can also be enhanced by the addition of a pat of compound butter.

Compound butters and other "dressings" for broiled and grilled meats:

To make a compound butter, use your food processor and prepare at least 4 ounces (8 tablespoons) of butter; if you have too much, keep the butter frozen to use another time.

Process the butter to a creamy texture, then add to it the seasoning or herb of your choice: cheese, herbs, aromatics; spices, wine, etc. Shape the flavored butter into a sausage 1 inch by 5 inches and store it in the freezer. You can cut slices as thick or as thin as you like to top your pieces of meat.

The Italian-style mustards mentioned at the beginning of this book on pages 39 through 41 are excellent condiments for broiled or grilled veal, chicken, or pork. These condiments keep a very long time in the refrigerator, and you can make 2 cups of each if you like when the fruit they are made of is in season.

STEAKS GRILLES AU BEURRE DE STILTON
{Grilled Steaks with Stilton Butter}

The little glaze poured on top of the steaks is optional.

SERVES 6

½ cup unsalted butter	*Coarsely cracked pepper from the mill*
2 tablespoons crumbled Stilton cheese	*6 sirloin strip, rib, or blade steaks, trimmed of fat and gristle*
2 tablespoons port wine, preferably tawny	*1 tablespoon olive oil*
Salt only if needed	*½ cup Golden Veal Stock (optional) (p. 20)*

1. Process butter, Stilton, and port together; add salt if needed and coarsely cracked pepper. Shape into a sausagelike 1-inch by 5-inch package and keep frozen in plastic wrap.
2. Brush the steaks with the olive oil. Preheat the grill or broiler. Cook the steaks to your desired doneness. Season well.
3. Top each steak with as many ¼-inch slices of frozen Stilton butter as you want (2 is an excellent measure). If you wish, pour the veal stock into the grill to lift most of the heavily caramelized meat pieces and pour a teaspoon or so of this glaze over the compound butter.

Recommended vegetable: The nice crisp green salad you like best.

STEAKS GRILLES A LA BEAUNOISE
{Grilled Steaks Beaune Style}

SERVES 6

1 tablespoon red wine vinegar
½ cup excellent red wine from Pinot
   Noir
1 small onion, chopped fine
1 shallot, chopped fine
2 cloves garlic, chopped fine
2 tablespoons chopped parsley stems
Small bouquet garni (see p. 82)
1 tablespoon dried tarragon
Salt

Pepper from the mill
1 egg yolk
6 tablespoons butter, melted and
   lukewarm
Dijon mustard to taste
2 tablespoons chopped parsley
1 tablespoon olive oil
6 sirloin strip, rib, or blade steaks,
   trimmed of fat and gristle
½ cup Golden Veal Stock (p. 20)

1. Reduce the vinegar, wine, onion, shallot, garlic, parsley stems, bouquet garni, tarragon, salt, and pepper to ¼ cup liquids and solids together. Add the egg yolk and fluff with a whisk until very foamy and white; remove from the heat and gradually whisk in the butter, dribbling it into the sauce. Strain into a small pot. Add mustard and parsley. Keep warm.
2. Brush the olive oil over the steaks. Grill or broil them to your preferred doneness. Deglaze the grill or broiler pan with the veal stock to obtain a very dark glaze. Add it to the sauce. Correct the final seasoning and spoon over the streaks in desired quantity.

Recommended vegetable: Any nice crisp salad of your choice.

STEAKS DE VEAU GRILLES A LA CHARTREUSE
{Grilled or Broiled Veal Steaks with Chartreuse and Hazelnut Butter}

You may use either ¾-inch chops boned and trimmed of all fat and gristle or ½-inch slices of veal top round sliced across the grain.

SERVES 6

½ cup unsalted butter
½ cup fine-chopped toasted
   hazelnuts
⅓ cup chopped chervil
1–2 tablespoons green Chartreuse
   liqueur
Salt

Pepper from the mill
12 slices of sirloin strip of veal,
   ¾ inch thick, or 6 slices of veal
   top round, ½ inch thick
1½ tablespoons olive oil
½ cup Golden Veal Stock (p. 20)

1. Place the butter, hazelnuts, chervil, and Chartreuse liqueur in the food processor; add salt and pepper and process into a compound butter. Using plastic wrap, shape into a sausagelike roll 1 inch by 5 inches and freeze.
2. Brush the meat with olive oil. Grill it to a juicy medium rare on a very hot grill and top each steak with one or two ¼-inch-thick pats of hazelnut and Chartreuse butter.
3. Deglaze the grill with the veal stock and pour a few drops of the very dark glaze on top of the steaks.

Recommended vegetable: Prepare a wonderful lamb's lettuce salad dressed with hazelnut oil.

COTES D'AGNEAU GRILLEES A L'AIOLI
{Broiled Lamb Chops with Aïoli and Pastis}

SERVES 6

12 rib or loin lamb chops, trimmed
   of fat and gristle
1 teaspoon powdered fennel seeds
1 egg yolk
1 teaspoon Dijon mustard
1 clove garlic, mashed

Salt
Pepper from the mill
½ cup plus 1 tablespoon olive oil
3 tablespoons chopped fresh parsley
1–3 teaspoons Pastis

1. Sprinkle both sides of the lamb chops with the fennel powder. Let stand for 1 hour.
2. Mix the egg yolk, mustard, mashed garlic clove, and a dash of salt and

pepper and slowly dribble in ½ cup of the olive oil, whisking constantly. Add 2 tablespoons of the chopped parsley and add Pastis to your taste. Let stand for 1 hour before using.

3. Brush the chops with the remaining tablespoon of the oil, then grill or broil them for 3 minutes on each side for the rib chops, or 5 minutes on each side for the loin chops, and season well. Spread each chop with ⅛ inch of the garlic sauce and sprinkle with the remaining tablespoon of the parsley.

Recommended vegetables: Grilled or broiled tomatoes and stir-fried fennel.

BLANCS DE VOLAILLES GRILLES
{Grilled or Broiled Chicken Breasts}

Excellent for all diets, especially those that are fat controlled. The chicken breasts used in these recipes must consist of only the filet, with no trace of skin or bone. Bone the chicken breasts or purchase them already boned and marinate them for 12 hours in 2 tablespoons lemon juice for each 6 filets. You can also marinate in buttermilk or yogurt. This procedure is standard for all grilled white meat of chicken or turkey.

Breast of chicken or turkey is best grilled over a barbecue or a ribbed grill; it is not as successful done in the broiler. Before grilling, brush very lightly with olive oil or any other oil of your choice. The grilling or barbecuing should be done on moderate rather than high heat to allow gradual penetration of the heat through the meat. Season with salt and pepper only after cooking.

GARNISHES:
- A plain pat of butter and more lemon juice
- A sprinkling of any freshly chopped herb
- The prune-plum mustard on page 41
- The apple-pear mustard on page 40
- The raspberry-rhubarb mustard on page 40

CAILLES GRILLEES A LA MOUTARDE DE CRESSON {Broiled Quails with Watercress Mustard}

SERVES 6

12 "frogged" quails (see p. 296)
2 tablespoons olive oil or other oil of
   your choice
Salt
Pepper from the mill

⅓ cup Golden Veal Stock (p. 20)
¼ cup heavy cream
1 tablespoon Dijon mustard
¼ cup chopped raw watercress leaves

1. Brush the quails with the olive oil. Broil them 4 inches away from the heat element for 3 minutes meat side up. Salt and pepper the seared side; turn the quails over and broil the skin side up for 3–5 minutes. Salt and pepper very well.
2. Deglaze whatever meat juices have gathered in the broiler pan with the stock. Add the heavy cream. Immediately strain into a bowl. Add the mustard and watercress. Correct the salt and pepper and serve each quail brushed with a thin layer of mustard.

Recommended vegetable: Prepare a crisp salad of endives, watercress, and oranges with a sherry vinegar and hazelnut oil dressing.

MAGRETS DE CANARD AU THE FUME {Grilled Duck Filets with Smoked Tea Butter}

Use the duck legs to prepare a *confit* (see p. 315).

SERVES 6

6 breasts of duck filets (see p. 314)
1 tablespoon Szechuan pepper
2 tablespoons corn oil
½ cup plus ⅓ cup Golden Veal
   Stock (p. 20)

2 tablespoons Lapsang Souchong tea
8 tablespoons butter
¼ teaspoon ground ginger
2 tablespoons chopped chives
Salt

1. Remove all traces of fat and gristle from the duck filets. Grind or crush the Szechuan pepper to a powder and sprinkle it evenly over the 6 filets. Brush the filets with corn oil. Let marinate for 1 hour covered with plastic wrap at room temperature.

2. Bring ½ cup of the veal stock to a boil. Add the tea. Let steep for 20 minutes. Place the whole content of the pot into a piece of cheesecloth and wring well to extract a dark, extra-bitter stock and tea mixture. Set it aside.

3. Put the butter in the food processor container and cream it for 30 seconds. Add the bitter tea extract, the ginger, and the chives; process until homogeneous. Add salt as needed. Shape into a sausage 1 inch by 5 inches, cover with plastic wrap, and freeze.

4. Grill the duck filets to medium rare, 3 minutes on each side. Top each filet with a ¼-inch-thick slice of tea butter; deglaze the grill with the remaining ⅓ cup of the stock and dribble a few drops of the very dark glaze over each filet.

Recommended vegetable: Stir-fried red, green, and yellow bell peppers (p. 378).

Variation: The tea butter is also excellent on veal steaks.

MAGRETS DE CANARD
A LA MOUTARDE DE PRUNEAUX
{Grilled Filets of Duck with Prune Mustard}

Use the duck legs to prepare a *confit* (see p. 315).

SERVES 6

2 tablespoons olive oil
2 teaspoons fine-grated lemon rind
6 breasts of duck filets (p. 314)
    trimmed of skin and gristle
½ pound pitted prunes

2 cups excellent Earl Grey tea
2 cloves garlic, mashed
Salt
Pepper from the mill
Chopped chives

1. Heat the olive oil with 1 teaspoon of the grated lemon rind. Let stand for 15 minutes to cool completely, then strain the oil into a ramekin and

brush the filets of duck with it. Let the filets stand for 1 hour at room temperature, covered with a plastic wrap.

2. Wash the prunes well, add them to the tea, and cook together until the prunes have swelled. Add the remaining teaspoon of the lemon rind and finish cooking until the prunes fall apart and form a compote. Add the garlic, mix well, and season with salt and pepper. Let the compote stand for 1 hour at room temperature, then strain it into a small bowl.

3. Grill the duck filets to medium rare, 3 minutes on each side. Season them well and serve them with the dark compote and sprinkled with chopped chives.

Recommended vegetables: Stir-fried Jerusalem artichokes garnished with scallion rings (p. 380) and a red pepper julienne.

NOISETTES DE PORC GRILLEES
{Grilled or Broiled Pork Noisettes}

You can use grilled or broiled ¾-inch-thick noisettes of pork, cut out of sirloin strip. *Remember*: if you want to be able to grill or broil them so they remain medium rare, you *must* freeze them a full 12 days before defrosting and using them.

Broil or grill pork on moderate heat to allow slow penetration of the heat through the tissues, and serve with any of the fruit mustards given on pages 38–41.

PANFRIED MEATS IN WHITE SAUCES

The use of flour in white sauces disappeared very early in the century, just as soon as there was a decent brand of cornstarch to use as a quick, instant thickening instead of the long drawn out procedures for preparing velouté or cloying béchamel. My mother, a working person all her life, had switched to white sauces made with a slurry of cornstarch before 1939 so that at home I never saw white meats glued to the plate by a milk and flour sauce. This is why when I arrived in the United States and saw the extensive use of béchamel or cream sauces by American cooks, I decided very quickly to teach the slurry method and the use of reduced heavy cream with a meat deglazing.

Only 5 types of meats are ever served with a white sauce:

- Cutlets of white meat of chicken (or 1 side of a breast, whole or sliced lengthwise)
- Mousses of white meat of chicken
- Veal steaks or escalopes, once in a while
- Pork, even more rarely
- Offal

You will see in the pages that follow that the chicken recipes by far outnumber the veal recipes.

A. Slurry method:

This method is what I call the "universal sauce" because it can be used with all meats to obtain a very quick sauce. If the meat is capable of rendering good caramelized juices, as is the case with veal and pork, one deglazes first with either a bit of stock (any type of excellent veal stock or even secondary stock) or a bit of light cream; then one adds the bulk of cream—*always light*—and mixed with a small amount of cornstarch, the sauce thickens over medium heat in a matter of seconds. Garnishes are added to the sauce to enliven its inherently bland taste.

If the meat will not render caramelized juices, as is always the case with white meat of chicken, one allows the bit of white transparent liquid to glaze in the pan first to reinforce the taste; then one adds either stock or light cream, and finally the slurried bulk of the cream and the garnish.

B. Reduced heavy cream method:

The best white sauce can be obtained simply by prereducing heavy cream and adding it to the pan in which the meat has cooked. The depth of taste of the sauce will again depend on the amount of caramelized juices the meat can produce. Veal and pork will produce quite a bit, since they can and must be seared, and a bit of stock must be added to the frying pan before the reduced heavy cream.

In the case of whole cutlets of chicken that are at least ½ inch thick, the heat must be kept rather low during the cooking to obtain amber clear juices.

One will glaze these cooking juices heavily, then dissolve the obtained glaze with a bit of stock, glaze again, and add the reduced heavy cream.

You will notice that when mushrooms are used in the sauce, the water of the mushrooms is used as a deglazer rather than stock.

Veal:

GRENADINS DE VEAU D'ARROMANCHES
{Sautéed Filets of Veal with Mushrooms and Cream the Old Normandy Way}

The same recipe can be applied to chopped veal patties, chops, escalopes, and scallopine.

SERVES 6

3 tablespoons butter
1 pound fresh mushrooms, sliced
Salt and pepper
A dash of nutmeg
1 cup heavy cream, or 1 cup light cream plus 1½ teaspoons cornstarch

3 veal tenderloins, cut into ½-inch slices
Chopped parsley

1. Heat 1 tablespoon of the butter in a skillet, add the mushrooms and toss them into the butter. Add salt, pepper, and nutmeg. Cover and stew until all juices have escaped from the mushrooms. Empty the mushrooms into a strainer placed over a bowl to collect the juices.
2. Meanwhile reduce the heavy cream to ⅓ cup or mix the light cream with the cornstarch.
3. Season the veal slices lightly and, in the same skillet the mushrooms cooked in, sear them for 2 minutes on each side in the remaining 2 tablespoons of the butter. Remove to a plate. Deglaze the pan with the mushroom juices, scraping well. Add the heavy cream or slurry of light cream and cornstarch and thicken. Add the mushrooms and reheat well. Return the slices of veal to the pan for 1 minute, or just enough time to reheat them through.

4. To serve, put the mushrooms on top of the meat and the sauce around it. Sprinkle with parsley.

Recommended vegetables: Plain blanched and buttered green beans and butter-fried potatoes.

COTES DE VEAU AUX ECHALOTES
{Veal Chops in Shallot Sauce}

This is the old shallot and cream sauce of Normandy adapted to veal. The recipe is adaptable to veal steaks, escalopes, or veal patties.

SERVES 6

4 tablespoons butter
1 pound shallots, sliced thin
Salt
Pepper from the mill
1½ cups heavy cream

6 loin veal chops
¼ cup stock of your choice
Chopped chives
Watercress bouquets

1. Heat 2 tablespoons of the butter in a large skillet. Add the sliced shallots and cook slowly until the vegetables have lost half their original volume and appear wilted and deep ivory in color. Season well with salt and pepper.
2. Add the heavy cream and simmer together until the cream has reduced to 1 cup.
3. Heat the remaining 2 tablespoons of the butter in 1 or 2 skillets. Cook the meat for 3 minutes on each side, searing and seasoning each side well. Discard the cooking fat, remove the meat to a plate, and keep it warm.
4. Add the stock and deglaze the pan well. Add the reduced shallot cream to the pan and cook together for a few minutes, or until the cream starts coating the spoon.
5. Serve the chops topped with the shallot cream and sprinkled with the chives. Garnish with watercress bouquets.

Recommended vegetables: A medley of root vegetables cut in julienne, blanched and stir fried in butter.

COEUR DE VEAU A LA CREME DE BASILIC
{Veal Hearts in Basil Cream Sauce}

SERVES 6

3 veal hearts
2 cloves garlic, chopped fine
2 tablespoons parsley
2 tablespoons butter or olive oil
⅓ cup Golden Veal Stock (p. 20)
1 ½ teaspoons tomato paste

1 ¼ cups heavy cream, prereduced to
   ¾ cup
¼ cup fine-scissored basil leaves
Salt
Pepper from the mill

1. Cut the veal hearts into slivers ⅛ inch thick and 1 inch long, taking care to remove all tough membranes and ligaments. Toss the meat with the garlic and parsley. Let marinate for 1 hour.
2. Over very high heat, quickly stir fry the seasoned veal heart slivers in the butter or oil. Remove to a plate. Add the veal stock to the pan and deglaze well. Add the tomato paste and reduced heavy cream. Add the meat to the sauce along with the scissored basil leaves. Correct the seasoning.

Recommended vegetables: A medley of true spaghetti mixed with the vegetable spaghetti on page 379.

White meat of chicken or turkey:
Cutlets may be either one whole side of a chicken breast, ½ inch thick, or the same piece recut into two ¼-inch pieces. Cutlets of turkey breast can be sliced against the grain of the meat from ¼–⅓ inch thick. The intensity of the heat with which one cooks the white meat of any bird depends on the thickness of the cutlets involved: ¼–⅙-inch-thick scallopine of turkey meat must be cooked extremely quickly over high heat, while whole chicken breast cutlets, boneless and ½ inch thick, must be cooked over medium heat, so that the heat penetrates slowly to the center of the meat; a whole chicken breast should coagulate in the frying pan without ever taking on any color. Searing the outside and browning it would result in an unpleasant bad hardening of the outside fibers while the inside remained soft.

The cutlets are done just as soon as they feel completely resilient to the touch; the cutlets may then have released some clear juices that must be glazed.

BLANC DE VOLAILLE DES CARAVANES
{Cutlets of Chicken with Ginger and Orange}

SERVES 6

6 large whole chicken breast cutlets, skinless and boneless	1 tablespoon fine-julienned orange rind, blanched
Salt	1/3 cup stock of your choice
Pepper from the mill	1 teaspoon cornstarch
1/2 teaspoon ground ginger	1 cup light cream
1/2 teaspoon dried orange rind	A dash of Grand Marnier
1 whole gingerroot, peeled, cut into 1/8-inch julienne and blanched	2 tablespoons toasted slivered almonds
3 tablespoons butter	6 orange slices

1. Trim the cutlets of all traces of fat and remove the long white tendon attached to the small filet. Season very lightly with salt and pepper and sprinkle the cutlets with a pinch of ground ginger and orange rind mixed. Let stand for 1 hour.
2. Sauté the julienne of ginger in 1 tablespoon of the butter and add the julienne of orange rind. Set aside.
3. Gently panfry the cutlets of chicken in the 2 remaining tablespoons of the butter. Season well with salt and pepper. When the cutlets feel resilient to the touch of the finger, remove them to a plate; keep them hot.
4. Reduce to a glaze any juices that escaped from the meat. Add stock and reduce again to a second glaze. Dissolve the cornstarch into the cream, add to the pan, and cook until the mixture begins to thicken. Correct the salt and pepper, and add a dash of Grand Marnier and the almonds.
5. Serve the cutlets topped with the cream sauce and a small portion each of ginger and orange rind. Decorate each portion with 1 orange slice.

Recommended vegetables: The saffron noodles on page 134 and a large bouquet of watercress.

BLANC DE VOLAILLES AUX ASPERGES DE PAUVRE {Chicken Cutlets with Leeks and Sour Cream}

"Poor people's asparagus" was the name given by the *Canuts*—the silk workers of Lyon—to leeks.

SERVES 6

6 medium-size leeks (white and light green parts only)	Salt
	Pepper from the mill
3 rashers of thick-sliced bacon	½ cup Golden Veal Stock (p. 20)
4 tablespoons butter	1¼ teaspoons cornstarch
6 chicken breast cutlets, skinless and boneless	1 cup light cream
	Chopped parsley

1. Wash the leeks. Cut them into slanted elongated slices ¼ inch thick. Blanch in boiling salted water for 3–4 minutes.

2. Cut the bacon crosswise into ¼-inch-wide "lardons"; render gently over medium heat. Set aside. Keep the lardons mellow for a true French taste. Discard the bacon fat from the pan; do not wash the pan.

3. To the pan, add 2 tablespoons of the butter and the leeks. Gently cook the leeks until they are tender. Set aside and keep warm. Do not wash the skillet.

4. Season the chicken cutlets with salt and pepper. Gently panfry them in the remaining 2 tablespoons of the butter in the same frying pan used to cook the bacon and leeks. Set them aside as soon as they are resilient to the touch. Keep warm.

5. Reduce any juices in the frying pan to a glaze without discarding the cooking butter. Add the veal stock; reduce to a glaze again; add the bacon. Dissolve the cornstarch into the light cream, add to the pan and thicken over medium-high heat.

6. To serve, top the chicken cutlets with the leeks and spoon the cream and bacon sauce over them. Sprinkle with chopped parsley.

Recommended vegetables: Any dish of grain: rice, wheat, etc., and plain green beans mixed with a julienne of carrots.

BLANC DE VOLAILLES AUX POIRES VERTES ET AU CHINON
{Chicken Cutlets with Green Pears and Chinon Wine Sauce}

SERVES 6

2 tablespoons currants	*1 shallot, chopped*
2 tablespoons pear brandy, Cognac,	*Bouquet garni (see p. 82)*
Armagnac, or plain brandy	*1 cup heavy cream*
4 pears, not too ripe and rather firm	*6 chicken breast cutlets, skinless and*
4 tablespoons butter	*boneless*
A dash of clove	*Salt*
1 cup Chinon, Bourgueil, or	*Pepper from the mill*
Zinfandel wine	*⅓ cup stock of your choice*
1 onion, chopped	*Chopped parsley*

1. Soak the currants overnight in the liqueur of your choice.
2. Peel the pears and slice them across in ⅙-inch slices. Sauté them in 2 tablespoons of the butter until tender but not mushy. Sprinkle with clove and let stand until ready to use.
3. Reduce together the wine, onion, shallot, and bouquet garni to ½ cup liquid and solids mixed. At the same time reduce the cream to ½ cup. Strain the reduction of wine into the cream.
4. Gently panfry the chicken cutlets in the remaining 2 tablespoons of the butter until resilient to the finger. Season well with salt and pepper. Set aside and keep warm. Reduce any juices in the pan to a glaze, then add the stock to the pan and reduce again to a glaze; add any juice that escaped from the meat, the wine and cream mixture, and the pears and the currants. Reheat well together and correct the seasoning.
5. Serve the cutlets topped with the pear sauce and sprinkle with parsley.

Recommended vegetables: A plain dish of buttered noodles mixed with a julienne of zucchini cut the same size as the noodles and stir fried.

BLANC DE DINDE A LA VALDOTAINE
{White Meat of Turkey in the Val d'Aosta Style}

Danish fontina works, but the real taste is in the Italian cheese.

SERVES 6

1 pound turkey breast, in 1 piece	*2 tablespoons fine-chopped parsley*
3 tablespoons butter	*½ cup stock of your choice*
Salt	*⅓ cup heavy cream*
Pepper from the mill	*½ pound fontina cheese (preferably*
2 cloves garlic, chopped fine	*Italian), slivered*

1. Slice the turkey breast across the grain of the meat into ¼-inch-thick scallopine. Sauté them quickly in 2 tablespoons of the butter; season them well. Preheat oven to 400°F.
2. Brush a baking dish with the remaining tablespoon of the butter. Alternate layers of scallopine with layers of garlic and parsley mixed. Deglaze the frying pan with the stock and reduce to a glaze. Add the heavy cream, mix well, and pour over the turkey.
3. Cover the turkey meat with the slivered Fontina. Bake until the cheese melts well but do not let it take on any color. Serve quickly.

Recommended vegetable: A plain green salad with *aceto balsamico* or *verjus* dressing (see pp. 44–45).

BLANC DE VOLAILLES AUX MOUTARDES
{White Meat of Chicken or Turkey with Fruit Mustards}

You can use any of the fruit mustards appearing on pages 38–41 as seasoning or sauce for chicken cutlets.

Simply panfry the cutlets, deglaze the pan with approximately ½ cup stock, and blend in as much of the fruit mustard as you like.

MOUSSES DE VOLAILLES
(Diverse Mousses of Chicken or Other Fowl)

Before you start making a mousse or mousseline of chicken or other fowl, make sure that you carefully reread the section on fish mousselines on pages 184–208. The directions and methods are exactly the same.

You will notice that the addition of reduced fish fumet is replaced in some of the recipes that follow by an addition of chicken glaze, which not only enlivens the bland taste of the chicken but also gives it firmness while cooking.

You can present a mousse of chicken either molded into quenelles by hand with 2 large sauce spoons, or molded into ramekins. Or, using a pastry bag and a plain 1-inch nozzle, you can pipe the mousse into thin sausage skins. I have purposefully used all possible methods in the 3 recipes that follow, but you will want to remember that they are interchangeable.

You will also notice that not only the white meat is used but also the dark meat from the legs. For taste, the dark meat is far superior to the white, but, of course, there is time involved in carefully removing every bit of sinew from the drumsticks.

The sauces accompanying these mousses are not necessarily white; as a matter of fact, they taste better when prepared with an essence of whatever bird you are using in the mousseline.

Although the portions given here are rather small, the extremely rich mousses may be served as main courses preceded by a high-protein salad to complement the nutritional content of the meal.

MOUSSE DE VOLAILLE TRUFFEE A L'ESSENCE DE POIREAUX
{Mousse of Chicken with Essence of Leeks}

This can be prepared from September through May with truffles and dried morels, and from July through September with "trumpets of death." *Please, no fake truffles!* We all know that truffles have priced themselves out of our lives. If you can afford them, by all means use them. If you cannot, substitute

14 dried morels (dried exclusively—the fresh ones have too tenuous a perfume); or a few dried or fresh black cantharella cornucopioides mushrooms also known as "trumpets of death." The look will be the same and the taste is certainly not to be disdained. No mushrooms at all? The plain mousse is eminently edible.

Please be careful not to use any of the dark green part of the leeks, or the dish will lose all its class. Also, *positively no light cream* in this dish! Prepare it only once a year, but do it as described here for maximum taste and texture.

SERVES 6

6 chicken wings or 2 carcasses, chopped into smaller pieces	3 cups heavy cream
1 cup butter	2 medium truffles, or 14 dried morels, or ½ pound fresh "trumpet of
3 cups Golden Veal Stock (p. 20)	death" mushrooms
8 medium-large leeks, without wood at the core	8 ounces white meat of chicken or turkey
Salt	3 eggs
Pepper from the mill	¼ teaspoon nutmeg

1. Brown the chicken wings in 2 tablespoons of the butter. Remove the browning butter to a cup. Add 1 cup of the veal stock and reduce to a glaze. Add the remaining 2 cups of the veal stock and reduce to 1¼ cups good essence. Set 1 cup aside to prepare the sauce and reduce the remainder to 1½ tablespoons very heavy glaze. Empty this glaze into a ramekin. Set aside at room temperature.

2. Slice 6 of the leeks into paper-thin slices. Blanch them in boiling salted water, then drain and blot them dry. Reheat the reserved browning butter in which the chicken wings cooked and sauté the leeks in it. Season with salt and pepper, cover and cook them until they fall into a purée. Add 1 cup of the heavy cream and reduce together until the cream has been well assimilated by the leeks, which will now form a loose purée. Put the leek purée in the blender to smooth well, then add it to the cup of chicken essence and simmer together for 10 minutes. Keep ready to use.

3. Soak the morels in a bit of lukewarm water; rinse them well and sauté them in 2 tablespoons of the butter. If using "trumpets of death," sauté

them in 2 tablespoons of the butter and let the water completely evaporate before you use them. Set aside.

4. To prepare the mousse, cut the chicken or turkey meat into ¾-inch cubes; place them in the food processor container. Add the eggs and process until a fine homogeneous purée results. You may either strain or not strain this purée (your choice entirely); in any case, chill it well for 2 hours (1 hour only in a convector refrigerator).

5. To finish and cook the mousse, cream ½ cup of the butter with 1½ teaspoons salt, 35 turns of the mill of aromatic pepper, and the nutmeg. Tablespoon by tablespoon, add the purée of chicken, then add the reserved chicken glaze (it will be semisolid).

    Turn the mixer down to low and add gradually, in a steady stream, the remaining 2 cups of the heavy cream. Chop 1½ tablespoons "trumpet of death" mushrooms or 2 large morels or the truffles and fold them into the mousse. Preheat the oven to 325°F. With 1 tablespoon of the butter, grease six or eight 2–3-ounce ramekins and spoon the mousse into the ramekins. Bake in a hot water bath covered with buttered parchment paper until a fine skewer inserted at the center of the mousse comes out hot and dry, about 15–20 minutes.

6. To present, slice the remaining 2 leeks into ¼-inch-thick slices, blanch them, and sauté them in the remaining tablespoon of butter until light golden; mix in the mushrooms.

    Unmold 1 mousse at the center of each of 6 luncheon plates. Top each mousse with an arrangement of black mushrooms and leek slices and spoon the sauce around the mousse.

Timing notes: Prepare the sauce, the mushrooms, and the mousse the day before so that all you have to do at dinnertime is bake the mousse and reheat the sauce.

Recommended vegetable: A pleasant, seasonal jardinière.

BOUDINS AUX TROIS VOLAILLES ET CELERI GLACE
{Boudins of Three Fowl with Glazed Celery Root}

This is a bit expensive, but different enough to be very attractive for a special occasion. Sausage skins are for sale in all good butcher shops.

SERVES 6–8

MOUSSE:

The breast meat of 1 duck (both filets)

The breast meat of 1 pigeon (both filets)

The breast meat of 2 quails or 1 filet of chicken

6 eggs

½ pound plus 2 tablespoons unsalted butter

Salt

Pepper from the mill

⅓ teaspoon freshly grated nutmeg

2 cups heavy cream

1 box salted sausage skins

SAUCE:

The wings of the duck

The legs of the pigeon, or the legs of the quails, or two chicken wings

4 tablespoons butter

1 quart Golden Veal Stock (p. 20)

1 cup heavy cream

1 cup blanched, "turned" celery root beads (see p. 368)

2 tablespoons chopped fresh parsley

1. Cube all the filets, place them in the food processor container with the eggs, and process until smooth. Strain through a drum sieve. Refrigerate for 2 hours.

2. Cream ½ pound of the butter, add 1½ teaspoons salt, 35 turns of the pepper mill, and the grated nutmeg. Add the puréed meat, tablespoon by tablespoon, until the mixture is homogeneous. Beat for 2–3 minutes to develop the elasticity. Gradually beat in the heavy cream on low speed. Test a nugget of the mousse by poaching it in salted simmering water (see p. 191); add more salt and pepper if necessary.

3. Rinse the sausage skins under cold water. Put the mousse into a pastry bag fitted with a 1-inch nozzle. Tie a knot at the end of the sausage skin length. Bunch the sausage skin over the nozzle so the end of the skin with its knot

it taut against the opening of the nozzle and push the forcemeat into the skin. Tie a knot at the other end of the sausage skin and twist the long white sausage into as many 4-inch links as you can make. Tie the sausages at each twist. Do not cut them.

4. Bring a large pot of water to a bare simmer. Immerse the sausage links and let them poach 5 minutes. Prick each sausage in four different places and continue poaching another 20 minutes. Remove from the water and cool completely. Keep refrigerated until ready to serve.

5. To prepare the sauce, brown all the wings and/or legs in 2 tablespoons hot butter. Add 3½ cups of the veal stock and reduce to 1 cup essence (see p. 268). Meanwhile bring the cream to a boil. Add the blanched celery root beads to the cream and finish cooking them in the cream, until the latter is reduced to ½ cup. Blend the essence into the reduced cream. Correct salt and pepper and add a bit more of the ½ cup remaining stock if needed to lighten the texture. Add the parsley.

6. To serve, peel off the sausage skin from around the links of poached mousse. Brown the links lightly in the remaining 2 tablespoons butter to reheat them well to their centers. Serve them topped with the celery sauce.

Recommended vegetables: A pilaf of coarsely cracked wheat (p. 424) with a large bouquet of parsley.

QUENELLES DE VOLAILLES AUX ASPERGES
{Quenelles of Chicken with Asparagus Sauce}

SERVES 6–8

4 large chicken legs
2 egg whites
Salt
Pepper from the mill
¼ teaspoon nutmeg
2½–2¾ cups heavy cream
1 quart Golden Veal Stock (p. 20)

1 pound asparagus, cleaned and
*   peeled*
1 teaspoon ground coriander
½ teaspoon dried orange rind
1 slice of excellent boiled ham,
*   ¼ inch thick, cut into ⅓-inch sticks*
1 tablespoon butter

1. Skin and bone the chicken legs. Remove all traces of sinews and tendons from the meat. Process the meat and the egg whites in the food processor. Strain the obtained purée through a drum sieve. Refrigerate for 1–2 hours.

2. Place the purée in the electric mixer bowl. Beat it on medium-high speed, adding approximately 1½ teaspoons salt, 30 turns of the pepper mill, and the nutmeg. Turn the mixer speed down to low and gradually add 1½ cups of the heavy cream. Make a test of the forcemeat: poach it in simmering salted water (see p. 191) and add up to ¼ cup more cream and additional seasoning if necessary.

    As soon as the forcemeat is ready, shape it into 6 large quenelles, using a large sauce spoon. Bring the stock to a simmer and poach the quenelles in the simmering stock. Keep them warm in the stock.

3. Meanwhile blanch the asparagus in boiling salted water until crisp-tender. Cut off the asparagus tips; reserve them for decoration. Put the cut-up asparagus stems and 1 cup of the stock (where the quenelles are waiting) in the blender container and process until a smooth purée results; strain it carefully into a saucepan.

4. Reduce the remaining cup of the cream seasoned with a pinch of salt and pepper and the coriander and orange rind by one-third. Blend the reduced cream with the asparagus purée. Reheat well without boiling and correct the final seasoning. Should the sauce be too thick, bring it back to coating consistency by adding stock as needed.

5. Gently sauté the ham sticks and the reserved asparagus tips in the butter to heat them through. Serve the quenelles garnished with ham and asparagus and topped with the sauce.

Recommended vegetables: Wilted spinach leaves and a few blanched then stir-fried silverskin onions.

LES VOLAILLES POCHEES AU SAC ET AU SEL
(Chicken Poached in a Bag or in Salt)

Poaching in a bag:
While I was growing up and until quite recently, one could purchase a pig's bladder in a French boucherie or charcuterie and use it as a tight glove into which one slipped a chicken. The funny-looking oblong package, not unlike a

smaller, irregularly shaped football, was then immersed in stock or salt water and poached for an hour or so. The resulting chicken was absolutely succulent.

Being unable to obtain a pig's bladder in the United States, I was rescued by nothing other than the "cook-in" plastic bag.

The problem with plastic bags is that it is extremely difficult to chase all the air out of them, so that they become all swollen and float to the surface of the water. To solve this minor inconvenience, I rub the bird(s) with soft butter, which makes the plastic film adhere to the skin; then I push hard to expel as much air as possible before tying the bag. Then I immerse the bag in the rapidly boiling salted water. To prevent the bird(s) from floating upward, I put on them a lid just about a size smaller than the pot. I turn the heat down to a simmer and cook until the juices accumulating in the two bottom corners of the plastic bag have turned clear. The sauce is then simply built by reducing those juices and blending them with reduced heavy cream.

If the birds must be kept warm over a period of time and/or prepared in advance, cook them only three-quarters done, remove the large pot from the heat and let it stand, covered. You will find out that the birds not only keep nice and hot but also that they finish cooking perfectly in their own accumulated heat. The only unpleasantness is the handling of these boiling hot bags, but who is the cook who has not eventually developed asbestos fingers?

It is a good idea, if one has the time and financial means, to prepare an essence of chicken to strengthen the chicken flavor in the sauce. Our meal-fed chickens are rather poor in flavor, and any outside help they can get does a lot for their final taste.

Poaching in salt:

The salt-cooking method is as ancient as the *confit*-cooking method and almost as universal. In searching for its origins, I, of course, turned to China, but found the method to exist also in Italy, where it is used for cooking ducks, which are then served with one of those wonderful sweet-sour fruit condiments such as the Italian Sapor or Saor (see recipe p. 345).

Using the salt method is unwieldly for large numbers of birds; I have found a duck or a chicken cooked in salt a welcome change of pace for a small meal for 4.

The 3 recipes below are examples of what can be done with the "bag and salt" methods of cooking. Notice that in the "bag" recipe the flavorings are under the skin of the chicken, but you could just as well leave them outside.

POULARDE MORILLEE POCHEE AU SAC
{Morel Chicken Poached in a Bag}

In the restaurant, 1 chicken serves 2 guests, but at home you will find that 2 chickens adequately serve 6–8. I transferred the idea of using truffles to that of using a morel hash trapped in butter.

SERVES 6–8

OPTIONAL ESSENCE:
> *6 chicken wings*
> *2 tablespoons butter*
> *3 cups Golden Veal Stock (p. 20)*

CHICKENS:

2 ounces dried morels	*Two 4½-pound chickens*
12 tablespoons unsalted butter	*2 "cook-in" plastic bags with ties*
Salt	*1 cup heavy cream*
Pepper from the mill	

1. If you prepare an essence, brown the chicken wings in butter until golden brown; discard the browning butter, add the stock, and reduce gently until ⅔ cup good essence of chicken is left. Set aside.

2. Rehydrate the morels for at least 1 hour in just enough lukewarm water to cover them. Reserve the soaking water. Remove the stems. Wash the pointed heads carefully under running water to discard all the sand in the folds. Drain well, pat dry, and sauté in 2 tablespoons of the butter. Season well with salt and pepper, then add the soaking water and let evaporate completely. Chop the mushrooms extremely fine by hand or in a food processor.

3. Cream 8 tablespoons of the butter with a dash of salt and pepper and add the chopped morels to obtain a compound butter. Put the compound butter in a small pastry bag fitted with a ¼-inch nozzle. Using your index finger, separate the skin of the chicken from the meat; slide the nozzle under the skin and pipe 4 tablespoons butter under the skin of each chicken. With your hand massage the butter to make an even ⅛-inch layer over the legs and breasts of each chicken. Season each chicken in its cavity and truss it.

4. Rub each chicken well with the remaining 2 tablespoons of the butter and fit the cook-in bags snuggly around each chicken. Twist the opening of each bag very well and tie. Immerse the chicken in boiling salted water, turn down to a bare simmer, and cook approximately 1 hour, covered with a lid a size smaller than the pot.

5. Meanwhile reduce the cream to ½ cup. When the chickens are done, empty the juices from the bag into the reduced cream. Add the essence now, if you are using it, and reduce together until approximately 1 generous cup well-bound sauce remains. Serve the sauce over the carved portions of chicken.

Recommended vegetable: The happy spring jardinière on page 387.

LE CANARD D'ANNA-MARIA
{*Anna-Maria's Duck in Salt*}

From the repertory of my Milanese cousin's mother. To save time, I prepared the fruit sauce with apple butter instead of starting with raw apples. Double the recipe to serve 6–8.

SERVES 4

One 4½-pound duck
1 small orange, stuck with 2 cloves
10 pounds salt
1 cup fresh grape juice, home crushed
   from fresh grapes
1¼ cups prepared apple butter
2 pears, grated

2 tablespoons Aceto Balsamico
   (p. 45) or 2 tablespoons any
   other vinegar plus 1 teaspoon honey
¼ teaspoon Angostura bitters
¼ teaspoon each fine-grated orange,
   lime, lemon, and grapefruit rinds
Salt
Pepper from the mill

1. Remove the fat pads from the duck cavity and add the orange stuck with the cloves. Truss the duck.

2. Preheat the oven to 325°F. Pour 2 pounds salt into the bottom of an oval, enameled, cast-iron roasting pan. Add the duck breast down. Cover with the remainder of the salt and bake for 2 hours.

3. While the duck bakes, mix the grape juice, apple butter, grated pears, vinegar, bitters, rinds, salt, and pepper from the mill. Bring to a boil and simmer until reduced to approximately 1 cup. Strain, blend to homogenize, and serve with the duck as soon as it is done.

4. To remove the duck from the salt, turn the pot upside down on a large board and break the salt; with a pastry brush, remove all traces of salt from the skin. Note that if the skin is too salty for your taste or your health, all you have to do is discard it. The meat is just as delicious.

Recommended vegetable: Vegetable spaghetti made with zucchini, carrots, and yellow squash (p. 379).

POULARDE AU GROS SEL ADOUCIE DE CHAMPIGNONS SAUVAGES
{Chicken in Salt, Sweetened with Wild Mushrooms in Cream}

Fresh wild mushrooms are to be found all over the American forests. Use any combination you like, or plain cultivated mushrooms.

The sweetness of the mushrooms and cream offsets the salt very pleasantly. Double the recipe to serve 6–8.

SERVES 4

One 4½-pound chicken
Pepper from the mill
10 pounds salt
⅓ pound fresh yellow chanterelles
  (Cantharellus cibarius)
⅓ pound oyster mushrooms
  (Pleurotus ostreatus)

⅓ pound fairy ring mushrooms
  (Marasmius oreades)
⅓ pound brown chanterelles
  (Craterellus cornucopioides)
Salt
2 tablespoons butter
1 cup heavy cream

1. Preheat the oven to 400°F. Season the cavity of the chicken with pepper. Truss it and bury the chicken breast down in the salt in an oblong, enameled, cast-iron braising pot. Bake it for 1 hour.

2. Meanwhile, clean and trim the mushrooms well, season them with salt and

pepper, and sauté in the butter until dry. Add the cream and reduce to a saucelike consistency.

3. To remove the chicken from the salt, turn the pot upside down on a large board and break the salt crust. Remove all traces of salt on the skin and completely skin the chicken. Cut it in portions and spoon the mushroom sauce over each portion.

VIANDES SAUTEES ET BRAISEES
(Meats Cooked by the Moist Cooking Techniques and Forming Their Own Saucelike Gravies)

Most of the ideas in the following recipes stem from the French women's cooking lore, and I shall indicate the origin at the beginning of each recipe. The three techniques applied are:

1. Sautéing
2. Fricasséeing
3. Braising

1. Les viandes sautées (sautéed meats):

The technique of sautéing is applied mostly to chicken legs, since white meat would become unpalatable and stringy when cooked in this manner. The sequence of cooking is the following:

a. Sear the chicken either lightly for a "sauté à blanc" if it is to be served with a white sauce, or to a deep golden brown for a "sauté à brun," which will result in a brown sauce. Season the meat well.

b. Discard the searing fat or oil.

c. Add a small amount of liquid: stock of any kind or part wine/part stock. Cover the meat and cook until tender.

The technique is still widely used in many restaurants and by many cookbook authors who like a small, not too plentiful sauce. The resulting gravy can indeed be called a sauce, since the stock or combination of stock and wine mix with the natural juices of the meat to form an excellent and very tasty gravy.

If a garnish of vegetables is added, the addition should be made 5–10 minutes before the end of cooking, depending on the nature of the vegetable.

LE POULET DE MAMAN
{My Mother's Onion, Potato, and Garlic Chicken}

This is probably my fondest memory of my mother's cooking. Prepared with excellent veal stock it becomes very special, but you may use any simple broth. The garnish of vegetables is potent enough to create a tasty gravy.

SERVES 6

½ pound butter
4 large potatoes, peeled and recut into olive-shaped pieces (see p. 368)
3 dozen silverskin onions, peeled
3 dozen large cloves garlic, peeled

6 chicken legs, separated into drumsticks and thighs
Salt
Pepper from the mill
⅔ cup Golden Veal Stock (p. 20) or any lighter broth of your choice
Chopped chives and parsley

1. Clarify the butter; use as much as you need to prepare this dish. Keep any leftover refrigerated in a small jar for later use.

2. In ½ cup of the butter, panfry the olive-shaped potatoes until they are crisp and golden. Set them aside without seasoning them. In the same butter, panfry the silverskin onions until they are also golden. Set aside on a plate. Change the butter only if it has browned too much; if not, slowly cook the garlic cloves in the same butter until they are semitender and light golden.

3. Still in the same skillet, brown the pieces of chicken slowly, salting and peppering them only after they have been seared. Continue turning the pieces until they are uniformly browned. Discard the fat, add the veal stock, cover and cook for 10 minutes.

4. After this time, mix the potatoes, onions, and garlic cloves. Salt and pepper them and add them to the pot. Cover again and finish cooking together, another 8–10 minutes.

5. To serve, transfer the preparation to a brown oval country dish and serve sprinkled with chives and parsley.

Recommended vegetable: Serve with any nice salad of your choice.

POULET BOUILLABAISSE
(Chicken with Bouillabaisse Seasoning)

Only fresh sun-ripened tomatoes, please, for the true Provençal taste!

SERVES 6

1 large onion, chopped	*2 shallots, chopped fine*
Olive oil as needed	*Small bouquet garni (see p. 82)*
8 chicken legs, drumstick and thighs	*½ teaspoon dried orange rind*
separated	*¼ teaspoon fennel seed*
Salt	*2 tablespoons butter*
Pepper from the mill	*6 basil leaves*
8 sun-ripened Italian plum tomatoes,	*¼ teaspoon saffron threads*
peeled, seeded, and chopped	*Parsley bouquets*
3 cloves garlic, chopped fine	

1. Sauté the onion in 2 tablespoons olive oil until golden. Remove to a plate, using a slotted spoon.
2. In the same oil, brown the chicken pieces until deep golden; season with salt and pepper. Discard the oil.
3. Add the tomatoes, 2 of the chopped garlic cloves, the shallots, bouquet garni, orange rind, and fennel seeds. Cook, covered, until the chicken is tender, 15–20 minutes.
4. Meanwhile mash together with a fork the butter, the remaining garlic clove, and the basil leaves. At the very last minute, also mash the saffron threads in.
5. When ready to serve, remove the chicken pieces to a deep dish. Add the compound garlic, basil, and saffron butter to the tomato sauce. Mix well and pour over the chicken. Decorate the dish with parsley bouquets.

2. Les viandes fricassées (fricasséed meats):
The fricassee is probably the roughest form of stew, and the easiest. Again, we will find ourselves here at the depth of the French women's food lore. The technique applies well to rabbit, chicken pieces, and small birds such as quails and squabs.

The sequence of cooking is as follows:

a. Flour the meat lightly and sear it "à blanc" or "à brun" (see p. 347). Note, however, that flouring is not a necessity and is not done with small birds that remain whole. If you do not flour, you must use the very best veal stock that will reduce to "saucelike" consistency without the help of a thickener.

b. Add just enough stock of your choice to barely cover the meat and cook, covered, until the meat is done. Any vegetable or fruit garnish used is added between 2–10 minutes before the end of cooking, depending on the nature of the garnish.

UNE PETITE PERDRIX ET UNE GROSSE POIRE
{A Small Partridge and a Great Big Pear}

This little recipe can be made with a nice squab in areas where partridge is not available.

The recipe came to my mind as I was looking at Chardin's wonderful *Perdrix morte, poire et collet sur une table de pierre* during the Chardin exposition at the Boston Museum of Art.

A wonderful intimate dinner for an anniversary or a celebration with a special friend.

SERVES 2

PARTRIDGE:

1 large partridge or squab
Salt and pepper
2 tablespoons butter
1 onion, chopped fine
1 very small carrot
1 cup excellent red wine (Petite Sirah, Pinot Noir, or an older Cabernet Sauvignon)

1 cup Golden Veal Stock (p. 20)
2 cloves
2 allspice berries
1 ounce pear brandy
1 small bouquet garni (see p. 82)
Watercress

SAUCE:

1 very large pear, not too ripe	*2 cloves*
4 tablespoons butter	*2 allspice berries*
1 teaspoon sugar	*2 slices of French bread*
1 cup of the same red wine as used	*Salt and pepper*
to cook the bird	*Juice and rind of 1 lemon*

1. Clean the partridge well. Salt and pepper the cavity and truss the bird. Heat 1 tablespoon of the butter in a small saucepan just large enough to contain the bird. Brown the onion and carrot until golden. Remove to a plate. Add the remaining tablespoon of the butter and brown the bird in it. Return the vegetables to the pot. Add the wine. Heat it and ignite it. Let it burn for 2–3 minutes so the flames lap the bird. Add the veal stock, salt, pepper, the cloves and allspice berries, pear brandy, and bouquet garni.

2. Cover the pot and cook a maximum of 20 minutes to obtain a medium-rare bird.

3. Prepare the sauce while the bird cooks. Peel and core the pear and cut it in half. Heat 1 tablespoon of the butter in a frying pan and cook the pear halves in it until tender. Remove the pears to a plate. Keep them hot. Add the sugar to the frying pan, caramelize it, then add the wine, the cloves and crushed allspice berries and reduce to ⅓ cup.

4. When the partridge is done, remove it to a carving board. Fry the bread slices in another tablespoon of butter. Mix the pear glaze and the cooking juices of the bird and reduce to approximately ½ cup good sauce. Correct the seasoning with salt, pepper, lemon juice and lemon rind; finally, fluff in the remaining 2 tablespoons of the butter.

5. On each plate serve a half bird on a slice of bread; arrange 1 pear half cut across in ¼-inch slices and fanned out like a cornucopia. In the hollow of the pear place a bouquet of watercress leaves. Spoon the sauce over each partridge half.

LAPIN AU GENIEVRE ET A LA BIERE
{Rabbit with Juniper and Beer}

I modified the very rough recipes of several of my great-aunts into this slightly bitter-tasting dish. Any gin will do if you have no Dutch gin.

SERVES 6

1 medium-size rabbit, cut up, or 1 box
   California rabbit properly
   defrosted in the refrigerator
4 tablespoons flour
Salt
Pepper from the mill
4 tablespoons butter
2 onions, chopped fine
1 carrot, chopped fine

1 ounce Dutch gin or other gin
2/3 cup dark beer
1 1/3 cups Golden Veal Stock (p. 20)
12 juniper berries, crushed
Small bouquet garni (see p. 82)
3 ounces fresh brisket of pork
   (unprocessed bacon)
36 silverskin onions, peeled
Chopped parsley

1. Pat the rabbit pieces dry with paper toweling. Mix the flour, salt, and pepper. Lightly dredge the rabbit pieces with the seasoned flour and pat smartly to discard excess flour.

2. Heat the butter in a large saucepan and in it brown the chopped onions and carrot. Remove to a plate with a slotted spoon. In the same butter, brown the pieces of rabbit until golden. Remove the browning fat to a small cup; set it aside. Add the gin to the pan, heat it well, and ignite it. Add the beer, stock, juniper berries, and bouquet garni. Bring to a boil, cover and cook until the rabbit is tender, 35–40 minutes.

3. Cut the pork into 1-inch by 1/3-inch "lardons" and brown the pieces well in the reserved rabbit browning fat. When ready, remove to a plate and add the silverskin onions. Brown them well. Add the brisket and onions to the rabbit stew during its last 10 minutes of cooking.

4. To serve, remove the rabbit pieces to a deep country-style dish. Reduce the cooking juices if they seem too thin and pour them over the meat. Serve sprinkled with parsley.

Recommended vegetable: Plain buttered noodles.

PETITS OISEAUX EN SAUVAGINE
{Wild Little Birds}

A combination of Provençal and Milanese ingredients. This is best applied to quails, but it also does very well with squabs, duck legs, and even Cornish hens.

SERVES 6

12 quails
Salt
Pepper from the mill
2 tablespoons olive oil
1 tablespoon unsweetened cocoa
  powder
2 cups Golden Veal Stock (p. 20)
  or other broth of your choice

24 cloves garlic, blanched and peeled
¼ teaspoon honey
2 tablespoons chopped parsley
Grated rind of 1 tangerine
1 clove garlic, chopped very fine
1 or 2 anchovies, mashed

1. Season the cavities of the quails with salt and pepper. Brown them very evenly in the olive oil. Discard the olive oil.

2. Mix the cocoa and 1½ cups of the stock, bring to a boil in a small pan, and pour over the quails. Add the blanched garlic cloves, the honey, and a bit of salt and pepper and bring to a boil. Turn down to a simmer, cover and cook until the birds are completely tender, or 45 minutes.

3. Remove the cooked birds to a deep country dish. Pour the sauce into the blender and process it to purée and homogenize it completely. If need be, lighten it with some of the remaining ½ cup of the stock. Strain into a clean saucepan.

4. Bring the sauce back to a full boil, add the parsley, grated tangerine rind, chopped garlic, and 1 or 2 mashed anchovies, depending on how much salt you think the sauce needs. Spoon over the little birds.

Recommended vegetables: A dish of plain risotto made with saffron (see method, p. 429) and watercress bouquets.

SALMIS DE PATTES DE CANARD *{Stewed Duck Legs}*

Another way to use duck legs after you have prepared the breasts as *magrets* (see p. 314).

(see p. 314)

SERVES 6

1 teaspoon allspice
6 duck legs
Salt
Pepper from the mill
3 tablespoons boiling water
2 tablespoons each dark and light
  raisins
3 tablespoons lemon juice

2 tablespoons confit *(rendered duck)*
  fat or plain oil of your choice
1 ½ cups stock of your choice
Grated rind of ½ a lemon
2 tablespoons ⅟₁₆-inch julienne strips
  of lemon rind, blanched
Chopped chives

1. Sprinkle the allspice evenly over the 6 duck legs; season with salt and pepper. Let them stand for 1 hour before cooking.
2. Meanwhile pour the boiling water over the mixed raisins, add the lemon juice and let stand.
3. In a sauté pan brown the duck legs evenly and very well in either duck fat or oil. Discard the fat or oil. Add the stock and the grated lemon rind. Cover and cook until the duck is almost tender, approximately 45–50 minutes.
4. Pour whatever sauce is in the pan into a measuring cup. Using a bulb baster, separate the lean from the fat. Return the lean sauce to the pan and add the blanched lemon julienne and the raisins with their juices. Correct the salt and pepper and simmer together for another 10 minutes. Serve on very hot plates, sprinkled with chopped chives.

Recommended vegetable: Plain pilaf.

3. Les viandes braisées (braised meats):

The only new insights in the following recipes are into the origins of the dishes rather than the cooking methods. The lamb shoulder is "Pied-Noir" cuisine as brought to France by the French families who came back home after Algerian independence. The *Coufidou* is the favorite stew of the Roquefort region; it can be made with either beef or lamb. As for the *Ris de Veau*, I was simply a bit bored with the sempiternal *Ris de Veau au Madère* and decided that mustard and watercress would liven up the bland sweetbreads considerably.

I insist on including braised dishes in a modern cookbook because, in spite of the fact that the technique demands a long cooking, it is essential that it be preserved for the future. Too many professional cooks do not know how to do a good *braisé*, and too many young cooks have what I call "an affluent society" approach to cooking: they use only the best cuts of meats and consequently use in their repertoire only the quick-cooking methods of panfrying, grilling, broiling, or steaming.

For a more detailed discussion of the techniques of braising, please go back to *The Making of a Cook*, pages 190–96. Here I will only outline the main steps of a *braisé*:

1. Use a thick round or oval cast-iron or enameled cast-iron pot.
2. Prepare a *fonds de braise* with 1 onion and 1 carrot, sliced thick and sautéed in butter or oil or other fat.
3. Remove the vegetables to a plate; in the same fat, brown the meat. Discard the browning fat.
4. Put the *fonds de braise* vegetables back around the meat. Cover the meat with barely enough stock (of your choice, but the best you can find), to cover if the meat is cubed; or if the meat is in one whole piece, with enough stock to come one-half to two-thirds of the way up the sides of the piece of meat. For your information, braising can also be done with water, with the addition of a good teaspoon of commercial meat extract.
5. *And this is the essential step*:
   Cover the meat *flush*—so there is no space between meat, stock, and foil—with aluminum foil forming an upside-down lid and climbing up the sides of the pot. Fold the excess foil back over the outside rim of the pot and cover with the pot lid. This is the most important point: The fact that there is no space for the steam to condense on the foil or on the pot lid means that the meat *braises instead of boils*. The stock in the pan first mixes with the juices that escaped from the meat and ultimately, by capillary action, finds its way back to the center of the meat, making it succulent instead of stringy.

The foil is a modern equivalent of the days when one prepared this type of dish on the hearth, burying the pot in hot embers and ashes and filling its specially hollowed lid with more embers. Nowadays one bakes in a preheated 325°F. oven.

6. You will know that the meat is done—when a skewer inserted at the center goes in and comes out without difficulty.
7. Strain the cooking juices into a measuring cup. Defat them by syringing the lean juices out with a bulb baster and reduce; and, if you want, butter the lean juices as you would any sauce.

This method of cooking will keep you alive under any conditions so long as even the toughest piece of meat is available. During the war, when gas was stringently restricted, my mother would start the cooking of whatever tough stringy cow we could obtain from the butcher in the morning during the 30 minutes or so that the gas supply lasted. Then she would bury the boiling pot in our "Norvegian Marmite"—a wooden crate filled with large sawdust flakes and old blankets. When mother came home at six o'clock, dinner was cooked and ready.

EPAULE D'AGNEAU DES PIEDS-NOIRS
{Pied-Noir Shoulder of Lamb}

This recipe will serve 8 if the shoulder is large, but it is recommended to choose it as small as possible.

SERVES 6

Olive oil as needed
1 small carrot, sliced thick
1 large onion, sliced thick
One 3–3½-pound boned shoulder
    of lamb
3 tablespoons fine-chopped mint
3 small cloves garlic, minced fine
Salt
Pepper from the mill

Small bouquet garni (see p. 82)
½ teaspoon ground cumin
2–3 cups stock or broth of your
    choice, the best possible
2 green peppers, peeled if desired
2 red peppers, peeled if desired
2 small zucchini
1 medium eggplant

1. Heat 2–3 tablespoons olive oil in an oval braising pot and brown the carrot and onion. Remove to a plate. Flatten the shoulder, sprinkle it inside with 1 tablespoon of the mint mixed with 1 clove of the garlic, and salt and pepper. Roll the shoulder and tie it well. Brown it evenly on all sides in the oil remaining in the pot. Discard the browning oil, return the onion and carrot to the pot, add the bouquet garni, cumin, salt, pepper, and enough stock to come two-thirds of the way up the sides of the meat. Cover with foil and pot lid. Preheat the oven to 325°F. Bring the pot to a boil and put to bake for approximately 45–50 minutes for medium rare, 90 minutes for well done.

2. Meanwhile, cut the peppers into ¾-inch squares. Sauté them in 2 tablespoons hot olive oil. Set aside. Cut the zucchini into ¾-inch cubes and also sauté them in hot olive oil. Mix the zucchini with the peppers.

3. Cube the eggplant, unpeeled, into ¾-inch cubes. Salt them. Let them stand for 30 minutes. Rinse them and pat them very dry. Sauté them in 2–3 tablespoons hot olive oil and, when nice and brown, add them to the peppers and zucchini.

4. When the meat is done, remove it from the pot and keep it hot. Defat the cooking juices. Add the vegetables and reduce together for approximately 10 minutes. The vegetables must be well done. Add the remaining chopped mint and garlic.

5. Serve the meat sliced, with the sauce on top and the vegetable garnish around it.

Recommended vegetable: A pilaf of rice with olives and lemon rind (see p. 425).

COUFIDOU AUX ECHALOTES
{Languedocian Stew with Shallots}

The pork rind may not seem appetizing, but while cooking, it melts to a gelatin in the sauce and gives it shine and texture.

SERVES 6–8

5 tablespoons oil or confit *(rendered duck) fat (see p. 315), as needed*

1 onion, sliced thick

1 carrot, sliced thick

One 3–3½-pound shoulder of lamb, cut into 1-inch cubes

Salt and pepper

1 tablespoon unsweetened cocoa powder

10 cloves garlic, chopped coarse

2 cups Cahors or Zinfandel wine

1 cup stock or broth of your choice

2 teaspoons tomato paste

Small bouquet garni (see p. 82)

⅓ cup pork rind, cut into ⅓-inch pieces

½ pound shallots

Chopped parsley

1. Heat 3 tablespoons of the oil or fat well in a round or oval braising pot. Sauté the onion and carrot. Remove to a plate. Brown the cubes of lamb well on all sides. Discard the browning fat. Return the vegetables to the pot. Season with salt and pepper.

2. Mix the cocoa powder, chopped garlic, and wine; add to the pot. Also add the stock and bring to a boil. Add the tomato paste and bouquet garni. Turn the heat down to a simmer. Preheat the oven to 325°F.

3. Cover the pork rind pieces with cold water, bring to a boil and boil 5 minutes. Drain and transfer to the braising pot. Cover the pot with foil and pot lid as described on page 355 and bake for 1½ hours.

4. Peel the shallots, brown them lightly in the remaining 2 tablespoons of the oil or duck fat. Set aside.

5. When the lamb is almost done, add the shallots to the braising pot and finish cooking the lamb.

6. When the lamb is completely done, transfer it and the shallots to a deep country dish. Defat the sauce, reduce it if need be; correct the seasoning, strain the sauce over the meat, and sprinkle with chopped parsley.

Recommended vegetable: A plain rice pilaf (p. 424).

RIS DE VEAU BRAISES A LA MOUTARDE ET AU CRESSON
{Braised Veal Sweetbreads with Mustard and Watercress}

As already mentioned in the salad chapter on page 155, the texture of sweetbreads is a matter of personal taste. Cook them the way you like; for this preparation I prefer them well done and almost melting on the tongue. The sauce as finished here with egg yolks the sole binder for the braising juices is a typical example of a "custard type sauce" (see p. 171).

SERVES 6–8

3 pairs veal sweetbreads
1 large onion, sliced thick
1 small carrot, sliced thick
2 tablespoons butter
Salt
Pepper from the mill
Small bouquet garni (see p. 82)

2–3 cups stock or broth of your
   choice
2 egg yolks
1–1½ tablespoons strong Dijon
   mustard
2–3 tablespoons heavy cream
⅓ cup chopped watercress

1. Soak the sweetbreads in water for 2 hours, renewing the water often. Place the sweetbreads between 2 plates and put 2 large, heavy cans on top of the second plate. This will squeeze the blood out of the sweetbreads so it does not turn brownish while braising.
2. Preheat the oven to 325°F. Sauté the onion and carrot in butter; add the sweetbreads, salt, pepper, and the bouquet garni. Cover with stock. Cover the pot with foil and the pot lid as described on page 355 and braise for 45 minutes in the oven. If you like the sweetbreads crunchy, 25–30 minutes of braising will be sufficient.
3. Remove the sweetbreads from the pot and clean them of all tough sinews and cartilages. Slice each in half lengthwise for easier serving. Keep warm.
4. Strain the cooking juices into a large saucepan; reduce them to ⅔ cup. In a heavy saucepan, fluff the egg yolks with a whisk, gradually add the hot cooking juices to them. The sauce will thicken noticeably. Add the mustard, heavy cream, salt, pepper, and finally the chopped watercress.

Recommended vegetables: A plain pilaf or creole rice and watercress bouquets.

VIANDES SANS SAUCES
(Meats Without Sauces)

The old favorite, breaded meats, served without any sauce but "noisette" butter mixed with lemon juice, are still very popular. Here are a few recipes to illustrate the method. In some cases, I like to replace the "noisette" butter with a very small concentrated essence of meat. Such is the case in the *Escalope d'Agneau à l'Anis* on page 363.

Watch your breading; it is important. Some cooks flour their meats before breading, some do not. This deserves a bit of explanation. If you want to be safe at all times and see your breading always stay on, by all means flour, but very lightly, so there is but a very thin veil of seasoned flour on the meat.

If you prefer not to flour, be careful: only very young meats can be breaded without problem because they contain a lot of liquid collagenous material in which the proteins will readily bond with those of the egg. To this category belong: milk-fed veal, small chicken cutlets from chickens no heavier than 3½ pounds, baby lamb (cutlets cut out of a leg no heavier than 4 pounds or chops with an eye no larger than 1¼ inches in the rib and 1½ inches in the loin). Any cutlet from larger animals that have reached maturity must be floured at all times.

Bread as follows:

- If you flour the meat, do so with seasoned flour.
- Apply your egg wash to the meat with a pastry brush. Use an anglaise made of: 1 egg well beaten with 1 teaspoon oil, 1 teaspoon water, and a large pinch each of salt and pepper. This will be sufficient to bread 6 good-size pieces of meat.
- Coat with either dry or fresh bread crumbs, plain, flavored, or blended with fine-chopped nuts. Once breaded, the meat must stand for at least 30 minutes on a rack to air dry. Keep the breading as thin as possible.
- The cooking of breaded meats is always done in oil or *clarified butter* (see p. 48) or a combination of the two, over rather high heat but not so high that the crumbing will instantly turn dark brown.
- In modern cuisine, the meat under the breading remains pink for veal, lamb, and liver; it turns a pinkish ivory white for chicken. Breaded veal sweetbreads prepared in the modern manner—that is, almost rare—will have a crunchy texture, since the short cooking time does not allow all membranes to melt properly and completely.

Arrange a work area for yourself with flour on the left, the bowl of anglaise in the center, and the crumbs or nuts on the right. The only implements you will need are a very supple, natural-bristle pastry brush and a stainless steel rack on which you will put the breaded pieces of meat.

ESCALOPES DE VOLAILLE A LA NOIX DE PECAN {Pecan Breaded Chicken Cutlets}

SERVES 6

3 tablespoons Jack Daniels whiskey
½ teaspoon grated lemon rind
6 medium chicken cutlets, each cut
   lengthwise into two ¼-inch slices
   (see cutlets, p. 332)
2 tablespoons flour
1 egg
1 teaspoon oil
1 teaspoon water

Salt
Pepper from the mill
⅓ cup fine-chopped pecans
¼ cup fresh bread crumbs from
   day-old French bread
½ cup butter
Juice of ½ a lemon
½ cup Golden Veal Stock (p. 20)

1. Blend the Jack Daniels and lemon rind and brush each cutlet with a small amount of the mixture. Let stand for 30 minutes. Dab dry with a paper towel.

2. Sift the flour onto waxed paper; mix the egg, oil, water, salt, and pepper and beat until homogeneous. Mix the pecans with the bread crumbs. Flour each thin cutlet very lightly, brush it with anglaise, and coat it with the mixed pecans and crumbs. Let dry for 30 minutes on a stainless steel rack before cooking.

3. Clarify the butter (see p. 48); in a skillet, heat it until it bubbles like champagne. Panfry the cutlets on each side until golden. Remove from the pan and keep hot. Do not discard the cooking butter.

4. To the skillet add the lemon juice, salt, pepper, and the veal stock; reduce to 3 tablespoons. Correct the seasoning and pour a trickle of glaze at the center of each cutlet.

Recommended vegetables: Watercress bouquets and a green salad.

MEDAILLONS DE RIS DE VEAU AUX NOISETTES {*Medallions of Sweetbreads in Hazelnut Crumbs*}

The sweetbreads are cooked in the modern manner. You can, if you prefer, braise them for 35 minutes and cool them before you slice and bread them.

Do not toast the hazelnuts too deeply since they will recook in the breading.

SERVES 6–8

2 pairs veal sweetbreads
1 teaspoon dried orange rind
2 tablespoons flour
Salt
Pepper from the mill
1 egg
1 teaspoon oil
1 teaspoon water

⅓ cup fine-chopped toasted hazelnuts
½ cup fresh bread crumbs from day-old bread
10 tablespoons butter
1 strip of fresh orange rind, 2 inches by ¾ inch
A dash of Grand Marnier
A dash of lemon juice

1. Soak the sweetbreads in water for 2 hours, renewing the water several times.
2. Put the sweetbreads in a large pot of cold water and bring to a boil. Turn down to a simmer, and simmer no more than 10 minutes. Drain, rinse under cold water, and cool completely.
3. Remove as much of the outside sinew and cartilage as you can, but do not separate the sweetbreads into nuggets; rather cut each of them crosswise into as many ⅓–½-inch-thick slices as you can.
4. Mix the dried orange rind, flour, and a good pinch of salt and pepper. Beat together until homogeneous the egg, oil, water, and another pinch of salt and pepper. Mix the toasted hazelnuts with the bread crumbs.
5. Flour the medallions of sweetbread, then brush them with the anglaise, and coat them with the mixture of hazelnuts and crumbs. Dry for 30 minutes on a stainless steel rack.
6. Clarify 8 tablespoons of the butter and heat it well in a large skillet or sauté pan. Roll the fresh orange rind backward to liberate the oil and immediately, using a fork, swish it around the bottom of the pan to flavor the butter well.
7. Cook the medallions in the orange-flavored butter until they are golden

on all sides. Remove to plates or a platter as soon as done. Keep hot. Discard half the cooking butter; add the remaining 2 tablespoons of the butter to the pan and let it cook to a dark "noisette" butter (see p. 48). Add the Grand Marnier and lemon juice and a dash of salt and pepper. Pour over the medallions.

Recommended vegetables: Watercress bouquets or the Pretty Green Salad with Edible Flowers on p. 156.

ESCALOPES D'AGNEAU A L'ANIS
{Escalopes of Lamb with Anise}

Always use a leg of lamb heavier than 4 pounds.

SERVES 8

One 5½–6-pound whole leg of lamb   *Salt*
1½ cups Golden Veal Stock (p. 20)   *Pepper from the mill*
1–1½ teaspoons of Pernod or Pastis   *1½ cups fresh bread crumbs from*
1 teaspoon powdered aniseeds   *day-old bread*
2 eggs   *2 tablespoons fine-chopped parsley*
Olive oil as needed   *2 cloves garlic, chopped fine*
2 teaspoons water   *⅓ cup clarified butter*

1. Completely remove the fell of the leg of lamb. Remove each muscle of the leg separately. Out of each muscle, cut as many ⅓-inch-thick escalopes as you can find. Always cut against the grain, *never with the grain* of the meat. Using a meat bat, flatten the escalopes to no more than ¼ inch.
2. With the tough muscles of the shank (called the *mouse* in French) and the stock, prepare ⅓ cup good simple essence of lamb (see p. 268). Flavor it with 1 to 1½ teaspoons Pernod or Pastis.
3. Sprinkle the anise powder over the escalopes; pat it well into the meat. Mix the eggs, 2 teaspoons olive oil, water, salt, and pepper. Brush the escalopes with this mixture. Mix the bread crumbs with the chopped parsley and garlic and coat the escalopes. Dry for 30 minutes on a stainless steel rack.

4. Panfry the escalopes in 1/3 cup olive oil or clarified butter to golden brown over medium-high heat so as to keep the meat medium rare under the crumb coating. Dribble the prepared essence in a thin stream over the escalopes.

Recommended vegetable: Prepare a salad of endives, oranges, and watercress with a good olive oil and lemon juice dressing.

FOIES GRAS

This small section is dedicated to two of the ways to cook foie gras. There are others: the liver can also be cooked wrapped in cheesecloth and immersed in a bath of melted *confit* fat, or it can be preserved in a glass jar. But these are the easiest ways to cook a fresh foie gras successfully.

FOIE GRAS FROID {Foie Gras to Be Eaten Cold}

This should be eaten with plain French bread. The sherry can be replaced by the same amount of French Sauternes or a semisweet muscat wine, or one half ounce of Cognac or Armagnac.

SERVES 8–10

1 duck foie gras
Fine salt (1/3 ounce salt per pound
*   of liver)*
A large pinch each of cinnamon,
*   nutmeg, and allspice*

The heads of two cloves, crushed
1/2 to 3/4 teaspoon pepper from the
*   mill, per pound of liver*
1/4 to 1/3 cup fino sherry per liver
1 tablespoon butter

1. Let the foie gras warm to room temperature. Weigh it.
2. Open each lobe lengthwise with one stroke of a very sharp paring knife. Gently tease out the artery and all the capillary vessels attached to it to prevent any spots of blood in the cooked liver.
3. Mix the salt, spices, and pepper, and sprinkle well all over the liver (inside and outside). Pour half the sherry into a terrine just large enough to contain

the liver, pack it, smooth side down, and add the remainder of the sherry. Cover with a piece of foil buttered with one tablespoon butter and marinate overnight in the refrigerator.

4. Bring the terrine back to room temperature and preheat the oven to 325°F. Bake, still covered with the foil, until the internal temperature of the liver shows 130°F; the cooking time varies with the size of the liver. Cool, chill overnight in the refrigerator and serve sliced with plain French bread.

ESCALOPES DE FOIE GRAS CHAUDES AU CARAMEL D'ORANGE
{Warm Slices of Foie Gras with Orange Caramel Sauce}

Cooking the foie gras in a very hot frying pan causes the fat to run immediately out of the liver slices.

SERVES 6

½ ounce sherry vinegar
⅔ cup fresh orange juice
⅔ cup Golden Veal Stock (p. 20)
¼ teaspoon fine-grated orange rind
12 slices of foie gras, ⅓ inch thick,
    cut slantwise out of the larger lobe
    of the liver

Salt
Pepper from the mill
⅓ to ½ teaspoon sugar
2 tablespoons butter
1½ tablespoons scallion greens cut
    slantwise into tiny slices

1. Mix the sherry vinegar, orange juice, veal stock, and finely grated orange rind in a saucepan and reduce to ⅔ cup. Set aside.

2. Season the liver slices with salt and pepper from the mill. Heat a frying pan until very hot, and add the slices of liver. Without using any fat at all, fry the slices very quickly, until dark brown on both sides. Remove to 6 heated luncheon plates.

3. Discard all the fat in the frying pan. Pat any excess fat off with paper towels and add the sugar, sprinkling it evenly over the surface of the pan. Let it turn to dark caramel. Add the prepared reduction and the butter. Correct the seasoning with salt and pepper. Strain over the liver portions and dot each portion with a few slivers of scallion.

Sparkling Fresh Vegetables

WHEN I WROTE *The Making of a Cook* in 1970, I as already keenly aware of the importance of good vegetables with pleasant textures and appealing, stable colors. And, of course, when I opened my restaurant this became particularly important to me. Successive visits to the great restaurants in France and surrounding countries had left me very disillusioned with the techniques of vegetable cookery applied by the French schools. The French still overcook their vegetables, and the situation is more painful because the quality of vegetables obtainable in France is far superior to anything produced anywhere in the United States, even in California.

The only vegetables I was trained to cook properly while working in my aunt's restaurant in France were the green beans, which always came out of rapidly boiling salted water bright green and perfect in their crisp tenderness. Paul Bocuse still serves a lovely green bean and almond salad in this style. Conversely, when I arrived in America, I found that vegetables cooked the American way, in a small amount of water to retain the vitamins, tasted raw and unfinished. I became fascinated by the Oriental method of stir frying vegetables, and I started using this method for myself, in my teaching and in my restaurant. Again, however, the grassy taste of the Oriental vegetables bothered me. My mind kept saying, no, either raw or cooked, but not that impossible in between where the flavor is neither that of the raw material nor that of the properly cooked one.

So I developed my own methods of cooking vegetables to my own taste, and these are outlined in the paragraphs that follow. Whatever technique I may use, in whatever season, I adapt the technique to the vegetable at hand and cook it according to its quality "of the day." Older carrots, for example, are blanched longer than younger ones, while very young carrots are often not blanched at all.

What I am trying to communicate to my readers is that one's taste in vegetable textures is extremely personal. Some people like vegetables grassy, others like them done medium well, still others like them mushy. So, use the seasoning ideas contained in this book with the textures that suit you. Your guests will be interested to see what you personally prefer.

I shall, in the following pages, discuss various methods of cutting vegetables for attractive presentation. You will see that I sometimes endorse the food processor wholeheartedly and sometimes warn of its shortcomings.

Good vegetables, like any other culinary presentation, require love, care, and time. All the recipes and techniques that follow apply strictly to fresh vegetables. Frozen vegetables are acceptable only when nothing else is available. Whenever possible, treat yourself and your guests to what nature has so lovingly made for you, and be sure that it tastes and looks the best you can make it look and taste.

SIMPLES LEGUMES CROQUANTS
(Simple Crisp-Tender Vegetables)

The only preparation these green and yellow vegetables require is that you wash them extremely carefully, dry them, shape them the way you like and stir fry them quickly until they reach the texture and degree of doneness you prefer. If preblanching is necessary, I will indicate it as the first instruction in the recipe.

CUTS OF VEGETABLES

A. The classic "olive" shape:

The classic olive can still be seen on many plates. The French school of vegetable cookery has not yet abandoned its way of "turning" the vegetables, but this method produces an awful lot of waste. If the scraps are kept to prepare soups, the damage to the budget is not too great, but if the scraps are not used, it is better not to adopt this type of cut.

1. To cut in olive shapes without too much loss: Carrots, turnips, zucchini, cucumbers, potatoes, rutabagas, Jerusalem artichokes, parsnips, celery root, gingerroot:
    a. Cut the *long* vegetables into 4 parts lengthwise. Discard the seeds, if any, or the woody center in carrots. You will be left with 4 flat long pieces the length of the vegetable and ¼–⅓ inch thick. Put them flat on a cutting board and, working at an angle, cut them crosswise into ½-inch-wide bands. Round off the sharp angles on each little band so the vegetable will roll easily in a skillet.
    b. Cut the *round* vegetables into parallelograms, with sides ⅓ inch by 1½ inches. Pare the angles of each parallelogram to form the vegetable pieces into ovals.

B. The old salpicons, mirepoix, paysanne, and Brunoise cuts (these are all cubes of sizes varying from 1/3 inch to 1/16 inch):

I personally use these only for soups, as vegetable salad garnishes, or as the *soffrito* or *fonds de braise* for small casserole-roasted or braised meats. Cutting these shapes presents no difficulty, but no machine can give you a good even square cut.

1. Cut slices of vegetables as thick as you desire the cubes to be. Recut the slices into strips of the same width, then cut the strips into cubes.

C. The juliennes:

Juliennes have become most popular, especially since the advent of the food processor, which is equipped with a number of julienning blades. Use the food processor if you must, but I prefer to slice the vegetables, then recut each slice into ¼-inch, ⅙-inch, or ⅛-inch sticks by hand. It is a personal choice that I have applied all through my years of teaching and as a restaurateur.

D. The spaghetti cut:

I was made aware of the possibilities for using the skins of vegetables such as zucchini and yellow squash when I read a restaurateur's ad in the *Gault & Millau* magazine and when, at approximately the same time, Myra Dorros, who was then one of my students and is now herself a teacher, used the skins of a yellow squash as a vegetable on her final examination plate.

To make the spaghetti cut, peel the skin of the zucchini or yellow squash into long bands ⅛ inch wide, either with a knife or with the "fine noodle" cutter of any pasta machine. Paper-thin slices of carrots can also be cut into spaghetti; of course, from spaghetti you can move on to vegetable noodles as my students Didi Davis and Linda Marino have done in their classes at the French Library in Boston and in their catering service.

E. Vegetable or fruit slices:

There is nothing wrong with simply slicing a vegetable that can be sliced. The slices should be approximately ⅛ inch thick. The slices can then be recut with a fancy cutter to obtain crinkle cuts, half moons, or other interesting shapes. Remember as always that in the same time it takes to slice a vegetable either by hand or by machine, you can always modify the cutting angle to obtain attractive ovals, and the ovals can themselves be cut into halves lengthwise to obtain half moons.

KEEPING PRECUT VEGETABLES

Both at home and in the restaurant, vegetables can be precut ahead of time, covered with plastic film, and stored in the refrigerator for 24–48 hours.

PREBLANCHING

All root vegetables, unless they are new and young, are better preblanched in boiling salted water for a minute or so before they are stir fried in hot fat. In the restaurant trade, the preblanching also sterilizes the outside of the vegetable and prevents it from drying out during the dinner service, or from oxidizing —and acquiring brown edges.

STIR FRYING: MEDIUM AND METHOD

Vegetables can be stir fried in pure clarified butter (see page 48), in any oil of your choice, or in a combination of the two. Heavy oils such as hazelnut and walnut should never be used alone, first because of their cost, but also because of their strong flavor. A mixture of one-third heavy oil with two-thirds clarified butter or corn oil is recommended. The clarified butter is necessary so the vegetables are not stained with dots of browned butter solids.

When stir frying, do not put the butter or oil directly into the sauté pan or skillet, but, with a pastry brush, first apply a thin layer of fat to the bottom of the cold pan. Heat well, then add the vegetables and stir fry over high heat for 1–2 minutes, constantly moving the vegetable pieces around the bottom of the pan. Season with salt and pepper and serve quickly.

It is essential that vegetables such as cucumbers, zucchini, and peppers, which contain a lot of moisture, be stopped from cooking before they lose their juices in the pan and turn mushy. *Stop cooking them when the first trace of vegetable juice appears in the pan.*

ASPERGES CHAUDES AU CARAMEL
{Orange Caramel Asparagus}

Use oranges and tangerines in combination, or either one of these alone.

SERVES 6

2 dozen asparagus, size of your choice
Salt
Pepper from the mill
⅓ cup orange juice
⅓ cup tangerine juice
½ teaspoon each grated orange and
    tangerine rind

½ teaspoon ground coriander
1½ teaspoons sherry vinegar
1½ tablespoons sugar
4 tablespoons butter, raw
1 tablespoon clarified butter or
    hazelnut oil
1 tablespoon chopped chives

1. Peel the asparagus and blanch them in boiling salted water, keeping them slightly undercooked. Drain and refresh under cold water. Cut the asparagus into 2-inch chunks, cut slantwise.

2. Place salt, pepper, orange and tangerine juices and rinds, coriander, and sherry vinegar in a saucepan and reduce to ¼ cup.
3. Meanwhile, cook the sugar to a deep caramel. As soon as the caramel is cooking to the dark (but not too bitter) stage, add the reduction of juices to dissolve the caramel. Bring it to a boil and fluff in the raw butter until melted and well emulsified.
4. Quickly stir fry the asparagus in the clarified butter or oil, and as soon as it is hot remove it from the heat and strain the orange caramel sauce over it. Mix well and add chives.

USES:

An excellent spring vegetable to serve with all roasted poultry, panfried chicken or turkey breast, pork roast, panroasted quail, roasted or braised pigeon.

CAROTTES A L'EAU DE NOIX
{Carrots in Walnut Wine Glaze}

A mixture of centuries: the carrots are crisp-tender, but the glaze is from the Middle Ages.

SERVES 6

1½ pounds carrots, preferably young, cut into olive shapes	¼ cup Golden Veal Stock (p. 20)
2 tablespoons butter or oil	Salt
3 tablespoons Nocino or Vin de Noix (p. 511)	Pepper from the mill
	Lemon juice as needed
	Chopped parsley

1. Blanch the carrots until crisp.
2. Add butter or oil to a skillet and stir fry the carrots until crisp-tender.
3. Meanwhile, reduce together the walnut liqueur or wine and the veal stock to obtain 2½ tablespoons excellent glaze. Toss the stir-fried carrots into the glaze. Add salt, pepper, lemon juice as needed, and chopped parsley.

USES:

For braised white meats or casserole-roasted quails, pigeons, or Cornish hens.

CONCOMBRES AUX HERBES {Herbed Cucumbers}

The cucumbers must be peeled, seeded, and cut into either olive shapes or half moons. The ends, which can be bitter, should be discarded. No blanching is necessary. If fresh herbs are not available, use dried ones, very well powdered.

SERVES 6

2 long hothouse cucumbers or 4
   small regular cucumbers
2 tablespoons clarified butter or 1½
   teaspoons oil of your choice

Chopped fresh watercress, tarragon,
   mint, dill, or chives, alone or in
   combination
Salt
Pepper from the mill

1. Peel, seed, and cut the cucumbers in the shape of your choice. Heat the butter or oil in a sauté pan or skillet. Stir fry the vegetables very quickly over very high heat.
2. Add the herb or herbs of your choice and mix well. Correct the seasoning and serve.

USES:

Excellent with all red and all white meats, and also with fish served as a main course.

COURGETTES VERTES ET JAUNES AUX HERBES DE PROVENCE
{Zucchini and Yellow Squash with Provençal Herbs}

There are two ways of cutting the vegetables for this presentation. If both varieties of squash are small and without visible seeds, slice them into ⅙-inch slices, then recut the slices lengthwise into ⅙-inch strips. Should the squash be older and larger, "box" each of them, that is, remove the skin of each in 4 longitudinal bands, leaving ⅛ inch of flesh attached to the skin. The center is good for a soup. Cut each long band on the slant into ⅙-inch-wide julienne strips.

SERVES 6

2 yellow summer squash (3 if
   smaller)
2 zucchini (3 if smaller)
1½ tablespoons clarified butter or
   other fat or oil of your choice

Salt
Pepper from the mill
Provençal herbs, fresh or dried

1. Prepare the julienne of vegetables as indicated above. Stir fry in clarified
   butter or oil and add the herbs. If the herbs are dried, powder them well
   before adding to the pan. Mix well.

USES:
   For all meats prepared in the "brown" manner. Also, for all fish.

JULIENNE DE COURGETTES ET CHAMPIGNONS AU BASILIC
{Julienne of Zucchini and Mushrooms with Basil}

This dish is a typical example of the superiority of hand cutting succulent
vegetables. Both zucchini and mushrooms are so full of moisture that cutting
by machine will start extraction of the juices and flood the skillet with the
vegetable water. The size of the julienne should not be smaller than ¼ inch.

SERVES 6

4 small, seedless zucchini
½ pound large mushrooms
2 tablespoons clarified butter or oil
   of your choice
Salt

Pepper from the mill
12 basil leaves, scissored very fine, or
   ¼ teaspoon very fine-powdered dried
   basil

1. Cut the zucchini into ¼-inch elongated oval slices. Recut the slices into a
   ¼-inch-wide julienne. Slice the mushrooms in ¼-inch-thick slices and
   recut those into ¼-inch-wide julienne sticks.
2. Heat 1 tablespoon of the butter or oil. Add the zucchini and stir fry for
   1–2 minutes. Remove to a plate. Heat the remaining tablespoon of the
   butter or oil and, over extremely high heat, add the mushrooms and stir fry

for 1 minute. Return the zucchini to the skillet. Stir fry for 1–2 more minutes. Season with salt and pepper. Add basil and serve immediately.

USES:

For all meats or fish.

EPINARDS DE PRINTEMPS AUX CHEVEUX D'ANGES {Young Spinach with Angel Hair}

It is essential to have small spinach leaves without too much "iron" taste in them. Any spinach that, tasted raw, can be easily and pleasurably eaten, can be prepared in this way. The color is strikingly beautiful and appetizing on a plate.

SERVES 6

2 pounds spinach
½ a red pepper
½ a green pepper
1 small carrot

2½ tablespoons clarified butter or
   oil of your choice
Salt
Pepper from the mill
A dash of nutmeg (optional)

1. Wash and stem the spinach. Blot dry, leaving a tiny bit of moisture on the leaves.
2. Peel the peppers and the carrot and cut all three into a ⅙-inch julienne. Blanch the carrot strips in boiling salted water for 1 minute.
3. Heat ½ tablespoon of the butter or oil in a large sauté pan, add the pepper and carrot strips, and stir fry for 1 minute. Set aside on a plate.
4. Heat 1 tablespoon of the butter or oil in the same skillet, and very quickly wilt half the spinach in the fat, turning the mass of leaves either with your hands or 2 wooden spatulas. Repeat with the remaining spinach and the remaining tablespoon of butter or oil.
5. Mix both spinach batches, season with salt, pepper, and the optional nutmeg, and serve topped with the tricolored angel hair.

USES:

For all meats, but best served with veal and white meats.

HARICOTS VERTS DIVERS {*A Variety of Green Beans*}

If young green beans, at the most ¼ inch wide, cannot be found, I always French the beans, which means that I peel off their strings on both sides with a paring knife. I leave to the individual cook the choice of preparation she or he prefers.

SERVES 6

1 pound green beans
2–3 tablespoons butter or compound butter (see following Variations)
Salt
Pepper from the mill

1. Prepare the green beans as you like best. Bring a large pot of water to a boil and blanch them for 7 minutes. Drain them and cool them under cold running water.
2. Put the beans in a large skillet, heat gradually, sautéing the beans until they have lost all their moisture. Remove from the heat and toss in the butter, cut in tiny pieces. Season with salt and pepper and serve.

Variations: Instead of plain butter, the following compound butters can be used:

- Basil butter
- Parsley and garlic butter
- Dill butter
- Oregano or any other Mediterranean herb butter
- Nutmeg butter

Also, plain butter and any of the following garnishes can be used:

- 2 tablespoons toasted, slivered almonds
- 2 tablespoons toasted coarse-chopped hazelnuts
- 2 tablespoons toasted pignoli nuts plus 1 tablespoon fine-scissored basil
- 1 recipe shallots, onions and garlic (page 410)

- Chopped mint
- The four fresh fine herbs, chopped (chervil, chives, parsley, tarragon)

USES:

For all red or white meats.

MAIS AUX CHAMPIGNONS *{Corn and Mushrooms}*

It appears American, but this dish is one of the more frequently encountered garnishes for *confits* in the Occitania (see p. 319). Use the best corn America has to offer, which is far superior to all French breeds of corn.

SERVES 6

1½ cups fresh corn kernels, or frozen, if need be	Salt
1 pound fresh mushrooms	Pepper from the mill
2 tablespoons butter	1 clove garlic
	1½ tablespoons chopped parsley

1. If using fresh corn, blanch it for 1 minute in boiling salted water. Do not blanch if using frozen corn; simply defrost under cold running water.
2. Trim the mushroom stems. Quarter the mushrooms, if large, leave whole if buttons only.
3. Heat the butter in a skillet, add the mushrooms, salt, and pepper and toss together. Cover for 2 minutes to extract the water; uncover, raise the heat and evaporate the water completely. The mushrooms should be well browned and the butter should be visible in the pan. Add garlic and parsley and brown lightly. Toss in the corn and reheat well together. Correct the seasoning and serve.

USES:

For all roasted meats, white and red, and especially for *confits* of birds (see p. 311).

Note: You can use any wild mushrooms you like, both yellow and brown chanterelles are the best.

MANGE-TOUT AUX AMANDES GRILLEES
{Slivered Snow Peas and Toasted Almonds}

The snow peas can be left whole if you prefer, but then they should be served without the almonds.

SERVES 6

> *½ pound snow peas*
> *2 tablespoons clarified butter or oil of your choice*
> *Salt*
> *Pepper from the mill*
> *2 tablespoons slivered toasted almonds or pignoli nuts*

1. Remove the ends of the snow peas and cut them crosswise into ¼-inch-wide strips to match the size of the slivered almonds.
2. Heat the butter or oil, add the snow peas and quickly stir fry for 2 minutes or so. Add salt, pepper, and the slivered nuts. Serve promptly.

USES:

For all meats.

NAVETS LIARDS {Sliced Turnips with Bacon and Chives}

This recipe can be used for blanched parsnips.

SERVES 6

1 pound small purple top turnips
2 slices of bacon
1½ tablespoons butter or oil of your choice

Salt
Pepper from the mill
1 tablespoon chopped chives

1. Peel the turnips, slice them into ⅛-inch slices, and blanch them for 1 minute in boiling salted water. Drain and pat dry.

2. In a large frying pan, cook the bacon, extracting all the fat. As soon as it is done, pat dry on paper towels and crumble into a small bowl.

3. Discard all the fat in the frying pan but do not wash the pan. Pat all the fat off with a paper towel and add the butter or oil. Stir fry the turnips for 1–2 minutes. They will turn golden and be salted by the bacon juices at the bottom of the skillet. Add the crumbled bacon, salt if needed, pepper, and the chives. Serve promptly.

USES:

Excellent for roasted or panfried pork, as well as for veal and all poultries.

POIVRONS DE TOUTES LES COULEURS
{Multicolored Sweet Peppers}

Ideally these peppers should be peeled for finer taste and complete digestibility. I leave to my readers the choice of peeling or not peeling. In the restaurant and at home, I always peel my peppers, either with a potato peeler or with a parer; at the beginning, peeling seems to take forever, but after several pepper dishes, it does not seem so bad anymore, and once the peeling becomes habit unpeeled peppers will be unattractive to the taste buds. The food processor also "juliennes" unpeeled peppers. If no yellow peppers are available, use 1 more each of the red and green peppers.

SERVES 6

3 red peppers
3 yellow peppers
3 green peppers
1 clove garlic

2 tablespoons clarified butter or oil of
    your choice
Oregano or Provençal herbs (optional)

1. Cut the peppers into 6 strips each. Peel those if you wish. Cut the strips lengthwise into ¼-inch julienne. Keep the peppers separated into 3 different bowls.

2. Peel and sliver the garlic clove. Heat the butter or oil in a large sauté pan, add the garlic slivers and let them brown over medium heat; then, using a slotted spoon, discard the garlic slivers. Raise the heat very high.

3. Add the green peppers and toss in the hot butter or oil for 1 minute. Add

the yellow peppers, toss them for 1 minute. Add the red peppers and continue tossing for 2–3 minutes. Add the herbs if you are using them. Serve immediately before the juices run out of the vegetables.

USES:

For all meats, especially those prepared with strong brown sauces, and for all broiled or grilled meats or fish.

RADIS ROSES SAUTES AU VINAIGRE
{Red Radishes Sautéed with Vinegar}

The vinegar is not essential if you prefer the peppery radishes by themselves, but you will find that they discolor completely without it.

SERVES 6

2 bunches of red radishes	Salt
1 1/2 tablespoons clarified butter or oil	Pepper from the mill
1 tablespoon sherry vinegar or other vinegar	Chopped parsley or chives

1. Clean the radishes of all black traces and slice them into ⅛-inch slices.
2. Heat the butter or oil in a frying pan or skillet. Add the radishes, toss well in the butter, add the vinegar, salt, and pepper. Continue stir frying until the radishes turn orangy red and become somewhat translucent. Add parsley or chives or a mixture of both.

USES:

For all white meats, especially chicken and turkey breast.

SPAGHETTI DE LEGUMES {Vegetable Spaghetti}

You can serve the vegetables either plain or, as I do here, with a sprinkling of any herb of your choice. For a Provençal touch, brown a good tablespoon of chopped garlic and parsley in the cooking fat or oil before adding the vegetables.

SERVES 6

2 large carrots	*Salt*
2 large zucchini	*Pepper from the mill*
2 large yellow summer squash	*1 tablespoon mixed fresh fine herbs,*
2 tablespoons clarified butter or oil of	*chopped (chervil, chives, parsley,*
your choice	*tarragon)*

1. Peel the carrots. Cut them lengthwise into ⅛-inch slices (use the food processor, a Mandoline or a Feemster). Cut the carrot slices into ⅛-inch-wide angel hair. Blanch for 1 minute in boiling salted water.
2. Peel the skins of the zucchini and the yellow squash along the whole length of each squash. Cut the skins into ⅛-inch-wide angel hair. Keep in 2 separate bowls.
3. Heat the butter or oil in a very large skillet. Add the carrots first, then the yellow squash, then the zucchini skins and stir fry together no more than 1 minute. Add salt, pepper, and fine herbs. Serve promptly.

USES:

Especially elegant with fish fillets, veal, and chicken.

TOPINAMBOURS SAUTES
(Stir-fried Jerusalem Artichokes)

We ate so many Jerusalem artichokes during the Second World War that I took a dislike to them. When they arrived in the eastern United States from California, I gave them a second try and, much to my amazement, loved them and their crunchiness. Instead of ginger and scallions, you can use a plain persillade of chopped garlic and parsley.

SERVES 6

1 pound Jerusalem artichokes (sun	*2 scallions*
chokes)	*2 tablespoons corn oil*
Juice of 1 lemon	*Salt*
1 small gingerroot, 2 inches by 1 inch	*Pepper from the mill*

1. Peel the artichokes, slice them into ⅛-inch slices, then cut those slices into ⅛-inch julienne strips.

2. Bring a pot of water to a boil, add the lemon juice and blanch the vegetables for 1 minute. Drain and refresh under cold water. Drain well, pat dry.

3. Peel the gingerroot and cut it into ⅛-inch cubes. Put these into a small strainer and blanch for 1 minute in boiling salted water. Cut the scallions into long ovals ¹⁄₁₆ inch thick.

4. Heat the corn oil in a large sauté pan. Add the ginger, raise the heat, and immediately add the Jerusalem artichokes. Toss for 2 minutes over high heat. Add salt and pepper. Add the scallions and serve immediately.

USES:

Serve with red or white meats, panfried or broiled.

TOMATES CERISES {Cherry Tomatoes}

These look striking on a plate and require no other preparation than removing their stems and washing them. Four or five tomatoes, according to size, will make up a portion. To cream the tomatoes, toss them after cooking in several spoons of reduced heavy cream.

SERVES 6

24–30 cherry tomatoes
1½ tablespoons olive oil
1 tablespoon chopped garlic and parsley mixed
Salt
Pepper from the mill

1. Wash and stem the tomatoes. In a large sauté pan, heat the olive oil, add the garlic and parsley mixture, and sauté until the garlic turns golden.

2. Add the tomatoes and toss into the hot oil until their skins are taut and threaten to split. Season with salt and pepper. Serve before the tomatoes lose their skins.

USES:

Serve with all meats.

LEGUMES CROQUANTS EN JARDINIERES
(Crisp-Tender Vegetables in Various Combinations for Different Seasons and Occasions)

These combinations of different vegetables served together on a dinner plate make color and taste combinations that are most appealing and varied.

Notice the order of "arrival" of each vegetable in the skillet or sauté pan, with the firmer ones coming first and the softer ones being added successively. The most succulent always come last, to prevent overcooking and loss of moisture. "Jardinière" is the name given by all French women to a vegetable medley.

JARDINIERE DE FIN D'ETE
{End of the Summer Vegetable Medley}

SERVES 6

1 small head of cauliflower	*1 red pepper, peeled*
1 bunch of broccoli	*1 zucchini*
⅓ pound carrots	*2 tablespoons oil of your choice*
⅓ pound white purple top turnips	*Salt*
1 green pepper, peeled	*Pepper from the mill*

1. Clean and pare the cauliflower and broccoli into small flowerets. In the same bath of boiling salted water, blanch first the cauliflowerets for 3–4 minutes, then the broccoli for 3 minutes.
2. Peel and cut the carrots and turnips into ⅙-inch julienne strips. Blanch for 1 minute in boiling salted water.
3. Cut the peppers into ⅙-inch julienne. Slice the zucchini (skin and pulp together) into ⅙-inch slices; recut those slices into ⅙-inch julienne.
4. Heat the oil in a large sauté pan. Add the cauliflower, the carrots, and the turnips together, then the peppers and the zucchini, and finally the broccoli, each at 1-minute intervals. Continue to stir fry over high heat for 1 more minute. Season with salt and pepper and serve immediately.

USES:
For all meats and almost all fish.

ASSIETTE DE LEGUMES A L'OCCITANE
{Occitanian Vegetable Plate}

SERVES 6

¼ pound button mushrooms	*1 large red pepper*
½ cup shoepeg corn kernels (frozen corn is acceptable, defrosted first)	*2 tablespoons corn oil or clarified butter* *Salt*
4 baby zucchini	*Pepper from the mill*

1. Clean and pare the button mushrooms. Rinse quickly under cold water, pat dry. Set aside.
2. Blanch the shoepeg corn for 1 minute. If using frozen shoepeg corn, put the block of frozen corn into a strainer and run hot water over it to discard the frozen "butter sauce."
3. Cut the unpeeled zucchini into olive shapes (see p. 368). Peel the pepper and cut into pieces the same size as the zucchini.
4. Heat the corn oil in a large sauté pan. Add the mushrooms and sauté until brown. Add the corn and zucchini and stir fry for 1–2 minutes. Add the red pepper and stir fry for another 2 minutes. Season with salt and pepper and serve promptly.

USES:

Serve with all meats. Especially good with roasted birds.

JARDINIERE A LA RUSSE *{Russian-style Vegetable Plate}*

The usual garnishes of borscht used as a vegetable.

SERVES 6

½ a white cabbage	*3 tablespoons sunflower seed oil*
2 large carrots	*1 tablespoon toasted sunflower seeds*
3 baby beets	*Salt*
2 tablespoons white wine vinegar	*Pepper from the mill*

1. Remove the core and large ribs of the cabbage. Cut the leaves into a ¼-inch julienne. Peel the carrots, slicing them crosswise into elongated ovals ¼ inch thick. Recut into ¼-inch julienne. Blanch the carrots for 1 minute in boiling salted water. Drain well.
2. Peel the beets. Slice ¼ inch thick, then recut the slices into ¼-inch julienne. Blanch in boiling salted water acidulated with the vinegar. Drain well.
3. Heat the oil in a large sauté pan. Stir fry the cabbage for 1–2 minutes. Add the carrots and beets. Stir fry for another minute. Add the sunflower seeds, salt and pepper and serve.

USES:
Best with all kinds of pork.

SYMPHONIE EN CHOU MAJEUR
{*Four-Cabbage Medley*}

SERVES 6–8

½ a white cabbage
½ a savoy cabbage
½ a red cabbage
2 tablespoons white vinegar
2 dozen baby Brussels sprouts

3 tablespoons clarified butter
1 teaspoon caraway seeds
Salt
Pepper from the mill

1. Remove the core and ribs of the white cabbage, cut into ¼-inch julienne. Blanch only if you like.
2. Remove the core and ribs of the savoy cabbage. Cut into ¼-inch julienne. Blanch for 1 minute in boiling salted water. Drain and pat dry.
3. Remove the core and ribs of the red cabbage. Cut into ¼-inch julienne and blanch for 1 minute in boiling water acidulated with the vinegar. Drain and pat dry.
4. Clean the Brussels sprouts and remove all stained outer leaves. Cut a cross into the root end of each sprout. Blanch in boiling salted water for 3 minutes. Drain well and pat dry.

5. Heat the clarified butter in a large sauté pan. Stir fry the white cabbage for 2 minutes. Add the savoy and red cabbages and stir fry for another minute. Add the Brussels sprouts and stir fry for another minute. Add the caraway seeds. Season with salt and pepper and serve promptly.

USES:

For all pork dishes, small birds such as quails and well-done pigeon . . . even the occasional pheasant.

DEUX CELERIS AUX NOIX {Two Celeries with Walnuts}

SERVES 6

4 large ribs of celery
1 medium celery root (celeriac)
2 tablespoons butter
¼ cup chopped walnuts

Salt
Pepper from the mill
1 tablespoon chopped parsley

1. Peel the celery ribs. Cut them crosswise into ⅛-inch-thick half moons. Peel the celery root, cut it into ⅛-inch slices, then cut each slice into ¾-inch-wide strips. Recut each strip into triangles.
2. In the same boiling water, blanch first the celery rib half moons for 1 minute, then the celeriac triangles for 2–3 minutes. Drain, rinse under cold water, and pat dry.
3. Heat the butter in a large skillet. In it sauté the chopped walnuts. Add both celeries and stir fry for 2–3 minutes. Season with salt and pepper, add the parsley, and serve.

USES:

Excellent with roast chicken or duck. Good also with red meats, but not with fish.

LA JARDINIERE DU PLEIN HIVER
{Midwinter Vegetable Medley}

The chestnuts found in the United States will tend to break and fall apart and must be reserved for puréeing. For this dish, use the French chestnuts sold cooked in glass jars—a bit of an investment but the vegetable dish is worth it.

SERVES 6

1 small celery root (celeriac)
½ pound silverskin onions
½ pound baby Brussels sprouts
3 tablespoons butter

½ pound French chestnuts (see above)
Salt
Pepper from the mill
1 tablespoon chopped parsley

1. Peel the celery root. Cut it into 1-inch by ½-inch parallelograms. Trim the angles of these to obtain olive shaped pieces. Blanch for 5 minutes in boiling salted water. Drain well.
2. Peel the silverskin onions, cut a cross into their root ends, and blanch them in salted boiling water for 4 minutes. Drain and mix with the celery root.
3. Remove the tough outer leaves of the Brussels sprouts. Cut a cross in their root ends and blanch for 5 minutes in boiling salted water. Drain well and mix with the celery root and onions.
4. Heat the butter in a large skillet. Add all the vegetables at once. Cook, stirring, for 2–3 minutes. Add the chestnuts and continue cooking until they are thoroughly heated through. Add salt, pepper, and chopped parsley and serve promptly.

USES:

For all wild meats and game birds. Also for chicken, duck, pork, and most beef and veal.

LA JARDINIERE DU PRINTEMPS
{Spring Vegetable Medley}

All the vegetables should be the small new ones and, except for the asparagus and peas, should not be blanched.

SERVES 6

¼ pound baby spring carrots	6 small asparagus
¼ pound white radishes	½ cup shelled baby peas
1 pound yellow squash, ¾ inch in diameter	3 tablespoons clarified butter
	Salt
1 young zucchini, ¾ inch in diameter	Pepper from the mill

1. Peel the carrots and radishes. Wash them; wash also the yellow and green squash. Cut all the vegetables in halves lengthwise, then recut each vegetable half into ⅛-inch-thick half moons.
2. Peel the asparagus and blanch for 1 minute in boiling salted water. At the same time, place the peas in a strainer and immerse the strainer for 1 minute in the asparagus blanching water.
3. Heat the butter in a large sauté pan. Stir fry the carrots and radishes for 1 minute. Add the yellow squash and stir fry for another minute. Add the zucchini, asparagus, and peas and stir fry for another minute. Season carefully with salt and pepper and serve immediately.

USES:

For all meats as well as for fish steaks, fillets, and mousselines.

LA JARDINIERE DES GRANDS JOURS
{A Medley for Special Occasions}

I used to serve this jardinière for mid-season special occasions and especially for catered dinners. For a more formal effect, arrange the individual vegetables in neat bundles of parallel sticks at the bottom edge of the dinner plate, alternating the colors. For 6 servings, use the vegetables listed below and the help of a colleague or a mate to arrange the plates.

SERVES 6

¼ pound small green beans, ¼ inch wide

¼ pound carrots, cut into ¼-inch julienne

½ a celery root, cut into ¼-inch julienne

¼ pound purple top turnips, cut into ¼-inch julienne

1 zucchini, cut into ¼-inch julienne

1 red pepper, cut into ¼-inch julienne

1 green pepper, cut into ¼-inch julienne

Butter as needed

Salt

Pepper from the mill

1. Blanch the beans, carrots, celery root, and turnips successively in the same boiling salted water. Drain well and pat dry.
2. Stir fry all vegetables individually in a tablespoon or so of butter. Season well with salt and pepper and arrange on a heated plate.

USE:

A good all-purpose vegetable to garnish any meat or fish.

LES LEGUMES A LA CREME
(Creamed Vegetables)

Any of the stir-fried vegetables in the preceding recipes can become creamed vegetables when blended with reduced heavy cream and seasoned with whatever herb or spice one desires. I would like only to mention the fact that a creamed vegetable should be cooked a little longer than a plain vegetable.

Below are a few recipes for vegetables that are particularly delicious when creamed. Such vegetables can be served plain, in a small pastry shell, or in an artichoke bottom. To prepare small pastry shells, see page 70. Here is the recipe for artichoke bottoms.

FONDS D'ARTICHAUTS {Artichoke Bottoms}

SERVES 6

6 very large artichokes
Water acidulated with lemon juice
⅓ cup white vinegar
2 tablespoons flour

2 tablespoons lemon juice
2 tablespoons corn oil
Salt
Pepper from the mill

1. Break the stems off the artichokes. This will pull off all the rough fibers on the artichoke bottom. Remove all leaves until the purple center leaves appear. Cut those leaves flush with the edge of the artichoke bottom to expose the choke. Remove the choke with a melon baller. Using a paring knife or a potato peeler, smooth and round the artichoke bottoms until all traces of green have disappeared. Immerse each one in lemon water as soon as it is ready.
2. Bring 1½ quarts water to a boil. Mix the vinegar, flour, lemon juice, and oil in a small bowl; add, stirring, to the boiling water. Add salt and pepper.
3. Immerse the artichoke bottoms in the boiling water and cook at a rolling boil until a needle can pierce and come out of an artichoke bottom without resistance. Drain, rinse under cold water, and keep refrigerated in salted water.

ASPERGES CREME MANDARINE
{Asparagus in Tangerine Cream}

SERVES 6

24–30 asparagus spears
2 strips of tangerine rind
1½ cups heavy cream
Salt

Pepper from the mill
1 teaspoon lemon juice
1 tablespoon mandarine liqueur

1. Peel and stem the asparagus. Cook them to your taste or for 7–10 minutes, depending on size, in boiling salted water. Drain well, reserving ⅓ cup cooking water.

2. Cut the asparagus into 1¼-inch chunks. Reduce the asparagus cooking water and tangerine rind to 1 very strongly flavored tablespoon water. Remove the tangerine rind, add the cream, and reduce until it coats the bottom of a spoon by ⅛ inch.

3. Add the asparagus to reheat well and correct the final seasoning with salt, pepper, lemon juice, and mandarine liqueur.

USES:

Served in a small pastry shell, it can be a first course. As a vegetable side dish it should be served with chicken or white meat turkey preparations.

COCOS A LA CREME DE PARMESAN
{Italian Flat Beans in Parmesan Cream}

This recipe is common to the Savoie and to the neighboring Valle d'Aosta, where the hardy Italian flat beans known as "*Cocos*" grow abundantly from late summer to late fall.

SERVES 6

1 pound Italian flat beans (pole
   beans or Kentucky wonders)
1½ cups heavy cream
½ cup freshly grated fine
   Parmigiano-Reggiano cheese

Salt
Pepper from the mill
A dash of nutmeg

1. String the beans. Bring a large pot of water to a boil and cook the beans until still bright green but truly tender. Drain and refresh under cold water.

2. Reduce the cream to a generous cup and add the cheese, stirring well until a cream forms. Add the beans, correct the seasoning with salt and pepper and a dash of nutmeg. Serve plain or in a pastry shell or artichoke bottom.

USES:
Excellent with all plain broiled or panfried veal dishes.

CAROTTES ET FEVES A LA CREME DE THYM
{Carrots and Fava Beans in Thyme Cream}

Instead of thyme in the cream, you could also use a pinch of rosemary or a combination of the two. This is a vegetable for the spring, when the favas have just come on the market.

SERVES 6

3 pounds fava beans, fresh in shells
½ pound baby carrots
Salt
1½ cups heavy cream

½ teaspoon fresh thyme flowers, or
¼ teaspoon crumbled dried thyme
Pepper from the mill

1. Shell the fava beans. Peel each kernel and split it in half. Place the halved kernels in a large conical strainer.
2. Peel the carrots and cut them into ⅙-inch slices.
3. Bring a large pot of water to a boil and add salt. Immerse the strainer containing the beans into the water for 5 minutes. Remove from the water and rinse under cold water. Add the carrots, cook for 3–4 minutes, drain and rinse under cold water. Mix the favas and carrots.
4. Reduce the cream flavored with the thyme to 1 small cup. Toss the vegetables with the cream and correct the seasoning.

USES:
For all white meats and for roast pork.

CHAMPIGNONS A LA CREME DE MADERE
{Mushrooms in Madeira Cream}

This is an old favorite. The flavoring can also be sherry or port and/or any herb of your choice, such as tarragon or chives.

SERVES 6

1½ pounds mushrooms
2 tablespoons butter
Salt
Pepper from the mill

1½ cups heavy cream
¼ cup Sercial Madeira
A dash of nutmeg

1. Clean the mushrooms. Wash them only if necessary. Slice or quarter them if they are large.
2. Heat the butter in a sauté pan, add the mushrooms, and sauté for 1 minute over high heat, tossing well. Season with salt and pepper. Turn the heat down and cover to extract the natural juices.
3. Uncover the pan, add the cream and reduce by one-third. Add the Madeira and nutmeg and reduce until the cream coats the vegetables. Correct the seasoning and spoon onto plates or into pastry shells or artichoke bottoms.

USES:

As a first course if topped with grated Gruyère or Parmesan. As a side dish for all red and white meats.

COURGETTES A LA CREME DE NOISETTES
{Creamed Zucchini with Hazelnuts}

SERVES 6

2 tablespoons hazelnut oil
4 small zucchini, cut into ½-inch cubes
Salt
Pepper from the mill

1½ tablespoons sherry vinegar
1½ cups heavy cream
2 tablespoons chopped hazelnuts, toasted and peeled

1. Heat the hazelnut oil well and in it sauté the zucchini pieces over high heat until they brown lightly. Season with salt and pepper and remove to a plate. Add the vinegar to the skillet and reduce slowly to a few drops. Set the pan aside.
2. Reduce the heavy cream by one-third. Return the zucchini to the skillet still containing the well-reduced vinegar. Add the cream and blend well. Add the hazelnuts and correct the salt and pepper. Serve plain, in pastry shells, or in artichoke bottoms.

USES:

As a pleasant first course in pastry shells or artichoke bottoms. As a side dish for chicken, turkey, duck, pork, and veal.

LES LEGUMES AU FOUR
(Baked Vegetables)

The reader will find grouped here a number of vegetables baked in a slow oven. These have long keeping capacities ideal for dinner parties or restaurant service. My previous books contain numerous ideas for baked vegetables not appearing in these pages, especially the Mediterranean eggplant gratins.

Pommes de terre au four (baked potatoes):
Through many years of baking potatoes in the United States, I have come to the conclusion that as far as I am concerned, the two best baking potatoes are the Maine and the new California breed that arrives on the market toward September and October. That does not mean that I do not like the russets from Idaho; I do, only I like to prepare French fries with them instead, and this is strictly a personal opinion.

There is no secret to baking a good potato. Scrub it, punch 4 or 5 holes in it with a skewer and bake it in a 400°F. oven until the skin is crisp and delicious. Everyone knows that the skin, wrapped around a "ton" of butter, is the most delicious fare in the world. A positive *no* to aluminum foil. Granted, the potato keeps better and waits longer for a dinner party or in a restaurant operation, but it also loses that wonderful skin and acquires an aluminum taste that is eminently unpleasant.

At home, time your baking of the potatoes so that they do not have to wait too long before being served. The restaurant cook will know how to stagger her/his batches of potatoes so the service maintains quality throughout the evening.

Here are a few "butters" or "creams" to garnish baked potatoes. Cut each potato through the center, squeeze it open and add a large spoonful or two to the potato pulp. Leave to your guest the pleasure of mixing the butter or cream into the pulp.

CREME AU LARD {Bacon Cream}

Crisp 6 slices of bacon over medium heat. Discard the bacon fat, crumble the bacon, and add 2 cups heavy cream. Reduce to ¾ cup and let cool. Add salt, if needed, and pepper from the mill. Put 2 tablespoons of this mixture into each potato.

SERVES 6

BEURRE DE MOUTARDE {Mustard Butter}

SERVES 6–8

Put ¾ cup unsalted butter, a large pinch of salt, 35 turns of the pepper mill, 2 tablespoons extra-strong Dijon mustard, 1 tablespoon each chives, chervil, tarragon, and parsley into the food processor and process until a smooth compound butter is obtained. Put 2 tablespoons of this butter into each potato.

RAGOUT DE CHAMPIGNONS {Mushroom Ragout}

SERVES 6–8

Heat 2 tablespoons butter in a skillet. Add 1 tablespoon each chopped onion and shallot. Sauté until golden. Add ½ pound fine-chopped mushrooms and sauté for 2 minutes. Season with salt and pepper. Add 3 tablespoons dry Madeira, a dash of nutmeg, and 1 cup heavy cream. Reduce to a thick purée. Put 2 tablespoons of this mixture into each baked potato.

CREME DE BASILIC AU PARMESAN
{Basil and Parmesan Cream}

SERVES 6–8

Reduce 1½ cups heavy cream to approximately ⅔ cup. While still hot, add 2 tablespoons fine-scissored basil leaves, ⅓ cup grated Parmigiano-Reggiano cheese, and pepper. Mix well. Let cool and spoon 1½–2 tablespoons of this cream into each baked potato.

BEURRE D'AIL CARAMELISE {Candied Garlic Butter}

SERVES 6–8

Peel 60 cloves garlic (approximately 4 heads). Brown lightly in 2 tablespoons butter. Add 1 cup good stock of your choice and cook until the garlic falls apart and the stock is reduced almost to a glaze. Cool until viscous. Put ½ cup butter in the food processor container. Add the garlic glaze and pepper and process until smooth. Add 1 tablespoon chopped parsley and correct the seasoning. Put 2 tablespoons of this compound butter into each baked potato.

Tomates au four (baked tomatoes):

These recipes are to be used only in the summer months when the tomatoes are ripe and full of sun-sweetened juices. Choose nice "naturally" round tomatoes; the more bumps they have, the more botanically natural they will be. Tomatoes are best purchased from the farms that grow them, during the summer to late fall months. Choose them not quite as large as "beefsteak tomatoes" and cut them into halves crosswise. For the following presentations, do not remove the internal juices or the seeds, and never peel the tomatoes.

Season the tomatoes with salt and pepper. Lightly top them with any of the mixtures in the following recipes, put a pat of butter on top of each tomato half, and bake until the top is nicely browned. At home, plan to do the baking 10 minutes before serving. In restaurants, you will have to stagger the baking so the portions come out as needed. The oven temperature should be 350°F. for larger tomatoes to 375°F. for smaller ones. Count on ½ a medium tomato per serving.

Toppings for baked tomatoes are always made of fresh, unsweetened bread crumbs with herbs, cheeses, and hams of different types.

USES:

Baked tomatoes do best with lamb, beef, and veal steaks and chops.

TOMATES PERSILLEES *{Parsleyed Tomatoes}*

SERVES 6

Mix ⅔ cup fresh bread crumbs with 1 large fine-chopped clove garlic and 2 tablespoons chopped parsley. Season the mixture with salt and pepper. Divide equally among 6 medium tomato halves. Top each half with ½ teaspoon unsalted butter.

TOMATES GRATINEES AU FROMAGE
{Cheese-browned Tomatoes}

SERVES 6–8

Mix ½ cup fresh bread crumbs with ⅓ cup grated Gruyère or ¼ cup grated Parmigiano-Reggiano or grana or 3 tablespoons fine-crumbled Gorgonzola or blue cheese. Divide among 6 medium tomato halves and top each with ½ teaspoon unsalted butter.

TOMATES GRATINEES AU JAMBONS
{Ham-topped Baked Tomatoes}

SERVES 6–8

With boiled ham: use the topping for parsleyed tomatoes above and add 2 tablespoons very fine-chopped boiled ham. Omit the salt in the crumbs.

With prosciutto-style hams: use ⅔ cup fresh bread crumbs, ¼ teaspoon extremely fine-grated lemon rind, and 2 tablespoons very fine-chopped air-dried ham. Omit the salt. Pepper them handsomely. Top each tomato with 1 teaspoon olive oil dribbled over the crumbs.

Baked squashes:

Spaghetti and butternut squash have always been two of my favorites. To avoid unnecessary oven cleaning, remember to put the squash on a jelly roll pan or a cookie sheet before baking.

Prick each squash several times with a skewer. Bake at 375°F. for at least 1 hour, or until a skewer inserted in the center comes out freely, cleanly, and feeling very hot to the back of the hand. To serve, open the squash either by cutting it into half or by removing the top. Remove the seeds, scoop out the meat, season with salt and pepper, and top with one of the creams that follows. Two large squash of either variety will serve 6–8.

For Spaghetti Squash use:

SAGE CREAM

SERVES 6–8

Reduce 1½ cups heavy cream, seasoned with salt, pepper, and ½ teaspoon rubbed sage, to ⅔–¾ cup. Spoon 2 tablespoons of the cream over each portion.

PARMESAN CREAM

SERVES 6–8

Eliminate the sage in the preceding recipe and add to the reduced cream ½ cup Parmigiano-Reggiano or grana cheese and a good grating of coarsely cracked pepper.

For Butternut Squash use:

SHERRY AND PECAN CREAM

SERVES 6–8

Reduce 1½ cups heavy cream to ¾ cup. Add 1½–2 tablespoons dry sherry, salt, pepper from the mill, and 2 tablespoons chopped pecans presautéed in 1 tablespoon butter.

CITRUS CREAM

SERVES 6 – 8

Reduce 1½ cups heavy cream to ¾ cup. Add a grating or two each orange, lemon, lime, and grapefruit rinds.

LES GRATINS DE LEGUMES
(Vegetable Gratins)

The origin of the word gratin is, according to modern researchers, to be found in the Latin name of the city of Grenoble, Gratianapolis. The preparation is indeed—even in America—a well-known one, made with potatoes and cream or with the large red pumpkins that grow all over the mountains and lower agricultural regions of the French Dauphiné. The gratin is closely related to older Celtic preparations that, all over Gaul, were called *fars* by our ancestors. The Savoie *farsmen*, which the dictionary translates as gratin, is probably the most typical of the "new style" gratins, made with potatoes after the discovery that potatoes were indeed edible. *Farsmen* or *farcements*, were, before the advent of potatoes, made with cereal gruels, pretty much like the *fars* and *farz* of Brittany. France remains full of these *fars* in which the medium passes from cereals to eggs, flour, and milk along the centuries (the *pachade* and *farinade* of Auvergne, the *clafoutis* of Limousin). Gratins and sweet *fars* are usually made in shallow flat dishes, *farcements* in tall or rounded ring molds, but the idea is the same. All bake in a slow oven for a nice long time. The most modern *farcons* made in Savoie with potatoes closely resemble the Dauphiné gratins.

USES:
     The basic gratin and the following variations may be served either as the main course of a meal consisting further of a salad and cheese, or as a side vegetable for all meats.

GRATIN DE BASE A LA CREME DIT GRATIN DAUPHINOIS
{Basic Cream and Potato Gratin Known as Gratin Dauphinois}

Here is the prototype of all gratins of potatoes on which many, many variations can be made; the best potatoes for gratins are: Maine, Idaho russet, California new baking potatoes, or Prince Edward Island potatoes.

SERVES 6

1 clove garlic	*Salt*
2 tablespoons butter	*Pepper from the mill*
4 large potatoes, peeled and sliced	*Nutmeg to taste*
into ⅛-inch slices	*1½ cups heavy cream*

1. Crush the garlic clove, rub it all around a shallow ovenproof baking dish to coat the dish. Discard all traces of the garlic. Butter the dish with all the butter.
2. Preheat the oven to 325°F. Add the potato slices to the dish. Season with salt and pepper and dust with nutmeg. Toss together well, pour the cream over the potatoes and shake the dish back and forth until the salt has dissolved. Taste the cream. It should be salted through.
3. Bake until the cream has reduced completely and breaks butter at its edge. During the baking, the crust will build rather rapidly. Break it several times so the brown cream is again submerged by the yet unbrowned cream in which the potatoes cook.

    The cooked gratin will keep at least 2 hours in a slow oven. In restaurant operation, prepare all dishes in advance and stagger the baking as needed.

LOWER CALORIE VERSION

The first question that pops up in class is always, "Can I make the gratin with milk because it is soooo rich?"

For me, it is such an excellent dish that I would rather enjoy it only once a month if need be for dietetic reasons. Using milk brings it down to the level of good old scalloped potatoes, and a tablespoon or so of cornstarch or flour should be used to prevent the milk from separating while baking. Light cream is a decent compromise, but the gratin still tastes much milkier and less opulent.

GRATIN DE POMMES DE TERRE AU FENOUIL
{Gratin of Potatoes with Fennel}

SERVES 6

Prepare the potatoes as described in the basic recipe (p. 399). Stir fry until quite tender the sliced meat of 2 young fennel bulbs. Add ½ teaspoon fennel seeds.

Prepare the baking dish as described in the basic recipe. Add first a layer of potatoes, then the fennel slices, then a second layer of potatoes. Bake as described in the basic recipe. You may need a bit more cream.

GRATIN DE POMMES DE TERRE AUX POIREAUX *{Gratin of Potatoes with Leeks}*

SERVES 6

Slice, wash, and cook slowly in butter the white part of 6 large leeks. Prepare the potatoes and the baking dish as described in the basic recipe (p. 399). Add a layer of potatoes, then a layer of sautéed seasoned leeks, then a second layer of potatoes and bake as described in the basic recipe. Use a little additional cream. *Careful*: very old, tough, end-of-the-season leeks must be blanched before sautéing.

GRATIN DE POMMES DE TERRE AU CELERI RAVE *{Gratin of Potatoes with Celeriac}*

SERVES 6

Following the basic recipe on page 399, peel, slice, wash, and blanch for 5 minutes 1 root of celeriac, approximately 2½ inches in diameter. Separate the potatoes by a layer of blanched seasoned slices of celeriac and use a little more cream.

GRATIN DE POMMES DE TERRE A LA MOUTARDE {Gratin of Potatoes with Mustard}

SERVES 6

This dish is not only a French variation of the basic gratin but also a genuine Viennese potato dish.

Following the basic recipe on page 399, mix the cream with 1 teaspoon cornstarch and ¼–⅓ cup excellent strong mustard. Build and bake the gratin as described, topping it with 1 cup fresh bread crumbs.

GRATIN DE POMMES DE TERRE AUX ANCHOIS {Gratin of Potatoes with Anchovies}

SERVES 6

Also a Viennese variation. Following the basic recipe on page 399, salt the cream with 4 mashed anchovy fillets and, between the layers of potatoes, sprinkle 2 tablespoons chopped garlic and parsley mixed. Add 1 teaspoon cornstarch to the cream to prevent it from separating.

GRATIN DE POMMES DE TERRE AUX HERBES FRAICHES {Gratin of Potatoes with Fresh Herbs}

Be careful of the potency of the herbs.

SERVES 6

> 1½ cups chopped watercress leaves
> 1 cup scissored basil leaves
> 1 teaspoon fresh thyme leaves
> 1 tablespoon each of the four French fine herbs: chives, chervil, parsley, and tarragon

Following the basic recipe on page 399, toss the potatoes with the herb mixture. You may replace the fresh herbs by a smaller amount of revived dried herbs and top the gratin with bread crumbs if you like.

A SPECIAL GRATIN OF POTATOES: THE CANTAMERLOU

Originating in the central mountains of France, the *Cantamerlou* was traditionally made by the shepherds tending herbs on the *aygade* (the high meadows). It takes its name from the fact that when the cream is poured into the very hot pan, one can hear a bird sing (in Occitanian Cantamerlou). The dish is best when prepared with morels or chanterelles.

1 pound morels, chanterelles, or	*1 clove garlic, chopped fine*
ordinary mushrooms	*4 Maine or Idaho potatoes, sliced thin*
¼ pound butter	*1 cup heavy cream*
Salt	*2 tablespoons sour cream*
Pepper from the mill	

1. Clean, wash, and dry the mushrooms, removing all dirt, stones, and other small twigs or leaves. Heat 1½ tablespoons of the butter and sauté the mushrooms in it until brown. Season with salt, pepper and the chopped garlic, set aside.
2. Heat the remaining butter in a skillet. Wash the potato slices 3 times under cold water. Pat them dry in a towel and toss them in the hot butter to coat them well. Season well. Transfer to a baking dish and bake at 325°F. until the potatoes are golden and tender. Mix in the prepared mushrooms.
3. Reduce the heavy cream to ½ cup. Add the sour cream, season with salt and pepper, and pour while still hot into the dish of potatoes. You should hear "birds sing." Serve immediately.

U S E S :

Serve this as a first course. It may be prepared in a large pan or—especially in the restaurant—in individual small oval dishes.

GRATIN DE RUTABAGAS A LA CREME DE XERES {Gratin of Yellow Turnips in Sherry Cream}

SERVES 6–8

1 very large yellow turnip	1 teaspoon cornstarch
Salt	3 tablespoons fino (dry) sherry
Pepper from the mill	1 clove garlic, crushed
2 cups heavy cream	3 tablespoons chopped chives

1. Peel and slice the turnip very thin. Blanch the slices in boiling salted water until crisp-tender. Drain well, add salt and pepper, and toss thoroughly.
2. Bring the cream and cornstarch to a boil. Remove from the heat. Add the sherry.
3. Preheat the oven to 325°F. Rub a 1-quart baking dish with the crushed clove of garlic. Add the turnip slices. Pour in sherried cream and add the chives. Shake the dish back and forth until all elements are well mixed. Bake until nicely browned. The cream should break butter at the edges of the dish.

USES:

Excellent with all poultry dishes, pork, and veal.

GRATIN NORMAND {A Normandy Gratin}

SERVES 6–8

1 pound Brussels sprouts	2 cups heavy cream
1 head of cauliflower	1 tablespoon cornstarch
Salt	4 tablespoons butter
Pepper from the mill	½ cup fresh bread crumbs

1. Peel and trim the Brussels sprouts. Cut a cross into the root end of each one. Blanch them in boiling salted water until crisp-tender. Remove from the water with a slotted spoon.
2. Trim the cauliflower to small flowerets approximately the same size as the sprouts; blanch these in the same water as the Brussels sprouts until crisp-tender. Remove from the water with a slotted spoon. Reserve 1 cup cooking water.
3. Mix the heavy cream into the cooking water. Place the cornstarch in a small bowl and gradually dilute it with the mixture.
4. Preheat the oven to 325°F. Butter a 1-quart baking dish with 1 generous tablespoon of the butter. Add the sprouts and cauliflower mixture. Pour and mix in the cream and cooking water mixture. Sprinkle with the bread crumbs. Bake until the cream has almost totally reduced, 45–60 minutes.
5. Melt the remaining butter and sprinkle it over the bread crumbs. Continue baking 10 more minutes until the crumbs are golden.

USES:

As a side dish with all poultry or as a main course if followed by a salad and a good Camembert or Livarot cheese.

GRATIN DE COURGETTES AUX RAISINS VINAIGRES *(Gratin of Zucchini with Vinegared Raisins)*

SERVES 6–8

½ cup currants	Pepper from the mill
2 tablespoons red wine vinegar	3 large onions
3 large zucchini	1 clove garlic, crushed
⅓ cup butter	3 cups heavy cream
Salt	1½ tablespoons cornstarch

1. Soak the dried currants in the vinegar until the latter has been totally absorbed.
2. Cut the zucchini into ⅛-inch-thick slices. Sauté them in 2 tablespoons of the butter until crisp-tender. Season well and set aside.

3. Peel and slice the onions into ¼-inch slices. Brown the slices in 2 tablespoons of the butter until golden brown. Season well.

4. Rub a baking dish with the crushed garlic clove. Butter the dish with the remaining butter. Alternate slices of zucchini with slices of onions and a few vinegared currants until all elements have been used.

5. Preheat the oven to 325°F. Mix the cream and cornstarch and bring to a boil, stirring. As soon as the cornstarch has thickened the mixture, season it well and pour over the onions and zucchini. Shake the dish to let the cream penetrate through the vegetables and bake until golden, approximately 1 hour. Be careful to let the cream reduce well.

USES:

Serve with all Mediterranean dishes of meat, with broiled chicken, and with veal.

LA MENOUILLE {*A Bean and Potato Gratin*}

La Menouille, which is a specialty of the cold and damp very northern provinces of France, is a vegetarian's delight. Solid proteins, solid starches; it is truly more a main course than a side dish and needs a good *daussade* as a table companion (p. 161).

SERVES 6

1 pound dried red beans
3 large onions
Bouquet garni (see p. 82)
2 potatoes, peeled and cut into
   ½-inch cubes
¼ pound butter

1 ½ cups red wine
Salt
Pepper from the mill
Dried savory or marjoram
1 cup fresh bread crumbs

1. Soak the beans overnight in cold water. Drain and cover with enough fresh water to reach 1 ½ inches above the beans. Bring slowly to a boil; skim. Add the whole onions and bouquet garni. Cook until tender. Drain and reserve the cooking water. Cut the onions up in small pieces.

2. Cook the potatoes until crisp-tender in the bean cooking water. Drain and again reserve the cooking water.

3. Preheat the oven to 350°F. Coat a baking dish with 2 tablespoons of the butter. Mix the beans with the potatoes and cup-up onions. Add the remainder of the bean and potato cooking water. Bring the wine to a boil. Season it well with salt, pepper, and savory or marjoram and pour into the baking dish.

4. Bake for 40 minutes, then sprinkle with the fresh bread crumbs and season again with salt and pepper. Dot with all the remaining butter and finish baking until golden, another 15–20 minutes. Cool lightly before serving.

GRATIN DE COURGE AU GRUYERE
{Gratin of Pumpkin and Gruyère Cheese}

SERVES 6–8

One 4–5-pound pumpkin, seeded
2 cups heavy cream
Salt
Pepper from the mill

1 clove garlic, crushed
2 tablespoons butter
1½ cups grated excellent Gruyère
  cheese

1. Bake the pumpkin in a 350°F. oven until tender enough to be easily pierced by a skewer.

2. Remove the lid and scoop out the meat, put it into a colander, and let it drain completely for 2 hours. Mash coarsely.

3. Bring the heavy cream to a boil. Add salt and pepper. Rub a 1-quart baking dish with the garlic clove and grease it with the 2 tablespoons butter.

4. Preheat the oven to 325°F. Mix the pumpkin meat with 1 cup of the heavy cream; season well. Turn the meat and cream mixture into the garlicked baking dish. Top with the remaining cup of the cream and bake for 35–40 minutes. Top with Gruyère and finish baking until golden, about 10–12 minutes.

USES:
   A main course if served with a salad, or a side dish for all white meats.

LES LEGUMES EN COMPOTES
(Vegetables Deeply Cooked in Stock)

Handed down to us from the Middle Ages, these vegetables, mostly of the onion family, are blanched if necessary and put to finish cooking covered with good stock in a large flat sauté pan. Although the best stock to use is definitely the Golden Veal Stock on page 20, the Secondary Stock as described on page 23 can be substituted without any problem. The technique is simple. If the vegetable is a strong one, it is first blanched; then it is drained, patted dry, and sautéed in a bit of butter. As soon as it is well coated with butter, add salt and pepper and just enough stock to cover. Cook over medium-low heat until the vegetable is tender and the stock is reduced to a nice glaze. Always handle such "candied in stock" vegetables with the greatest care. They are as fragile to serve as they are delicious to eat. Vegetables "en compote" are best served in tartlet shells (see p. 67) or small bread croustades.

CROUSTADES

Cut the crust off the required number of white bread slices. Flatten them with a rolling pin. Butter them lightly on both sides and fit each slice into a tartlet mold. Bake in a 325°F. oven for approximately 8–10 minutes, or until golden. See page 68 for an *amuse-gueule* using rye bread croustades.

ENDIVES EN COMPOTE
{Endives Cooked in Cream and Stock}

SERVES 6

12 large Belgian endive
3 tablespoons butter
Salt
Pepper from the mill
2 cups stock of your choice

2 cups heavy cream
6 tartlet shells (see p. 67) or
*   croustades (preceding recipe)*
2 tablespoons chopped chives

1. Cut out the root end of each endive and remove the core. Cut any stained leaf tip away. Let water run into the leaves and squeeze them dry in a towel. Cut the endive crosswise into ⅓-inch-wide strips.
2. Heat the butter in a sauté pan, add the endives and sauté for a few minutes until well coated with butter. Season with salt and pepper. Add the stock and cream and let cook until the endives are very tender and well coated with the reduced cream and stock.
3. Correct the seasoning and spoon into warm tartlet shells or bread croustades. Sprinkle with chives just before serving.

USES:

Best with all chicken dishes (solid meat as well as mousses), but also pleasant with veal and pork.

ECHALOTES AU VIN ROUGE
{Shallots Candied in Red Wine}

When peeling the shallots, always break the bulb into 2 half bulbs; the vegetables will cook faster and taste better.

SERVES 6

2 tablespoons currants
1½ cups red wine (Côtes-du-Rhône or Zinfandel)
1½ pounds shallots
3 tablespoons butter
Salt

Pepper from the mill
1 cup stock of your choice
⅓ teaspoon very fine-grated lemon rind
Chopped parsley

1. Soak the currants in the red wine for 2 hours.
2. Peel the shallots. Heat the butter in a sauté pan, toss the shallots into it, and sauté over medium heat until the bulbs are uniformly golden. Season with salt and pepper.

3. Add the wine and the currants as well as the stock and the lemon rind and cook until the shallots are tender, approximately 40 minutes.
4. Serve as a garnish, sprinkled with the chopped parsley.

USES:

Good with all meats, especially red meats, roasted, panfried, or broiled.

COMPOTE DE POIREAUX AUX PETITS POIS ET AMANDES GRILLEES
{Compote of Leeks with Peas and Toasted Almonds}

It is essential to blanch the vegetables, or the cream may separate during the cooking.

SERVES 6

*12 medium-large leeks (white and
   light green parts only)
3 tablespoons butter
Salt
Pepper from the mill
2 cups stock of your choice*

*2 cups heavy cream
½ cup blanched baby peas
¼ cup slivered toasted almonds
6 tartlet shells (see p. 67) or
   croustades (see p. 407)*

1. Cut each leek into ⅓-inch slices. Bring a pot of water to a boil and blanch the leeks in it for 2–3 minutes. Drain and pat dry.
2. Heat the butter in a sauté pan, toss the leeks in it, add salt, pepper, the stock, and the heavy cream and cook until the leeks are coated with the well-reduced mixture.
3. Correct the seasoning and, just before serving, add the peas and toasted almonds. Spoon into individual tartlet shells or croustades.

USES:

Excellent with all meats.

TROIS LEGUMES CONFITS EN BARQUETTES DE COURGETTES
(Three Candied Vegetables in Zucchini Boats)

This makes a nice formal presentation. The onions, shallots, and garlic cloves should be cooked separately and blended together just before serving.

SERVES 6

½ pound shallots, peeled
¼ pound silverskin onions, peeled
4½ tablespoons butter
Salt
Pepper from the mill
1 quart stock of your choice
3 large heads of garlic

2 very large zucchini or yellow
*   summer squash, each at least 6 inches*
*   long*
2 tablespoons olive oil
3 tablespoons pignoli nuts, toasted
Chopped chives

1. Sauté the peeled shallots and onions, each in 1½ tablespoons butter, in separate pans, until golden. Season with salt and pepper. Add stock over each vegetable to cover and cook until tender.

2. Blanch the garlic cloves in their skins. Peel them and sauté in the remaining 1½ tablespoons of the butter until golden. Add the remaining 1½ cups of the stock and cook until tender. The cloves must remain whole.

3. Cut the zucchini or yellow squash in halves lengthwise. Cut each half in half again crosswise. Round off the ends of each chunk with a paring knife. Empty the centers of the squash chunks with a melon baller, leaving only ⅓ inch of pulp. You will obtain 8 small containers. Salt each one lightly and let stand for 30 minutes. Rinse the "*barquettes*" under cold water and pat dry. Heat the olive oil in a large sauté pan and cook the "*barquettes*" in it, turning them often until they are crisp-tender. Season them well inside.

4. Mix the shallots, onions, and garlic cloves. Correct the seasoning and mix in the pignoli nuts. Spoon into the "*barquettes*" and serve sprinkled with chopped chives.

USES:
For all meats, but especially tasty with pork.

POIREAUX RABASSES {*Truffled Leeks*}

Les Rabasses, in northern Comtat Venaissin, the area of Avignon and Vaison la Romaine, are the black truffles that grow at the foot of some oaks in the Garrigue. They can be imported into the United States (see p. 50) raw or canned. If you have canned truffles, use the category know as "Première Cuisson"; others will not be as good. If you have no truffles, enjoy the leeks candied in their butter and stock sauce by themselves. They are still a treat. Notice the 2 alternate presentations for this dish.

SERVES 6

VEGETABLE PRESENTATION:

2 medium-large truffles	*Salt*
6 large leeks (white and light green parts only)	*Pepper from the mill*
	2 cups Golden Veal Stock (p. 20)
1½ tablespoons butter	*Chopped parsley*

SALAD PRESENTATION:

All ingredients for Vegetable Presentation above	*1½ tablespoons* Aceto Balsamico *(p. 45) or other vinegar*
⅓ cup heavy cream	*Salt*
1½ tablespoons Madeira	*Pepper from the mill*
	6 tablespoons walnut oil

1. Brush the truffles well if they are uncooked, then cut them into ⅙-inch slices.
2. Blanch the leeks for 3 minutes in boiling salted water. Drain and cool. Cut each leek in half lengthwise, leaving ⅔ inch uncut at the root end. Coat a 1-quart baking dish with 1 tablespoon of the butter. Preheat the oven to 325°F. Slide 3 slices of truffles into the cut of each leek and arrange the leeks in the bottom of the baking dish. Season with salt and pepper. Add the veal stock, top with a piece of parchment paper buttered with the remaining ½ tablespoon of the butter, and bake until tender. Turn the leeks once while baking. The vegetables are done when the stock has turned to a glaze. The baking time will vary with the size of the leeks. Serve topped with chopped parsley.

3. To serve as a salad, remove the leeks to a serving dish. Deglaze the baking dish very well with the cream, add Madeira, *aceto balsamico*, salt, and pepper and whisk in the walnut oil. Spoon the dressing over the lukewarm leeks.

U S E S :

As a vegetable with any meat, but especially with beef tournedos, white meat or mousse of chicken, or veal steaks. As a salad, make it a dish in itself, presenting each leek on a leaf of lettuce, or serve as the garnish of a good terrine (see p. 112).

LES LEGUMES EN PUREES
(Puréed Vegetables)

Purées are most delightful in the depth of winter, especially with game birds or any other meats made to taste "wild" by artful marination. The basic rule of the classic cuisine has not changed: thin vegetables will need a binder, while the starchy ones will build a good solid purée, often so solid that it must be diluted with milk or cream. Purées are useful for using older vegetables that would not fry easily. However the purée is made, it must be buttered extravagantly and be stiff enough to hold together on a plate without running into a sauce.

PUREE DE CHOUX A L'ITALIENNE
{Italian Cabbage and Potato Purée}

SERVES 6

1 head of white cabbage   *Salt*
8 tablespoons butter   *Pepper from the mill*
4 cloves garlic, slivered   *2 large baking potatoes*
3 ounces diced pancetta

1. Discard the ribs and cut the cabbage into 1/4-inch-wide shreds. Wash and pat dry.
2. Heat 4 tablespoons of the butter in a sauté pan, add the garlic slivers and sauté until golden. Remove to a plate. In the same butter, sauté the diced

pancetta until golden; return the garlic to the pan, add the cabbage and toss well together. Season with salt and pepper, cover, and cook until the cabbage is reduced to a purée, 40–45 minutes.

3. Meanwhile, bake the potatoes in their skins. When they are soft, scoop out the pulp and strain it directly into the pan containing the cooked cabbage. Mix very well, correct the seasoning and whisk in the remaining 4 tablespoons of the butter. Serve very hot.

USES:

Particularly delicious with pork, but also good with all other meats.

PUREE DE COURGETTES AU CRESSON FRAIS
{Purée of Zucchini Peppered with Watercress}

SERVES 6

4 medium zucchini
8 tablespoons butter
2 cloves garlic, mashed
2 tablespoons parsley

2 baking potatoes
Salt
Pepper from the mill
½ cup chopped fresh watercress leaves

1. Remove both ends of the zucchini. Wash and quarter lengthwise. With a paring knife, trim off all seeds. Cut the zucchini into small pieces.
2. Heat 3 tablespoons of the butter in a skillet. Add the garlic and parsley and cook until golden. Add the zucchini and toss into the mixture. Season with salt and pepper, cover, and cook until reduced to a purée. Purée in the food processor or blender to obtain an even texture. Return to the cooking pot and keep hot.
3. Bake the potatoes in a 400°F. oven until tender. Strain the potato pulp into the purée of zucchini. Add the remaining 5 tablespoons of the butter and correct the seasoning. Just before serving, add the watercress. Serve piping hot.

USES:

For all meats, but also for game birds and meats prepared in strong marinades.

PUREE AU FER {*Spinach Purée with Garlic Chips*}

Obviously, a remedy for iron deficiencies; butter well to tame the strong iron taste. If you really object to it; blanch the spinach, but bid goodbye at the same time to the color and most of the vitamins.

SERVES 6

2 baking potatoes   *Salt*
4 pounds fresh spinach   *Pepper from the mill*
¼ cup olive oil   *4 tablespoons butter*
¼ cup garlic chips (slivers)

1. Bake the potatoes for 1 hour at 400°F.
2. Stem and sort the spinach. Wash it well and extract the moisture with a salad spinner. Put ½ pound spinach at a time in the food processor container and chop very fine, but without extracting the water.
3. Heat the olive oil in a large sauté pan. Add the garlic slivers and brown very lightly, no more than 2 minutes. Remove from the pan with a slotted spoon and drain on paper towels. To the same oil, add the spinach and toss it until well coated. Season with salt and pepper and cook until all the water has evaporated. The spinach is ready when approximately 1½ cups of it is left and it is shining with olive oil.
4. As soon as the potatoes are soft, strain the pulp into the hot spinach, mix well, add the butter, correct the seasoning, and serve.

USES:
    As a vegetable for all meats, white and red.

PUREE DE COURGE JAUNE ET ROUGE {*Purée of Winter Squash*}

This can be made either with butternut or buttercup pulp. If using butternut squash, do not bake. Peel and slice the squash and cook it in a skillet before adding the cream and sherry to it.

SERVES 6

2 large buttercup squashes
Salt
Pepper from the mill

½ teaspoon grated orange rind
3 tablespoons fino (dry) sherry
1½ cups heavy cream

1. Bake the squash for approximately 1 hour at 350°F., or until a skewer inserted at its center comes out clean. Slice off the top of the vegetable, scoop out and discard the seeds. Scoop out and immediately strain the pulp into a clean saucepan. Add salt, pepper, orange rind, and sherry and keep warm.

2. Reduce the cream to ¾ cup. Add to the squash purée. If the purée is too thin, return to the heat and reduce a bit more. Correct the seasoning and serve.

U S E S :

To accompany venison or any game bird, as well as meats marinated to imitate venison.

PUREE CREME D'ARTICHAUTS AU CITRON
{Purée of Artichokes with Lemon}

SERVES 6

6 very large or 9 large artichokes
1 large baking potato
1 cup heavy cream
¼ teaspoon fine-grated lemon rind
4 tablespoons butter

Salt
Pepper from the mill
1 tablespoon very fine-chopped fresh
   tarragon

1. Boil the artichokes in boiling salted water until almost tender, or until a skewer inserted into the stem end comes out freely.

2. Meanwhile, bake the potato. Season the cream with the lemon rind and reduce it to ½ cup.

3. Remove the artichokes from their water. Scoop the meat from the leaves. Clean the artichoke bottoms and sliver them. Heat the butter in a large sauté pan. Add the artichoke meat. Season with salt and pepper and cook

over medium heat until the vegetable pulp falls apart. Purée in the food processor until very smooth.

4. As soon as the potato is cooked, strain its pulp into the artichoke purée. Dry the purée over medium-high heat, add the lemon cream and the tarragon. Correct the seasoning and serve.

U S E S :

For chicken, veal, chicken or turkey mousse, even white fish mousses and mousselines. Also, very good with lamb and beef.

LES TIMBALES DE LEGUMES
(Vegetable Timbales)

These vegetable puddings, molded in small 2–3-ounce buttered cups and baked in a hot water bath, are a welcome change in the usual vegetable repertoire.

Different techniques can be applied to obtain various textures for the timbales. The vegetables can be puréed or shredded and the eggs can be left whole for a true pudding appearance or separated to obtain a "souffléed" and more airy appearance.

The timbales can be served as vegetables or, as indicated in the chapter on bread, as a pleasant first course. I've included here a few typical examples.

TIMBALES DE CAROTTES AU PASTIS
{Timbales of Carrots Flavored with Pastis}

SERVES 6

3 tablespoons butter	*Pepper from the mill*
1 onion, chopped fine	*4 eggs*
1 teaspoon aniseeds	*1 teaspoon cornstarch*
½ pound carrots, shredded	*1 cup heavy cream*
Salt	*1½ tablespoons Pastis, Pernod, or ouzo*

1. Heat 2 tablespoons of the butter and in it sauté the onion until translucent. Add the aniseeds, carrots, salt, and pepper. Toss well in the butter and

cook, covered, over medium heat until the vegetables are soft and show signs of breaking. Cool.

2. Transfer the vegetables to the blender or food processor. Add the eggs, cornstarch, and heavy cream and process until smooth. Correct the seasoning, add the liqueur, and process again to blend the flavors well.

3. Preheat the oven to 350°F. Butter 6 custard cups with the remaining tablespoon of the butter and fill them with the carrot custard. Bake in a hot water bath for 30–35 minutes. Cover each custard with a piece of nonstick parchment paper to prevent the formation of a skin.

4. To serve, simply unmold the timbales onto each plate.

USES:

Excellent with all veal and poultry dishes.

TIMBALES SOUFFLEES AU CRESSON
{Souffléed Watercress Timbales}

This has a slightly bitter taste and a very airy texture. If you object to the bitterness, blanch the watercress. To serve as a first course, spoon the sauce over the top of each timbale.

SERVES 6

TIMBALES:

3 tablespoons butter
1 cup chopped watercress leaves
½ teaspoon cornstarch
¼ cup heavy cream

Salt
Pepper from the mill
3 eggs

SAUCE:

1 onion, sliced very thin
1 tablespoon butter
⅔ cup heavy cream
Soy sauce to taste
Pepper from the mill

1. To prepare the timbales, heat 2 tablespoons of the butter in a saucepan. Add the watercress and wilt it for 1 minute in the butter. Mix the cornstarch and the heavy cream into a slurry and add to the watercress. Bring to a boil to thicken. Cool slightly. Correct the seasoning with salt and pepper.

2. Separate the eggs. Add the yolks to the watercress one by one, whisking well. Beat the whites to a good foam and fold into the watercress.

3. Preheat the oven to 325°F. Butter 6 custard cups with the remaining tablespoon of the butter and fill them with the mousse. Bake in a hot water bath until a skewer inserted at the center comes out clean, approximately 20–25 minutes.

4. While the timbales cook, prepare the sauce. Sauté the onion in the butter until golden. Add the cream and reduce to ½ cup. Season with soy sauce to your taste and pepper from the mill.

USES:

Unsauced, this is excellent with veal steaks and chops and with chicken breasts. A nice first course with the sauce.

TIMBALES D'ASPERGES A LA CREME D'OIGNONS {Timbales of Asparagus with Onion Cream}

SERVES 6

TIMBALES:

2 pounds medium asparagus	4 eggs
3 tablespoons butter	1 teaspoon ground coriander
1 tablespoon cornstarch	Salt
1 cup heavy cream	Pepper from the mill

SAUCE:

2 tablespoons butter	1 cup heavy cream
1 strip of orange rind, 2 inches by ½ inch	Salt
	Pepper from the mill
1 onion, sliced very thin	Reserved asparagus tips
1½ tablespoons cider vinegar	

1. To prepare the timbales, peel the asparagus. Cut off the tips and blanch them for 3–4 minutes in boiling salted water, drain, and reserve for the sauce. Cut the asparagus stems into 2-inch-long chunks and blanch them for 2 minutes.

2. Heat 1 tablespoon of the butter in a skillet. Add the asparagus stems and cook until tender, or another 5–6 minutes. Purée in the blender together with the cornstarch, cream, and eggs. Add coriander, salt, and pepper to taste and process again for 1 minute to blend well.

3. Preheat the oven to 325°F. Butter 6 custard cups with the remaining 2 tablespoons of the butter and ladle the custard mixture into the cups. Bake in a hot water bath until a skewer comes out clean, 20–25 minutes.

4. While the custards bake, prepare the sauce. Melt the butter in a saucepan. Add the orange rind and let stand for 1 minute. Discard the rind. Add the onion and cook until golden. Add the vinegar and cook until completely evaporated. Add the cream and reduce to coating texture (approximately ⅔ cup). Correct the seasoning and strain the onion out. Add the reserved asparagus tips and reheat well.

5. To serve, unmold the timbales onto individual plates and spoon the sauce over them.

USES:

This can easily be a first course as well as a vegetable for all white meats. Use the sauce only if used as a first course.

TIMBALES DE BROCCOLI A LA CREME BRUNE
{Timbales of Broccoli with Brown Cream}

SERVES 6

TIMBALES:

1½ cup broccoli flowerets and peeled stems	*Pepper from the mill*
	4 eggs
3 tablespoons butter	*1½ teaspoons cornstarch*
Salt	*1 cup heavy cream*

SAUCE:

4 tablespoons butter
1 tablespoon sesame seeds
⅔ cup heavy cream
Salt
Pepper from the mill

1. Blanch the broccoli for 1 minute in boiling salted water. Heat 2 tablespoons of the butter in a small skillet, add the broccoli, salt, and pepper and cook, covered, for another 5 minutes, until very soft. Cool.
2. Transfer to the blender container. Add the eggs, cornstarch, and cream and process until smooth. Season well with salt and pepper.
3. Preheat the oven to 325°F. Butter 6 custard cups with the remaining tablespoon of the butter and fill them with the broccoli pudding. Bake in a hot water bath until a skewer inserted in the center comes out clean.
4. While the custards bake, prepare the sauce. Heat the butter, add the sesame seeds, and cook until the butter solids precipitate into a fine brown layer at the bottom of the pan. Add the heavy cream and whisk well to obtain a light coating texture. Correct the seasoning.
5. Unmold the custards onto individual plates and spoon the sauce over them.

USES:

Topped with its sauce, this makes a fine first course. Without sauce, it is an interesting vegetable for veal or poultry.

LES LEGUMES-FRUITS
(Fruits as Vegetables)

The Anglo-Saxons and Scandinavians have been much less resistant to fruit used as vegetables than the French. Only twenty years ago, I used to wrinkle my nose at all fruit served with meats. But, the world being so truly "stuck" on duck and orange, I decided I should try a few other fruits and ended by loving them.

There is only one problem. A fruit and a piece of meat on a plate form a "whole" that no other vegetable except a starch should break, so omit other vegetables and serve a nice salad, before or after.

Also, the red meats do not always mix well with fruit, and it may be wise to reserve other types of vegetables for them. There is an exception, try some nicely browned lamb chops with the oranges on page 423.

POMMES AU VERMOUTH {Vermouth Apples}

SERVES 6

6 large baking apples
2 tablespoons butter
6 teaspoons sugar
Salt

Pepper from the mill
½ cup Secondary Stock (p. 23)
½ cup dry vermouth

1. Peel, halve, and core the apples. Butter a baking dish. Put the apples in it flat side down.
2. Preheat the oven to 350°F. Sprinkle the apples with sugar, salt, and pepper; pour over them the secondary stock mixed with vermouth. Bake, basting with their natural juices, until golden and tender, 40–50 minutes.

USES:
Serve with duck, goose, pork, or chicken.

POMMES SAUTEES AU BEURRE {Butter-fried Apples}

This is the favorite fruit vegetable of the French, traditionally served with blood sausage.

SERVES 6

6 large russet or Red Delicious apples
3 tablespoons butter
Salt
Pepper from the mill

1. Peel, core, and slice the apples. Heat the butter in a large skillet and sauté the apples over high heat until nicely browned. Season with salt and pepper.
2. If your skillet is not large enough to hold all the apples at once, split into 2 equal batches.

USES:

For all poultry dishes, especially duck and goose, as well as pigeon and quails. Also excellent with pork.

POIRES-LEGUMES {Butter-fried Pear Halves}

SERVES 6

6 medium Bosc pears, very firm   Salt
2 tablespoons butter   Pepper from the mill
1 teaspoon ground ginger or ⅛   Scallion rings
    teaspoon ground cloves

1. Peel, halve, and core the pears. Do not rub them with any bleaching agent, such as lemon juice; the darker they are, the better.
2. Heat the butter in a large sauté pan. Add the pears, flat side down, and brown well. Turn over and brown the other side. Remove from the heat. Sprinkle with ginger or cloves, salt, and pepper and let stand, covered, for 5 minutes.
3. To serve, cut the pear halves into ¼-inch slices while still holding them in shape. Flatten each pear half to fan it out. Transfer to individual plates with a long spatula and dot with scallion rings.

USES:

Serve with roast chicken, duck or goose and with roast veal and pork.

ORANGES-LEGUMES {*Butter-fried Orange Slices*}

Difficult to prepare, the orange slices must be seared in very hot fat and just heated through. Any overcooking will cause them to fall apart and will create a bitter aftertaste.

SERVES 6

4 large navel oranges	*Soy sauce as needed*
2 tablespoons clarified butter or	*¼ teaspoon fine-grated orange rind*
olive oil	*¼ cup orange juice*
Pepper from the mill	*1 teaspoon Dijon mustard*

1. Peel the oranges to the juice and slice them across into ¼-inch slices.
2. Heat the butter or oil until very hot. Add the orange slices. Sear quickly, turn over, sear again. Remove from the heat. Pepper the orange slices well. *Positively do not salt them!*
3. To the pan add soy sauce to your taste, grated orange rind, and orange juice and reduce to one-third. Add the mustard and mix well. Correct the salt level with more soy sauce if needed.
4. Arrange the oranges on individual plates and dribble a few drops of the sauce over them.

USES:
   Serve with all white meats, with poultry, and with roast lamb.

BANANES-LEGUMES {*Butter-fried Bananas*}

SERVES 6

6 medium bananas, ripe but firm
2 tablespoons butter
Salt
Pepper from the mill
1 teaspoon ground coriander

1. Peel the bananas. Cut them in half lengthwise, then in half again crosswise. Proceed to cook them in 2 batches.
2. For each batch, heat 1 tablespoon butter in a large skillet and sear half the bananas until brown on both sides. Arrange all the bananas on a warmed platter, and season them with salt, pepper, and ground coriander.

U S E S :

For all poultry dishes with the exception of quail or pigeons, and for pork and veal.

LES CEREALES LEGUMES
(Cereals as Vegetables)

Cereals include not only rice and barley but also cracked wheat, couscous, and polenta.

BASIC PILAF OF RICE OR WHEAT

Pilafs keep very well in a slow oven. All the garnishes indicated under "Orzo" Pilafs are usable also for both rice and cracked wheat (see p. 141). It is preferable to use coarse cracked wheat for better taste and texture. The method of cooking is identical but:

• Converted rice will need twice its volume of stock to swell to the correct consistency.
• Wheat will need liquid equal to its own volume.

The broth used may be any you have, but not the very rich Golden Veal Stock, which is too thick and too gelatinous.

S E R V E S 6

4 tablespoons butter
2 onions, chopped so very fine by hand that they appear mashed
1 cup converted rice or coarse cracked wheat

2 cups hot broth for rice, or 1 cup hot broth for wheat
Salt
Pepper from the mill

1. Heat the butter in a heavy braising pot. Add the onions and toss into the butter until the steam stops rising. Add the rice or wheat. Toss into the hot butter until so very hot that when touched with the top of your finger, you cannot stand the heat.

2. Add the hot broth and mix well by fluffing with a fork. Cover the pot with several layers of paper towels and the pot lid and cook either on top of the stove over medium-low heat or in a 325°F. oven for 15–20 minutes, or until all the broth has been absorbed.

3. Add salt and pepper to correct the seasoning and any garnish you like (see p. 141). The pilaf will keep, if transferred to a glass baking dish and covered with foil, for 1–4 hours.

RICE AND WHEAT PILAF GARNISHES:

⅓ cup toasted slivered almonds

¼ cup toasted pignoli nuts, mixed with 3 tablespoons currants

3 tablespoons chopped walnuts mixed with ⅓ cup diced Camembert

¼ teaspoon each grated lemon and orange rinds mixed with ¼ cup chopped black olives

¼ teaspoon grated orange rind plus a pinch of saffron mixed with 2 tablespoons scissored fresh basil

2 tablespoons each toasted cashew nuts, unsweetened crumbled coconut flakes, and currants

2 tablespoons each chopped toasted almonds or hazelnuts and chervil

½ teaspoon fennel seeds or aniseeds

TRIPLE PILAF AUX CEPES
{Pilaf of Three Cereals with Boleti}

I have used, with a mixture of 3 cereals, the delicious seasonings of the Lombardian Risotto al Barolo. You can use any good red wine. The best French one to use would be a good Côtes-du-Rhône, and the best American one would be a solid Zinfandel.

SERVES 10–12

½ *pound butter*	*1 cup wild rice*
4 onions, chopped fine	*1 cup coarse cracked wheat*
1 carrot, chopped fine	½ *pound sliced fresh mushrooms,*
1½ teaspoons Quatre-Epices *(p. 35)*	*preferably Boleti or chanterelles*
1 bottle Côtes-du-Rhône or Zinfandel	Salt
1 quart Secondary Stock (p. 23)	*Pepper from the mill*
Bouquet garni (see p. 82)	*1 clove garlic, chopped*
1 cup converted rice	*Chopped parsley*

1. Heat 2 tablespoons of the butter in a sauté pan. Add the onions and carrot and sauté until golden. Add the *quatre-épices*, the wine, and the broth. Bring to a boil, add the bouquet garni and reduce to 6 cups. Remove the bouquet garni. *Do not strain.*

2. Heat 4 tablespoons of the butter in a braising pot. Add the converted rice. Toss in the butter until very hot. Add 2 cups of the prepared wine and broth reduction. Cover with paper towels and the pot lid and cook until tender.

3. Heat 4 more tablespoons of the butter in a large saucepan. Add the wild rice. Toss quickly. Add 3 cups of the reduced liquid and cook, covered, over very low heat, without boiling hard, until all the liquid has evaporated and the grains have fluffed open, approximately 30 minutes.

4. Heat 4 more tablespoons of the butter in another saucepan, add the cracked wheat and toss well in the butter. Add the last cup of broth. Remove from the heat and keep covered until all broth has been absorbed.

5. Heat the remaining 2 tablespoons of the butter in a skillet. Add the sliced mushrooms, salt, and pepper and sauté until all the juices run out of the mushrooms. Add those to the wheat. Continue sautéing the mushrooms until golden. Blend together the rice, wild rice, wheat, and mushrooms and season with chopped garlic and chopped parsley. Correct the salt and pepper if necessary.

USES:

For all red meats. Also for game birds and all white meats cooked as "brown" sautés or stews.

COTELETTES VEGETARIENNES
(Vegetarian Cutlets)

You can vary the herbs during the seasons and cover the whole map of the world. Some of the best seasonings are:

- A pinch of curry
- A pinch of cayenne pepper or a dash of Tabasco
- Provençal herbs, powdered
- Fresh chopped basil
- Fresh chopped fine herbs
- A generous quantity of *Quatre-Epices* (p. 35)
- Cinnamon and allspice, alone or in combination
- A generous quantity of fresh chopped dill (use a large quantity)

BASIC VEGETARIAN CUTLETS

SERVES 6

CUTLETS:

½ cup butter	*Herbs or spices of your choice (see*
1 large onion, chopped	*above)*
½ pound mushrooms (cultivated or	*1½ cups scalding Secondary Stock*
wild, of your choice)	*(p. 23) or other broth of your*
Salt	*choice*
Pepper from the mill	*2 eggs*
1½ cups coarse cracked wheat	

BREADING AND PANFRYING:

3 tablespoons flour	*Pepper from the mill*
1 egg	*⅔ cup dry bread crumbs*
1 teaspoon each oil and water	*⅓ cup very fine-powdered almonds*
Salt	*Butter or oil as needed to panfry*

1. Heat the butter in a sauté pan. Add the onion and sauté until translucent. Meanwhile, chop the mushrooms coarse (¼-inch cubes) and add them to

the onion; cook until brown. Season with salt and pepper. Add the cracked wheat, tossing it well into the hot ingredients, then add the boiling stock and mix well. Cover and let stand until all the liquid has been absorbed. Then beat the eggs and add them to the hot mixture. Correct the salt and pepper. Cool. When easy to handle, shape into 6 cutlets.

2. To prepare the breading, spread the flour on a sheet of waxed paper. Beat the egg, oil, and water together with a good pinch each of salt and pepper. Mix the bread crumbs and almonds and spread on another sheet of waxed paper. Flour the cutlets, brush them with egg, and coat them with crumbs on both sides. Let dry on a stainless steel rack for at least 1 hour.

3. Panfry in butter or oil until golden. Serve piping hot.

USES:

To replace meat in a vegetarian meal. This goes well with any other vegetable.

RISOTTI

As is by now well known in America, the rice to use for risotto is the Italian, arborio or vialone, produced in the valley of the Po River. These types of round-grained rice are available in all Italian neighborhoods. In all European countries where very large colonies of Italian families live, these 2 types of rice are available on the supermarket shelves. The arborio rice will cook in approximately 18 minutes, while the vialone will take slightly less time, maybe 16 minutes.

The texture of a risotto is always a question of personal taste, which explains why every existing teacher always indicates a different amount of liquid to prepare it. Italian books written in Italian for Italian cooks are much more understanding of the fact that no one rice will behave like another, and the books simply skip specifying the amount of broth to use, concentrating on the fact that the rice must be "al dente," the broth boiling and added to the rice in small quantities.

The total amount of broth used is of course in direct relation to the texture sought by the cook, and it can be safely said that if a cook likes risotto very al dente, it will be enough if 2½ cups broth are used per cup of rice. The more puddinglike one wants the rice, the more broth one will have to use. For medium-firm kernels, 3 cups broth will do, and for almost soft rice, 4 cups. A light, not too gelatinous broth is best.

I was taught to cook risotto by a cousin-in-law who is Milanese and insists that a good risotto is never stirred with a wooden spoon, which breaks the grains of rice while cooking, but is fluffed upward with the tines of a fork. I have applied this method gratefully and successfully for the last twenty years.

These questions of texture and stirring technique will probably never be resolved. It is simpler to cook the risotto several ways and decide which one likes best. In any case, leave the rice slightly wet before serving it. It will absorb any excess broth by the time it reaches the table.

Here are several risotti that I have found very successful. The risotto with asparagus purée is definitely a first course, but the risotti with vegetable jardinières are definitely main courses for vegetarians or for those who still practice the rules of fasting on Fridays and Lent days.

RISOTTI POUR VEGETARIENS
{Risotti for Vegetarians}

This is the basic recipe for risotto. To transform it into a complete vegetarian meal, add to it any of the jardinières given on pages 382–88, or any of the simple stir-fried vegetables (pp. 370–81), and, of course, some good Parmigiano cheese.

SERVES 6

½ cup butter
2 medium onions, chopped very fine
1½ cups arborio or vialone rice
3–5 cups boiling light broth of your
  choice

Jardinière of vegetables of your
  choice (see pp. 382–88)
Parmigiano-Reggiano cheese

1. Heat the butter in a braising pot. Add the onions and cook until translucent. Add the rice and cook until well coated and heated through. It should be too hot to touch with the *top* of your finger.

2. Add about 1 cup boiling broth. Continue cooking over low heat until completely absorbed. Repeat, adding broth until the rice reaches the consistency you prefer.

3. Add a last cup of broth and at the same time the chosen vegetable garnish. Remove from the heat. By the time you serve, all the liquid will have been absorbed.

4. Add Parmigiano-Reggiano cheese as you like.

RISOTTO A LA PUREE D'ASPERGES
{Risotto with Asparagus Purée}

SERVES 6

1 pound medium-size green asparagus
1 quart boiling water
Salt
½ teaspoon ground coriander
Pepper from the mill

½ cup butter
2 onions, chopped very fine
1½ cups arborio or vialone rice
Parmigiano-Reggiano cheese as needed

1. Peel and trim the asparagus. Cut into 1½-inch chunks. Bring the water to a boil, add salt and the asparagus tips. Boil them for 4 minutes. Remove from the water with a slotted spoon. Cool under cold water and reserve.

2. Add the remainder of the asparagus pieces to the water and cook for another 5 minutes. Cool them. Process the asparagus and the cooking water in the blender to obtain an asparagus-flavored broth. Strain into a clean saucepan to discard any threads. Add the ground coriander and season with salt and pepper.

3. Heat the butter in a braising pot. Add the onions and cook until translucent. Add the rice and toss in the hot butter until well coated and too hot to touch.

4. Keep the asparagus broth simmering and add it 1 cup at a time. You will probably need the whole amount. Cook the rice to your taste. During the last addition of broth, also add the asparagus tips.

5. As soon as the rice is done, add Parmigiano cheese to your taste and serve promptly.

USES:

A first course during asparagus season.

LES POLENTES
(Polentas)

My province of Savoy has, from the eighteenth century on, borrowed from the Italian Piemonte its fondness for the cornmeal mush known in Italy as polenta and has Frenchified the name to *polente*. The 3 polentas that follow the basic recipe are the ones I have found most successful.

BASIC POLENTA

Notice that I indicate part cornmeal, part corn flour; it gives a softer texture, but the recipe can be executed entirely with cornmeal if you prefer. Croutons are best prepared entirely with cornmeal.

SERVES 6

3 cups water or light broth   *Salt*
½ cup cornmeal   *Pepper from the mill*
½ cup corn flour   *Nutmeg*
1 cup cold water

1. Bring the water or broth to a boil. Mix the cornmeal and corn flour with the cold water to make a slurry. Add the slurry, stirring well, to the boiling liquid. Continue stirring over medium-low heat until the polenta has so thickened that a spoon stands in the center of it.* Be careful: if you have a

---

* The method described here is known as *"polenta au baton"* (made with a stick). In a further Frenchification, French cooks attempt to prepare polenta by the pilaf method applied to rice and wheat on pages 424–26. All the garnishes used for rice can then be applied to polenta.

large-surfaced pan, this will never happen. Bunch the polenta on one side of the pan and try to stand the spoon in it this way before you start being frustrated. It works in approximately 5 minutes.

2. Season with salt, pepper, and nutmeg.

USES:

Serve with a good rabbit stew to soak up the sauce.

CROUTONS DE POLENTE A LA PUREE D'AIL
{Polenta Croutons with Garlic Purée}

SERVES 6

2 large heads of garlic, separated into cloves	Pepper from the mill
2 tablespoons butter	1 quart cold water or light broth
1 ½ cups Golden Veal Stock (p. 20)	1 cup cornmeal
Salt	2 tablespoons flour
	¼ cup clarified butter

1. Blanch the garlic cloves in boiling water for 1 minute. Peel them. Heat 1 tablespoon of the butter in a small saucepan and toss the garlic in it until golden. Add the veal stock and cook slowly until the garlic falls to a purée. Season with salt and pepper.
2. Bring 3 cups of the water or light broth to a boil. Mix the cornmeal with the remaining cup of the water and pour the mixture, stirring, into the boiling liquid. Stir until a wooden spoon stands at the center of the pot. Blend the garlic purée into the polenta and cook again to evaporate any added liquid.
3. Butter a cookie sheet with the remaining tablespoon of the butter. Pour the polenta onto the sheet. Shape it into a rectangular or square cake uniformly ½ inch thick. Let cool completely. Cut into croutons, either square or rectangular (with a knife), or into rounds (with a cutter).

4. Season the flour with salt and pepper. Flour the croutons on both sides. Heat the clarified butter in a large skillet. Add the croutons and fry them until golden on both sides.

USES:

These croutons can replace the classic bread croutons served with small birds, such as quails or pigeons, and also with any veal grenadins or any tournedos of beef.

GRATIN DE POLENTE AUX CHAMPIGNONS
{Baked Polenta with Mushrooms}

This dish can be a main course for a vegetarian dinner or even a country style dinner, if followed by a pleasant salad of bitter greens. It is best made with Boleti Eduli mushrooms.

SERVES 12

2 quarts light broth or salted water
1 cup cornmeal
1 cup corn flour
Salt
Pepper from the mill
¼ teaspoon fresh grated nutmeg
½ pound fontina or raclette cheese
1½ cups heavy cream

4 tablespoons butter
1 pound sliced mushrooms (any wild
 species or cultivated)
1 teaspoon anchovy paste
2 tablespoons chopped parsley
1 large clove garlic, chopped fine
⅓ teaspoon fine-grated lemon rind

1. Bring 6 cups of the broth or water to a boil. Mix the cornmeal and corn flour with the remaining 2 cups of the broth or water. Pour, stirring, into the boiling liquid. Continue stirring until the spoon stands by itself in the mixture. Add salt, pepper, and a dash of nutmeg. *Keep hot.*
2. Cut the cheese into ⅛-inch slices. Scald the cream, add a dash of nutmeg, salt, and pepper.
3. Preheat the oven to 325°F. Butter a 2-quart baking dish with 1½ teaspoons of the butter. Spread half the polenta evenly on the bottom of the dish. Top with half the cheese and half the cream. Add the remainder

of the polenta. Top with the remainder of the cream and the remainder of the cheese. Bake for 45 minutes, or until the cheese is golden.

4. Meanwhile, heat the remaining 2½ tablespoons of the butter in a large sauté pan. Add the mushrooms of your choice and sauté until well coated with butter. Add the anchovy paste, parsley, garlic, lemon rind, and pepper and toss well. Continue cooking until half the mushroom water has evaporated. Do not cook until dry; the mushrooms will form a sauce for the polenta. Correct the final seasoning.

5. To serve, spoon out individual portions and top each serving with a large spoonful of mushrooms.

USES:

As mentioned above, this is an excellent vegetarian main course. In smaller quantity, it makes a delicious side dish for all brown stews.

GRATIN DE POLENTE A LA SCAROLE
{Baked Polenta with Escarole}

SERVES 12

2 large heads of escarole
Salt
3 tablespoons butter
Pepper from the mill
2½ cups heavy cream
⅔ cup grated Parmigiano-Reggiano cheese

2 quarts light broth or water
1 cup cornmeal
1 cup corn flour
¼ teaspoon fresh grated nutmeg
¼ pound sliced fontina or raclette cheese

1. Wash the escarole very well. Bring a large pot of water to a boil and salt it. Add the escarole and blanch for 5 minutes. Drain and let cool completely. Squeeze the cooled escarole into a towel to remove the excess moisture and chop fine.

2. Heat 2 tablespoons of the butter in a large skillet. Add the escarole, toss in the butter, and add salt and pepper. Cover and cook for 5 minutes until wilted. Add 1½ cups of the heavy cream and reduce by half. Add the

Parmigiano cheese and mix well until the contents of the pan are well bound.

3. Bring 6 cups of the broth or water to a boil. Mix the cornmeal and corn flour with the remaining 2 cups of the broth or water. Pour, stirring, into the boiling liquid. Continue stirring until the spoon stands by itself in the mixture. Add salt, pepper, and the nutmeg. *Keep hot.*

4. Preheat the oven to 325°F. Butter a 2-quart baking dish with the remaining tablespoon of the butter. Spread half of the polenta evenly over the bottom of the dish. Spread the escarole mixture over the polenta. Top with the remainder of the polenta, and spread with the remaining cup of the cream, lightly seasoned, and the slices of fontina. Bake until golden brown, approximately 30–35 minutes; the cream will be absorbed by the polenta.

U S E S :

This is a fine main course for vegetarians; in smaller portions, it can also be a side dish for veal chops and escalopes, or for chicken or turkey.

A Dessert Sampler

ALL DESSERTS DEPEND on the very classic techniques of pastry, cake, and custard making. So that in each section of this chapter, I have listed and, when necessary, explained the techniques involved in the making of desserts.*

You will notice the large amount of rich mousses, chocolate desserts, and extravagantly buttery cakes and the relatively small amount of fruit-based desserts. I have listed here what the American public at large likes. When people go out to eat, they will order those extravagant desserts that they never eat at home where they try to stay on a lean diet.

BASIC DEFINITIONS, TECHNIQUES, AND INGREDIENTS

Ribboning, or *bringing to the ribbon stage*: beating egg yolks or whole eggs and sugar together until a thick foam builds; the ribbon is reached when, lifting the beater 4 inches above the batter, the batter falls back from the beater

---

* For more detailed descriptions of these techniques see *The Making of a Cook.*

into a 1-inch-wide flat ribbon that folds upon itself. *Careful*: A ribbon is never round and straight, and it is never measured or appreciated by lifting the beater more than 4 inches above the mass of eggs and sugar beaten. Ribboning is nowadays done with an electric mixer, unless one is a masochistic purist.

Folding: technique applied to introduce and blend foam (egg whites, whipped cream) into preparations that will then become mousses, cakes, soufflés, etc.

To fold, use a large rubber spatula. Cut *at the center* of the bowl and all the way down to its bottom. Now turn your wrist toward the center of the bowl as you bring the spatula upward, lifting the batter from the bottom and depositing it at the center. Repeat the same movement evenly while you turn the bowl counterclockwise with your left hand, or clockwise with your right hand if you are left-handed, until the batter is homogeneous. *Do not overfold.* Overfolding brings on deflation of the foam in mousses and the formation of gluten tunnels in cakes. In cakes, tunnels also result from stirring an ingredient into a batter instead of folding it in.

Where ribboning is better done by electric mixer, the best folding is always done by hand with a rubber spatula. Folding can be done with an electric mixer set on "folding" speed only when ordinary commercial cakes are involved. Cakes leavened exclusively by egg foams must be hand folded.

The basic rules of good folding are:

- When you start, the heavy ingredients (ribboned egg yolks and sugar, melted chocolate, creamed butter) are always at the bottom of the bowl, below the foam.
- The heavy ingredients are more often than not called "the base" (of a soufflé, of a mousse, or of a cake).
- The base must be lightened by mixing one-quarter of the total volume of the foam into it before folding in the remainder.
- Dry ingredients such as flour, starch, cocoa powder, or ground nuts are sprinkled over the bulk of the foam and folded into the base at the same time as the foam. This is a Swiss method that I learned in Zurich, and it gives the very best volume to all sponge cakes, nut meringues, and chilled or frozen mousses.

CREME ANGLAISE

Crème anglaise is the base for most dessert sauces. It is, when stabilized with gelatin, the base for all Bavarian creams, and it is the base for all ice creams made in the French manner. The basic recipe is usually made with milk, but in many preparations you will see the milk replaced by heavy or light cream. This is a personal interpretation and method of execution; the classic *crème anglaise* is less rich in egg yolks.

4 egg yolks	*1 cup scalding milk*
¼ cup sugar	*1½ teaspoons pure vanilla extract*
A pinch of salt	*Liqueur or spirit of your choice*

Mix the egg yolks and sugar thoroughly *without* ribboning. You will see a thin layer of foam appear on the surface of the mixture. These are the tiny air bubbles that were attached to every angle of every sugar crystal. They appear as soon as the sugar starts to melt. The layer of air bubbles will help you cook the custard in a matter of minutes and without using a thermometer.

Add the salt and gradually blend the milk into the egg yolk/sugar base, using a wooden blunt-ended spatula. Proceed very gradually and be sure to scrape into the angle of the saucepan to dissolve all the egg and sugar. Notice that on the surface of the mixture, you still have a thin blanket of air bubbles.

Put the saucepan over medium-high heat. Stir constantly with your spatula until the blanket of tiny air bubbles breaks into larger bubbles that go to the edge of the pan and finally break open. This disappearance of the blanket of air is due to the increase of pressure as the contents of the pot heat from bottom to top; the increasing pressure forces the air to reintegrate the atmosphere. The custard is done when all the air bubbles have disappeared.* Remove your pot from the heat and look at the spatula; it should be evenly coated with a thin layer of custard, and if you pass a finger through it, a "path" will be clearly visible in the cream. Now whisk the custard at full speed with a wire whisk to cool it and to prevent further cooking and coagulation. Strain into a bowl to

---

* Prepared on gas heat, the custard is a cinch and is done in 1 minute flat; on electricity, it is much more demanding of your attention. Use medium-high heat and negotiate the heat by taking your pot off the burner every so often to lightly cool the pan.

discard any egg white chalazas and flavor with *both* vanilla and the liqueur or spirit of your choice.

Gelatin as stabilizer:

Gelatin is often added to *crème anglaise* or the egg yolk and sugar base of mousses to stabilize them, make them more homogeneous, or make them even stiff enough to unmold.

Melt the gelatin on top of a double boiler with 1–2 tablespoons water. When the gelatin is well liquefied, add to it a good ¼ cup of either the *crème anglaise* or the ribboned base of a mousse; stir well to homogenize and add the mixture to the bulk of the cream or ribboned egg yolk foam.

This method is particularly important in frozen soufflé and biscuit mixtures, for it prevents the gelatin from getting trapped in the wires of the whisk and forming those abominable threads that are the bane of cooks.

Agar-agar as stabilizer:

Whipped cream stabilizer is easier to use and does just as good a job as gelatin. Add the stabilizer to the cream during whipping (see below).

It is essential *not to whip the cream too stiff* for these preparations. For the quantity of agar-agar to use, follow manufacturer's directions. Agar-agar can be purchased in all pastry equipment supply stores.

Whipped cream:

The cream used in dessert preparations should be the clean, heavy kind with no cheesy taste. Crème fraîche is fine over the berries of fruit pies, but it is better replaced by sweet heavy cream in the making of cooked desserts.

The texture of the heavy cream to be folded into Bavarian creams and mousses is really very important, for the texture of the finished product depends on it. The most a cream should be beaten for any of these preparations is "until barely mounding." This can be explained as follows:

When one whips cream, it must be extremely cold so the butterfat in emulsion in the milk remains stiff rather than oily. A warm cream never beats because the butterfat is already as soft as oil, and the fat molecules are, therefore, never teased together by the friction of the beater. When the cream is very cold, the molecules of butterfat tend to move closer to one another while one whips and end up bonding to one another.

When the cream barely mounds, it is ready to be folded into a mousse base. As one folds the cream into the base, the folding motion will bring on a continued bonding of fat molecules so that by the time one has finished folding, the cream will have reached a stiff texture and blended smoothly into the base. Should one have whipped the cream very stiff, the molecules of fat would have further bonded during the folding, provoking the breaking of the cream into butter molecules and whey. I am sure each reader will be able to relate this statement to the personal experience of a mousse started with great enthusiasm and ending in the trash can because, once frozen, it was a mess of water crystals and ice-cold butter particles.

In Bavarian creams, stiffly beaten cream results in a dessert that could be used to play football. As a matter of fact, many authors recommend the use of beaten egg whites in Bavarian creams, stating that they are lighter than whipped cream. The classic texts are clear on the subject: Bavarian creams are made of stabilized *crème anglaise* into which one should fold *exclusively* heavy cream, *properly whipped*.

Chocolate:

You will notice that, all through this chapter, I mostly recommend the use of Swiss, French, or Belgian bittersweet chocolate. My reason is that these chocolates all have been 51 percent and 53 percent pure cocoa in their composition. So, if you are in an area where semisweet chocolate is produced with an equally high percentage of chocolate, by all means use the equivalent American product. Such chocolate is expensive, but I believe it is far better to have no chocolate dessert at all than a chocolate dessert made with inferior chocolate.

Melt the chocolate over a double boiler and stir well over heat until its color turns a high reddish brown, then cool before adding to any preparation. Keep stirring the chocolate as you cool it.

Since the introduction on the market of hazelnut oil, I have started to blend it with melted chocolate for glazes. It tastes better than the usual vegetable shortening or paraffin oil.

CREPES

Thousands of years ago, one cooked flat cakes on hot stones, and we still love to eat crêpes either as main luncheon courses or as dessert. I truly enjoy making them once in a while as an impromptu dessert for the family or in class. In spite of their horrible commercialization all over France and the United States, they are still good if nicely prepared. The 2 recipes that follow were served in the restaurant as desserts for the simple country dinners of the *cuisine de misère*.

CREPES AU BEURRE DE CIDRE
{Crêpes with Cider Jelly Butter}

SERVES 12

CREPE BATTER:

2 tablespoons dried currants	A pinch of salt
2 tablespoons applejack	½ cup each sweet cider and heavy
⅔ cup sifted all-purpose flour	cream
⅓ cup buckwheat flour	¼ teaspoon Quatre-Epices (p. 35)
3 eggs	¼ cup melted butter

CIDER JELLY:

1 gallon sweet unpasteurized cider
1 tablespoon cider vinegar
4 tablespoons unsalted butter

1. Chop the currants fine; cover them with the applejack and let stand at room temperature. Mix both flours into a bowl. Break the eggs into the center of the flour and, using a whisk, gradually mix the eggs and the flours. Add the salt and, successively, the cider and the heavy cream; strain the batter, add the *quatre-épices* and the melted butter and let stand for 40 minutes at room temperature. Mix the currants and their soaking liquor into the crêpe batter.

2. Empty the sweet cider into a large sauté pan, reserving ⅓ cup for later use. Bring the cider to a boil and let it reduce, skimming at regular intervals, until a brown caramellike syrup results. There should be approximately ⅔ cup. To the bright hot caramellike syrup, add the vinegar and the reserved fresh cider and dilute until the mixture resembles a pancake syrup. Add the

butter and let it simmer into the syrup until melted. Whisk well to homogenize.

3. Cook the crêpes in a No. 18 crêpe pan and serve each one spread with a layer of cider jelly and folded. To cook a crêpe, heat your pan to hot. Pour 3 tablespoons batter into the lip of the pan held at a 45-degree angle to the stove. Tilt the pan toward yourself until the batter covers the bottom. Cook for 2 minutes, turn over with a spatula and cook another minute on the second side.

CREPES A L'ANIS ET AU BEURRE DE MIEL
{Anise-flavored Crêpes with Honey Butter}

From the Périgord, where they are made in large quantities during carnival season.

SERVES 12

1 cup sifted all-purpose flour
1 teaspoon well crushed aniseeds
3 eggs
A pinch of salt

1 cup whole milk
¾ cup unsalted butter
½ cup liquid honey, preferably from
*   clover pollen*

1. Make a well in the flour, add the anise powder and the eggs. Mix the eggs into the flour with a whisk; add the salt and the milk very gradually. Melt ¼ cup of the butter and add to the mixture, whisking well; strain into a bowl or a pitcher. Let stand for 40 minutes at room temperature.

2. To prepare the honey butter, cream the remaining ½ cup of the butter, gradually whisking the honey into it.

3. Cook the crêpes and spread each of them with ½ teaspoon honey butter. To cook the crêpes, see Step 3 of the preceding recipe.

BAVARIAN CREAMS

The amount of gelatin one uses determines whether a Bavarian cream is un-moldable or not. If you wish to unmold a Bavarian cream, use 1 envelope gelatin per basic recipe; if you prefer the cream soft, use only 1 teaspoon gelatin per basic recipe and serve the cream in balloon glasses or champagne cups.

BASIC BAVARIAN CREAM

PROPORTIONS:
If you look at the recipes that follow, you will see that the proportions of 1–1¼ cups base (either custard or fruit purée) mixed with 1 cup heavy cream, whipped, are, with a few variations, fairly standard. The whipped cream for a Bavarian should be almost too soft, never stiffer than *barely mounding*.

DIRECTIONS:
1. Prepare the *crème anglaise* (see p. 438) and stabilize it with 1 envelope or 1 teaspoon gelatin, depending on the texture you have chosen (see above). Melt the gelatin in a small saucepan placed over a double boiler, add a tablespoon or so of water, and mix until the gelatin is liquid. Blend some of the *crème anglaise* into the gelatin, then reverse the process and add the gelatinized part of the cream to the bulk of the custard and mix well. Strain into a stainless steel bowl; cool.
2. Whip the heavy cream so it barely mounds. It should seem almost too soft. Keep refrigerated.
3. Brush a 1-quart mold with 1 tablespoon corn or hazelnut oil. Set the mold to drip upside down on paper toweling.
4. Put the bowl containing the cream into another one filled with ice cubes and salted water. Stir with a spatula until the cream starts setting. Imme-diately remove from the bath of ice and whip the heavy cream into the base of *crème anglaise*. The heavy cream will finish whipping to the correct stage and texture while you whip the 2 creams into one another.
5. Pour into the oiled mold and refrigerate until set.

BAVAROISE AUX NOISETTES
{Hazelnut Bavarian Cream}

Yes, this is custard upon custard, but who cares, the taste is worth all the custards. This can be unmolded. It will fill a 1-quart mold, or 6–8 individual custard cups.

SERVES 6–8

BAVARIAN CREAM:

1¼ cups milk
⅔ cup well-toasted, peeled, and
  chopped hazelnuts
4 egg yolks
⅓ cup sugar
A pinch of salt

1 envelope gelatin
2 tablespoons dark rum
2 tablespoons hazelnut liqueur
  (p. 512)
1 tablespoon hazelnut oil
1 cup heavy cream, softly whipped

CHOCOLATE SAUCE:

3 egg yolks
¼ cup sugar
A pinch of salt
1 cup scalding milk
1 ounce dark unsweetened chocolate, chopped

1. Bring the milk to a boil. Place the hazelnuts into the blender container, add the milk, and process together. Refrigerate and let steep for 24 hours. Strain, squeezing well through several layers of cheesecloth. Bring back to a boil.
2. Follow the basic steps for Bavarian Creams given in the preceding recipe. Prepare the *crème anglaise* with the yolks, sugar, hazelnuts, milk, and gelatin. Flavor it with rum and hazelnut liqueur. Cool over ice. Whip the already softly whipped heavy cream into the *crème anglaise*. Rub the mold with hazelnut oil and turn the mixture into it.
3. To prepare the chocolate sauce, prepare a second *crème anglaise* with the yolks, sugar, salt, and scalding milk. As soon as it is done, add the chopped chocolate. Chill.
4. Serve the cream unmolded and topped with the bitter chocolate sauce.

LE FROMAGE BAVAROIS DE CAREME
{Carême's Bavarian Cheese}

I adapted this directly from Carême's own words for a course in "historical" French cuisine. His measurements were pre–1789 Revolution style and he calls gelatin *"colle"* (glue). Usually I roast the coffee beans myself to obtain the totally fresh aroma; if you want to do that, you will need 6 ounces pure mocha java beans; roast them in a skillet until the beans break their fat and start shining. Orange flower water can be purchased in any gourmet shop. This will fill a 2-quart mold or 12 individual molds.

SERVES 12

BAVARIAN CREAM:

2/3 cup coarsely ground French roast mocha java coffee

2 cups scalding milk

1 cup sugar

A pinch of salt

1 1/2 envelopes gelatin

1 tablespoon almond or corn oil

1 1/2 cups heavy cream

CARAMEL TOPPING:

2/3 cup sugar

1/3 cup plus 2 tablespoons water

1/2 teaspoon orange flower water

1 cup heavy cream

1. Add the coffee to the scalding milk. Let steep for 2 hours, covered. Strain through several layers of cheesecloth. Dissolve the sugar and salt into the coffee infusion. Soften the gelatin with 1/4 cup of the coffee; blend into the rest of the infusion and stir until the gelatin has dissolved. Strain again through a very fine strainer into a stainless steel bowl.

2. Oil a 2-quart mold or 12 custard cups. Turn upside down on paper toweling to drain. Beat the heavy cream until it barely mounds; keep it cool.

3. Put the bowl containing the coffee-flavored milk into another, larger one containing ice cubes. Stir until the mixture starts to set; immediately whip the already lightly whipped cream into the coffee custard and turn into the molds. Chill for 4 hours.

4. To prepare the caramel cream topping, melt the sugar with 2 tablespoons of the water and cook it to the brown caramel stage. Dilute it with the remaining ⅓ cup of the water and cool it. Add the orange flower water. Whip the heavy cream until stiff, gradually adding the diluted caramel.

5. To serve, unmold the Bavarian cream and decorate it with large rosettes of caramel cream.

BAVAROISE AUX POIRES ET AU POIVRE
{Pear and Green Peppercorn Bavarian Cream}

The dried pears are used to intensify the pear taste; and the pears are not skinned during their cooking for the same reason. The cream is presented here in balloon glasses, but it can also be molded if one doubles the amount of gelatin used.

SERVES 6–8

2 dried pear halves
3 very ripe Bartlett pears
Juice of ½ a lemon
A pinch of salt
⅓ cup plus ¼ cup sugar
1½ teaspoons gelatin
2 tablespoons green peppercorns with
1 tablespoon of their canning
liquid

2 tablespoons pear brandy
1 cup heavy cream
3 egg yolks
1 cup scalding milk
1 ounce dark unsweetened chocolate,
chopped

1. Soak the dried pears overnight in enough water to cover. When they are soft, discard the water and core them. Dice the pears and put them in a saucepan. Wash the fresh pears, stem and core but do not peel them. Cut them into small slivers and add to the dried pears along with the lemon juice and salt. Cook over medium heat until a compote forms. Add ⅓ cup of the sugar and let it dissolve. Purée in the blender and strain to discard all traces of skin. Soften the gelatin in the tablespoon of green peppercorn canning liquid and dissolve it into the hot pear purée. Turn into a bowl and cool.

2. Rinse the peppercorns under cold running water until their dark outer skins split and only the pale green corns are left. Add these to the pear purée.

3. Add the pear brandy to the cream and whip until the cream barely mounds. Keep it refrigerated. Cool the purée of pears over ice. As soon as it starts setting, whip in the cream. Turn into balloon glasses and refrigerate.

4. Mix the egg yolks with the remaining ¼ cup of the sugar, dilute with the scalding milk, and thicken over medium-high heat. As soon as the custard is ready, add the chopped bitter chocolate and mix well. Cool completely. When cold, pour ¼ inch chocolate custard over the cold Bavarian cream and chill again. Serve with small cookies of your choice.

Variations: Using the basic proportions given above, you can work out other formulas for yourself. Try some of the following:

- Pistachio Bavarian Cream and Raspberry Purée Topping
- Bergamot Bavarian Cream (see p. 465)
- Apricot Bavarian Cream with Kirsch and Pistachio Sauce
- Pear Bavarian Cream with Cassis and Maine Blueberry Sauce
- Orange and Madeira Bavarian Cream
- Rhubarb and Strawberry Bavarian Cream
- Blueberry Bavarian Cream
- Royale of Lemon-Lime Bavarian Cream
- Satsuma and Orange Caramel Bavarian Cream

SABAYONS FROIDS
(Cold Sabayons)

As sweet—almost unbearably cloying—as they are when served warm, sabayons become pleasant and refreshing when they are transformed into a cold cream and served over poached fruit. Here are 2 different cold sabayons. I taught the first in Annecy with the sour cherries of the Savoie countryside and presented the second at the Phelps vineyards during my demonstrations in 1981. The techniques of cold sabayon follow those of Bavarian creams. The only differences are that their base is made with wine instead of milk and that the lightly whipped cream is folded into the cold sabayon base.

Serve cold sabayons in balloon glasses with the cream entirely covering the fruit. Top each portion with any decoration appropriate to the components of the dessert.

SABAYON FROID AUX GRIOTTES
{Cold Sabayon with Sour Cherries}

Sour cherries are best because of their tartness. If using sweet Queen Annes or Bings, double the lemon juice.

SERVES 8

1½ cups heavy cream
¼ cup kirschwasser or framboise
¾ pound sour cherries, stemmed
  and washed
1½ cups tawny or ruby port
5 tablespoons sugar

2 teaspoons gelatin
Juice and rind of 1 lemon
A pinch of salt
3 egg yolks
8 mint leaves

1. Whip the cream until it barely mounds, gradually adding the kirsch or framboise. Keep refrigerated.
2. Put the cherries in a saucepan. Add the port and bring to a boil. As soon as the cherries come floating to the surface of the wine, use a slotted spoon to remove them to a bowl. Set 8 cherries aside for decoration and sprinkle the remainder with 2 tablespoons of the sugar. Let steep together until the sugar has melted and the cherries have lost all their juice. Reserve the juice. Pit the cherries and distribute them equally at the bottom of 8 balloon glasses.
3. Reduce the cooking port to ¾ cup and dissolve the gelatin in the reserved cherry juice.
4. Grate the rind of the lemon into a ½-quart saucepan made of heavy enameled cast iron. Add the egg yolks and the remaining 3 tablespoons of the sugar and beat with a sauce whisk until you reach the ribbon stage. Add a few drops of lemon juice and the salt. Mix the reduced port with the gelatin-stabilized cherry juice. Set the saucepan with the ribbon mixture over medium-low heat and cook, gradually whisking in the port and juice.

When all the juices have been incorporated and the egg foam feels warm to the top of the index finger, remove to a bowl and stir over ice until the mixture is cold. Fold in the whipped cream. Ladle an equal amount of sabayon over the poached cherries in the balloon glasses and refrigerate for several hours.

5. To serve, decorate each glass with 1 of the reserved cherries and a mint leaf.

LES QUATRE SAISONS D'UN RAISIN
{The Four Seasons of a Grape}

A true fall dessert. The grapes are used 4 times: as grapes, as grape juice, as wine, and as brandy. Hence, the name.

This can be served either in individual balloon glasses or in one large elegant 1-quart crystal dish.

SERVES 12

2 pounds ripe Gewürztraminer or white seedless grapes	*6 egg yolks*
A tiny pinch of Quatre-Epices *(p. 35)*	*⅓ cup plus 1 tablespoon sugar*
	1½ teaspoons gelatin
2 cups Gewürztraminer wine as heady and spicy as possible	*A pinch of salt*
	1 egg white, lightly beaten
½ cup Marc de Gewürztraminer	*Several small grapes or maple leaves of various colors*
2 cups heavy cream	

1. Reserve 24 grapes for the decoration. With approximately 1 pound grapes, prepare 2 cups grape juice, crushing the berries in the blender and squeezing the juice through several layers of cheesecloth to strain it of all pits and skins.
2. Mix the grape juice, the *quatre-épices*, and the Gewürztraminer wine in a heavy saucepan and reduce to 1⅓ cups.
3. While this mixture reduces, peel the remaining grapes (this step is optional) and distribute them equally among the serving glasses. Spoon a drop of Marc de Gewürztraminer over them.

4. Whip the heavy cream until it barely mounds. Flavor it with 2 tablespoons Marc de Gewürztraminer. Keep refrigerated.

5. When the wine and juice mixture has properly reduced, beat the egg yolks and ⅓ cup of the sugar and the salt to the ribbon stage. Set over low heat and gradually whisk in the reduction of wine and juice until you have a thick foamy custard that feels warm to the top of the index finger. Melt the gelatin and add to the reduction. Add the remaining Marc de Gewürztraminer. Turn into a mixing bowl and cool, stirring over ice. As soon as the custard is cooled, fold in the whipped cream.

6. Ladle the sabayon into the serving glasses. Refrigerate for at least 4 hours. The mixture will remain as foamy and fluid as a warm sabayon.

7. Dip the reserved grapes in the lightly beaten egg white, then roll them into the remaining tablespoon of the sugar sprinkled onto a plate. Let dry to set the sugar crystals. Decorate each glass with 2 crystallized grapes and 1 grape or maple leaf.

MOUSSES FROIDES ET GLACEES, PUDDINGS FROIDS
(Cold and Frozen Mousses, Cold Puddings)

No French or even vaguely Continental restaurant in America will ever be able to survive without serving a chocolate mousse. I am still laughing at a telephone inquirer who, having been told that I served *no* snails, *no* onion soup, and *no* chocolate mousse in the summer months, promptly told me, "You are not a French restaurant."

Closing the list of mousses, you will find a chilled marbled chocolate mousse (p. 456). All the other recipes are frozen mousses that you can present either as soufflés or between 2 layers of meringue under the name of *Biscuit Glace* or frozen mousse cake.

Here are a few words on their preparation, which can be a bit tricky. I have always followed, with some variations, the basic proportions of Henri Paul Pellaprat, the most modern of the French classicists.

The basic Pellaprat recipe consisted in ribboning 5 egg yolks with ⅔ cup sugar, adding whatever flavoring one wished, folding in 3 beaten egg whites, then folding in 2 cups whipped cream.

That was basically a very nice recipe, but the frozen mousse always showed

bothersome and unpleasant crystals in its final texture. So I increased the number of egg yolks per recipe to 8 for more lecithin and a smoother texture, and
I introduced into the ribboned egg yolks either some gelatin or some whipped
cream stabilizer to help absorb the water content of the mousse and eliminate
the formation of crystals during freezing. I also set the average quantity of
liqueur at ½–⅔ cup maximum, which also influences the mellowness of the
texture.

Cooks should also know that the efficiency of the freezer has a great deal
to do with the final texture of such frozen desserts. A fast freezing unit will
always give better results than the smaller home freezers.

If possible, place a cake rack on the freezing shelf of your freezer and set
the mousse to freeze on it, but do not worry too much if you have to set the
dish or pan directly on the freezing unit. The thickness of both the soufflé dish
and the meringue layers will protect the bottom of the mousse in any case.

All the recipes that follow can be made in the containers and according
to the techniques given below. They will serve 12–16.

To prepare a frozen mousse cake:

Use 10-inch round cake pan. First use the bottom of the pan to trace the circles
on which you are going to bake the meringue layers on a buttered and lightly
floured rigid cookie sheet. Then line the bottom of the cake pan with a paper
circle. Cut as follows: put the cake pan upside down on the table. Cover it with a
sheet of parchment paper. Secure the paper on the bottom of the pan with
your left hand. Using the back of a knife blade, scrape around the edge of the
pan bottom until a circle of paper results; turn the cake pan right side up and
grease it very lightly.

Fit the paper circle into the bottom of the pan. Measure the circumference
of the cake pan. Cut a band of parchment 1½ inches longer than that circumference and as wide as the cake pan side is high. Fit that paper around the
lightly greased sides of the cake pan. The pan is ready to receive the meringue
layers and the frozen mousse. Butter and flour an unbendable cookie sheet.
Trace two 10-inch circles using the bottom of a 10-inch pan as a pattern.
Prepare the meringue and, using a spatula, spread it over each circle. Bake at
325° until set and dry, approximately 20 minutes.

When the meringue layers are cooked, handle them with care; trim the
edges so they will fit exactly into the 10-inch pan.

Choose the better looking of the 2 meringue layers and put it at the bottom of the pan *smooth* side down. That smooth side will become the top of your *Biscuit Glace.* Pour the finished mousse over the first meringue layer. Top the mousse with the second layer of meringue *smooth side up.* Wrap the whole pan in plastic food wrap and freeze.

To serve, unmold the frozen mousse cake onto a cake platter; powder the top with confectioners' sugar and cut into wedges.*

An important problem—adding the gelatin correctly:

Melting the gelatin and adding it directly to the ribboned egg yolk must be avoided at all costs or one will find the gelatin neatly wrapped around the electric beater in maddening strings. Proceed as follows: Melt the gelatin with a tablespoon or so of water over a double boiler. Remove the double boiler from the heat but leave the gelatin over the hot water. Gradually blend ⅓ cup of the ribboned mixture into the gelatin, then reverse the process and gradually whisk the gelatinized egg foam back into the remainder of the yolk mixture. Do not melt the gelatin into the liqueur, or you will lose most of the flavor and aroma.

Ideas for other frozen mousses:

Since I am giving only a few recipes in detail here, cooks may want to try their hands at preparing other frozen mousses and frozen mousse cakes using the following ideas as combinations:

- Almond and orange rind layers enclosing a mousse flavored with pure malt whiskey and candied fruit macerated in Drambuie
- Walnut meringue layers enclosing an Armagnac and cardamom mousse
- Blanched almond meringue layers enclosing the raspberry frozen soufflé in *The Making of a Cook* (p. 490)
- Cocoa meringue layers enclosing the lemon-lime mousse in *The Making of a Cook* (p. 487)
- Cocoa and blanched almond meringue layers enclosing a green Chartreuse and chocolate chip mousse

---

* In a restaurant this is not a dessert for the dessert cart. Although if made with gelatin it will never fall apart, it is better to keep it frozen. Unmold it on the bottom of a 10-inch cake pan; trace the portions; keep it covered with plastic wrap at all times and store it in the freezer.

- Hazelnut meringue layers enclosing a Mandarine Napoléon and tangerine rind mousse
- Vanilla and aniseed meringue layers enclosing an espresso mousse flavored with Kahlua or Tia Maria
- Blanched almond meringue layers enclosing a pistachio nut and kirsch mousse
- Toasted coconut meringue layers enclosing a rum and candied ginger mousse
- Pignoli nuts and cocoa meringue layers enclosing a Galliano mousse

See also the variations indicated after some of the recipes that follow.

BISCUIT GLACE AUX PRUNEAUX D'ARMAGNAC
{Prune, Walnut, and Armagnac Frozen Mousse Cake}

Give yourself plenty of time. You will need at least 2 weeks to soften the prunes properly. Make yourself a great big jar of them; you will enjoy them year round as a little nightcap. This recipe is a personal tribute to my favorite Occitanian ingredients: the prunes of Agen, the walnuts of the Périgord, and Armagnac.

SERVES 16

PRUNES:

        30 large, soft pitted prunes
        3 cups Armagnac
        6 allspice berries
        1/4 teaspoon each black and white peppercorns
        1 strip of orange rind, 2 inches by 1/2 inch

MERINGUE LAYERS:

        3 egg whites
        1 cup fine-ground walnuts
        1/3 cup sugar

MOUSSE:

The prunes and ½ cup of their preserving Armagnac	*1½ teaspoons gelatin*
6 egg yolks	*3 egg whites*
⅔ cup plus ½ cup granulated sugar	*2 cups heavy cream*
A pinch of salt	*Confectioners' sugar*
	16 walnut halves

1. Prepare the prunes. If they have been preserved with sulfur dioxide, blanch them in boiling water before adding them to the Armagnac. Soak the prunes in the Armagnac, add the allspice berries, the peppercorns, and the orange rind. Shake well and steep for at least 2 weeks.

2. When you are ready to prepare the dessert, start with the meringues. Beat the egg whites and fold in the ground walnuts mixed with the sugar. Prepare the cake pan and bake at 325°F. in two 10-inch round layers (see p. 451 for instructions).

3. Purée 15 of the prunes with ¼ cup of the Armagnac in the blender. Mash 15 more prunes with a fork and reserve on a plate. Ribbon the egg yolks and ⅔ cup of the granulated sugar with the salt; add the prune purée and the melted gelatin (see instructions on p. 452).

4. Beat the egg whites; then beat the cream with the remaining ¼ cup of the Armagnac until it barely mounds. Fold the egg whites into the prune base, then fold in the cream. Pour half of the prune mousse over the first walnut meringue layer. Freeze immediately. Keep the remainder of the mousse refrigerated in the warmest part of the refrigerator. As soon as the first layer of prune mousse is solidified, spread the mashed prunes gently over it. Top with the remainder of the mousse and the second walnut meringue layer, then wrap the whole cake pan in plastic wrap and freeze.

5. To serve, unmold, dust heavily with confectioners' sugar, then trace the portions with the back of a knife. Melt the remaining ½ cup of the sugar to the caramel stage. Dip the walnut halves into the caramel; cool them on a lightly buttered plate. Put a walnut half at the center of each portion.

BISCUIT GLACE A L'ALSACIENNE
{Alsatian Frozen Biscuit}

Inspired by the wonderful Truffles au Marc de Gewürztraminer by the Pâtisserie Gross in Obernai, Alsace.

SERVES 12–16

MERINGUE LAYERS:

> *3 egg whites*
> *¾ cup plus 2 tablespoons fine-ground unblanched almonds*
> *2 tablespoons cocoa powder*
> *⅓ cup sugar*

MOUSSE:

9 egg yolks	*2 ounces Swiss, French, or Belgian*
¾ cup granulated sugar	*bittersweet chocolate, chopped*
A pinch of salt	*3 egg whites*
2 teaspoons gelatin	*2 cups heavy cream*
½ cup Marc de Gewürztraminer	*Confectioners' sugar*

1. To prepare the meringues, whip the egg whites. Mix the almonds, cocoa powder, and sugar and fold into the whites. Prepare the cake pan and bake at 325°F. as described on page 451 in two 10-inch circles. Cool.
2. Ribbon the egg yolks with the granulated sugar and salt. Melt the gelatin in a double boiler (see p. 452) and blend into the egg yolk and sugar base along with ¼ cup of the Marc and the chopped chocolate. Beat the egg whites, then beat the cream with the remaining ¼ cup of the Marc and fold them successively into the yolk/sugar base.
3. Build the *biscuit* as indicated in Step 4 of the preceding recipe and freeze overnight. To serve, unmold and dust with confectioners' sugar.

Variation: You can replace the almonds in the meringue with the same amount of hazelnut, and the Marc de Gewürztraminer in the mousse by Grand Marnier.

MOUSSE MARBREE {*Marbled Chocolate Mousse*}

A white chocolate mousse served alone is too sweet; this is why I marble a dark, bitter chocolate mousse into it. Serve in champagne cups or in a large crystal dish.

SERVES 12–16

WHITE MOUSSE:

> *8 ounces white chocolate*
> *4 tablespoons butter*
> *4 egg whites*
> *1 cup heavy cream*
> *3 tablespoons green Chartreuse*

DARK MOUSSE:

7 ounces Swiss, French, or Belgian bittersweet chocolate	*5 eggs, separated*
	1 tablespoon sugar
1 ounce unsweetened chocolate	*1¼ cups heavy cream*
1½ tablespoons butter	*3 tablespoons green Chartreuse*

DECORATION:

2 ounces Swiss, French, or Belgian bittersweet chocolate, at room temperature

1. Melt the white chocolate and the butter together. Cool. (*Do not overheat* or the chocolate will separate; if it does, add heated light cream, bit by bit, until the emulsion rebuilds.) Beat the egg whites and fold them into the white chocolate base; whip the cream with the Chartreuse until semistiff; fold into the lightened chocolate. Refrigerate until ready to use.

2. Melt the dark chocolates and the butter together. Beat the egg yolks until pale yellow; blend the cooled chocolate into them. Beat the egg whites with the sugar and fold into the egg and chocolate base. Whip the cream with the Chartreuse to the semistiff stage and fold it into the lightened chocolate.

3. Pour the white chocolate mousse into the bottom of the cups or crystal dish. Top with the dark mousse and fold them into each other to marble. Refrigerate and just before serving sprinkle with tiny chocolate curls made by scraping the room temperature chocolate with a potato peeler.

Note: The mousse freezes and defrosts extremely well.

BLANC MANGER A LA RUSSE
{Russian-style White Cream Pudding}

This is extremely easy if one splits the cooking into 2 stages.

SERVES 12

4½ cups heavy cream

½ cup milk

1½ envelopes gelatin

⅛ teaspoon salt

½ cup kirschwasser

½ teaspoon pure bitter almond extract

3 ounces bittersweet chocolate

1 pound fresh sour cherries

½ cup ruby port

⅓–½ cup sugar

1 tablespoon cornstarch per cup of cherry juice

1. Divide the cream, the milk, the gelatin, and the salt in halves. Keep in separate containers. Heat half the cream and soften half the gelatin in half the milk. Add the milk and gelatin mixture to the hot cream. Stir until dissolved. Cool and add ¼ cup of the kirsch and ¼ teaspoon of the almond extract. Cool over ice, and as soon as it starts setting, ladle into 12 champagne cups. Cover with plastic wrap and refrigerate until solid.
2. Grate the chocolate with a potato peeler and add 1 teaspoon of the chocolate to each cup, sprinkling it evenly over the layer of cream.
3. Repeat Step 1 with the remaining cream, milk, gelatin, salt, kirsch, and almond extract. Cool and ladle into the cups on top of the chocolate. Refrigerate again until firm.
4. Clean and pit the cherries, place them into a saucepan, and cover them with the port. Bring to a boil and, as soon as the cherries come floating to the surface, remove them to a bowl and sprinkle them with the sugar. Let the sugar melt completely, then transfer to a saucepan again. Measure the cherry juice and mix the proper amount of cornstarch with the port. Bring the cherries and their juice to a boil, blend in the cornstarch and port mixture and cook until clear and thickened. Cool. As soon as cool, spoon it equally over the 12 portions of solidified cream. Serve with cookies.

TARTS AND TARTLETS

Before giving the reader and cook a few recipes for pies that are a bit different, I feel compelled to repeat some of the basic techniques of pastry making.* I still am—and always will be—that type of pastry cook who enjoys making unsweetened pastry doughs by hand and who believes that handmade pastry has it all over the machine-made product for texture and taste. However, it is a fact that the food processor has opened the world of pastry making to thousands of people, and I can only encourage those who want to use the food processor to prepare any and all of the pastries indicated here in what I have called for years "the magnificent machine." There is no doubt that it is better to make a pastry in the food processor than it is to throw away the product of hands that simply will not function. But the reader must understand that the teacher in me simply does not believe in hands that will not work, since it is my function to make them function. So the choice remains the reader's. Those who firmly believe in the food processor will want to consult the excellent volumes that have been published on its use. I use the food processor myself only to prepare sweet pastry containing a large amount of sugar (see p. 460). It will soon become apparent that I also believe in only one type of shortening: *pure butter*. You may use salted or unsalted butter, but make sure that you use only grade AA 93 score to avoid any kind of rancidity. Taste the butter before you prepare a pastry. If you use salted butter, do not add any additional salt.

BASIC SHORT PASTRY AND ITS VARIATIONS

MAKES TWO 8-INCH PIES
OR ONE 9-INCH TWO-CRUST PIE
OR ONE 10-INCH PIE

1½ cups sifted all-purpose flour, preferably unbleached
9 tablespoons very cold butter
½ teaspoon salt, if using unsalted butter
4½ tablespoons ice-cold water

* For a more extensive discussion of the techniques of basic pastry making, see *The Making of a Cook*, pages 389–411.

1. Make a well in the flour. Add the butter cut into tablespoon-size chunks. Add the salt if used. With your fingertips, mash the butter into the flour until the particles of butter are the size of large peas.
2. Mix in the ice-cold water 1 tablespoon at a time, introducing it with your fingertips. Several balls of irregularly textured dough will soon form; press them into 1 large ball.
3. With the heel of your hand push very large pieces of the dough 6 inches forward until all the dough has been used. Gather it back into a ball and repeat the operation. Refrigerate the pastry for an hour or so before using it.

VARIATIONS OF THE BASIC SHORT PASTRY:

Decreasing butter:

Notice the large quantity of butter used to shorten the strong American flour properly. With a softer French flour, one would use only 6½–7 tablespoons butter.

Adding sugar:

One can add 2 tablespoons sugar to the basic pastry, which will then require a maximum of 3½ tablespoons water.

Adding flavorings:

The following ingredients can be used to flavor any pastry: liqueurs and/or flavoring extracts, powdered spices of your choice, fine-grated citrus fruit rinds, fresh chopped herbs of your choice.

Mixing flour and fine-ground nuts:

You may remove one-quarter to one-third of the total amount of flour and replace it with the same amount of fine-ground nuts such as almonds blanched or not, hazelnuts skinned or not, walnuts, pignoli nuts, macadamia nuts, etc. If you use nuts in a pastry, remove 1–2 tablespoons butter since the nuts contain a certain amount of oil.

Preparing the pastry with a liquid other than water:

Instead of pure water you can use a combination of water and wine, a combination of water and liqueur, milk, light cream, buttermilk, yogurt, or sour cream, whole eggs well beaten and liquefied, egg yolks well blended into water or milk.

To introduce these ingredients into the dough, proceed exactly as you would to introduce plain water. Differences in texture will occur. Because of protein content, a pastry made with milk, cream, or any proportion of egg will be stronger than one made with water only, and it will become less quickly soaked by liquids such as fruit juices when standing after baking.

A pastry made with buttermilk, yogurt, or sour cream will be extremely fragile and tender and break easily because the lactic acid in the dairy product will soften considerably the strands of gluten in the pastry.

PATE SUCREE {Sweet Pastry}

This *pâte sucrée* (or *pasta frolla* to the Italians) used to be a mess to prepare until we acquired electric machines and clear plastic food wrap. The pastry is now made entirely in the food processor or with an electric mixer.

10 tablespoons butter, at room temperature	A pinch of salt, if using unsalted butter
⅓–½ cup sugar to taste	Flavoring of your choice
1 whole egg	1⅓–1½ cups sifted all-purpose unbleached flour

1. Put the butter, sugar, egg, and salt if used into the food processor container and process until smooth; add flour through the funnel and process 15–30 seconds or until a ball of dough forms.
2. The dough will be very soft and cookielike. Empty it onto a sheet of clear plastic wrap. Stretch a second sheet of plastic wrap over the dough and flatten it to a thickness of ⅓–½ inch in a round and regular shape. Refrigerate for 1 hour. Should you cool it longer, the dough would turn into a hard piece of concretelike material that would break at any attempt to roll it out. So, if you have refrigerated the dough too long, let it mellow a bit at room temperature before you roll it out.
3. Roll out to a thickness of ⅛ inch between its 2 sheets of plastic wrap, then lift the top sheet and invert the dough into your pie plate; fit it well and as regularly as you can. By now, the dough will have become too soft for the plastic sheet to be lifted without tearing the pastry. Refrigerate again until the plastic lifts easily. Finish arranging the edges of the pastry in an aesthetic pattern and proceed with your pie filling and baking.

Consider the same variations in flavoring as for regular short pastry, as well as the replacement of some of the flour by a certain amount of very fine-ground almonds (see p. 459). Avoid using heavy cream, sour cream, or any acid material such as yogurt or buttermilk; the egg is the best binding material for a sweet pastry.

PATE FEUILLETEE {Puff Pastry}

As soon as I started working in a restaurant context, I immediately abandoned the old-fashioned complicated techniques of the classic puff pastry. Although I still faithfully teach them in depth to the students who come to me for professional training, I generally use the more modern techniques described below, which I already recommended in *When French Women Cook* (1976).

> *2 cups less 1 tablespoon sifted all-purpose unbleached flour*
> *1 tablespoon cornstarch*
> *1 cup (½ pound) unsalted butter*
> *¾ teaspoon salt*
> *⅓–½ cup ice-cold water*

1. Make a well in the flour. Add the cornstarch. Cut the butter in 1½-tablespoon chunks; add salt. Mash the butter into the flour with your fingers until the particles of butter are the size of whole macadamia nuts.
2. Mix in the ice-cold water 1 tablespoon at a time, introducing it with your fingertips. Press the small balls of dough that will form into a large one. With the heel of the hand, lightly push the ball of dough forward into large pieces and gather it into a ball again. Shape into a rectangle 6½ inches by 4½ inches. Refrigerate for 1 hour, preferably in the vegetable crisper.
3. Roll the dough 6 inches away from you and 6 inches toward you, keeping it 6½ inches wide and never less than ⅓ inch thick. Do not bear down on the dough; roll it out parallel to the counter top in 1 or 2 decisive strokes.
4. If the dough becomes wider than 6 inches, block it on each side by placing the rolling pin parallel to the edge of the dough and tapping it gently. The edge will straighten up. Fold the dough in three. Now turn it by 90 degrees so that it looks like a book ready to be opened. With a bit of pressure applied with the rolling pin at the top and bottom seams, pinch the layers of dough slightly to prevent any butter from escaping. Roll out the dough

again and fold it a second time, exactly as described above. You will have given 2 "turns." If the package of dough is less than 6 inches wide, tap it gently with the rolling pin and flatten it. To keep track of the turns, punch 2 small depressions on the surface of the dough with your fingertip. Put the dough on a lightly floured plate; cover loosely with a sheet of foil and put to cool in the vegetable crisper of the refrigerator. Let the dough rest for 1 hour or longer if you wish.

5. Finish the dough by giving 2 more series of 2 turns each, exactly as described above. The rest period, always in the vegetable crisper, should never be less than 30 minutes. After turns 3 and 4, punch 4 small depressions on the surface of the dough. After turns 5 and 6, trace an X. That will remind you that the pastry is finished and may be used at any time.

6. Roll out after chilling deeply for 1–2 hours. Cut the dough neatly, perpendicular to the counter top, so it rises straight up. After cutting patty shells or pieces of any shape, put them *upside down* on a baking sheet. This will keep the baked product from being narrower at the top than at the bottom. Use a buttered unbendable baking sheet rinsed under cold water or ever so lightly floured. Follow the same procedure if you cut the dough according to a paper pattern. For good coloring while baking, brush the top of all pastries with glaze made of 1 egg yolk mixed with 3 tablespoons milk.

A collection of pleasant tarts and tartlets:

In the recipes that follow, I have used many variations on the making of the pastry, thus illustrating by example the explanations given on pages 458–62.

T A R T E   P O I V R E E   {Peppery Tart}

Use a 9-inch white porcelain plate.

SERVES 8

PASTRY:

1 cup plus 2 tablespoons sifted flour
1/3 cup very fine-ground blanched
   almonds
1/2 teaspoon ground ginger

1/2 cup butter
A pinch of salt
3 1/2–4 tablespoons ice-cold water

FILLING:

5 not-too-ripe Bosc pears

⅔ cup ginger marmalade

1½ tablespoons lemon juice

1½ tablespoons dark rum

3 tablespoons unsalted butter

Coarsely cracked black pepper

Heavy cream (optional)

1. With the flour, almonds, ginger, butter, salt, and water, prepare the pastry as described on page 458. Put it to rest for 1 hour in the refrigerator. Roll out the dough into a circle 11 inches in diameter and ⅙ inch–⅛ inch thick. Build an elegant edge according to your personal taste. Preheat the oven to 375°F.

2. Cut the pears into halves. Remove the stems and cores with a melon baller. Slice the pear halves across into ⅙-inch slices. Flatten them to fan out the slices and, using a spatula, transfer them into the pastry shell. Arrange the pear halves so as to alternate the root ends with the stem ends. Bake the pie for 15 minutes in the lower part of the oven.

3. Melt the ginger marmalade without straining it. Cool it slightly and add to it the lemon juice, rum and butter. Pour evenly over the pear slices. Bake for another 30–35 minutes in the top part of the oven, or until the pear juices and the marmalade have bound and reduced very well together. Remove from the oven and immediately sprinkle the top of the candied pears with the cracked pepper, using as much or as little as you like (¾ teaspoon is a good measure).

4. Serve with the heavy cream on the side, if you like.

TARTELETTES EN VENITIENNE
{*Venetian-style Tartlets*}

Use any red berry or berries in combination for the filling, but use strawberries exclusively to prepare the purée for the glaze, and serve as soon as glazed. Use 8 individual tartlet shells.

SERVES 8

PASTRY:

2 cups sifted all-purpose flour

3 tablespoons sugar

¾ cup plus 1 tablespoon butter

1 egg yolk

1 tablespoon wine vinegar

⅓ cup ice-cold water

FILLING:

1½ cups extremely fine-chopped blanched pistachio nuts

⅓ cup sugar

5 tablespoons butter

2 egg yolks

½ teaspoon vanilla extract

5 tablespoons kirschwasser

Salt

1 quart strawberries

1 quart raspberries

Sugar to taste

1 teaspoon red wine vinegar

1. With the flour, the sugar, ¾ cup of the butter, the egg yolk, and the vinegar diluted into the ice water, prepare the pastry following the directions on page 458. Roll out into a large sheet and cut into eight 3-inch circles. Butter all tartlet shells with the remaining tablespoon of the butter and fit 1 circle of pastry into each. Preheat the oven to 375°F.

2. Put the chopped pistachios, ⅓ cup sugar, butter, egg yolks, vanilla, 2 tablespoons of the kirschwasser, and a pinch of salt in the blender container. Process until a smooth pistacho cream is obtained. Spoon an equal amount of cream into each tartlet shell. Bake for 12–15 minutes, or until golden and set. Cool completely.

3. Clean the strawberries and raspberries; select the smallest strawberries, mix them with the raspberries, and fill the shells with the berries, mounding them a bit.

4. Purée all the large berries in the blender; add sugar to your taste, a tiny pinch of salt, and the red wine vinegar. Mix well and strain into a bowl. Just before serving, spoon the strawberry purée over the berries mounded into the tart shells. Serve promptly.

TARTE A LA BERGAMOTTE ET AUX CANNEBERGES {Bergamot and Cranberry Tart}

Essence of bergamot is not easy to find in the U.S.A., so I have substituted a combination of 4 citrus rinds, which are quite a good imitation. Use a 9-inch flan ring.

SERVES 8

PASTRY:

1½ cups sifted all-purpose flour
½ teaspoon salt
1 drop essence of bergamot or ¼
   teaspoon each fine-grated orange,
   lime, lemon, and grapefruit rinds

9 tablespoons butter
4 tablespoons orange juice
½ tablespoon lemon or lime juice

FILLING:

1 cup heavy cream
2 tablespoons Grand Marnier
1 cup scalding milk
2 drops essence of bergamot or ½
   teaspoon each fine-grated orange,
   lime, lemon, and grapefruit rinds

4 egg yolks
⅓ cup sugar
A pinch of salt
1 envelope gelatin

TOPPING:

1 pound fresh cranberries, washed
   and sorted
1 cup sugar
1 cup water

A pinch of salt
Grated rind of ½ an orange
3 tablespoons Grand Marnier
½ cup chopped blanched pistachios

1. Prepare the pastry as described on page 458, using the flour, salt, essence of bergamot or citrus rinds, butter, and fruit juices. Rest the pastry for 1 hour in the refrigerator.

2. Preheat the oven to 425°F. Roll the pastry out ⅛ inch thick and fit it into a 9-inch flan ring placed on a buttered pastry sheet. Line the pastry with aluminum foil. Fill with beans or aluminum nuggets and bake for 7–10 minutes.

3. To prepare the filling, whip the cream with the Grand Marnier until it barely mounds. Keep refrigerated. Flavor the scalding milk with the essence of bergamot, or, if using the rinds, add them to the milk and let them infuse, covered, for 30 minutes. Reheat the milk when you are ready to cook the custard.

4. Mix the egg yolks, sugar, and salt and gradually dilute with the flavored milk. Thicken over medium-high heat and, as soon as the custard coats the spatula, strain it into a clean bowl. Melt the gelatin in a double boiler and

dissolve it into the cream. Strain the custard into a bowl, which you will place in another bowl containing salt water and ice. Stir until the custard starts setting. Immediately remove from the ice and whip in the whipped cream. Turn into the pastry shell and let set completely in a cool room. Avoid the refrigerator, which makes the crust soggy.

5. To prepare the topping, put the washed cranberries in a pot with the sugar and water, salt, and grated orange rind. As soon as the berries have popped open, strain the mixture into a bowl and add the Grand Marnier. Let cool completely and, before the sauce sets, spread a thickness of ¼ inch over the cold bergamot cream. Sprinkle with chopped pistachios and serve.

SERPENT AUX PRUNEAUX
{A Feuilleté with Prunes, Apples, and Walnuts}

In the southwest of France the women prepare a cake with a phyllo type dough made with goose fat and called a *tourtière* or *pastis*. Here I have replaced the fat with butter and walnut oil and succumbed to my love for apples cooked to a a very dark brown color—I remain uninspired by the pale apples in the Gascony *tourtières*. The serpent shape comes from the fact that when women did not own ovens, the cake was cooked rolled around the bottom of a *cocotte*, a round iron cooking pot, which was embedded from bottom to top in the hot cinders of the hearth. The *pastis* was then said to be *"en cabessal"* because the rolled serpent resembles the *cabessal* or rolled cloth on which women carried jugs of water on their heads.

SERVES 12

FILLING:

*1 pound natural prunes, pitted and
    dried without sulfur dioxide*
Armagnac
¼ cup butter
*3 Granny Smith or Pippin apples,
    peeled and cut into 6 large slices
    each*

⅓ cup sugar
*½ cup very coarse-chopped walnut
    meats*

PASTRY:

2½ cups sifted flour (11–12 percent protein content) (see p. 48)
¼ pound butter, melted
1 tablespoon lemon juice
A pinch of salt

1 egg, beaten
½ cup warm water, between 95°F. and 100°F.
2 tablespoons walnut oil
2 cloves

1. Soak the prunes in just enough Armagnac to cover them for 24–36 hours, or until the liqueur has been almost completely absorbed.

2. Heat the butter in a large skillet, brown the apples well on both sides, sprinkle them with the sugar and cook until they caramelize. Remove to a plate. Dissolve the caramel in the skillet with any Armagnac left at the bottom of the prune soaking bowl. Mix apples, prunes, and walnut meats and toss them all in the little bit of caramel in the skillet. Remove to a lightly buttered plate.

3. To prepare the pastry, make a well in the flour, add 1 tablespoon of the melted butter, the lemon juice, a pinch of salt, and the beaten egg. Beat well together, then gradually add the water. Progressively bring the flour into the well and, as soon as the flour has been absorbed, start kneading as you would a noodle dough (see p. 125) until it is smooth and elastic. Butter a plate, place it over a pot of warm water, put the dough on it and cover it with an inverted bowl. Let stand for 30 minutes. Keep *warm*—not cold, not hot.

4. Mix the remaining melted butter with the walnut oil. Stretch a tablecloth over a card table. Flour the tablecloth lightly. Put the pastry on the tablecloth, roll it out as far as it will naturally let itself be rolled, then brush it with some of the butter and oil. Now stretch it over your hands and that of a helper's while you both turn the dough clockwise and gently pull it from under. Continue the stretching until the dough has pulled thin enough to cover the whole surface of the table. Anchor the pastry at all 4 angles of the table. Brush it again with the mixture of melted butter and walnut oil. At the end of the pastry closest to you, arrange the mixture of prunes, apples, and walnuts so it covers only 2 inches of the pastry in one direction and the whole length of the pastry in the other. Cut all thick edges with scissors and, holding the tablecloth with both hands, force the sheet of pastry to roll forward, enclosing the fruit; roll until you have rolled all the pastry into a big cigarlike package. Tuck one end under and shape it into a pointed

serpent head, sticking a clove on either side of the face to make eyes. Twist the other end of the package into a tapered end that will look like the thin tail of a serpent.

5. Preheat the oven to 375°F. Transfer the serpent to a buttered unbendable pastry sheet and brush it with the remaining butter and oil mixture. Roll it into a loose coil and bake until deep golden, or approximately 40 minutes. Serve lukewarm.

ALLUMETTES MEXICAINES
{Chocolate Cinnamon Puff Pastries}

A pleasant after-dinner "munchy" variation on a classic little pastry.

MAKES 2 DOZEN COOKIES,
2 INCHES BY 1 INCH

1 ¾ cups sifted all-purpose flour
⅓ cup sifted Dutch cocoa powder
½ pound butter, quite cold
⅓–½ cup ice-cold water

½ teaspoon salt
1 ½ cups confectioners' sugar
½ teaspoon cinnamon
1 egg white

1. Mix the flour and the cocoa. Cut the butter into large chunks and mix it into the flour with your fingertips. Gradually add the water and salt; press the small balls of dough that will form into a large one. With the heel of your hand, push the ball forward in large pieces and gather them into a ball again. Shape into a rectangle 6½ inches by 5½ inches. Refrigerate for 1 hour.

2. Following the directions given on pages 461–62, give the dough 6 turns, 2 at a time at 30-minute intervals. Rest the dough for at least 1 hour in the refrigerator before using it.

3. Mix the confectioners' sugar, cinnamon, and egg white gradually to obtain a semifluid glaze. Preheat the oven to 400°F.

4. Roll the pastry out into a rectangular sheet ¼ inch thick. Brush the glaze evenly over the sheet and, with a pizza wheel, cut rectangles 1 inch by 2½ inches and transfer them to a buttered pastry sheet. Refrigerate for 15 minutes, then bake for 12–15 minutes. Cool on a rack; enjoy while very fresh and barely lukewarm.

CROUTE NORMANDE {Normandy Apple Dessert}

If you can find unpasteurized heavy cream that will lightly sour and thicken within 24 hours of its gathering, serve a large serving spoon of it beside each portion of tart; we served it in the restaurant during that blessed fall of 1978 when U.S. customs let into Boston several thousand cases of true Normandy crème fraîche; I felt compelled to prepare a "croûte" to go under the cream.

SERVES 8

PASTRY:

1 cup plus 2 tablespoons sifted flour
⅓ cup fine-ground unpeeled hazelnuts
9 tablespoons butter
1 tablespoon Calvados
3½ tablespoons ice-cold water

TOPPING:

8 Granny Smith or Pippin apples,
  peeled, cored, and cut into quarters
¼ pound butter
¼ cup plus 1 tablespoon sugar

1 cup dry cider
¼ cup Calvados
¾ cup heavy cream
1 egg, beaten

1. Mixing the flour with the ground hazelnuts, butter, Calvados, and ice water, prepare a pastry as described on page 458.
2. To prepare the topping, recut the apple quarters in such a manner that the trace of core disappears and the piece of apple will lie flat on the bottom of a skillet. Heat the butter in a large skillet and in it brown the apples on both sides. Sprinkle them with sugar, then add some cider to dissolve it when it has caramelized. Repeat sprinkling and turning the apples at regular intervals until all the sugar and cider have been used. When the apples are done, remove them to a lightly buttered plate. Add the Calvados to the skillet, reduce by one-half, and add the cream. Let it reduce until it coats a spoon heavily. Strain into a small bowl. Preheat the oven to 425°F.
3. Roll out the pastry ⅛ inch thick. Fit the sheet of pastry over the bottom (used alone without the mold sides) of a 10-inch springform mold. Brush the edge of the pastry with beaten egg. Cut ¾-inch-wide strips out of the remaining pastry pieces and fit those, with their ends overlapping, around

the perimeter of the round sheet of pastry to form an edge. Using a fork, imprint the tines into the pastry edge to seal both layers and as a decoration. Brush the edge and what has now become the bottom of the pie with a bit of beaten egg. Also prick the bottom of the pastry very heavily with the fork and sprinkle it with sugar. Bake until golden brown. Transfer to a rack and cool.

4. To finish the tart, fill the shell with the caramelized apples and spoon caramel Calvados cream over them. Serve promptly.

TARTE AUX BIMBRELLES
{Blueberry, Lime, and Jack Daniels Tart}

Bimbrelles is the name given to blueberries in the Vosges Mountains. Try to use wild blueberries, which are as delicious in the U.S.A. as in the Vosges. The combination of blueberries, bourbon, and lime has always been a favorite of mine. Serve the tart promptly to prevent the berries from juicing.* Use a 9-inch white porcelain pie plate.

SERVES 8

PASTRY:

1½ cups sifted all-purpose flour

1 tablespoon sugar

½ teaspoon very fine-grated lime rind

A pinch of salt

9 tablespoons butter

1 tablespoon Jack Daniels

2½ tablespoons natural plain yogurt

TOPPING:

6 tablespoons unsalted butter

⅔ cup sugar

Juice of 2 limes

Fine-grated rind of 1 lime

A pinch of salt

2 tablespoons flour

3½ tablespoons Jack Daniels

2 eggs

2 egg yolks

½ cup unstrained lime marmalade, melted

1 quart blueberries, picked over, washed, and dried

* In a restaurant put the glazed berries over the individual servings of custard.

1. With the flour, sugar, grated lime rind, salt, butter, liquor, and yogurt, prepare a pastry following the directions given on page 458. Roll out the pastry ⅛ inch thick and fit it into a 9-inch white porcelain pie plate. Preheat the oven to 375°F.

2. To prepare the filling, cream the butter and add the sugar, 2 tablespoons of the lime juice, the lime rind, salt, flour, 2 tablespoons of the liquor, and the eggs beaten with the egg yolks. Pour into the pie shell and bake for 35–40 minutes. Cool completely.

3. Mix the remaining ½ tablespoon liquor into the melted marmalade and cool. Toss the blueberries into the cooled jam. Spoon them into the prepared lime pie. Serve promptly.

CREMES GLACEES
(Ice Creams)

Everyone sings it: "I scream, you scream, we all scream for ice cream." The word scream is far from being an exaggeration. I have discussed the feeling with all those of my contemporaries who, for health reasons, have been radically forbidden "to touch the stuff": As soon as one cannot have it anymore, one craves it badly.

When I came to America, after several years of pleasant trips and stays in London and the English countryside, I knew that ice cream making was not an area in which the French necessarily excelled. In my opinion, the best ice creams in the world are to be found in the Scandinavian and Anglo-Saxon countries, quickly followed by Italy.

The French ice creams are too hard, and with a few exceptions not rich enough in egg yolks and heavy cream. Yes, even in the best, much admired restaurants in the nation.

Ice cream textures and tastes are entirely a question of personal taste. I like them sinfully rich and would rather eat a little of a very rich ice cream than a steady diet of those ordinary ice creams sold in shops and supermarkets.

Generalities:
The basic technique used to prepare ice cream is that of the Crème Anglaise explained on pages 438–40.

You will notice:

a. The more egg yolks an ice cream formula contains, the smaller the crystals will be and the smoother the texture of the ice cream.

b. The more sugar and the more liqueur you use in an ice cream, the less it will freeze and the softer it will remain. Only "lean" ice creams can be molded into bombes.

c. Any ice cream mixture is better if it is deep chilled for 24 hours before being processed in a machine.

d. The way an ice cream is frozen is most important. It is necessry to mix the crushed ice used to pack the ice cream machine with one-tenth of its weight (no more, or the ice cream crystals will be too large) in coarse salt. If this question of weight bothers you, simply figure it this way: 1 standard ice cube tray contains 1 pint (2 cups) water, and 1 pint weighs 1 pound. You will need 6 trays of well-crushed ice cubes to pack an average machine; the total weight is 6 pounds or 96 ounces of water turned to ice. You will need no more than 9.6–10 ounces salt.

e. To serve, remove ice cream from the freezer to the refrigerator 15 minutes before serving, so you can scoop it into dishes or glasses easily.

To prevent a mess:

Empty the ice cubes into a heavy-duty plastic trash bag; mix in the salt and, with a mallet or hammer, pound the ice until well crushed.

Set the ice cream bin into the machine, pour the salted ice all around, and process. A good machine churns a batch of 1½–2 quarts ice cream in 20–25 minutes and will stop by itself as soon as the ice cream is ready.

A very important word about sanitation and freshness:

It is essential to realize that an ice cream base is—along with meat stock—one of the most active bacterial development grounds there is. Two safeguards are:

1. Use only an ice cream freezer with a removable container that can be sterilized.

2. Keep the ice cream in a deep freezer, well sealed in plastic containers.

Ideally, an ice cream churned today should be served tomorrow to give it the 24 hours of necessary ripening. Any ice cream left over should not be served more than 48 hours after being churned. The flavor of ice cream deteriorates rapidly in the freezer, which explains why commercial ice creams so often have such a "blah" taste.

Basic formulas and their variations:

There follow three basic formulas for making ice creams. They are arranged in increasing degrees of richness.

FORMULA I: CRÈME GLACÉE DES PERDEURS DE POIDS
{Dieters' Ice Cream}

The batch for 12 people will contribute 100–110 calories to the daily diet, depending on whether it is made with whole or skim milk. The ice cream molds easily for a bombe.

SERVES 12

1 quart milk, whole or skim
8 egg yolks
1 cup sugar
A pinch of salt
2 tablespoons pure vanilla extract

1. Scald the milk. Mix thoroughly the egg yolks and the sugar. Add salt. Gradually blend in the scalding milk.
2. Thicken over medium-high heat (see Crème Anglaise, p. 438). Cool by whisking well. Add the vanilla. Strain into the *sterilized* container of your ice cream maker. Chill overnight.
3. Pack the machine with ice as indicated on page 472 and churn. Ripen for 12–24 hours before serving.

Variations: In any of the variations indicated below, make sure to use the tablespoon of vanilla; it is necessary to alleviate the egg yolk taste, and its alcohol base helps to soften the texture of the ice cream.

   a. *Liqueurs*: Add 1/3–1/2 cup of any liqueur of your choice.

   b. *Chocolate*: Add either 3 tablespoons cocoa or 1/2 cup bittersweet chocolate, chopped into chips, before preparing the custard.

   c. *Coffee*: Infuse 1/3 cup ground Italian roast coffee in the scalding milk for 1 hour. Strain before making the custard.

d. *Citrus fruit*: Infuse rinds of the type and in the quantity you like in milk for 2 hours before you cook the custard.

e. *Nuts*: Infuse toasted nuts (½ cup, ground fine) in the milk for 2 hours before making the custard. Strain before cooking.

f. *Praline*: Prepare praline and crush before mixing with eggs and milk to cook into a custard. Add ¼ cup rum if using almonds and/or hazelnuts and ¼ cup bourbon of your choice if using pecans or cashews. To make praline, cook 2 cups sugar to the caramel stage and add 1⅔ cups chopped nuts of your choice. Pour over a buttered cookie sheet and cool completely. Break into pieces and crush coarse or fine, as you prefer.

FORMULA II:
LA SEULE ET UNIQUE CREME GLACEE
{Basic Ice Cream for Ice Cream Lovers}

Needless to say, this is my favorite formula. One portion will be approximately 255 calories.

SERVES 12

> *1 quart light cream*
> *12 egg yolks*
> *⅔ cup sugar*
> *A pinch of salt*
> *2 tablespoons pure vanilla extract*

1. Scald the light cream. Mix the egg yolks and the sugar very well; gradually blend in the scalded cream. Add the salt.
2. Thicken over medium-high heat (see Crème Anglaise, p. 438). Immediately whisk very quickly to stop the cooking. Add the vanilla. Chill overnight and churn in an ice cream machine (see instructions, p. 472).

CREME GLACEE A LA CARDAMOME
{Cardamom and Bourbon Ice Cream}

Use the bourbon you like best—my personal taste calls for Jack Daniels—and use the dehydrated pineapple without artificial colorings available in health food stores.

This ice cream is very soft and cannot be molded into a bombe.

SERVES 12

2 slices natural dehydrated pineapple,
   chopped into ¼-inch cubes
⅓ cup bourbon of your choice
12 egg yolks
⅔ cup sugar
A pinch of salt

2 tablespoons pure vanilla extract
1½ tablespoons cardamom powder
2 cups heavy cream
2 cups light cream
¼ cup sour cream

1. Macerate the candied pineapple bits in the bourbon for 48 hours.
2. Mix thoroughly, but without making too much foam, the egg yolks, sugar, and salt. Add the vanilla and cardamom. Scald together the heavy and light cream mixed. Gradually stir it into the yolk/sugar mixture. Thicken over medium-high heat (see Crème Anglaise, p. 438). Whisk well to cool, add the sour cream, mix well, and strain the ice cream mixture over the pineapple. Cool completely. Chill overnight.
3. The next day, process in the ice cream machine (see instructions, p. 472) and ripen for 24 hours.
4. Serve in crystal glasses, by itself and without decoration.

CREME GLACEE A LA LAVANDE, AU THYM SAUVAGE ET AU MIEL
{Lavender, Thyme, and Honey Ice Cream}

If you can find it, use pure lavender honey or evergreen honey as dark and resiny as possible. Lavender flowers can be found in health food stores.

SERVES 12

6 cups light cream
2/3 cup dried lavender flowers
1 1/2 teaspons dried thyme leaves
12 egg yolks
2/3 cup dark natural honey

A pinch of salt
Rind of 1 orange
1/4 cup sugar
1/4 cup slivered toasted almonds,
   chopped

1. Scald the cream. Put the lavender and the thyme in the blender container. Add the scalding cream and process until the 2 dried spices have been pulverized into the cream. Let steep overnight. Strain through a very fine strainer or through several layers of cheesecloth.

2. Mix the egg yolks, the honey, and the salt. Scald the lavender and thyme cream. Gradually add it to the mixture of egg yolks and honey. Thicken over medium heat (see Crème Anglaise, p. 438). As soon as it is thick enough to coat the spatula, remove from the heat and strain again to remove any egg white particles that might have clung to the yolks and chill overnight.

3. Process in an ice cream machine (see instructions, p. 472) and ripen for 24 hours.

4. Cut the orange rind into 1/8-inch slivers. Blanch them in plain water and drain well. Mix 1/4 cup water with the sugar to make a syrup. Add the orange rind slivers and cook them until translucent. Cool.

5. To serve, scoop the ice cream into crystal cups; top with a small teaspoon of orange rind and syrup and dot with a few chopped toasted almonds.

CREME GLACEE A LA SAVOYARDE
{A Savoie-Inspired Caramel and Pear Ice Cream}

In the fall, the women of Savoie bake fresh peeled pears with sugar and butter and dissolve the cooking juices with the cream from their cows! This dessert is obviously inspired by that farm dish.

SERVES 12

6 ripe Bartlett or Bosc pears
1 tablespoon butter
1 3/4 cups sugar
5 cups light cream
12 egg yolks

A pinch of salt
2 tablespoons vanilla extract
A dash of ginger
Pear brandy as needed (Poire William)

1. Peel and core the pears. Preheat the oven to 375°F. Butter a baking dish large enough to hold them in 1 layer. Add the pears, sprinkle with ½ cup of the sugar. Add a dash of water to the dish and bake until the pears are tender and their juices have caramelized.

2. Remove the pears to a plate. Sliver and reserve them.

3. Dissolve the caramel in the baking dish with 1 cup of the light cream. Strain into the remaining 4 cups of the cream. Heat the cream mixture well.

4. Put 1 cup of the sugar and a few tablespoons of water in a pot and cook to the deep brown caramel stage. Dissolve the caramel with the cream mixture.

5. Blend the egg yolks and the remaining ¼ cup of the sugar well. Gradually add the caramel cream. Thicken over medium heat (see Crème Anglaise, p. 438) and strain into a bowl. Add salt, vanilla, and ginger. Chill overnight.

6. The next day, process in the ice cream machine (see instructions, p. 472) and ripen for 24 hours.

7. To serve, mix the sliced pears with a dash of pear brandy (or any other suitable liqueur). Scoop 3 small scoops of caramel ice cream into a large balloon glass and top with a few slices of pear.

CREME GLACEE A LA PISTACHE SAUCE CHOCOLAT {Pistachio Ice Cream with Chocolate Sauce}

Yes . . . superexpensive, but worth every penny of its unreasonable price.

SERVES 12

ICE CREAM:

1 pound shelled pistachios

4 cups light cream

10 egg yolks

1 cup sugar

¼ cup kirschwasser

A pinch of salt

SAUCE:

⅓ cup sugar

1 cup hot single-strength espresso coffee

3 ounces bittersweet chocolate (preferably French, Swiss, or Belgian)

1 egg yolk

A pinch of salt

Pistachio liqueur to taste

1. Blanch the pistachios and skin them. Set ¼ cup of the nuts aside.

2. Put the remaining nuts in the blender container. Scald the cream; start the blender and add the cream. Process until the pistachio nuts are puréed. Empty into a bowl and let steep overnight. Strain through several layers of cheesecloth. Reheat the pistachio milk to the scalding point.

3. Mix the egg yolks and the sugar. Dilute gradually with the pistachio milk and thicken over medium-high heat (see Crème Anglaise, p. 438). Strain again to discard egg white stragglers; add kirsch and salt. Mix well. Chill overnight.

4. Process in the ice cream machine (see instructions, p. 472). Ripen overnight.

5. To prepare the sauce, dissolve the sugar in the boiling hot espresso coffee. Add the chocolate and mix until smooth and homogeneous. Add the egg yolk while still hot. Add a pinch of salt. Let cool and add pistachio liqueur to suit your personal taste.

6. To serve, scoop the ice cream into balloon glasses. Top with a large tablespoon of chocolate sauce and sprinkle with a few of the reserved pistachios.

FORMULA III:
LES VELOURS GLACES *{Frozen Velvets}*

These are extremely rich ice creams made with many egg yolks and a lot of heavy cream. They are not, however, any richer than the "Parfaits" of the classic cuisine, which were made with 32 egg yolks for each 6 cups heavy cream. Their great advantages are their "oh, so smooth" texture and the fact that they need no churning and will remain soft enough to scoop without having to mellow in the refrigerator. Serve less than you would in a portion of regular ice cream.

The basic formula consists of 32 egg yolks and ⅔ cup sugar to each quart of heavy cream. As you will see, the recipe can stand many variations.

VELOURS GLACE AU QUATRE THES
{Four-Tea Frozen Velvet}

Orange flower water is available in all "gourmet" shops.

SERVES AT LEAST 20

1 quart water
½ cup Earl Grey tea
⅓ cup Green Gun Powder tea
½ cup Jasmine tea
¼ cup Lapsang Souchong tea
6 cups heavy cream

1¾ cups sugar
24 egg yolks
1 envelope gelatin
⅓ teaspoon salt
2½ teaspoons orange flower water
2 tablespoons toasted coconut

1. Bring the water to a boil. Add all the teas at once. Remove from the heat and let stand for 2 hours. Strain to obtain 3 cups very strong tea.

2. Mix the tea with 3 cups of the heavy cream and bring to the scalding point. *Do not boil or simmer.* Mix the sugar and the egg yolks; dilute with the tea-flavored cream and thicken over medium-high heat (see Crème Anglaise, p. 438). Melt the gelatin with a teaspoon of water in a double boiler and add to the mixture with the salt. Strain, add the orange flower water and cool immediately.

3. When the cream is cold, whip the remaining 3 cups of the heavy cream to the Chantilly stage and fold them into the tea cream.

4. Turn into a shallow stainless steel pan. Cover well with plastic wrap and aluminum foil. Freeze without churning.

5. Serve in balloon glasses or champagne cups sprinkled with toasted coconut flakes.

VELOURS GLACE AU BASILIC ET A LA MENTHE {Basil and Mint Frozen Velvet}

SERVES AT LEAST 20

1 quart heavy cream
28 egg yolks
1 cup sugar
2 tablespoons mint extract
1 cup fine-chopped fresh mint leaves

1 cup fine-scissored fresh basil leaves
A pinch of salt
2 tablespoons each Sambucca, Genépy
*   and Crème de Menthe liqueurs*
mixed

1. Scald the heavy cream. Mix the egg yolks and the sugar. Dilute with the scalded cream. Thicken over medium-high heat (see Crème Anglaise, p. 438). Strain and cool.
2. Add the mint extract, the chopped mint, the scissored basil leaves, and the salt. Pour into a flat stainless steel pan. Freeze immediately. Stir several times during the freezing process and keep well covered with plastic wrap and foil between and after stirrings.
3. To serve, scoop into champagne cups and top each portion with a tablespoon of the mixture of liqueurs.

GLACES AUX FRUITS {Fruit-flavored Ice Creams}

This is an excellent way to obtain maximum flavor from fresh berries and pulpy fruit. To obtain exactly 1 pound purée from most fruits other than berries, purchase 1½ pounds fruit; for berries, purchase 1¼ pounds. This recipe contains the basic formula for these desserts.

SERVES ABOUT 12

1 pound sugar
⅓ cup water
1 pound thickish fruit purée
A pinch of salt
2 cups heavy cream

1. Dissolve the sugar in the water to make a syrup. Add the fruit purée and mix well. Add the salt. Cool and blend in the heavy cream.
2. Process in the ice cream machine (see instructions, p. 472) and ripen for 24 hours. Or pour into a tray and freeze until semisolid; beat and, when smooth, return to freezer and let ripen for 24 hours.

GLACE AUX POIRES {Pear Ice Cream}

SERVES ABOUT 12

1 pound dried pears
2 fresh Comice or Bartlett pears, very
  ripe, stemmed and cored but not
  peeled
Juice of 1 lemon

1¾ cups sugar
A pinch of salt
2¼ cups heavy cream
Pear brandy (Poire William)

1. Soak the dried pears overnight. Discard the water; remove the stems and cores. Put the soaked pears, the unpeeled fresh pears, and the lemon juice in the blender container. Process until puréed and strain well.
2. Bring the pear purée to a boil and add the sugar and salt. Stir until the sugar has melted. Cool. Blend in the heavy cream and the pear brandy and chill. When deep chilled, process in the ice cream machine and ripen for 24 hours.
3. To serve, scoop into champagne cups and top each portion with a teaspoon of pear brandy.

CREME GLACEE CITRON-LIMETTES
{Lime-Lemon Ice Cream}

Truly a one, two, three ice cream, made and churned all in a matter of 1½ hours. It's especiallly good served with a fresh raspberry or strawberry purée.

SERVES 10–12

ICE CREAM:

1 quart heavy cream
Fine-grated rinds of 2 lemons and 2
    limes
1½ cups lemon juice

1½ cups lime juice
3 cups sugar
⅓ teaspoon salt

SAUCE:

2 packages frozen raspberries

1. Bring the cream to a boil. Add the citrus rinds and let stand for 20 minutes, stirring occasionally. Cool completely.
2. Blend the citrus-flavored cream with the 2 juices, the sugar, and the salt and stir well until the sugar has melted.
3. For the best texture this should be churned in an ice cream machine (see instructions, p. 472), but if you have no machine, put it to freeze in a stainless steel tray. Store covered with plastic wrap and aluminum foil. The mixture need not be broken up or beaten during freezing.
4. To prepare the sauce, defrost and drain the berries, reserving the syrup. Purée them in the blender. Strain well to discard the seeds. Dilute the purée with as much syrup as you like to sweeten it.
5. Scoop the lemon-lime cream into balloon glasses or champagne cups and serve topped with 2–3 tablespoons raspberry purée.

SORBETS
(Sherbets)

There are 2 types of sherbert. One is the "entremet" sherbet served between first and main courses, the other is a light dessert.

The classic sorbets served to this day in upper-class French restaurants are all made from a base of sugar syrup mixed with some fruit purée. The syrup is made with equal weights of sugar and water, that is to say, for each pound of sugar (2 cups) one should have 1 pint (2 cups) of water. The syrup can be prepared in bulk and kept refrigerated.

It is easy to prepare a syrup-based sherbet, provided one has the proper equipment: a saccharometer and a narrow container in which one can first blend the fruit purée and syrup, then float the saccharometer. The saccharometer offered for sale may be graded either in Baumé degrees or by sugar density level. To be able to use either of these measurement systems, you must know that to prepare sorbets: the degree Baumé 17 corresponds to density 1,1335, the degree Baumé 18 corresponds to density 1,1425. To obtain a good sorbet, the thermometer should float between those two numbers. Add sugar syrup to the fruit purée until the saccharometer indicates that level. One usually adds the juice of 1 or 2 lemons to cut the sweetness and set the color of the fruit purée. Last, one churns the sorbet and ripens it for 24 hours in a well-sealed container.

Corrections are easy: If a sorbet is too crystally when it comes out of the machine, all one has to do is let it mellow, add a bit more syrup, and churn it again. If on the contrary the sorbet is too soft and does not set well, one should add fruit purée.

The amount of syrup one will need depends on the natural sweetness of the fruit. Tart berries, for example, require almost equal amounts of syrup and purée, while peaches, which are very sweet when very ripe, will need less.

I am not always fond of the results obtained with sugar syrup, since unfortunately our commercially grown fruit does not always reach us at the peak of ripeness and flavor. So I have, as you will see in the following pages, often used jams made with the same fruit: strawberry jam for strawberries, raspberry jelly for raspberries, etc., instead of sugar syrup. In some cases, a different but compatible jam or jelly may be used.

A certain amount of lemon juice is still needed to temper the sweetness and bring out the natural esters in the fruit. If after freezing, such a sherbet tastes just too sweet, the best remedy is to mellow it and whip it in the electric mixer as one adds to it enough heavy cream to break the sweetness. This addition is done to taste.

BASIC SHERBET SYRUP

2 pounds sugar
1 quart water

Mix sugar and water. Bring to a boil and simmer for 2 minutes. Store in *sterilized* jars. If the syrup is kept for more than 2 weeks, reboil it for 2–3 minutes and add 1 tablespoon boiled water for each cup of syrup to correct the density, which increases with reboiling.

Sorbets for entrements:
Made with various syrups.

SORBET AU SAUTERNES ET AU STILTON
{Sauternes Sorbet with Stilton Flakes}

I have made it with Château d'Yquem using a bit less sugar; you can use much lesser wines, but always the French Sauternes.

SERVES 18

*3 ¼ cups white grape juice, made from
    fresh grapes, put through the
    blender and strained
    (approximately 3 pounds grapes)
1 cup sugar*

*1 ½ cups excellent Sauternes (French,
    please)
Juice of 1 lemon
A pinch of salt
6 tablespoons fine-flaked Stilton cheese*

1. Mix grape juice, sugar, Sauternes, lemon juice, and salt and stir until the sugar has melted. Pour into the ice cream freezer bin and process (see instructions, p. 472). Store in very tightly sealed plastic containers and ripen for 24 hours. *Consume within 48 hours.*
2. Scoop into 4-ounce glasses and serve each portion dotted with 1 teaspoon Stilton flakes.

SORBET AU CHATEAUNEUF-DU-PAPE ET AU ROQUEFORT *{Châteauneuf-du-Pape and Roquefort Sorbet}*

This recipe obviously follows the pattern of the preceding one. It is dedicated to my good friends who produce the Mont-Redon Châteauneuf-du-Pape. It should be eaten within 48 hours of processing.

SERVES 18

3½ cups grape juice, made from
 fresh Red Emperor or Ribier
 grapes, put through the blender
 and strained (approximately 3
 pounds grapes)
1¼ cups sugar

1½ cups excellent Châteauneuf-du-
 Pape
Juice of 1 lemon
A pinch of salt
6 tablespoons fine-flaked Roquefort
 cheese

1. Mix the grape juice, sugar, Châteauneuf-du-Pape, lemon juice, and salt.
   Stir until the sugar has melted. Pour into the ice cream freezer bin and
   process (see instructions, p. 472). Store in a tightly sealed plastic container
   and ripen for 24 hours. *Consume within 48 hours.*
2. Scoop into 4-ounce glasses and serve each portion dotted with 1 teaspoon
   Roquefort flakes.

SORBET AU MARC DE GEWURZTRAMINER
{Marc de Gewürztraminer Sorbet}

This can be executed with any other white wine and any other marc from any
other areas of France, as well as any Italian grappa. It is extremely good as
an entremets for any dinner of venison or game birds.

SERVES 12

3 cups fresh grape juice, made from
 white grapes put through the
 blender and strained (2½–3
 pounds grapes)
1⅓ tablespoons lemon juice

⅔ cup sugar
A pinch of salt
1⅓ cups Alsatian Gewürztraminer
10 tablespoons Marc de
 Gewürztraminer

1. Mix the grape juice, lemon juice, sugar, and salt and stir to dissolve the
   sugar. Add the wine and 2 tablespoons of the Marc de Gewürztraminer.
2. Pour into the ice cream machine freezing bin and process (see instructions,
   p. 472). Turn into a plastic container with a tight-fitting lid and ripen
   overnight.
3. To serve, scoop into 4-ounce glasses and top each portion with 2 teaspoons
   marc.

Sorbets pour desserts (dessert sherbets):

The basic formula for the fruit and jam sherbets is as follows: for each pound of fresh fruit, use 24 ounces jam or jelly of the same or a compatible fruit. However, you may have to experiment a bit, for when fruit is sweet and very ripe (a rarity unless it is locally grown and hand picked), the quantity of jam can dip as low as 18 ounces per pound of fresh fruit.

Always start with the lesser amount, and if the texture is too crystally, gradually add more melted jam. Since no churning is necessary, pour a small amount of sherbet into a custard cup, freeze it and check it for texture and taste, adding more jam only if necessary. Freeze in a shallow plastic tray with both plastic wrap and aluminum foil.

The smooth texture will be produced by the cooked sugar in the jam as well as the pectin, which acts as a stabilizer. Lemon juice is necessary to cut the sweetness and brighten the fruit esters.

ASSIETTE DE FRUITS FRAIS AUX TROIS SORBETS
{Fresh Fruit Plate with Three Sherbets}

These can be served in combination as presented here, or each sorbet can be served separately.

SERVES 12

PAPAYA SORBET:
> 1 1/3 pounds papaya pulp
> 12 ounces apple jelly, melted and cooled
> 6 ounces lime marmalade, melted and cooled
> Juices of 1 lime and 1 lemon
> A pinch of salt

PINEAPPLE SORBET:
> 1 pound pineapple meat
> 24 ounces pineapple jam, melted and cooled
> Juice of 2 lemons
> A pinch of salt

TWO-ORANGE SORBET:

1 quart orange juice

2 cups tangerine juice

3 cups granulated sugar

1 cup heavy cream

½ teaspoon salt

Grated rind of 2 oranges

6 tablespoons confectioners' sugar

2 tablespoons each Grand Marnier and
Mandarine Napoléon

FRUIT GARNISH:

36 large strawberries

12 slices of fresh pineapple

12 small slices of papaya

12 small slices of honeydew melon

36 slices of red banana, cut slantwise
across the bananas

12 mint bouquets

1. To prepare the papaya sorbet, place the pulp, apply jelly, lime marmalade, and the lime and lemon juices in the blender container and process until a smooth purée results; add salt. Strain into a stainless steel flat dish or small plastic tray. Cover with plastic wrap and aluminum foil and freeze. Ripen for 24 hours.

2. To prepare the pineapple sorbet, place the well-cleaned cut-up meat, the jam, the lemon juice, and the salt in the blender container. Process to a smooth purée and strain into a stainless steel or plastic tray. Freeze as indicated above. Ripen for 24 hours.

3. To prepare the orange sherbet, mix orange and tangerine juices. Add the granulated sugar and stir until the latter has completely dissolved. Add ⅔ cup of the heavy cream, the salt, and the grated orange rind. Pour into the freezing bin of the ice cream machine and process until semistiff (see instructions, p. 472). Lightly whip the remaining ⅓ cup of the cream. Beat the confectioners' sugar, Grand Marnier, and Mandarine Napoléon into it and add to the semistiff sorbet; finish processing until completely homogenized. Pour into a shallow tray and freeze as indicated above.

4. To serve, place 1 scoop of each sorbet at the center of a luncheon or dinner plate. Place a bouquet of mint at the center of the 3 balls and surround the sorbets with an arrangement of the fruit and fruit slices, alternating the colors for better presentation.

COUPE ANGELA BELLA {Sambucca Espresso Cream Cup}

SERVES 12

SORBET:

4½ cups sugar
2 quarts water
⅓ teaspoon salt
1½ cups heavy cream
1⅓ cups Sambucca liqueur

CUSTARD:
4 egg yolks
¼ cup sugar
A pinch of salt

½ cup double-strength espresso coffee
½ cup heavy cream
1 teaspoon aniseeds

1. Bring a mixture of 4 cups of the sugar, the water, and the salt to a boil. Cool. Add 1 cup of the heavy cream and pour into the freezing bin of an ice cream machine. Process until semisolid (see instructions, p. 472). Lightly whip the remaining ½ cup of the heavy cream, with the Sambucca, and add to the sorbet; finish processing until solid. Pour into a plastic container with a tight-fitting lid, freeze, and ripen for 24 hours.
2. To prepare the custard, mix well the egg yolks, the sugar and salt. Dilute with the espresso and the cream mixed and thicken over medium-high heat. Add the aniseeds while the mixture is hot and let cool. Cover with plastic wrap and keep refrigerated overnight. Strain before using.
3. To serve, scoop the Sambucca sorbet into balloon glasses or champagne cups and spoon 2 tablespoons of the cold espresso cream onto each portion.

RED BERRY MESS

No fancy French name. Made and composed in Newton Centre, Massachusetts, for a very American public, who loved it.

SERVES 16

SORBET:

1 pound fresh blueberries
  (exclusively wild or Maine, please)
1 pound fresh raspberries
12 ounces black currant jam, melted
  and cooled

12 ounces raspberry jam, melted and
  cooled
Juice of 2 lemons
A pinch of salt

GARNISHES:

3 packages frozen raspberries in
  syrup
1 teaspoon red wine vinegar
1 pint fresh blueberries (cultivated
  are fine here)

1 pint small strawberries (the best
  are Louisiana)
1 pint fresh raspberries
2 cups cassis liqueur
2 cups heavy cream

1. Process the blueberries, raspberries, black currant and raspberry jams, well mixed, in the blender to obtain a fine purée. Add lemon juice and salt and strain into a stainless steel tray. Cover with plastic wrap and aluminum foil and freeze. Ripen for 24 hours.

2. Defrost the frozen raspberries and reserve the syrup. Purée the berries with the vinegar. Strain to discard all seeds and add as much syrup as you like to sweeten the purée.

3. Clean the fresh blueberries, strawberries, and raspberries. Mix them in a bowl.

4. To serve in portions, scoop 2 balls of sherbet into a balloon glass. Add 2 tablespoons berry mixture. Top with 3 tablespoons raspberry purée, 2 tablespoons cassis liqueur, and 2 tablespoons heavy cream. Serve promptly.

SORBET AUX ABRICOTS {Apricot Sherbet}

The key to this recipe consists in using dried apricots, which are very concentrated in flavor and can be prepared year round.

SERVES 12

SORBET:

½ pound dried apricots (the best California fruit)

Water as needed

Juice of 2 lemons

A pinch of salt

24 ounces excellent apricot jam

¼ cup kirschwasser

RASPBERRY SAUCE:

2 packages frozen raspberries in syrup

Lemon juice to taste

1. Soak the apricots overnight in water. Discard the water and rinse the fruit well.
2. Place the apricots, just enough water to cover, the lemon juice, and the salt in a pot. Bring to a boil and cook until the apricots break down and lose shape. Add the apricot jam and melt it into the apricots. Cool to lukewarm for easier handling.
3. Purée the apricot mixture in the blender or food processor. Strain it into a stainless steel or plastic tray through a tamis or conical strainer to discard all traces of skin. Mix in the kirschwasser.
4. Cover the tray with plastic wrap and aluminum foil and freeze. Ripen for 24 hours.
5. To prepare the sauce, defrost the berries; strain and reserve the syrup. Purée the berries; strain again to discard the seeds. Dilute the purée with syrup as needed to obtain the sweetness and texture you like. Brighten with a few drops of lemon juice.
6. To serve, scoop the sorbet into balloon glasses or champagne cups and spoon over each portion 2½–3 tablespoons raspberry purée.

SORBET TIRETAINE {Apple Butter and Calvados Sherbet}

Serve with a plateful of cookies of your choice.

SERVES 12

SORBET:

Two 28-ounce jars apple butter
One 12-ounce jar apple jelly
8 ounces ginger marmalade
1 cup Calvados

1 ½ cups heavy cream
¾ cup freshly squeezed lemon juice
2 teaspoons Quatre-Epices *(p. 35)*
1 ¼ cups heavy cream

1. Mix together the apple butter, apple jelly, and ginger marmalade. Heat until well melted. Purée in the blender to smooth completely. Add the Calvados, heavy cream, lemon juice, and *quatre-épices* and strain into a stainless steel or plastic tray. Cover with plastic wrap and aluminum foil and freeze. Ripen for 24 hours.
2. To serve, scoop into balloon glasses or champagne cups and top each portion with 2 tablespoons heavy cream.

SORBET AUX POIRES ET AU GINGEMBRE
{Pear and Ginger Sherbet}

SERVES 12

1 pound fresh pears, net weight cored
   and stemmed but unpeeled
24 ounces ginger marmalade, melted
   and cooled
Juice of 2 lemons

A pinch of salt
1 ¾ cups heavy cream
1 teaspoon ground ginger
¾ cup ginger liqueur

1. Mix the pears and ginger marmalade. Add lemon juice and salt. Purée in the blender and strain into a flat stainless steel tray. Freeze.
2. Empty the frozen sherbet into the food processor container and start the machine, adding 1 cup of the heavy cream through the spout. Refreeze and ripen for 24 hours.
3. To serve, scoop into balloon glasses or champagne cups. Using the remaining ¾ cup of the cream, top each portion with 1 tablespoon cream flavored with ground ginger and ginger liqueur.

SORBET DE MELON A L'EAU DE NOIX
{Melon Sherbet with Walnut Wine}

You must make the walnut wine first or bring it back from a trip to France. If no walnut wine is available, use white port.

1 pound very ripe and very sweet melon meat (a mixture of cantaloupe and cranshaw is best)	*A pinch of salt*
	Juice of 1 lemon
	1 cup Vin de Noix (Walnut Wine)
24 ounces apple jelly, melted and cooled	*(p. 511)*
	2 cups diced cantaloupe meat

1. Put the pound of melon meat and the melted apple jelly into the blender container and purée. Add salt and lemon juice as well as ½ cup of the walnut wine. Strain into a flat stainless steel or plastic tray; cover with plastic wrap and aluminum foil and freeze. Ripen for 24 hours.
2. To serve, macerate the diced melon in the remaining ½ cup of the walnut wine. Scoop the sorbet into glasses or cups and top each portion with 2 tablespoons melon cubes and their maceration juices.

A FEW POPULAR CAKES

Before giving the recipes, I would like to remind the users of this book of the different types of cakes to be found in the general body of pastry cookery.

Genoises:
Made by ribboning whole eggs and sugar, then folding in flour, then folding in melted butter.

The *folding* technique is the most important and is given a special paragraph on page 437. In *génoises*, a certain quantity of nuts or pure cocoa can replace some of the flour.

Biscuits:
Also known as *sponge cakes* in American culinary terminology. The egg yolks they contain are first ribboned with the sugar; then the egg whites are beaten

until they can carry the weight of an uncooked egg in its shell. One-quarter of the total volume of egg whites is mixed into the ribboned egg yolk and sugar base. The remainder of the beaten egg white is put over the lightened yolk and sugar base, and the dry ingredients (flour, starch, cocoa, nuts) are sprinkled over all. The whole mass of whites and dry ingredients is folded at once into the yolk and sugar base until the mixture is homogeneous.

Butter cakes:
Those whose recipe begins: *cream* the butter. The sequence then follows: add the sugar; beat until fluffy. Add the egg yolks one by one, beating steadily. Add the flour or any other dry ingredients without beating to prevent tunnels in the finished cake; simply flatten the flour into the buttery mixture with a large rubber spatula. Then beat the egg whites and fold them into the heavy base to lighten it. Some butter cakes contain baking powder; if they do, you will always notice a certain amount of liquid or milk in the recipe; it is there to allow the baking powder to react.

Those butter cakes containing baking soda instead of baking powder will always contain an acid (sour cream, buttermilk, lemon juice, vinegar) to make the baking soda react.

Pound cakes:
Rich butter cakes made with equal quantities of butter, sugar, eggs, and flour.

Torten:
Of Germanic origin; most of them are cakes made with layers of nut meringues, or nut and cake or bread crumb layers, separated by rich buttercreams.

About cake decoration:
The decorations for the cakes included here are extremely simple and easily executed by any amateur cook.

I do not like complicated flowers, plastic glazes, or fancy writings because they do not taste good, they only look good, and also because they are difficult for the lay person to do. The disappointment of a gorgeous look, to which a correspondingly gorgeous taste is not attached, has its measure of cruelty.

My philosophy is to have a good-looking cake with totally edible decorations rather than a smashing presentation that deflates the spirit when tasted.

Ripening cakes:

To taste its best, a cake must ripen for at least 12 hours in the refrigerator and be brought to room temperature 15–20 minutes before serving.

Buttercream fillings:

All the buttercreams in this book are based either on a custard or on a sugar syrup. With the modern electric mixer these are a cinch to make. If your cream should break a little, add a tablespoon or so of butter, and make sure that all the while you blend the egg yolk foam and butter you keep your mixer on "creaming" speed. High speed will cause some buttercreams to separate. No buttercream is ever a perfect magical formula that "works" because Madeleine or some other expert wrote it—Madeleine, all other experts, and the lay cook alike have to contend with different ingredients, different temperatures, different mixture speeds, and different mixers every time they make a buttercream. Bring very cold creams to room temperature before you rebeat them and expect their color to lighten as you beat them and thus introduce air into them.

CHRISTMAS POUND CAKE

SERVES 12–16

5 ounces candied ginger, in large pieces	1 cup sugar
6 rings natural dehydrated pineapple	1 teaspoon ground ginger
2 ounces ginger-flavored brandy	½ teaspoon salt
2 ounces very dark rum	4 extra-large eggs, separated
⅔ cup unsalted, lightly toasted macadamia nuts	2 cups sifted all-purpose flour
1¼ cups plus 1 tablespoon unsalted butter	2 tablespoons cornstarch

1. Remove the granulated sugar from the pieces of ginger. Cut the ginger into ⅓-inch cubes. Cut the pineapple pieces into the same size pieces. Mix the 2 fruits together and cover with the liqueurs. Macerate for approxi-

mately 48 hours, or until the fruit has absorbed at least 75 percent of the liqueur.

2. If your macadamia nuts are salted, wipe the salt off. Chop the nuts in approximately ⅓-inch pieces.

3. Butter two 1-pound loaf pans each with ½ tablespoon of the butter.

4. Cream 1¼ cups of the butter until fluffy. Add the sugar and beat until at least half of the sugar has melted. Add the ground ginger, the salt, and the egg yolks one by one.

5. Mix the flour and cornstarch. Dust each loaf pan with 1 tablespoon of the mixture. Flatten the remaining flour into the butter-sugar-egg base; add at the same time the fruit, nuts, and any macerating rum left over.

6. Preheat the oven to 275°F. Beat the egg whites until they can carry the weight of an uncooked egg in its shell without its falling into the batter by more than ¼ inch. Add one-quarter of the egg white, stirring it into the cake batter; fold in the remainder.

7. Turn into the prepared loaf pans and bake for 1½ hours, or until a skewer inserted at the center of each cake comes out hot and dry. Cool on racks and ripen for 48 hours. Serve sliced. No decoration is neecessary.

GENOISE A LA PIEMONTAISE
{Hazelnut Chocolate Cream Cake}

This is my personal execution of a torta seen in the windows of Alemagna in Milan. It follows the *Génoise* method (see p. 492). Toast the hazelnuts deeply, but take care not to brown them too much.

SERVES 12–16

CAKE :

6 eggs
1 cup sugar
A pinch of salt
1 cup plus 2 tablespoons sifted all-purpose flour

2 tablespoons cornstarch
½ cup butter
2 tablespoons dark rum

SYRUP FOR SOAKING:

> 6 tablespoons water
> 6 tablespoons dark rum
> 6 tablespoons light Crème de Cacao liqueur
> 1 tablespoon sugar

FILLING AND ICING:

1¼ cups milk
2 cups chopped, peeled, toasted
   hazelnuts
4 egg yolks
½ cup granulated sugar
A pinch of salt

12 ounces Swiss, French, or Belgian
   bittersweet chocolate
1 cup unsalted butter, at room
   temperature
Confectioners' sugar

1. Preheat the oven to 350°F. Ribbon the eggs, sugar, and salt with an electric mixer (see p. 436).

2. Mix the flour and cornstarch. Butter a 10-inch round cake pan with 1 tablespoon of the butter. Melt the remaining butter and cool it. Dust the cake pan with a veil of the flour and starch mixture.

3. As soon as the ribbon has formed, add the rum; beat again until the ribbon re-forms. Fold in the flour and cornstarch mixture; fold in the butter. Turn into the prepared cake pan and bake for 40–45 minutes, or until the cake recesses by ⅛ inch from the sides of the pan. Unmold immediately onto a cake rack and cool.

4. To prepare the soaking syrup, mix the water, rum, Crème de Cacao, and sugar and let the mixture stand until the sugar has completely dissolved.

5. To prepare the filling, bring the milk to a boil. Place 1 cup of the hazelnuts in the blender container and add the scalding milk. Process until the hazelnuts are puréed. Empty into a bowl and let steep for 2 hours. Strain the hazelnut milk through several layers of cheesecloth.

6. Mix the egg yolks, granulated sugar, and salt. Reheat the strained hazelnut milk and gradually stir it into the egg and sugar mixture. Thicken over medium-high heat (see Crème Anglaise, p. 438). Immediately add 6 ounces of the bittersweet chocolate and stir well to melt it. Cool completely. Cream the butter in an electric mixer and gradually add the cooled chocolate custard until a smooth buttercream results.

7. Cut the cake into 2 layers. Saturate the bottom layer with half of the syrup.

Spread with a ⅓-inch-thick layer of buttercream. Put the second layer on top and saturate it with the remaining syrup. Coat the top and sides evenly with the rest of the buttercream. Coat the sides of the cake evenly with the remaining cup of the chopped hazelnuts. Cut a 12-inch by 2½-inch band of waxed paper, wrap it around the cake and gently squeeze to imprint the hazelnuts into the sides of the cake.

8. To finish the decoration of the cake, melt the remaining 6 ounces of the chocolate and spread it ⅟₃₂ inch thick over a cookie sheet. Chill the cookie sheet until the chocolate dulls. Using a pastry scraper, pull the chocolate toward you to make chocolate curls. Spread or arrange the curls on top of the cake. Dust with confectioners' sugar.

GATEAU DE TROUVILLE {Trouville in Normandy Cake}

Everyone always seems to go to chic Deauville because of its shops and its "Parisian" atmosphere. The truth of the matter is that the true Normandy is still in Trouville on the other side of the bridge, on the right bank of the Dives. The Normands, the fish market, the cheese and antique shops, the pastry shop at the center of town have not changed since I can remember, and that goes back to 1934. . . . "The Cake," as I always called it, is still done, and I have reconstructed it for you from taste memory. It follows the *Génoise* method (see p. 492).

SERVES 12–16

CAKE:

½ cup plus 1 tablespoon butter
6 eggs
1 cup light-brown sugar

A pinch of salt
1 cup sifted all-purpose flour
3 tablespoons pure cocoa powder

FILLING AND DECORATION:

4 eggs, separated
⅓ cup light-brown sugar
A pinch of salt
8 ounces Swiss, French, or Belgian
   bittersweet chocolate

½ cup heavy cream
½ teaspoon cinnamon
1½ cups sliced, blanched, toasted
   almonds

1. Butter a 10-inch round cake pan with 1 tablespoon of the butter. Preheat the oven to 350°F. Ribbon the eggs, the light-brown sugar, and salt very heavily (see p. 436). While the eggs and sugar ribbon, mix thoroughly the flour and the cocoa. Melt and cook the remaining ½ cup of the butter until it turns very brown and the milk solids at the bottom of the pan toast to a light color. (*Do not burn them, please!*) The butter has now reached the "noisette" stage.

2. As soon as the cake base is ribboning properly, fold in the mixture of flour and cocoa, then fold in the "noisette" butter. Turn into the buttered pan and bake 40–45 minutes, or until the cake shrinks ⅛ inch away from the edge of the pan. Unmold immediately onto a rack and cool completely.

3. To prepare the chocolate mousse, ribbon the egg yolks and the brown sugar with the salt. While the yolks are ribboning, melt the chocolate and cool it; beat it into the ribboned mixture. Beat the egg whites until they can hold the weight of a raw egg in its shell without its sinking into the foam by more than ¼ inch. Fold them into the mousse base; beat the cream with the cinnamon until quite stiff; fold it into the lightened mousse. *Deep chill* before using to fill the cake.

4. When you are ready to finish the cake, cut it into 3 layers. Fill the layers with two-thirds of the chilled mousse. Put the layers back together and spread the sides and top of the cake with the remaining one-third of the mousse. Spread the cake all over with the sliced toasted almonds. Ripen for 24 hours before serving.

GATEAU APRY {*Apricot and Cognac Cake*}

A truly good-looking cake with plenty of taste, this follows the *Génoise* method (p. 492).

SERVES 12–16

CAKE:

1 tablespoon butter	*⅔ cup sifted all-purpose flour*
6 eggs	*1 tablespoon cornstarch*
1 cup sugar	*½ cup very fine-ground blanched*
A pinch of salt	* almonds*
1½ teaspoons bitter almond extract	*4 tablespoons melted butter, clarified*
2 tablespoons Cognac or Armagnac	

FILLING:

5 egg yolks
¼ cup plus 3 tablespoons water
½ cup sugar

A pinch of salt
¼ cup Cognac or Armagnac
1 cup unsalted butter

DECORATION:

Apricot liqueur as needed
1 cup blanched, chopped pistachios
½ cup blanched, chopped almonds
½ pound dried apricots, soaked
* overnight in barely enough water*
* to cover them*

1 cup water
1 cup sugar
16 whole pistachio nuts, blanched

1. Butter a 10-inch round cake pan with 1 tablespoon of the butter. Preheat the oven to 350°F. Ribbon the eggs and the sugar with the salt (see p. 436). Add the almond extract and Cognac and ribbon again. Mix the flour and cornstarch together. Reserve 1½ teaspoons of the mixture to dust the cake pan, and fold the remainder, along with the ground almonds, into the ribboned egg and sugar mixture. Fold in the melted butter. Turn into the prepared cake pan. Bake for 40–45 minutes, or until the cake shrinks by ⅙ inch from the edge of the pan. Unmold immediately onto a cake rack and cool.

2. To prepare the buttercream filling, beat the egg yolks in the electric mixer. While they foam up, mix 3 tablespoons of the water, the sugar, and the salt and bring it to a boil. Cook until the syrup lifted from the pan with a teaspoon falls back into the bulk of the syrup, forming a heavy, uninterrupted thread. Remove from the heat. Cool for 1 minute, add the remaining ¼ cup of the water and the Cognac or Armagnac, and pour immediately over the foaming egg yolks in a thin stream. Beat until completely cold. Cream in the butter tablespoon by tablespoon.

3. Cut the cake into 2 layers. Saturate the layers with apricot liqueur. Fill the center with half the buttercream. Put the cake back together and spread a ⅟₃₂-inch layer of cream all over its top and sides. Coat the sides of the cake with the chopped pistachios and almonds mixed. Make a 12-inch by 2½-inch band of waxed paper and press it around the cake to imprint the nuts. Put the rest of the buttercream into a pastry bag fitted with a small

star tube and pipe 16 rosettes of cream all around the top of the cake to correspond to the 16 portions.

4. Rinse the soaked apricots. Bring the water and sugar to a boil in a flat sauté pan. As soon as the syrup boils, turn it down to a simmer, add the apricot halves and cook them for 5 minutes meat side down and 5–7 minutes skin side down. Drain and cool on a rack. Prop 1 apricot half over each rosette of cream and slide 1 whole pistachio nut at a 45-degree angle between the cream rosettte and the apricot. Reduce the syrup and brush it lightly over each apricot with a fine brush or a tiny espresso spoon.

Note: The cake will look even better if you do not hesitate to use 1 or 2 drops of green food coloring in the buttercream. If you do not want to use food coloring, you can squeeze the juice out of 1 large leaf of spinach.

TORTE LUDMILLA

Why Ludmilla? I have no idea. It might as well have been Maroussia or Katya. The cake was part of a Russian-inspired menu and looks rather sober but tastes like something out of *The Nutcracker*. The cake must age for 2 days for the top meringue layers to soften. If you are among those who like the meringue layers crisp, ripen for only 24 hours. This uses the Biscuit or Sponge Cake as well as Torte method (see pp. 492–93).

SERVES 12–16

MERINGUE LAYERS:
3 egg whites
A pinch of salt
1/3 cup plus 1 tablespoon sugar
1 cup fine-ground hazelnuts

1/2 teaspoon grated orange rind
1 tablespoon butter
2 teaspoons flour

CAKE:
6 eggs, separated
1 1/4 cups sugar
1 tablespoon vanilla
6 ounces Swiss, French, or Belgian
    bittersweet chocolate, melted

2 cups fine-ground hazelnuts
1 teaspoon grated orange rind
1 tablespoon butter
2 teaspoons flour

BUTTER CREAM:

> *3 egg yolks*
> *¼ cup plus 1½ tablespoons sugar*
> *1½ tablespoons water*
> *2 tablespoons Mandarine Napoléon or Grand Marnier*
> *½ cup unsalted butter, at room temperature*

DECORATION:

> *Mandarine Napoléon*
> *Confectioners' sugar*
> *2 dozen blanched whole pistachios*

1. Beat the egg whites with the salt and 1 tablespoon of the sugar. As soon as they are stiff enough to carry the weight of a raw egg in its shell without its sinking by more than ¼ inch into the foam, fold in the remaining ⅓ cup of the sugar thoroughly mixed with the hazelnuts and the grated orange rind.

   Preheat the oven to 325°F. Butter and flour a large cookie sheet, shaking the excess flour off. Using the bottom of a 10-inch pan, trace 2 circles on the sheet and fill those with an even ⅙-inch-thick layer of hazelnut meringue. Bake for 20–25 minutes. Loosen with a long spatula and gently transfer to cool on a cake rack.

   Do not turn oven off.

2. To prepare the cake batter while the meringue layers are cooling, ribbon the egg yolks and the sugar (see p. 436). Add the vanilla and ribbon again. Melt the chocolate in a double boiler, cool it, and add the ribboned yolks and sugar. Beat the egg whites. Mix one-quarter of their volume into the base, then slide the remainder of them on top of the lightened base. Sprinkle the ground nuts and orange rind over the egg whites and fold until the batter is homogeneous. Turn into a 10-inch cake pan greased with the butter and sprinkled with the flour. Bake in the 325°F. oven until a skewer inserted at the center of the cake comes out clean, hot, and dry, or approximately 40 minutes. Unmold onto a cake rack.

3. To prepare the buttercream, beat the yolks in the electric mixer. While they fluff up, cook the sugar and water until a spoonful of syrup lifted from the pot will fall back to a thick, unbroken thread. Add the liqueur and pour immediately over the egg yolks, continuing to beat until a ribbon forms

and the mixture is cold. Beat the butter into the egg and sugar base, tablespoon by tablespoon, until the buttercream is smooth.

4. To assemble the cake, put the first meringue layer smooth side down onto a platter. Cover it with half the buttercream (there should be a ¼-inch layer, not more). Brush 1 side of the chocolate almond cake very generously with Mandarine liqueur. Invert that side onto the buttercream. Brush the other side with the same amount of liqueur, cover with the remainder of the buttercream, and top with the second meringue layer set smooth side up. Smooth the cake side, making sure that the successive layers of meringue, cream, cake, cream, and meringue are apparent. Wrap the cake, on its plate, in clear plastic wrap and refrigerate it for 24–48 hours.

5. To serve, unwrap the cake; powder it with confectioners' sugar strained through a superfine tea strainer. Trace a crisscross pattern of lines on top of the cake with the back of a knife. Place a pistachio at the center of each diamond formed by the crisscrossed lines.

CHARLOTTE DES CHARTREUSES
{A Chocolate and Green Chartreuse Charlotte Cake}

This is a late version of a cake that was originally made with kirschwasser and pistachio liqueur. The results are even better with green Chartreuse.

SERVES 12

CAKE:

6 eggs, separated
⅔ cup sugar
A pinch of salt

2 tablespoons green Chartreuse
6 tablespoons cocoa powder
1 tablespoon butter

ALMOND PASTE:

¼ pound ground blanched almonds
¼ pound confectioners' sugar
1 egg white
Green Chartreuse as needed

FILLING:

> *12 ounces Swiss, French, or Belgian bittersweet chocolate*
> *6 tablespoons butter*
> *1½ cups heavy cream*
> *2 tablespoons green Chartreuse*

1. Preheat the oven to 325°F. Prepare the sponge cake batter. Ribbon the egg yolks, sugar, and salt. Add the Chartreuse and ribbon again. Beat the egg whites until they can carry the weight of a raw egg in its shell without its sinking into the foam by more than ¼ inch. Mix one-quarter of the whites into the egg and sugar mixture. Slide the remainder of the whites over the lightened mixture, sift the cocoa powder over the whites and fold until homogeneous.

   Grease a 16-inch by 12-inch by 1-inch jelly roll pan with the butter and line it with nonstick parchment paper. Turn the batter into the pan. Bake for 20–25 minutes. Remove from the oven and cool completely in the baking pan; cover the cooled cake with slightly dampened paper towels. Set aside.

2. To prepare the almond paste, put the almonds and confectioners' sugar in the food processor container and process to a superfine powder. Add three-quarters of the egg white and 2 teaspoons green Chartreuse. Working between layers of waxed paper, roll the paste out into a paper-thin sheet as long and as wide as the jelly roll pan.

3. Invert the cake onto another sheet of waxed paper. Remove the parchment paper, trim the edges of the cake, brush it with a bit of green Chartreuse, and immediately put the sheet of almond paste on top of the cake, making sure their edges correspond. Brush the almond paste with a bit of Chartreuse and roll very tightly. Cut the obtained roll into ⅙-inch slices. They will look like black and white pinwheels.

4. Brush a 9-inch round cake pan with some Chartreuse. Brush each slice of cake with Chartreuse and arrange the slices of cake in a regular pattern on the bottom and side of the cake pan. Too little liqueur will make the cake difficult to unmold; *be generous.*

5. To prepare the filling, melt the chocolate with the butter. Cool well. Beat the cream until it barely mounds. Add the Chartreuse, mix well, and immediately fold into the cooled chocolate. Turn into the prepared cake

pan. Pack it well and cover the pan with plastic wrap. Chill for 24 hours before serving. Unmold onto a cake plate; the cake pattern constitutes its decoration. Cut it in wedges as small or large as you care to enjoy.

UNE ASSIETTE DE PETITS FOURS SECS ET CHOCOLATS
(An After-Dinner Plate of Cookies and Chocolates)

The same batter is usually used to prepare a variety of cookies. I am including here only the 2 kinds that I truly love. Readers interested in macaroons will want to refer to the chapter on Magaly and the Provence in my book *When French Women Cook*. For those who like madeleines, they can be made with the plain pound cake batter on p. 494, omitting the nuts and fruit from the batter.

BASIC TUILES

This is the basic recipe taught to me by my Aunt Claire and reworked for use with American flour.

MAKES TWO DOZEN 2-INCH COOKIES

1 cup nuts, chopped fine	*1 tablespoon cornstarch*
2/3 cup sugar	*3 tablespoons butter, melted*
A pinch of salt	*1/2 teaspoon each orange flower water*
3 tablespoons sifted all-purpose	*and Armagnac*
unbleached flour	*3 egg whites*

1. Mix the nuts, sugar, salt, flour, and cornstarch. Add the melted butter, the orange flower water and Armagnac, and then the egg whites one by one. Refrigerate before baking—the longer, the better.
2. Preheat the oven to 375°F. Butter a cookie sheet well and drop ½ teaspoonfuls of batter onto the sheet, leaving 2-inches between each cookie to allow for spreading. Flatten the batter very thin with a wet fork. Bake until golden. When done, keep the cookie sheet on the lowered hot oven

door. Lift the cookies with a flexible-bladed knife and shape into tuiles by
letting the cookies fold around a rolling pin.

TUILES AUX AMANDES *{Almond Tuiles}*

Follow the basic recipe, using I cup blanched almonds chopped into ⅛-inch
pieces and replacing the orange flower water with ½ teaspoon natural bitter
almond extract.

TUILES AUX NOISETTES *{Hazelnut Tuiles}*

Follow the basic recipe, using 1 cup unblanched hazelnuts chopped into ⅛-inch
pieces and replacing the orange flower water with 1 teaspoon dark rum.

TUILES AUX NOIX *{Walnut Tuiles}*

Follow the basic recipe, using 1 cup walnuts chopped into ⅛-inch pieces and
replacing the orange flower water with 1 teaspoon Armagnac or Cognac.

TUILES AUX MACADAMIAS *{Macadamia Tuiles}*

Follow the basic recipe, using 1 cup macadamia nuts chopped into ⅛-inch
pieces and replacing the orange flower water with 1 teaspoon white rum.

TUILES AUX NOIX DE PECAN *{Pecan Tuiles}*

Follow the basic recipe, using 1 cup pecans chopped into ⅛-inch pieces and
replacing the orange flower water with 1 teaspoon Jack Daniels.

TUILES AU CHOCOLAT {Chocolate Tuiles}

Each and every tuile offered in this list can be coated with chocolate *couverture*. For each 2 dozen cookies, use:

> *6 ounces Swiss, French, or Belgian bittersweet chocolate*
> *1½ teaspoons hazelnut oil*

Melt the chocolate and oil in a double boiler. Brush the back of each tuile with ⅟₁₆ inch of chocolate *couverture* and cool until the chocolate has solidified again.

BASIC CROQUIGNOLLES

The formula that follows is a basic vanilla sugar cookie known in classic pastry work as "pâte à Croquignolles." It is versatile enough to make a variety of little cakes of different shapes that look awfully good on a dessert plate.

MAKES 36 CIGARETTES OR 24 CORNETS

BASIC BATTER:

2 egg whites	*1¼ cups sifted flour*
1¼ cups heavy cream	*3 tablespoons cornstarch*
2½ cups confectioners' sugar	*A pinch of salt*

1. Beat the egg whites until they can carry the weight of a raw egg in its shell without sinking into the foam by more than ¼ inch. Set aside.
2. Whip the cream until semistiff. Spoon the cream over the egg whites.
3. Mix the confectioners' sugar, flour, cornstarch, and salt. Sift over the egg whites and cream and fold all the elements of the batter together until smooth and homogeneous.

   The batter is ready to use as described below.

CIGARETTES A LA GANACHE
{Ganache-filled Cigarettes}

36 CIGARETTES

COOKIE BATTER:
> *1 recipe Basic Croquignolles (preceding recipe)*

FILLING:
> *8 ounces Swiss, French, or Belgian bittersweet chocolate*
> *2 tablespoons butter*
> *1 cup heavy cream*

CHOCOLATE COVER:
> *4 ounces Swiss, French, or Belgian bittersweet chocolate*
> *1 teaspoon hazelnut oil*

1. Prepare the cookie batter. Preheat the oven to 375°F. Trace circles 2½ inches in diameter onto a floured and buttered cookie sheet. Spread the batter paper thin on each circle. Bake for 5–6 minutes. Loosen from the cookie sheet with a flexible-bladed knife. Quickly turn the cookies upside down; then roll them around a pencil. Gently slip them off the pencil to cool on a rack.

2. To prepare the filling, melt the chocolate and butter together. Cool until no heat can be detected in the chocolate when tested with the top of the finger. Whip the cream until it mounds lightly and fold it into the chocolate. Stuff the chocolate cream into a pastry bag fitted with a plain ¼-inch nozzle. Pipe it into both ends of each cookie.

3. To coat the ends of the cookies with chocolate, melt the chocolate with the hazelnut oil. Dip both ends of each cookie ¾ inch deep into the chocolate; cool on the ½-inch-wide blade of a long spatula to prevent the chocolate from sticking to any cake rack. Place a small object under the tip of the spatula blade so the cookies will stay balanced on it and not tip forward.

CORNETS A LA CREME {*Cream-filled Cornucopias*}

The cream to fill those lovely little cornucopias can be flavored with anything one likes; I have often presented them filled with hazelnut pastry cream, but this time I chose lime rind and dark rum.

24 CORNETS

"CORNET" BATTER:
    1 recipe Basic Croquignolles (p. 506)

FILLING:
2 cups milk	*½ cup flour*
Fine-grated rind of 1 lime	*1 envelope gelatin*
6 egg yolks	*4 tablespoons dark rum*
½ cup sugar	*1 cup heavy cream*
A pinch of salt	*24 candied violets*

1. Prepare the cookie batter. Preheat the oven to 375°F. Trace as many 3-inch circles as you can on an unbendable buttered and very lightly floured cookie sheet. Bake for 5–6 minutes, or until light golden. Loosen each cookie from the sheet with a flexible-bladed knife. Turn each cookie upside down and quickly roll it around a wooden or metal cone to obtain a cornucopia. Cool on a rack; store in canisters.

2. To prepare the filling, scald the milk, add the lime rind, and steep for 2 hours. Strain. Ribbon the egg yolks and the sugar with a pinch of salt. Blend in the flour; dilute with the lime milk and bring to a boil to thicken over medium heat. Melt the gelatin with 1 tablespoon water in a double boiler; blend it with ¼ cup of the egg yolk mixture, then blend this mixture into the bulk of the yolks. Strain into a clean bowl and cool completely. Add 2 tablespoons of the rum.

   Whip the cream with the remaining 2 tablespoons of the rum. Fold it into the egg yolk and lime mixture; cover with plastic wrap and refrigerate until set.

3. To fill the cornucopias, stuff the lime cream into a pastry bag fitted with a small star tip. Just before serving the cookies, fill each of them with cream and place a candied violet at the center of the cream.

BONBONS

MISS JUDY'S CHOCOLATE TRUFFLES

We served rum balls and these truffles after the big Friday and Saturday night dinners at the restaurant in Newton Centre. The recipe given here was perfected by the chocoholic in the place, "Miss Judy Flew" herself!

MAKES EIGHTEEN 1-INCH TRUFFLES

*8 ounces Swiss, French, or Belgian
    bittersweet chocolate
4 ounces unsalted butter
2 tablespoons scalding heavy cream
½ cup sugar*

*3 tablespoons water
½ teaspoon cinnamon or 2 tablespoons
    liqueur of your choice (green
    Chartreuse is best)
Dutch processed cocoa butter*

1. Melt the chocolate with the butter; blend in the hot cream bit by bit.
2. Bring the sugar and water to a boil and cook until a spoonful of syrup lifted from the pot will fall back in an unbroken thread. Using a wooden spoon, gradually whisk the sugar syrup into the chocolate mixture. Cool a bit and add the cinnamon or liqueur. Refrigerate for several hours. The chocolate will solidify.
3. Using a melon baller, remove chunks of chocolate from the pot. Roll each one between your hands, then roll in cocoa powder. Keep cool.

PATES DE PISTACHES AU KIRSCH
{Pistachio Balls with Kirsch}

Thanks to the food processor, this confection has become extremely easy to prepare. The "bugaboo" remains the peeling of the nuts . . .

MAKES 24 BALLS

*1¼ cups blanched and peeled
    pistachio nuts
1⅓ cups confectioners' sugar
2 tablespoons kirschwasser
Egg white as needed*

*1 drop green food coloring, only if
    the pistachios are too pale
6 ounces Swiss, French, or Belgian
    bittersweet chocolate
1 teaspoon hazelnut oil*

1. Place the pistachios in the food processor container; chop coarse. Add the confectioners' sugar and process to a superfine meal. Add the kirschwasser and food coloring, if used, then the egg white, tiny bit by tiny bit, until a ball of pistachio paste forms. Knead with your hands and divide into twenty-four ¾-inch balls. Deep chill.
2. Melt the chocolate and the hazelnut oil; stir well to homogenize. Dip the chilled pistachio balls into the chocolate and cool on a very lightly buttered sheet. Refrigerate for 10 minutes to set the outside of the chocolate, then let harden in a very cool place.

HOMEMADE WINES AND LIQUEURS

For as long as I have lived, I have seen every single one of the women in my family prepare homemade wines and liqueurs.

These are three of my personal favorites.

The berry wines are short-lived; they are prepared with the spring berries in the Annecy market and happily consumed before the end of July.

VIN DE FRAMBOISES {Raspberry Wine}

1 bottle dry white wine (Sauvignon, Aligoté, or any Pinot Chardonnay)
2 pounds raspberries, crushed
1½ cups sugar
1 tablespoon lemon juice
⅓ cup Eau de Vie de Framboise

1. Empty the wine into a glass bowl. Add the raspberries and let the fruit macerate for 1 full month in the refrigerator. Stir well every day; keep covered with plastic wrap.
2. Strain through several layers of cheesecloth, pressing to discard all the raspberry seeds.
3. Mix the liquid obtained with the sugar and bring to a boil, stirring constantly. Add the lemon juice and let cool completely. Add the framboise.
4. Patiently let the wine filter through a stainless steel China cap strainer

and store it in 2 bottles. Seal the bottles and keep them standing in the cellar or in the refrigerator. This tastes best deep chilled.

Variations: The same recipe can be used to prepare blueberry, cassis, blackberry, strawberry, and red currant wines.

VIN DE NOIX {Walnut Wine}

This recipe is for my friend Aileen Martin, who each summer provides me with the green walnuts I need to prepare this, my favorite witch's brew. Among other places in the U.S.A., California is filled with walnut trees. Dear walnut producers, how about packaging some green walnuts picked between June 24 and July 5 and mail-ordering them?

The making of the wine requires no work; it ages all by itself.

MAKES 1¼ QUARTS

*1 bottle excellent red wine
(Zinfandel, Pinot Noir, French
Côtes-du-Rhône)
¼ teaspoon each black and white
peppercorns
½ teaspoon allspice berries*

*4 green walnuts, well crushed and
internally still milky
¾ cup sugar
1 strip orange rind, ½ inch by 2 inches
⅓ cup vodka
⅓ cup green Chartreuse*

1. Bring the wine to a boil, add peppercorns, allspice berries, crushed green walnuts, and sugar. Remove from the heat and stir until the sugar has melted. Add the orange rind. Cool completely. Blend in the vodka and the green Chartreuse.
2. Turn into 1 large jar without straining; seal and put to age for at least 40 days in a dark cupboard. Filter into a decanter and enjoy for drinking (slightly chilled) or cooking (see p. 371).

TOASTED HAZELNUT LIQUEUR

6½ ounces peeled toasted hazelnuts, chopped
2½ cups boiling water
2½ cups vodka
½ a vanilla bean or 2 tablespoons pure vanilla extract
¾ cup sugar

1. Put the hazelnuts into a 6-cup glass jar or container. Pour the boiling water over them. Let cool completely. Add the vodka and the vanilla. Let steep for approximately 2 weeks in the refrigerator.
2. Remove one-third of the mixture from the jar. In it dissolve all the sugar, then add this to the bulk of the infusion. Let age for several months.
3. Filter through a coffee filter and store in 1 or 2 well-sealed bottles.

Index